OTHER BOOKS BY PETER GAY

Savage Reprisals (2002)
My German Question (1999)

THE BOURGEOIS EXPERIENCE: VICTORIA TO FREUD
Education of the Senses (1984)
The Tender Passion (1986)
The Cultivation of Hatred (1993)
The Naked Heart (1995)
Pleasure Wars (1998)

Reading Freud: Explorations and Entertainments (1990)
Freud: A Life for Our Time (1988)
A Godless Jew: Freud, Atheism, and the Making of Psychoanalysis (1987)
Freud for Historians (1985)
Freud, Jews and Other Germans: Masters and Victims in Modernist Culture (1978)
Art and Act: On Causes in History — Manet, Gropius, Mondrian (1976)
Style in History (1974)
Modern Europe (1973), with R. K. Webb
The Bridge of Criticism: Dialogues on the Enlightenment (1970)
The Enlightenment: An Interpretation Vol. II: The Science of Freedom (1969)
Weimar Culture: The Outsider as Insider (1968)
A Loss of Mastery: Puritan Historians in Colonial America (1966)
The Enlightenment: An Interpretation Vol. I: The Rise of Modern Paganism (1966)
The Party of Humanity: Essays in the French Enlightenment (1964)
Voltaire's Politics: The Poet as Realist (1959)
The Dilemma of Democratic Socialism: Eduard Bernstein's Challenge to Marx (1952)

SCHNITZLER'S CENTURY

Schnitzler's Century

The Making of Middle-Class Culture

1815 ▼ 1914

Peter Gay

W · W · NORTON & COMPANY · NEW YORK · LONDON

For information about permission to reproduce selections from this book, write to Permissions,
W. W. Norton & Company, Inc., 500 Fifth Avenue, New York, NY 10110

The text of this book is composed in Cochin with the display set in Cochin
Composition by Tom Ernst
Manufacturing by Quebecor Fairfield
Book design by Antonina Krass
Production manager: Julia Druskin

Library of Congress Cataloging-in-Publication Data

Gay, Peter, 1923–
        Schnitzler's century : the making of middle-class culture, 1815–1914 / Peter Gay.
            p. cm.
        Includes bibliographical references and index.
        ISBN 0-393-04893-4
            1. Civilization, Modern — 19th century. 2. Civilization, Modern — 20th century. 3.
        Europe — Social life and customs — 19th century. 4. Europe — Intellectual life — 19th
        century. 5. Europe — Civilization — 19th century. 6. Middle classes — History — 19th
        century. 7. Nineteenth century. 8. Schnitzler, Arthur, 1862–1931. I. Title.

        CB415.G39 2001
        940.2'8'08622 — dc21

                                                                                        2001034557

ISBN 0-393-32363-3 pbk.

W. W. Norton & Company, Inc., 500 Fifth Avenue, New York, N.Y. 10110
www.wwnorton.com

W. W. Norton & Company Ltd., Castle House, 75/76 Wells Street, London W1T 3QT

1 2 3 4 5 6 7 8 9 0

For
ROBERT DIETLE
and
MARK MICALE
in friendship and gratitude

Contents

List of Illustrations   xi

Preface   xix

Overture   xxvii

Part I ▩ FUNDAMENTALS

ONE   Bourgeoisie (s)   3

TWO   Home, Bittersweet Home   35

Part II ▩ DRIVES AND DEFENSES

THREE Eros: Rapture and Symptom   63

FOUR   Alibis for Aggression   97

FIVE   Grounds for Anxiety   129

Part III ⬛ THE VICTORIAN MIND

SIX   *Obituaries and Revivals*   157
SEVEN   *The Problematic Gospel of Work*   191
EIGHT   *Matters of Taste*   221
NINE   *A Room of One's Own*   253

Coda   281

Notes   291
Bibliography   315
Acknowledgments   317
Index   321

List Of Illustrations

p. 1: "Beard Trimming Chart," copyrighted by W. W. Bode, San Francisco, circa 1880. From the collection of the Prints and Photographs Division, Library of Congress.

p. 2: "McCounter Jumper repents of an Easter Trip in a Third-class Carriage," from *Judy*, April 21, 1869. The illustration supports Sigmund Freud's comment to his fiancée, Martha Bernays, on August 29, 1883: "One could show that the 'people' are quite unlike us in the way they judge, believe, hope, and work. There is a psychology of the common man that is rather different from ours." Reprinted from John Gloag, *Victorian Comfort: A Social History of Design from 1830–1900*. London: Adam & Charles Black, 1961.

p. 34: "Changes at Home," by Hablot K. Browne (aka "Phiz"). David's mother is breast-feeding his little half brother, a perfectly respectable activity permitting the presence of witnesses—within the family. Reprinted from Charles Dickens, *The Personal History of David Copperfield*. London: Caxton Publishing Company, n.d.

p. 61: *Les trois grâces*, by Jean-Baptiste Regnault. Reproduced with permission of Musée du Louvre and Réunion des Musées Nationaux/Art Resource.

p. 62: *Arthur Schnitzler*, by Ferdinand Schmutzer, 1912. Schnitzler, who greatly liked this portrait, was fifty, at the height of his powers. Etching of Schnitzler: Schiller-Nationalmuseum, Deutsches Literaturachiv, Marbach.

p. 96: "Monument to Napoleon" (1841), by George Cruikshank. Drawn to "celebrate" the return of the emperor's body to France in the previous year: a wry tribute to the price of aggression. The sarcastic text Cruikshank wrote for this engraving begins: "On the removal of Napoleon's remains, I prepared the above design for a monument, but it was not sent because it was not wanted." Reprinted from Richard A. Vogler, ed., *Graphic Works of George Cruikshank*. New York: Dover Publications, 1979.

p. 128: "Four-Pointed Urethral Ring," from John L. Milton, *Pathology and Treatment of Spermatorrhoea* (1887). Reprinted from Peter Gay, *Education of the Senses. The Bourgeois Experience: Victoria to Freud*. New York: W. W. Norton & Company, 1999.

p. 155: "Names, Numbers, and Location of the Organs," reprinted from S. Wells, *New Physiognomy, or Signs of Character*. New York, 1871.

p. 156: "To the preacher of morals in Cologne on the Rhine," by Olaf Gulbransson, *Simplicissimus*, October 25, 1904. The cartoon is accompanied by a poem that assaults what the magazine persistently called the immorality of Catholic priests, who know nothing of love but everything about illicit sex. Reprinted from *One Hundred Characters from Simplicissimus, 1816–1914: Simplicissimus and the Empire*, a catalogue for an exhibition of the Goethe-Institute for Promoting the Study of the German Language Abroad and for International Cooperation, Munich, selection and commentary by Fritz Arnold, 1983.

p. 190: "The Emancipator of Labor and the Honest Working-People," by Thomas Nast, *Harper's* (February 7, 1874). Nast was an inventive and vigorous draftsman, indefatigable in putting social injustice and political corruption in the pillory, but his imagination failed when it came to trade unions or radical proposals to regulate the economy. Then, like many bourgeois, he sided uncritically with the manufacturers. Reprinted from Morton Keller, *The Art and Politics of Thomas Nast*. New York: Oxford University Press, 1968.

p. 220: *"Mais si, ma femme ..."* by Honoré-Victorin Daumier (November 13, 1846). Translates as "But yes, my dear, I assure you the gentleman is doing a landscape . . . Isn't that true, sir, that you are doing a landscape?" A relatively unassuming instance of the great nineteenth-century confrontation: artist vs. philistine, which (according to avant-garde opinion) was synonymous with artist vs. bourgeois. Reprinted from Charles F. Ramus, ed., *Daumier, 120 Great Lithographs*. New York: Dover Publications, 1978.

p. 252: Floor plan for a fairly sizable two-story house, designed for a comfortably off middle-class family, offering adequate private space on the second floor. Reprinted from a reissue of Catherine Beecher, *A Treatise on Domestic Economy*. New York: Schocken Books, 1977.

SCHNITZLER'S
CENTURY

Genuss ohne Liebe ist doch kein Genuss —
Still, pleasure without love is no pleasure
—Arthur Schnitzler, *Tagebuch*, vol. II, June 10, 1893

Preface

 THIS BOOK IS THE BIOGRAPHY OF A CLASS, the middle class in the nineteenth century from 1815 to 1914. I have used as my guide Arthur Schnitzler, the most interesting Austrian playwright, novelist, and short story writer of his time. Why Schnitzler? He was hardly the archetypal bourgeois. There were vast, unknown numbers of his class born in the nineteenth century less affluent, less talented, less articulate — less neurotic — that is to say, more representative than he. If by "representative" we mean "average," Schnitzler would not have suited my purposes, since the last epithet one would attach to him is "mediocre." But, as I discovered in the course of my research, he was endowed with qualities that make him a credible and resourceful witness to the middle-class world I am depicting in this book. He will appear in each of the chapters that follow, sometimes briefly as an impetus to broader investigations, sometimes as a participant. I have found the man enormously interesting (if by no means always likeable), but that would not have been cause enough to appoint him as a kind of master of ceremonies for the far more inclusive drama I have explored and tried to understand. I had better, more objective reasons.

True, Schnitzler was Viennese to his bones. He traveled relatively little—he was born in Vienna in 1862, died in Vienna in 1931, and (except for brief visits to London, Berlin, and Paris, and short vacations in northern Italy) lived in Vienna. But with his lively, discriminating appetites, he touched on an extraordinary spectrum of styles and ideas, and captured his tastes and feelings for posterity in the diary he conscientiously kept for many years. He had privileged, never naïve, access to the middle-class mind of his time, to that of his contemporaries and of his own. His culture, in short, was cosmopolitan; indeed, his life and work document that it is not necessary to undertake long voyages in order to be well traveled. The mind can, and with Schnitzler it did, receive and work through impulses from faraway places and across generations. Modern French and English literatures (not excluding the American) were his reading matter, to say nothing of the major Scandinavian and Russian novelists and dramatists. He was equally receptive to music and art from many countries. I might say that I have traveled with him to Norway and Italy, the United States and Russia. As I have intimated, he proved to be genial, reliable, and immensely informative.

Schnitzler was a man of the nineteenth century whose life reached deeply into the twentieth. And since the nineteenth century was, as it were, pregnant with its successor, it is also our history. His bridging two centuries meant more than mere physical survival. It has often been said, and compellingly, that the years of World War I made an irreparable breach between two eras. But what held true in the domain of political action—the consequences of that war were to unleash twenty years later an epoch of unprecedented mass mobilization and mass murder—did not hold true in the regions of high culture. The stirring upheavals in the arts, literature, and thought that we call Modernism and associate with the twentieth century were all incubated, in numerous areas well underway, years before 1914. A subversive thinker like Friedrich Nietzsche, who drastically altered the contours of the ways of philosophy, and who, though he went mad and fell silent in 1889, was a portent of a world of thought we still live in today, is a splendid instance of just how much we still live off our Victorian ancestors.

A small sampling of artists may make my point: Henrik Ibsen, George Bernard Shaw, and after them August Strindberg, who revolutionized the drama, had become famous—or notorious—well before 1900, and Anton Chekhov, a luminary in their company, was dead by 1904. Arnold Schoenberg discarded key signatures and entered unexplored domains of music with his second string quartet in 1908. The most enduring Modernist novelists—Proust and Joyce, Mann and Hamsun—launched their careers around the turn of the century. By that time Chekhov had grown into as towering a figure as a writer of short stories as he had become of plays. Academic painting, under pressure from independent artists for decades, saw the rebels increase in numbers and influence well before 1900; a sequence of radical schools—Impressionists, Post-Impressionists, Expressionists, and in Germany and Austria Secessionists who defied the art establishment—acted as pitiless critics of Salon artists; Vassily Kandinsky, who had been moving away from representative painting for some years, produced his first abstraction in 1910. I could extend the list at will; in poetry, architecture, city planning, a new culture was being born. It is perhaps significant that there was a turn-of-the-century school of painters led by Pierre Bonnard and Edouard Vuillard that called itself the Nabis, a Hebrew word for prophet. The future was in their sails.

Schnitzler, too, danced on the edge of bourgeois respectability in his fictions and more than once ventured beyond it. In 1897, he wrote a brilliantly conceived and wittily realized comedy, *Reigen*. It consists of ten amorous dialogues between two lovers, with one of the pair reappearing in the next installment and so around the circle, with each episode culminating in sexual intercourse—an act that not even so audacious a nonconformist as Schnitzler tried to show onstage. Despite this concession to prudence, the text proved unprintable for several years and unplayable on stage for many more. Then, in 1900, in a long story, *Lieutenant Gustl*, as dazzling as *Reigen*, he constructed the young lieutenant's stream of consciousness, exploring from the inside the mortal anxieties of a boastful young Austrian officer who faces a duel he has provoked.

The story attests to Schnitzler's wide reading; he had happened upon the avant-garde, difficult narrative technique that he used in *Gustl* in a short story by the French writer Edouard Dujardin, *Les lauriers sont coupés*. Schnitzler was modest enough to recognize his limitations as a creative artist, and did not claim to be in the immortal company of Tolstoy or Chekhov, but he bristled at the suggestion by so-called benevolent critics that through his years as a prolific author he had in essence been conventionally unconventional, only recycling his earliest dramas about irresponsible bachelors and adulterous love affairs. He was, he protested in some indignation, more imaginative, more inventive, in a word more modern than that.

He was right; but still, are we entitled to take Schnitzler's testimony as usable evidence for the Victorian bourgeoisie? The question presupposes the existence of a single definable entity, the middle class. This is a vexed issue to which I am devoting a whole chapter, the first, in this book. Historians have wrestled with it for years and in the end the solution may turn out to be mainly a matter of emphasis. Certainly Schnitzler thought that there was such a creature as the bourgeois. We shall see that he showed little respect for him—and her—and was disposed to equate "bourgeois" with "boring." In return, many bourgeois would doubtless have called his sense of life eccentric if not bohemian. Yet, as I shall show in some detail, in most important respects, Schnitzler was a solid bourgeois in his own, highly individualistic way. He dutifully chose a profession, medicine, his father wanted him to enter. He desperately wished that his mistresses were still virgins. He tried, like millions of other bourgeois, to sabotage the efforts of the women he loved to practice a profession. He despised such aristocratic anachronisms as the duel. He thought himself to be open-minded in high culture, but it will appear that he could not reconcile himself to Schoenberg's atonal compositions and had his doubts about Joyce's *Ulysses*. He was addicted to work. He cherished his privacy. But this book, though it starts with Schnitzler, does not end with him. As I have said before: if we may call it a biography at all, it is one of a class.

———

❧ I HAVE WRITTEN THIS BOOK AS A SYNTHESIS rather than as a summary. In the early 1970s, I became interested in the Victorian bourgeoisie as a historical topic relatively neglected by my profession. There were, of course, competent books on the nineteenth-century middle class, but the subject did not attract the attention of many historians, certainly not the most interesting ones. The beckoning areas of research lay elsewhere: in women's history, labor history, black history, and what called itself, a little pretentiously, the "new" cultural history. For well over two hundred years, ever since the eighteenth-century philosophes secularized historical causation, the historical profession has periodically experienced such moments of exhilarating discontent; a time when the generally accepted limits of historical research seemed narrow, even stifling.

Much of this dissatisfaction was fruitful, leading to hitherto unasked questions and unsuspected answers. But it was also confusing, notably after postmodern merchants of subjectivism invaded the field; instead of widening historians' horizons, they quite unreasonably threw doubt on the search for truth about the past to which most historians have long been committed. In this heady atmosphere, my own way of doing history, cultural history informed by psychoanalysis—informed, not overwhelmed—seemed to me an appropriate direction to follow and, given the general indifference, the nineteenth-century middle class a highly promising subject. I did not know then, and would not know for some years, how revisionist my work would turn out to be; I certainly had not planned for it. I simply went my own way, following where the evidence led me.

The result was a massive five-volume study that I collectively titled *The Bourgeois Experience: Victoria to Freud* (1984 to 1998), which concentrated on such unconventional topics as sexuality and love, aggression, the inner life, and middle-class tastes. Though my choice of subjects plainly announced the impact of Freud on my thinking, I took care to link my perspective on the past to the "real" world that is the historian's common home. There were, in short, a great many facts in my pages. Some of them will reappear in this book; I found them simply too enlightening, simply too tempting, to do without. Those who have read my five volumes may remember these prize exhibits: William Ewart Gladstone, the classic Victorian, gently, piously, stroking his wife's breasts to alleviate a stoppage that kept her from breast-feeding her infant; the mid-century American Laura Lyman seducing her absent husband with inflammatory letters promising that on his return, "I'll drain your coffers dry next Saturday I assure you"; lower-middle-class art lovers as the first to appreciate the revolutionary canvases of Cézanne; the pioneer of Italian unity, Giuseppe Mazzini, in English exile, infuriated on discovering that officials had been opening his mail; the avant-garde poet Charles Baudelaire praising the bourgeoisie for its taste in art; the German steel magnate Alfred Krupp refusing a title of nobility. There are necessarily some others.

But this is not to say that this book, moderate in size if not necessarily in its conclusions, is merely a *Reader's Digest* condensation of the bulky texts that preceded it. I have introduced a great deal of new material and subjects like work and religion that, though they had a place in my five-volume study, deserved more consideration than I had given them before. The fundamental reinterpretations of generally accepted views about the Victorian bourgeoisie that figured largely in *The Bourgeois Experience*, notably on middle-class attitudes toward sexuality, aggression, taste, and privacy, will prominently reappear here. But not even they are simply old wine in a new, trim bottle. I have rethought them and, I think, complicated them even further.

▓ ONE MATTER REQUIRES CLARIFICATION AT THE outset: my generous employment of the name "Victorian." Customary usage has long defined "Victorian" as pointing to British, and even more narrowly, to English tastes, morals, and manners. Its meaning has never been wholly confined to the reign of Queen Victoria, since it is generally recognized that there were Victorians before her accession in 1837 and after her death in 1901. In short, her name has been loosely applied to the nineteenth century that dates roughly from Napoleon's final defeat in 1815 to the outbreak of World War I in 1914. But there were also Victorians outside her realm. In recent years, historians of American culture have domesticated the term, and I believe that it can be properly generalized even further. This is not to say, of course, that French or German or Italian "Victorians" were precisely like their British contemporaries; this book is, in addition to being a venture in generalization, also a celebration of differences. But there is, I am convinced, a strong family resemblance among bourgeois for all these differences, and it is this resemblance that my way of using "Victorian" is designed to underscore.

But now to raise the curtain.

Overture

"A DIARY IS FOUND, OF COURSE THE MOST recent one (about Emilie). Big scenes with my father." In the chapters that follow, I want to explore the implications of this laconic entry. By exploiting a seemingly fugitive domestic skirmish, an unwanted invasion of a schoolboy's closely held confessions, as a clue to the Victorian middle-class experience, I am not claiming that such an encounter was common. But it should play the role of a brief overture that rehearses the motifs that will recur, greatly amplified and wide-ranging, in the ambitious composition it introduces. This traumatic confrontation opens up the macrocosm of nineteenth-century bourgeois culture. It carries the weight of that well-remembered moment in *A la recherche du temps perdu*, in which the taste of a madeleine dipped in lime-blossom tea retrieves for Proust's narrator—and will retrieve for the reader—a rich, long-forgotten past. This diary entry is my madeleine.

The protagonists: Arthur Schnitzler, a sixteen-year-old about to leave for a day's classes at the Akademische Gymnasium, and his father, Dr. Johann Schnitzler, an eminent throat specialist and professor at the university. The time: the morning of March 18, 1879. The place: an upper-middle-class apartment in Vienna. The object of contention: a little red book that the father has purloined from a locked drawer in his son's desk, a surreptitious, indiscreet record to which the young man had confided some precocious erotic exploits, in detail, and not about Emilie alone.

Recounting the incident some thirty-five years later in his autobiography, Schnitzler, by then Austria's most prominent and most controversial writer, expanded on the brisk sentences he had devoted to it in his diary. Evidently the encounter had left an indelible mark on him. He recalled the "terrible reprimand" his father had launched against him on that March morning. The lecture had culminated in the professor's consulting room with the son obliged to leaf through Moritz Kaposi's three-volume standard treatise on syphilis and skin diseases complete with explicit and repellent illustrations. Schnitzler acknowledged that the lesson had had its uses: it ended his visits to the various "Greek goddesses" he had frequented—Venus, Hebe, and Juno, he called them—and made him more prudent in his sexual exploits.

But not all of its aftermath had been quite so salutary. Schnitzler pointedly commented that he had not given his father the key to his desk drawer and he strongly, if by and large silently, objected to his father's "underhanded method." He saw it as an act of perfidy that no good intentions could excuse. "If indeed we could never establish a wholly unreserved relationship between us, surely the inextinguishable memory of that breach of trust was in part responsible for it." The father had broken a bond with his son that could never be wholly repaired.

This was not the only intrusion into his privacy that the young Schnitzler had to endure. Three months after his father's well-meant invasion, one of his Gymnasium teachers, inspecting written material his class had smuggled into the examination room, got a good look at the opening pages of Schnitzler's new diary that contained some excited passages about his current infatuation. Graciously, he did not comment on this intimate text or betray its existence to Dr. Schnitzler, but his very access drove Schnitzler to despair: an unauthorized person had seen his most personal papers! He told a friend that nothing would do now but to shoot himself.

Obviously, Schnitzler did not carry out this pubertal-romantic gesture. Rather, in July 1882, he destroyed his diaries one by one because, he decided, they consisted of tedious "blather about frictions at home" and a few comments, some gushing and some frigid, about "Fännchen," his love of the moment. But he did not dispose of them all: some passages were clearly too interesting to be lost to posterity. Schnitzler's distaste for his daily entries wrestled with a certain affection for his youthful transgressions, and so he copied out the essentials, starting with the terse reference to his father's crime. Looking back, one can see why: the adult's violation of his boyish private space rankled and helped to shape his outlook on the world he would so closely observe and so fiercely anatomize. That the emotional charge animating the clash between the Schnitzlers, though lasting only an hour or so in a life intensely lived, should survive for decades in a mind of exceptional retentiveness, wit, and subtlety, makes it a clue worth pursuing. As he put it in *Paracelsus*, a one-act play of 1887 that provides a key text to his psychological preoccupations, life is a mysterious game; the soul opens its gates only rarely and only to the perceptive and persistent inquirer. "Dream and waking, truth and lie flow into one another. Safety is nowhere." Safety is nowhere—it might serve as Schnitzler's motto, and, we shall see, as that of his class.

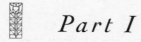

Part I

FUNDAMENTALS

McCounter Jumper *repents of an Easter Trip in a Third-class Carriage.*

ONE

Bourgeoisie(s)

 EVERYTHING IN THE SCENE STARRING
Arthur Schnitzler's diary speaks of prosperity: the boy
inhabiting a room of his own complete with desk; his attending a
Gymnasium, which only a select minority of Vienna's families could
afford; his father's well-appointed consulting room. The ambiance
exudes an aura of comfort, with expensive music lessons—Schnitzler
became a competent amateur pianist—and with servants hovering in the
background. At the time of this closet drama, the Schnitzlers were living
in Leopoldstadt, Vienna's Second District. It was being rapidly transformed into a quarter populated by Jews, most of them poor, who were
immigrating by the thousands from the countryside and the eastern
reaches of the Austro-Hungarian Empire in search of a better life and
relief from anti-Semitic outrages: around 1880, nearly half of Vienna's
Jews lived there. But during Schnitzler's childhood, he recalled, it was
"still genteel and respectable." As a young man, he mainly frequented
"good Jewish middle-class circles," which is to say, his own.

Through the years, he would not confine himself to his thriving, well-
educated Viennese world as he traveled across the range of respectabil-

ity, at times beyond. As a physician, he had professional, if rather distant, connections with the medical world. As a writer, he came to make friends with publishers, journalists, novelists, playwrights, critics, actors, to say nothing of actresses. As a bachelor—he did not marry until 1902, at forty—he spent many evenings in his favorite haunt, the café Griensteidl, with friends like Richard Beer-Hofmann, Felix Salten, Hugo von Hofmannsthal, all of them writers, trading literary gossip, manuscripts, sometimes mistresses. And, as will emerge, as a lover he ventured among women from the petty bourgeoisie of the outer districts, the Vorstadt. He was crossing boundaries, knew it, and used in his writings the knowledge he stockpiled by living hard.

1

SCHNITZLER'S EXCURSIONS UP AND DOWN THE social ladder provide an instructive glimpse of a wider social reality. They are just one instance of an important characteristic of nineteenth-century urban life: the Victorian bourgeoisie was sizable, diverse, and deeply fissured.* One other telling illustration of this complexity will suffice. In the 1850s, the marchese Massimo d'Azeglio, painter, novelist, and politician, then prime minister of Piedmont, noted that in his country, "the hierarchical instinct dominates the whole of society." To capture these subtle gradations, one needed "a whole series of subcategories" more refined than merely "nobility, bourgeoisie, people and plebs." He believed a little complacently that such shadings were more nuanced at home than elsewhere, but there he was mistaken. Everywhere, the slightest subdivisions in the middling ranks could generate social discrimination, economic nepotism, envy, and gossip, to say nothing of marital strategies wherever bourgeois clustered in appreciable numbers. The historian attempting to understand the nineteenth-

---

*As I noted in the preface, but want to reiterate here, I am using the term "Victorian" very broadly in this book, to include all of Western civilization, and synonymous with "nineteenth century."

century bourgeoisie must come to terms with pervasive conflicts among those who defined themselves as "middle class" as much as with the qualities that made them kin.

Not unexpectedly, conflicts within the middling orders were more pronounced than peaceful cooperation. Tariffs on imports were a boon to domestic manufacturers but a burden on merchants. Distribution of largesse from the central government, whether paintings donated to provincial museums or subsidies provided to struggling industries, led to disputes about favoritism among cities or regions. The issue of state support for sectarian schools became a contentious issue between devout and secular citizens. The location of the railroad network, which speedily spread through most of Europe in the 1840s and 1850s, became a matter of virtual economic life and death across the map. And, as we shall see, limitations on the right to vote on the basis of income were sore points between bourgeois safely at home in the political elite and bourgeois aspiring to join them. Some of these contests were trivial: in the late nineteenth century, Munich and Berlin engaged in a rivalry, carried on mainly in the press, over which was the cultural capital of Germany. But most of the time, the stakes were higher than this. Economic self-interest, religious agendas, intellectual convictions, social competition, the proper place of women became political issues where bourgeois battled bourgeois.

These divisions were so acute that it is tempting to doubt that the bourgeoisie was a definable entity at all. This nominalism can only be fed by the recognition that all collective statements necessarily oversimplify the rich diversity of social life and likely slight singular variations. But unless historians reduce every report on the past into a collection of biographies, a literally impossible task, they must, however circumspectly, gather into diverse baskets substantial similarities, shared family traits. I have written this book in the conviction that while it may be hard to live with generalizations, it is inconceivable to live without them.

At all events, for at least two centuries, journalists and politicians, ideologues and historians, intent on making partisan, or at least intelligible points, have ignored glaring exceptions to their global statements about the bourgeoisie. And grand simplicities about it have long been particular favorites among its detractors. Yet it will emerge that there are ways of gathering Victorian bourgeois into a single class, even if its internal strains are as interesting as its fragile unity. The nineteenth-century British practice of resorting to the plural—the "middling ranks" or the "middle classes"—has much to commend it.

▓ THOUGH AVERAGE VICTORIANS WERE NO DOUBT impatient with fine discriminations, their linguistic conventions document their awareness that the bourgeoisie was one and many at the same time. They retained the collective name but subdivided it: the Germans had their *Grossbürgertum* and *Kleinbürgertum,* the French the *grande, bonne,* and *petite bourgeoisie.* In the course of years, they sliced these rough divisions even more exquisitely: the Germans drew a distinction between the bourgeoisie of property and that of cultivation— *Besitzbürgertum* and *Bildungsbürgertum.* Everywhere, popular locutions underscored the intricacies of class hierarchies: in France, the epithet *l'aristocracie financière* paid homage, in an amalgam of jealousy and disdain, to the political weight of bankers, as did the term *Geldaristokratie* for the German aristocracy of money. Contemptuous of the bottom of the heap, Germans nicknamed the lowest segments of their *Bürgertum,* the lowest paid in the army of clerks, proletarians in stand-up collars, *Stehkragenproletarier.* Such oxymorons were essential to the search for precision.

In the professions, gifted bourgeois—painters, singers, poets, eminent professors, or natural scientists—carved out careers outside the familiar economic hierarchies to establish a ranking of prestige rivaling that of wealth. Their grateful society showered them with medals, provided them with access to privileged circles, invited them to marry into the gentry, or buried them in national shrines. It even bestowed on a handful of them titles of nobility. The German painter Adolph Menzel was elevated to Adolph von Menzel; the English poet Alfred Tennyson, to Alfred, first lord Tennyson.

Less dazzling, though still gratifying rewards awaited other Victorian bourgeois. A phalanx of lawyers, physicians, middling bureaucrats, bankers, merchants, and industrialists, the solid core of the bourgeoisie, respected and respectable, were content with being of the middle classes, even proud of it. Some tycoons, like Alfred Krupp, the preeminent munitions maker in the German empire, politely rejected the offer of a title, saying that he would "rather be the first among industrialists than the last among knights." Another example: In Austria, Friedrich Lohmeyr, scion of a dynasty of glass manufacturers that took great pride in its craft origins, refused ennoblement, a rare and striking gesture in a society in which the imperial court scattered titles by the thousands. Mainly the upper crust of the bourgeoisie, the great plutocrats, some of them aching to escape into the aristocracy, and its lowest counterpart, poverty-stricken petty bourgeois afraid of being plunged into the mass of plebeians, monitored the prospects of their status closely and anxiously.

🎴 WHAT FURTHER COMPLICATES ANY ATTEMPT TO define the nineteenth-century bourgeoisie is the fact that it had a history. It was not static; many bourgeois harbored great expectations, of wealth, of prestige, of fame, of social ascent. They were not wholly unrealistic; there was a measure of upward social mobility in the Victorian century for the unusually talented, unusually lucky, or unusually unscrupulous. Only the very few could even dream of emulating John D. Rockefeller or Andrew Carnegie, but the rise of these two to stunning riches made for tales that fostered fantasies. A slender minority of enterprising bourgeois climbed economically, and soon after that socially, at vertiginous speed. The brothers Eugène and Adolphe Schneider, sons of a modest provincial notary, became the steel kings of France in one generation. And Carnegie himself had arrived in the United States from Scotland with his indigent family, yet made himself into one of the wealthiest men in the world, the stuff of legends.

One could recount many such stories, a number of them even true, of rags transformed into riches within a few decades. Aristide Boucicaut, the son of a lowly hatter, founded the Parisian department store Le Bon

Marché and was worth 22 million francs at his death in 1877. George Peabody, born in 1795 to an impecunious branch of an old American family in a small Massachusetts town, had to leave school at eleven to work in a general store, but soon managed his own wholesale dry goods store in Washington, with branches in New York and Philadelphia. By 1827, he was worth $85,000; only a decade later, having become an international trader, he moved to London and went into banking. Twenty-five years later, in 1852, he had amassed a fortune of over $3 million, perhaps some $50 million in today's currency.

Arthur Schnitzler's father, the highly esteemed laryngologist Dr. Johann Schnitzler, belongs among these favorites of fortunes, one of many Jews—even unconverted Jews—whom the century of widespread liberation granted an entrance into the world of success. His life graphically demonstrates how far a bourgeois could go in that age with ability and ambition, especially if decorated with agreeable manners. Born in the Hungarian town of Gross-Kanizsa in what his son called "indigent, indeed shabby circumstances," the son of a skillful but illiterate and alcoholic joiner, he made his way to Vienna in a wagon, and there, like other penniless students, financed his medical education by giving lessons. Yet he climbed up the social and professional ladder to reach the summit with a professorship at the university and the prestigious title of *Regierungsrat,* coveted in a society in which waiters invariably addressed their regulars as Herr Baron or at least Herr Doctor, whether earned or not. No doubt ability counted for much in such life histories, but so did opportunities. In these social and economic success stories the cooperation of the historical moment was an essential prerequisite.

That moment of course appeared particularly sustained and alluring in the United States; the country, a virtually legendary beckoning giant, invited daydreams of easy success among Europeans desperate or enterprising enough to leave their continent behind. Germans looking westward for opportunities they could not hope for at home imagined the golden land overseas as the land of unlimited possibilities—*das Land der unbegrenzten Möglichkeiten*—although they discovered after they landed that the country often proved reluctant to give them access to the secret map that showed the way to wealth and security.

Numerous newcomers to the United States accumulated fortunes, growing with its western and southern reaches, and in the burgeoning cities. But others remained mired in the shallows of the New World as they had been in the Old. After midcentury, the glut of Victorian success literature, modern fairy tales predictably addicted to happy endings, had become an international mainstay for publishers. Horatio Alger's vastly popular confections, mainly recounting the climb of a penniless orphan—he perpetrated more than a hundred narratives chronicling a near-miraculous rise in the world—was a tribute to the power of the imagination. Far from documenting an open society, Alger and his imitators displayed wishful thinking at its most inflamed, in which all too real barriers to quick wealth melted away. In fact, the spectrum ranging from success to failure in America was very wide and far from predictable. Ascent was on a ladder with many broken rungs.

2

ONE TRAIT THAT DISTINGUISHED NINETEENTH-century bourgeois publics from one another was their habitual, though not unchangeable, mind-set concerning the authorities that governed them—here, as elsewhere, the definition of the Victorian bourgeoisie depends heavily on attitudes. Obviously enough, the more unchecked the holders of power, the more subservient their middle-class subjects, the less able they were to mount initiatives not just in politics but also in the arts, literature, or education. Two extreme middle-class types coexisted in Victorian civilization, the one forceful, the other inert, with mixed types in between.

A comparison between two nineteenth-century cities, Manchester and Munich, will mark the outer limits between bourgeois enterprise and bourgeois complaisance. The citizens of Manchester, a booming textile town, produced an efficient and magnanimous army of self-started philanthropists. In 1846, they founded Owens College—it was granted a university charter in 1880—from a private legacy of about £100,000. Two years later, the year of revolutions across the Continent that left

Britain unscathed, three local merchants invited the German conductor and piano virtuoso Karl Halle, long resident in France, to take Manchester's musical life in hand. In his long and impressive career—he died Sir Charles Hallé in 1895—he energetically transformed the city into one of the preeminent centers of music in the Western world. Before long, the Hallé Orchestra, launched in 1858 (typically Hallé's private property), secured an international reputation. There was more for Manchester's leading citizens to be proud of through the decades: they built themselves an assertive Gothic town hall, an art museum, and great libraries. In 1895, Her Majesty Queen Victoria graciously consented to have the exalted term "Royal" added to the name of the new Manchester conservatory. But that was pure decoration; local capitalists had already donated all the necessary funds.

Munich, the capital of Bavaria's Wittelsbach monarchy, could not have been more different. In twenty-three years of rule beginning in 1825, the art-loving Ludwig I had set the tone for, and largely financed, the city's cultural institutions. He was his country's unrivaled first builder, giving welcome employment to a swarm of architects, masons, carpenters, glaziers, framers, sculptors, muralists, and gardeners. The king's record is impressive: he was responsible, among other things, for moving the university to Munich from the provincial town of Langhut; building the Glyptothek, which provided a magnificent backdrop for classical sculpture, and the Alte Pinakothek, which housed a fine collection of old masters. Not content with these monuments to high culture, he permanently altered the appearance of Munich, commissioning churches, exhibition halls, and broad avenues. Only his forced retirement in 1848, compelled to abdicate over a pathetic (and expensive) affair with the dancer Lola Montez, kept him from completing yet another project, the Neue Pinakothek, designed to display his superb collection of contemporary German art.

Under his successors as under his benevolent autocracy, the Wittelsbach spirit, and money, were active wherever Bavaria's, and Munich's, high culture needed attention and support. Maximilian II kept Ludwig's program alive, though at a more restrained pace, and invited humanists from northern Germany to settle in his capital. And it is only too well known that without Ludwig II, Richard Wagner's Bayreuth would have remained a pipe dream. It was typical of Bavaria's cultural style that the conductor Hermann Levi, who raised the city's opera and orchestra to the highest levels in Germany, perhaps in Europe, should be a civil servant. And, a few insubordinate gestures apart, the city's *Bürger,* at once pampered and patronized, followed their dynasty's lead. Even a private organization like the *Kunstverein,* which brought together practicing artists and art-loving amateurs, had to obtain the king's permission for its statutes and met under the vigilant eyes of the Royal Academy. It was not until late in the century that some enterprising Munich citizens began to organize their own exhibitions. It had taken them many long years before they dared to throw away the crutches of all-knowing authority.

Nineteenth-century Manchester and Munich were extremes. Most cultural capitals of the time — Vienna, Paris, London, and, after the 1860s, Berlin — were mixed types, combining private and public sources of inspiration and of funds wrestling for supremacy, with the pressures from the top usually prevailing. But Manchester and Munich were not alone. Amsterdam's celebrated Rijksmuseum and Concertgebouw were the creations of a few cultivated and enterprising merchants. Berlin's Philharmonic Orchestra, which rapidly vaulted to the top of Germany's finest ensembles, was founded by its musicians in 1882. Similarly the Boston Symphony Orchestra was the product of Brahmin, which is to say private, initiative. And in serving literature and the arts, Birmingham was in many respects the twin of Manchester. After midcentury, it opened a major free public library complete with branches and founded an art museum, the first financed from local taxes and the second from the profits garnered by the municipal gasworks, remarkable exercises in democratic culture. Filled with justified pride, the citizens of Birmingham placed an eloquent inscription in the museum's entrance hall: "By the gains of industry we promote art." Nothing could contrast more sharply with the servile, but accurate, legend that Munich's grateful town fathers engraved into a copper plate they placed next to the corner stone of the Alte Pinakothek: "Bavaria owes the building and its art treasures to the noble disposition of its rulers, the House of Wittelsbach."

Together, these two lapidary texts attest to the coexistence of bourgeois self-reliance and bourgeois dependency in the Victorian age.

THE QUESTION WHETHER THE BOURGEOISIE OF any country should be counted among the self-assertive or the submissive raises the tragicomedy of the nineteenth-century middle classes in politics. Nothing can advance—and complicate—the search for a definition of the Victorian bourgeoisie more fruitfully than this line of inquiry. For the historian, the study of past politics entails more than tracking the pursuit of power under specified rules; showing classes in action, it points directly at fundamental self-appraisals, at expectations and anxieties. The most energetic among Victorian bourgeois had to confront royal arbitrariness, aristocratic claims, clerical interference, time-honored cultural habits. Yet the quest for political power obsessed middle-class activists across most Western societies. "The middle class must govern," the Zurich politician and physician Johannes Hegetschweiler asserted in 1837, tersely summing up the agenda of those bourgeois across Europe smarting under their lack of access to public influence. For their part, obedient and indifferent bourgeois could only dream of power, much of the time not even that, and remain content with scratching a living and avoiding disputes with local potentates. "The Tuscan bourgeois," wrote Stendhal in the mid-1820s, hard as it was for him to admit it, "of a timid disposition, enjoys his quiet and his well-being, works to enrich himself and a little to enlighten himself, but without ever dreaming of taking his place in the government." All he and his kin aimed to do was to avoid work and annoyance. The same charge could be leveled against bourgeois in other countries.

A preponderance of discontented Italian opinion echoed Stendhal's rebuke through the decades. In fact, nineteenth-century Italian bourgeois, before their country's conclusive unification in 1870 and even after that, serve as a model of tameness. The elites essentially running the country were highly concentrated and rarely questioned. That celebrated Italian motto in praise of idleness, *Dolce far niente*, seemed to be inscribed over the entrances of banks, shops, and factories. Middle-class initiative and inventiveness, without which capitalism must stagnate, were rare.

Four decades after Stendhal, in the 1860s, another observant French visitor, Hippolyte Taine, literary and political historian and perceptive psychologist, virtually copied his precedessor. "Is there in Rome any degree of moral energy?" he asked, and responded skeptically, "Most of my friends reply, no; the government has demoralized men." Aided by the church, it had systematically obstructed independent thinking. "People are extraordinarily intelligent, adroit, and calculating, but no less egotistical." It followed that "as enterprise and action are prejudicial and regarded unfavourably, indolence becomes honourable." All that other eyewitnesses could add was that the country was beset by crippling corruption, that well-to-do northern *borghesi* were blasé about the appalling poverty and illiteracy in the country's southern regions, and that their own endemic attitude toward work was one of unabashed aversion. And it was true: Italian industrialization failed to match that of other European countries, and its most spectacular advances, as in the steel industry, were mainly generated by the state rather than through individual enterprise. The Italian bourgeoisie, witness to historic transformations in the peninsula, mainly sat and waited.

Other political cultures, however, experienced drastic shifts, learning to cope with world-shattering inventions and devising political instruments, like the widening of the suffrage, to keep the social peace. Each bourgeoisie took its own path, though most also responded to stimuli from their neighbors: the European revolutions of 1848 were sparked in France with the embers rapidly leaping across frontiers. These revolutions were essentially middle-class efforts with the working classes their weapon and their victim, and by and large failures. Yet by around 1900, the grip of the middle classes on political power was far tighter than it had been only a century before, even though it was far from complete.

———

THIS IS HOW MOST HISTORIANS WOULD SEE THE matter today; but most contemporary students of politics thought the middle classes in political control, at least in France; in fact, largely so since the French Revolution. If observers had any doubts about this straightforward diagnosis, they were largely stilled after the revolution of 1830, which, too, started in France. It dethroned the Bourbon dynasty that had reclaimed power fifteen years earlier after Napoleon's Waterloo, and elevated the more pliant Orléanists to the place they had left vacant. Countless caricatures of the new king, Louis Philippe, depicted him as a bourgeois with his happy marriage, large family, and modest walks complete with umbrella. Did he not embody the class he served? As early as 1836, Michel Chevalier, public servant, travel writer, and, later, adviser to Napoleon III, could sum up his sense of bourgeois political power in one short sentence: "Today it is universally recognized that the middle class rules in France." Only a few years after that, Heinrich Heine, in French exile, called his time "an industrial, bourgeois age."

Alexis de Tocqueville, the most profound political commentator of the century, lent this thesis his lasting prestige. In his memoirs, he paid the bourgeoisie a reluctant tribute: "In 1830, the triumph of the middle class was definitive and so complete that all political power, all the privileges, all the prerogatives, the entire government, found themselves locked, and, as it were, piled up within the narrow confines of that single class." And so, "it made itself at home in all offices, prodigiously augmented its numbers and grew used to living almost as much off the public treasury as from its own efforts." This conquest, Tocqueville believed, had produced a dramatic change in the French mentality: the mind-set distinctive of the middle class had been elevated into the mind-set dominant across class lines. It was, to him, not a welcome development.

From the left, Karl Marx advanced a view of middle-class supremacy substantially like that of Tocqueville. Even the Bourbon Restoration of 1815, he argued, despite its reactionary schemes to revive the eighteenth-century Old Régime, despite its ostentatious religiosity and royalism, was a bourgeois state managed by one powerful branch, the large landowners. Then, from 1830 until 1851, when Louis Napoleon, the Nephew, imitated his Uncle, Napoleon I, by making himself master of France with a coup d'état, other sectors of the middle class—merchants, manufacturers, bankers—had manipulated the régime in their behalf. And in times of popular insurrection, as in June 1848, when workers went into the streets to claim some of the benefits of the Revolution, the bourgeoisie had joined other butchers of the masses and taken the lead in establishing the repressive régime of the Party of Order. Finally, Marx noted, under the Second Empire, though Napoleon III kept the threads of authority in his hands, the bourgeoisie continued to prosper. What is particularly arresting about such confident declarations and others like them is their tone: they sound as though they were expressing a familiar and unarguable truth when in fact it was highly problematic. Bourgeois activists on the political battlefields, struggling to enlarge their share in political power, knew better. A number of countries, including most of the crazy quilt of German states small and large, were governed by absolutist regimes constrained by no constitution at all, or by a council called into session only to ratify the prince's will.

The compass of the bourgeois electorate and the degree of bourgeois influence never quite matched. Even John Stuart Mill, the great liberal, acknowledged that those who govern must rely on a handful of sage, largely invisible counselors. The elites making things happen were always far more exclusive than the voting public, and they normally made decisions out of sight. A cabal of generals, a camarilla of bishops, a cluster of confidential advisers to the ruler, a consortium of bankers directed affairs in ways of which citizens, even the well informed, knew little and over which they had no control. Most of the indictments leveled at governments presumably in thrall to secret pressures were driven by the appetite of journalists for sensational disclosures and by the paranoia of the ignorant. But at least some of these suspicions proved true enough. One thinks of the enormous political power of French banks like the Péreire brothers' Crédit Mobilier or J. P. Morgan's almost single-handed rescue of U.S. credit in 1907.

Still, bourgeois clamoring for the right to join what the French call the *pays légal* thought that this would give them leverage to exert pressure on the shaping of policy, especially when joined by a free press that permitted sympathetic journalists to speak for them. That pressure, to be sure, was significantly compromised in most countries: citizens subservient to landowners, employers, or local magnates casting their vote in the open normally bowed to the wishes of their masters. A troop of censors and undercover agents, most conspicuously in the years between 1815 and 1848, when Prince Metternich was Europe's policeman, inhibited all but the most tepid criticism of the state, its rulers, and its actions. In a pseudo-parliamentary régime like Bismarck's German Reich, founded in 1871, in which the cabinet was responsible not to the legislature but to the emperor, the vote by itself did little to move the levers of power.

What is more, régimes lording it over a limited electorate soon mastered the art of manipulating election returns by threats, bribery, and the sheer manufacture of results. The votes of government employees could be counted on as a matter of course, and others, too, could be made all too predictable. Politics, a new experience for unnumbered thousands of Victorian middle-class men, was proving to be a disillusioning business for idealists. And yet, in countries like the United States and Britain, with the emergence of modern political parties, legalized oppositions, and a partly unshackled press, the possibility of making votes count was always in the cards.

❧ DEBATES OVER CRITERIA FOR POLITICAL FITNESS, a legacy from the eighteenth century, became a staple in public debates across Europe and the United States in the Victorian age, dramatizing once again the divisions characterizing the middling orders. Ideological discord pitted bourgeois liberals against bourgeois democrats and both against bourgeois conservatives. Who should be eligible to vote, or (an even narrower elite) to serve in the legislature? The most widely canvassed instance of those controversies figured prominently in the

Frankfurt parliament of 1848, sitting amidst revolutionary risings in the German states. The delegates' agenda was to write a constitution for a united Germany still to be founded—a pathetic failure after Prussia's Friedrich Wilhelm IV, to whom the parliament offered the crown, contemptuously rejected it. In their debates, the suitable extent of the suffrage aroused fervent emotions. The democrats, in a permanent minority, bravely lectured their fellow delegates to persuade them that mere wealth does not guarantee independence of mind, that bureaucrats and professors, always held up as ideal voters, are no freer than intelligent workingmen. But the liberals objected that an illiterate peasant or a destitute laborer was scarcely a creature rational enough to fulfill a citizen's duty. More, they warned that a radical extension of the suffrage would only produce a modern form of Caesarism: the rule of an autocrat resting his authority on the assent, real or manufactured, of the masses too infatuated to see than when they enthusiastically endorsed a leader, they were voting themselves not into freedom but into a new slavery.

The notion of modern Caesarism, emerging to prominence around midcentury, deeply engaged bourgeois in their political debates. Marx disliked the term, but other contemporaries found it significant: Caesarist demagogy, counting on the susceptibility of the great unwashed for colorful campaigns, primitive slogans, and the cult of personality, was a promising technique for bypassing the middle-class voter. It was a way, Bismarck said cynically, of bringing down parliamentarism by means of parliamentarism. In 1866, as Prussia's prime minister, he proposed a German parliament elected through universal manhood suffrage, and reassured one of his worried political allies: "In a country with monarchical traditions and loyal sentiments, universal suffrage would lead to monarchical elections by eliminating the influence of the liberal bourgeois classes."

Middle-class politicians, alert to this danger, far more threatening than old-fashioned monarchism, lobbied for a limited expansion of the suffrage in their own behalf. They wanted the right to vote extended, but not too much. The Caesars would piously protest that they were the servants of the people, who had expressed its will by choosing them. But after midcentury, few liberals were deceived by this rhetoric. They knew their political interests and their political history too thoroughly for that, remembering only too well that Napoleon I and Napoleon III had exploited plebiscites with universal manhood suffrage to hoist themselves into power and to keep themselves there.

This baldly summarized, the middle-class bid for political influence may seem nothing better than a single-minded contest for power to secure self-centered, mainly financial ends. But so jaundiced a reading of the Victorian bourgeoisie in politics reduces complex human beings to simple moneymaking machines. Doubtless legislation benefiting industrial, agricultural, and business interests was a widespread, scarcely disguised endeavor in nineteenth-century politics. It was supported by rationalizations that identified the dividends accruing to capitalists with the welfare of society as a whole. But interests were more than merely economic. Idealistic bourgeois were intent on abolishing slavery, outlawing childhood labor, introducing divorce, granting citizenship rights to members of religious minorities. Much of the time, the appeal to conscience, which figured large in nineteenth-century rhetoric, may have been a convenient veil thrown over the lust for money and control. But it was too, often enough, the authentic voice of a self-critical superego seeking an outlet in political action.

3

BOURGEOIS CAMPAIGNING FOR THE EXTENSION of the suffrage had a wide field to conquer: except for the United States, the right to vote in constitutional states was narrow. It barred most bourgeois, and even after reforms grudgingly introduced, it often continued to bar them. In this atmosphere, only a new country, the proud, self-assertive republic of the United States, could break through the old distinction between inhabitants qualified and those unqualified to share in making public policy. From the early decades of the century, American orators and editorialists distanced their blessed country from reactionary Europe. By the 1850s, the United States boasted universal suffrage, though its practice was tarnished by two weighty exceptions: slaves and women. But (at least in law) the first of these were enfranchised after the Civil War, while the second had to wait until the end of the century: in 1890, the new state of Wyoming extended the vote to women, promptly followed by Colorado, Idaho, and Utah. But cultivated Europeans, basking in their (largely imaginary) superiority, liked to protest that the United States, a country of wild cowboys, sprawling cities, vulgar and boastful democrats, and no discernible high culture, had nothing to teach them.

On that Continent, though, bourgeois made massive strides, if intermittently. In France, with a population of well over 26 million, the charter adopted in 1814 to guide the Bourbon Restoration confined the suffrage to citizens paying more than 300 francs in taxes. In practice, this meant that about ninety thousand, a mere 1 percent of adult males, had the right to vote. To be eligible as a candidate for the legislative Chamber, one had to pass through a second, even more selective sieve: at least 1,000 francs paid in direct taxes. This conferred the privilege of sitting in the Chamber to a handful of fifteen thousand Frenchmen. Together, they produced a régime of landowning gentry who associated with upper-level bureaucrats and with aristocrats, both normally landowners as well. What with a heavy representation of prominent lawyers, plutocrats aspiring to a title, and public officials wanting nothing more than to remain public officials, bourgeois interests faded into the background.

The overthrow of the Bourbons in 1830 changed less than at first appeared. Apart from the accession of a new dynasty and a decimation of old-line bureaucrats, the political public remained much as before. The biggest gainers in the Chamber were the lawyers, while businessmen increased their numbers slightly. That bourgeois influence over policy grew is undeniable; as disgruntled aristocrats withdrew to their estates, an increasing number of prosperous middle-class Frenchmen became seriously involved in their country's political culture, and this made a difference in legislation. But this was not quite the bourgeois régime of current legend.

True, in 1831, the July Monarchy almost trebled the number of eligible voters. But this meant only that perhaps 250,000 Frenchmen, around 3 percent of adult males, now had the vote. Similarly, Belgium, split off from the Dutch Netherlands in 1830, enacted a constitution that gave the suffrage to about the same percentage of adult males. Half a century later, government by property owners still found vigorous defenders. In the Italy of 1870, after an exhilarating decade of military action and international diplomacy that consolidated the state, the country had a total population of 27 million, with about half a million adult males eligible to vote—some 8 percent. The much-touted electoral reform of 1882 quadrupled this figure by lowering the voting age and the required amount of taxes paid. But impressive as this sounds, it made little dent in the political domination by the few for the few: elections were corrupt and managed by the holders of power. The middle classes remained unimpressive in size, adding up (including the petty bourgeoisie of small businessmen, landowners, and clerks) to roughly 750,000, and were largely concentrated in the northern regions. And late in the century in Sweden, only a third of adult males enjoyed the privilege of the vote, and this after several extensions.

All these laborious evolutions read like reluctant concessions to liberal bourgeois agendas. Yet one country was widely hailed as a model of how to ease the middle classes into political culture: Great Britain. A series of acts between 1832 and 1885 widened the franchise until it became inclusive enough to give respectable workingmen the vote. The famous First Reform Act, many argued, had decisively broken the iron hold that the oligarchy, nobles and gentry, had long enjoyed in Parliament. In fact, it only rationalized and broadened that oligarchy. The power of personal patronage decreased, but members of Parliament were unpaid and had to depend on their own wealth or on that of a patron. The Second Reform Act, of 1867, continued the march to a wide franchise, and two important pieces of legislation responded to the needs of the larger political public that this act had decreed into being. The law of 1870 establishing universal education was intended to make the masses ripe for legitimate political participation. And the act of 1872 established the secret ballot, which greatly increased the privacy of the vote, an impressive victory for that supreme bourgeois value.

Yet, all pronouncements to the contrary, nineteenth-century Britain, much like other countries, was not in the hands of the bourgeoisie—not yet. In 1859, in his celebrated essay on liberty, John Stuart Mill declared the governing class to be "chiefly the middle class." More than a dozen years earlier, Friedrich Engels had already flatly described the "ruling class" of Britain, "as in all other civilized countries, the bourgeoisie." Half a century later, near the end of his life, he recognized this pronouncement to be an unacceptable generalization as he wondered at the "meekness" of the "wealthy middle class." It had left, he concluded, "the landed aristocracy in almost exclusive possession of all the leading government offices." His second thoughts were more accurate than his first. Still, commoners were making their inroads.

❧ NOT ALL THE HISTORY OF VICTORIAN BOURGEOIS politics is a success story. Sharply contrasting with Great Britain, in Schnitzler's country the bourgeoisie, particularly its liberal wing, suffered catastrophic reverses. In that multinational conglomerate known since 1867 as the Austro-Hungarian Empire, the *Bürgertum* never established a secure mass base, and was doomed to witness the noisy triumph of unchecked nationalists, racist anti-Semites, and narrowly partisan politicians. A petty bourgeois party, the Christian Socials, careful to stress its middle-class nature, prospered by promising to address the grievances of small shopkeepers dwarfed by department stores and of trained artisans displaced by industry. In 1897, the adroit anti-Semitic politician Karl Lueger became mayor of Vienna.

Even in its best days, the liberal Austrian bourgeoisie had not been disposed to take the lead in politics. When the revolutionary fervor of 1848 reached Hapsburg lands and reform was in the air, the middle classes loyally supported the neo-absolutist regime of the new emperor, Franz Joseph. In these exhilarating days, a handful of middle-class activists, though firmly declaring their allegiance to the throne, permitted themselves, as bourgeois, to offer a petition expressing their wish for a share in decision making. But they left the pervasive impression of a largely inert collection of loyal servants, fortunate enough to profit from the course of events rather than imposing themselves on them. Compared to their German neighbors, Austrian bourgeois were smaller in number and less enterprising in commerce and industry. Private initiative was slow to foster industrialization, and owed more to the state than to venture capitalists. The régime had nothing to fear from bourgeois radicals, whether in its Italian possessions, in Hungary, or in German Austria. They welcomed the liberalization of the laws, they did not make it happen; they took advantage of whatever press freedom the government allowed them and, in 1873, of an electoral reform that gave the vote to some 6 percent of adult males.

For Austria's Jews, the decades after 1848 were filled with hopes realized by the legalization of Jewish religious services, the removal of onerous taxes, the opening of professional and governmental careers. In 1860, when the liberals captured Vienna, prospects for Jews were brighter than ever. This was the time, Freud recalled, when "every Jewish boy carried a minister's portfolio in his satchel"; the time, too, when Dr. Johann Schnitzler could launch his remarkable career. In those years, anti-Semitism still seemed a relatively innocuous marginal phenomenon. When Schnitzler was a schoolboy in the early 1870s, there was only one anti-Semite in his class at the Gymnasium, and his classmates despised this boy as snobbish and stupid. That would change.

In this climate, Schnitzler and his literary friends thought they could afford to pay little attention to politics. His copious diaries suggest that from the late 1890s, when racial anti-Semitism had become an oppressive presence, he discussed this unpleasant matter with his friends, a little. In late November 1897, after Lueger had taken office in Vienna and there were disturbances in the streets, Schnitzler sat with his friends and, he noted, "even we talked politics." But that, at least until the outbreak of World War I, was a rare moment for him. He voted, when he did vote, for the Social Democrats, but he thought politics—he meant politics as usual: acting on partisan motives, libeling opponents, opportunistically shifting positions—a poor substitute for society's great task, which was to alleviate hunger. "The great politicians," he wrote in his diary, "were either monomaniacs or great gamblers with human beings." This kind of indifference to, or revulsion against, public activity was a luxury that an Austrian humane bourgeois could little afford.

One reason why the meekness of Austria's bourgeoisie has gone little noticed is that contemporary commentators seriously overstated middle-class activity in politics and culture alike. They transformed wishes into realities, but only in their minds. In 1869, in his authoritative history of music in Vienna, Eduard Hanslick, the czar of local reviewers, noted against all the evidence that the city's unsurpassed reputation for musicianship rested largely on its influential Society of Austrian Friends of Music, which he praised as a "purely bourgeois creation," animated by "the active enthusiasm of the music-loving middle class." In truth, the protectors and chief officials of that society were almost without exception aristocrats, and the crown and courtiers kept it alive with indispensable patronage.

Hanslick, himself a good bourgeois, was not alone in misleading his readers. In the early 1880s, a French journalist writing under the pseudonym of Count Paul Vasili, a professional traveler who had already published a study of Berlin, visited Vienna and concluded that whether "commercial, industrial, or agricultural," the bourgeoisie, dominating "all the liberal professions and occupying the largest share among state employees, finds itself the most powerful element in public life." Professors, scientists, artists, and litterateurs recruit their "most illustrious representatives" from the middle class. That was only natural: it was all due to the bourgeois character, "its incessant labors, its intelligence, its wealth." No wonder, he concluded, "the bourgeoisie has become a preponderant factor in the political affairs of Austria." A liberal Viennese bourgeois reading this appreciation around 1900 would have sighed for the good old days, although even those days had been less glorious for the middle classes than they appeared in retrospect.

Elsewhere, however, hopes for a place at the table with the makers of policy were firmly lodged in the minds of politically impassioned bourgeois. In short, from the beginning of the nineteenth century, the political map of Western countries was a checkered document, ranging from monarchs governing without a constitution to monarchs negotiating with their parliaments, from republics with a presidential system to republics in which the legislature held sway. However impermanent, Napoleon's conquest of Europe had stirred up lasting middle-class political awareness east of the Rhine, an awareness that countries to the north of France and across the Channel already possessed in good measure. Metternich, who more than any other statesman tried to stuff back into the bottle the genie of middle-class aspirations that the age of Revolution and Napoleon had set loose, told Czar Alexander I in 1820 that it was "principally the middle class of society" that had been touched by "the moral gangrene" of "presumption." And that presumption, taking many forms, did not die down.

4

IT HAS LONG BEEN ROUTINE TO DRAW THE SOCIAL profile of the Victorian middle class as a pyramid, very broad at the bottom, very steep on the way up, very narrow at the top. Statistical surveys in Belgium, the Netherlands, Germany, and elsewhere confirm this convenient image. In France at mid-nineteenth century, a school-teacher earned roughly 1,500 francs a year, a salary he could double if he secured, after long, devoted service, an appointment as a principal. Skilled craftsmen who clung to petty bourgeois status made perhaps 1,800 to 2,000 francs, which was also the pay of a government official at the outset of his career. A shopkeeper with a thriving business hoped for 5,000, but would not go bankrupt with merely 4,000 francs. Beyond this lay the land of plenty. Lawyers, physicians, engineers earned at least 8,000 francs, and depending on their location, their skill, and their social adroitness, could realistically expect several times that; a higher public servant like a prefect earned 12,000 francs a year and might double that if he succeeded in keeping his post, which is to say the favor of his superiors, for long years. Above that, the ascent induced vertigo: virtuosi, bankers, publishers, entrepreneurs, and speculators breathed the thin, bracing air of the economic stratosphere. For scale one might note that in his early years, Claude Monet sold his paintings at 300 francs apiece—more than two months' salary for a teacher.

The model of a pyramid proves practical as long as it is conceived as an elastic construction. With the passing decades, the middling and upper segments of the bourgeoisie swelled in numbers, wealth, and political consequence; the lower segments increased in numbers alone. The appetite for the services of the lowest among the middle orders — clerks for the private and public sector, sales personnel, bookkeepers, customs officials, mail carriers — grew more voracious with the irresistible rise of industry, banking, trade, insurance, government. In Germany between 1882 and 1907, while the number of industrialists and mine owners slightly declined, that of factory workers doubled and that of white-collar employees multiplied sevenfold. The state swelled into a major employer; in the Austria of 1841, imperial and local governments employed some 130,000 bureaucrats, while around the turn of the century the number had risen to about 340,000. This distension of the bourgeois pyramid was so spectacular that contemporaries endowed its lower strata with names of their own: *Mittelstand* in Germany, *nouvelles couches* in France.

These "new layers" attest to a destabilizing social reality that pervaded the Victorian century: it was an age of explosive and ubiquitous change. This is a crucial point to which I will return. Let me say here only that while change had many beneficiaries, the petty bourgeoisie, the *Mittelstand*, was not among them. Its denizens struggled bravely to have something left over after they bought their food and paid their rent. They enjoyed few luxuries and defined as a luxury an activity or a possession that better-situated bourgeois took for granted: a dinner in a restaurant, a visit to a concert hall, a holiday away from home, a new overcoat, comfortable furniture. They clipped the pictures on their walls, except perhaps for a religious print, from a magazine; they pushed their children into the workforce at the earliest legal moment and at times lobbied against protective labor legislation that would keep their offspring from contributing to the family's keep. Their apprehensions over dropping into the proletariat were very real, one reason why so many of them were almost comically insistent on bourgeois formal manners and bourgeois ethical standards for their children. They might let themselves go after payday, they might enter domestic arrangements that good bourgeois would disdain, but they were respectable people. They were *not* proletarians!

This grim disclaimer, more panic-stricken than self-assured, suggests that perceptions almost as much as realities helped to generate an underlying identity for the middling ranks amidst their diversity and their persistent, at times irreparable internal strains. That identity, it seems, rested in large part on negatives. In August 1883, Freud wrote to his fiancée, Martha Bernays, responding to her account of boisterous working-class visitors at a fair in Hamburg. "One could show," he told her, "that the 'people' are quite unlike us in the way they judge, believe, hope, and work. There is a psychology of the common man that is rather different from ours." The "rabble," he added, give way to their feelings with a spontaneity and directness that well-schooled bourgeois have learned to control. Why don't we bourgeois get drunk? he asked rhetorically. Because the discredit and discomfort of a hangover give us more pain than drinking gives us pleasure. Why don't we fall in love with someone new every month? Because every breakup tears away a piece of our heart.

This is an extremely enlightening text. It secures for feelings—and the professional study of feelings, psychology—a place in the search for the Victorian middle class. The bourgeois character, it proposes, is largely built from prohibitions, from things that middle-class people will not do and words they will not allow themselves to say. But if the bourgeois motto is self-abnegation, that is not because their passions are feeble but because their passions are harnessed—in Freud's word, "refined"—in ways that those of coarse peasants or laborers, or for that matter self-indulgent aristocrats, are not. The modern bourgeoisie, on this showing, is the class that sublimates its raw urges more thoroughly than any other class and does so many times, above all in the nineteenth century, to its regret. Refined, though, does not mean denied: that many good Victorian bourgeois, men and women alike, took their pleasure not at the table alone but no less, respectably, in bed, is a central thesis of this book. In that respect, Schnitzler, with his avid pursuit of sexual conquests, was not typical of his class, for bourgeois pleasure was generally guarded, tempered, shot through with abstentions.

Yet another negative element pushed nineteenth-century bourgeois toward a sense of shared identity: they were in a distinct minority in every town and every city. It was this striking fact that sent so many of them to the suburbs. In every urban setting about which we have reliable figures, the middle classes amounted to anywhere from 10 to 15 percent, rarely more, of the populations among which they lived. They encountered the proletarian majority (without necessarily getting to know it) as servants in the household, construction workers at their site, laborers skilled and unskilled in the factory. They encountered it, too, as denizens in the slums, to say nothing of beggars or strolling prostitutes whose obtrusive and obnoxious visibility reminded them, if they had an ounce of philanthropy left, that the society they were so profitably building was not without its casualties, including casualties they had made.

To be sure, bourgeois found convenient ways to segregate themselves from the masses that virtually swamped them. They could, as we have seen, limit the size of the political public by imposing property qualifications on the right to vote. They could huddle together in privileged, expensive neighborhoods. They could underscore their distance from the lower orders by educating their children in separate schools far beyond the reach of the poor. They could choose a route for walking to their office through streets that let them avoid the most unprepossessing quarters of town. And they could distinguish themselves from their "inferiors" by their clothes, their food, their accent, their tastes. By whatever means, they saw to it that Freud was right when he told Martha Bernays: "There is a psychology of the common man that is rather different from our own."

In times of upheaval—and the century from the French Revolution to the outbreak of World War I had more than its share of barricades—the presence of the lower-class majority could be ominous. It generated defensive maneuvers on the part of the bourgeoisie, including alliances of convenience with aristocrats or demagogues with whom, except for social anxiety, they had little in common. It was in these times that bourgeois became leading actors in what I have called the Party of Order. Even as it slowly receded in people's minds, the memory of the

French Revolution obsessed most bourgeois for at least half a century. Exhilarating for some and frightening to most, it substantially supported the mentality that united bourgeois of all stripes.

5

THERE ARE MORE NEGATIVES STILL IN THE Victorian century: the bourgeoisie was defined by its antagonists, a ferocious and growing sect of avant-garde writers and artists. These enemies of the middle class were a fertile source for facile generalizations that gratuitously discounted the variations among bourgeois—fertile and only too natural: the enemy is always a single recognizable villain, sporting none of the virtues and all of the vices. Painters and novelists, dramatists and literary critics, political radicals, journalists with advanced opinions, aristocrats infuriated by middle-class insurgency, let the world know that the nineteenth-century bourgeoisie was hypocritical, materialistic, vulgar, and incapable of generosity and love. When convenient, the scourges of the bourgeoisie could produce an alternate character portrait of the *Bürger* no less dismissive than the first: grasping, unscrupulous, power-hungry, parvenu, and callous, exploiting the laboring classes on whose backs he had grown fat. As they saw it, the financiers and factory owners whom an indulgent Thomas Carlyle had celebrated as captains of industry were nothing better than robber barons.

These distinctive perspectives on the middle classes were not necessarily incompatible. To the mind of most hostile polemicists, the spineless clerk stood (or, perhaps better, knelt) at one end of the bourgeois spectrum with the ruthless entrepreneur towering over the other. Emile Zola, for one, packed both caricatures into one; he used the very name "bourgeois," a succulent insult he rolled on his tongue, as an indictment. "Bourgeois, and what is more, provincial bourgeois!" he threw back at the Catholic writer Barbey d'Aurevilly, whose impudent dismissal of Goethe and Diderot had offended him.

All this was strong stuff; but probably the most intemperate hater of the Victorian bourgeoisie was Gustave Flaubert. Fighting down occasional twinges of affection, he conducted a lifelong crusade against the class—his own—which, he said, made him want to vomit. In May 1867, he told his beloved *chère bon maître*, George Sand: "Axiom: Hatred of Bourgeois is the beginning of all virtue." By then such venom was nothing new for him. Fifteen years earlier, he had summed up his rage in a single word. Writing to his closest friend, the playwright Louis Bouilhet, he signed himself "Bourgeoisophobus."

Though Schnitzler held his fellow bourgeois in low esteem, he was far less vitriolic than these French bourgeoisophobes, and simply took his class prejudices for granted: in his exhaustive diaries, he rarely made his disdain explicit. In 1893, after an evening visiting a respectable family, he coolly judged the occasion to have been "bourgeois and dull." Three years later, he berated an acquaintance for holding "stupid bourgeois views." That was about all.

Loathing and contempt for the middling orders were, to be sure, not an invention of the Victorians; they could draw on age-old habits of derision. Jesus had driven the moneychangers and pigeon sellers from the temple and medieval theologians had excoriated merchants for taking interest on loans. Early modern aristocrats and patricians had sneered at businessmen, bankers, and manufacturers as so many plebeians: pushy, philistine, dissatisfied with their god-given place in the social hierarchy. And well before the nineteenth century, Goethe's Werther, perhaps the first and most conflicted among modern anti-bourgeois, had felt uncomfortable with the burghers among whom fortune had flung him. They struck him as incurably mediocre and incapable of the higher flights of the imagination.

This was mockery that romantics, especially the Germans, were to take up with gusto early in the nineteenth century. But these anticipations still lacked the single-mindedness of Victorian detractors of the bourgeoisie, for these reached a focused intensity of abuse not known before. The vehemence of bourgeois-hating zealots was countered by bourgeoisophilia, but that was far less noisy. Nineteenth-century merchant patricians of long standing in commercial centers like Amsterdam or Hamburg, Antwerp or Lübeck, could smile at detractors yapping at their heels and not bother to answer them. They had their family dynasties, imposing mansions, prestigious art collections, and local political supremacy to fall back on. The portraits of their sixteenth- and seventeenth-century ancestors with the attributes of their trade or craft, weighing gold or superintending a workshop, show that nineteenth-century middle-class self-respect and self-confidence had a solid tradition behind it. In the Victorian era, both bourgeoisophobia and bourgeoisophilia were democratized.

In the mid-1870s and after, Vienna's champions of the bourgeoisie, defying the devastating economic collapse of May 1873, were not left behind. Editorials and essays rang with voices celebrating its *Bürgertum*. When, in April 1879, a gigantic, meticulously organized parade marked Emperor Franz Joseph and Empress Elisabeth's silver anniversary, Vienna's leading liberal newspaper, the *Neue Freie Presse*, wrote editorially: "However festive, however cordial, however splendid the tributes brought the imperial couple, the tribute of Vienna's bourgeoisie has outdone them all. It bestowed the loveliest and the best that the capital has to offer: itself. Art, science, commerce, trade, industry, everything that makes for the wealth, the energy and the pride of our country, cooperated to give witness to the patriotism and the loyalty of Vienna's bourgeoisie to the Kaiser."

The Victorian middle classes, then, had their hearty boosters, although far less effective in the market of advanced opinion than their opponents. These opponents had, it seems, if not precisely monopolized, certainly enlisted most of the talented partisans in the Victorian debates over the identity of the bourgeoisie. Still, bourgeoisophiles made their mark and enlisted vocal support. In 1826 James Mill, Bentham's friend and Utilitarian ideologue, spoke for many when he maintained that "the value of the middle classes of this country"—note the plural—"their growing number and importance, are acknowledged by all. These classes have long been spoken of, and not grudgingly, by their superiors themselves, as the glory of England." This was the first line of defense to which bourgeois under attack could retreat; even their betters had kind words for them.

Proud bourgeois did not corner the market on such sentiments. Even

Marx and Engels, not known to harbor much affection for the *Bürgertum,* felt compelled to pay it a few wry compliments in the midst of their heated critique: "The bourgeoisie, during its rule of scarce one hundred years," they wrote in a famous passage of the *Communist Manifesto,* "has created more massive and more colossal productive forces than have all preceding generations together." As unreconstructed city dwellers, they approvingly commented that "the bourgeoisie has subjected the country to the rule of the towns. It has created enormous cities, has greatly increased the urban population as compared with the rural, and has thus rescued a considerable part of the population from the idiocy of rural life." If even the century's leading Communists could acknowledge the historic contributions of the bourgeoisie, there was some hope for its reputation.

🌺 BOURGEOISIE, THEN, OR BOURGEOISIES? IT IS tempting to evade the question by making the answer depend on the perspective of the inquirer. The striking diversity of nineteenth-century middle-class political aspirations, attitudes toward authority, tastes in art and music, economic resources, to say nothing of the varied developments in the middling ranks in country after country, supports the plural solution: the middle classes. Nothing I am saying in this book should be taken as slighting this multiplicity—on the contrary, I offer evidence for it in each chapter. At the same time, though, this historical tapestry, as it evolved through the decades, reveals certain patterns, a set of opinions and attitudes that crossed national frontiers and united social ranks. They permitted bourgeois to recognize one another from certain unmistakable signs. No doubt, Tocqueville and Marx and other contemporary students of society unduly slighted the distinctions among bourgeois. But even as one recognizes, even admires, the colorful and changing scenes in Victorian middle-class life, a pervasive unity emerges.

This is how most nineteenth-century bourgeois thought of themselves. Styles of thinking and feeling, some already adumbrated and others to appear in later chapters, greatly mattered to the self-definition of the middle class. It would be too easy to assert that a bourgeois was someone who considered himself, or herself, a bourgeois; ideological self-deception, whether conscious or unconscious, and plain wishful thinking were endemic in these gazes in the mirror. Still, the historian dare not ignore these self-definitions; they rested on consistent, really profound perceptions.

The standard by which Victorians hoped to live was that of free individuals who set their own course, though within a given, gladly accepted framework of family, society, and state. Institutions, especially religious commitments, were authoritative markers, so many monitory uplifted fingers, which demanded a good measure of conformity. Yet this social and spiritual discipline implied a realm of individual autonomy. The Victorians richly elaborated this ideology, launched on its triumphant course a century before, to make it their own. In the early decades of the Enlightenment, Richard Addison and Voltaire had led an international family of insubordinate modern thinkers to challenge time-honored values by heaping sincere praise on stock exchange traders and rejecting the bellicose knight as their social ideal. They were setting the stage for a new hero: the pacific, tolerant, secular bourgeois, the man who prefers prudence and profits to glory, and who disdains aristocrats for making a fetish of organized murder they called war. In 1778, Beaumarchais had taken the Enlightenment's disrespect for the old model to the theatre with his subversive *Le Mariage de Figaro*. In the last act, Figaro, the servant, assails his employer, Count Almaviva, with fighting words: "Nobility, fortune, rank, appointments, all that makes you so proud! What have you done to deserve so many advantages? You took pains to be born, and nothing more." It was on such an aggressive stance that liberal Victorian bourgeois could build.

Their new hero was a man in a frock coat, perhaps wearing galoshes, carrying a briefcase and certainly an umbrella, thinking on his business and his family. He was, or at least claimed to be, a loving husband, a doting father, an honest business partner, a moderate in politics and the consumption of wine, and addicted, if at all, to inexpensive pleasures. He read the newspaper at breakfast, and, religious or not, probably went to church. His wife was an indispensable presence in this self-portrait. Yet she had her own story. If she had not fully accepted her assigned role as helpmeet, housekeeper, and mother—and increasing numbers of middle-class women did not—she was bound to be more restless, more rebellious, than her spouse. The history of bourgeois women throughout the Victorian decades was more eventful, in many ways more gripping, than that of their husbands. They had more to aspire to.

Still, whatever its imperfections in reality, the family was the icon that the nineteenth-century middle class worshipped, domestic felicity the motto that, as it were, hung over the marital bed. "The home life of a people," wrote an anonymous American in a London periodical, *The Leisure Hour*, in 1869, "is the best index of its character." We can see these bourgeois families, harmoniously at lunch, in Impressionist canvases; watch them gazing at the exhibits at the Great Exhibition of 1851 in London, complete with children, in contemporary illustrations; and observe them on stage, entangled in amorous complications, in Schnitzler's dramas, multifarious and interesting, in their full sober glory.

CHANGES AT HOME.

TWO

Home, Bittersweet Home

THE QUARREL BETWEEN ARTHUR
Schnitzler and his father over the little red diary reads
like a major skirmish in the familial warfare to which the young man
was regularly exposed. That highly charged tangle of love and hate, at
times blazing into action so typical of two generations at odds is as old
as recorded history, probably even older—it is significant that Freud
should take a Greek tragedy, Sophocles' *Oedipus Rex*, as his principal
illustration of this intimate conflict. But among Victorians like the
Schnitzler family, the rebelliousness of adolescents emerged with
exceptional clarity. There were few buffers in the modern family (sociologists have been calling it the "nuclear family" for half a century) to
soften the antagonism between the combatants. The household in
which Arthur Schnitzler grew up included his father who, we know,
was a distinguished throat specialist and a formidable presence in his
son's life; his mother, Louise, the daughter of a reputable Viennese
physician; and two siblings with whom he got along admirably: his
brother Julius, also to become a physician, and his sister Gisela, who
married one—in short, a fairly typical constellation for the professional

upper middle class. Tolstoy said that happy families are all alike, but in times of stress, too, one bourgeois family is much like the others.

The nineteenth-century middle-class family, essentially populated by parents and children alone, was not a radical innovation. Nor was it the spawn of those bugaboos of conservatives, the French Revolution and the burgeoning industrial society. Rather, the Victorians transformed it from a fact into an ideology. To be sure, the modern family did not impose a rigid prescription on itself. Catastrophes within the wider clan could add one, perhaps two, members to a household, as it made a haven for a widowed grandmother or an orphaned cousin. And, perhaps surprisingly, its mean size, some 4.75 persons, had remained largely unchanged from the seventeenth to the nineteenth century. Schnitzler's Vienna was right on target: in 1890, the average household size in that city was 4.68 persons. But for all its history, the Victorian family has long been praised, and blamed, for making us what we are today. When, since the end of World War II, cultural critics have lamented the decay of the family—the high incidence of divorce and of unorthodox domestic arrangements—it is against the nineteenth-century ideal that they have measured the contemporary situation and found it falling short.

Commonplace though the adolescent Schnitzler's situation may have been, it seemed exceptional to him as victim. To his mind, not yet seventeen, the stakes were high: he was bidding for grown-up status. "Annoyances at home," he noted in June 1879, "because of my emancipation." Later that year, in November, he once again registered his parents' dissatisfaction with his companions and his slovenliness. And they kept up their reproaches, all tersely chronicled. As late as 1892, he told his diary: "Disagreeable discussion at home—My thirty years, and no private practice, and as for literature, no prospects as far as earnings go."

Yet for all his insubordinate moods, Arthur Schnitzler was by and large an obedient young man, just as he had been an obedient adolescent. Since early boyhood, he recalled, he had dreamt of becoming a physician, "like Papa." But these fantasies had centered on the pleasures of riding around town in a comfortable carriage and stopping at bakeries to buy sweets. Reality would prove less delectable. Dr.

Schnitzler's repeated hints that as the son of a physician and a professor, Arthur had a head start over his rivals, struck the "beneficiary" as tactless and profoundly irritating. But when in the fall of 1879 he matriculated in the University of Vienna, Schnitzler selected the faculty of medicine "as a matter of course." The father wanted his son to become a doctor, and so the son went to medical school and became a doctor. Such traditional paternal authority survived well into the age of the modern family.

Schnitzler took his course from duty rather than inclination, for he was, and always remained, in love with words, with their magical powers, their vast expressive possibilities, their uncanny capacity for masking as much as revealing the truth. He had been scribbling plays and poems since he was a boy; by the time he was eighteen, he had completed twenty-three dramas and started thirteen more. "I feel it already," he noted as a first-year medical student, "science will never become for me what art already is." He would say so again, often. He haunted theatres and concert halls; at the end of 1879, summing up the season as he would later count his orgasms, he logged fifteen visits to the Stadttheater, fourteen to the Burgtheater, eleven to the opera, and at least nineteen concerts. Medicine had too few attractions to compete with music and the stage. Significantly, foreshadowing the psychological explorations that became the hallmark of his fiction, the only department of medicine that really interested him was psychiatry, with its esoteric methods: hypnotism and suggestion.

For some time, Schnitzler remained under his father's tutelage. Following paternal guidance, he visited foreign capitals to bolster his professional competence, and for five years, until his father's death in 1893, he worked as his assistant. He had already published short stories and one-act plays, and after his father died, he allowed his practice to fade away gradually that he might devote himself to dramas and stories. It was, at least consciously, his final liberation from paternal control. In his early thirties, then, Schnitzler went his own way, the way of literature, after treading water for years as a physician. The best he could say for medicine, which bored him, was that his practice brought him women patients who were young, pretty, and eminently seducible.

In his rather straitlaced world, the profession of writer struck many proper bourgeois as not quite respectable, and in any event almost bound to be unremunerative. As a student, Schnitzler's father also had committed literature by writing plays; what worried him was his son's failure to make the kind of splash, either in the theatre or in medical periodicals, that promised a profitable future. Many middle-class families objected on principle to making a living by one's pen; devoted to the gospel of work, they had little tolerance for grown men who invented stories, in short told lies for a living. Yet there were contemporaries whose careers described some of the twists that Schnitzler went through before he settled in his vocation. Charles Baudelaire, captivated by poetry, managed after serving a short stint to escape the study of law, which his family had strongly recommended as suitable preparation for the diplomatic service. And Gustave Flaubert, presumably doomed to a hated legal career by his father (also an eminent physician who, like Schnitzler's father, showed no understanding for his son's literary bent), was saved for literature by suddenly experiencing severe, apparently life-threatening seizures that disqualified him for the patient immersion that the law requires. Whether his illness was epileptic or hysterical in nature has never been settled, but whatever it was, it served him well. Compared to these contemporaries, Schnitzler had shown exceptional patience with his family's demands. Once launched as a writer, though, he never looked back; the main traces that his medical years left on his fictions are occasional characters, like the protagonist in *Professor Bernhardi*, one of his most enduring dramas.

1

THE ANECDOTAL EVIDENCE FOR THE INSURGENCE, or at least the insurgent feelings, of pubertal sons against their fathers throughout the ages is ample. What can be more familiar from experience, or from history, than the young executive whom his father has taken into the firm and who cannot wait for the old man to retire? Or for the impatient crown prince who wants nothing more than to see his father die sooner rather than later? It was in Vienna, during Schnitzler's lifetime, that another local physician, Sigmund Freud, enlarged this duel into a triangle and gave these conflicts their rationale and their name. The Oedipus complex, Freud insisted, was neither a self-revelation nor an arbitrary invention; he had stumbled on it through his pioneering self-analysis and confirmed it by reading literary masterpieces.

At its simplest, the triangle that Freud thought universal in child-hood —he took adolescent rebellions to be a second edition of early encounters—would seem to be the case of a child loving one and hat-ing another parent. But, though this was a striking and convenient for-mulation, Freud learned to distrust its classic simplicity; it was far too schematic to mirror faithfully the inner turmoil of a growing child. The boy who wants his father out of the way that he might have sole access to his mother does not just abominate his father but admires him as well; he want to outdo him but, at the same time, follow in his foot-steps. Nor is his attitude toward his mother unequivocal; the maternal figure he wants to marry in the morning he angrily strikes in the after-noon. To understand that oedipal combat and oedipal love coexist makes the complex more lifelike than the original, all too clear-cut ver-sion. Freud found the term "ambivalence" appropriate for this amal-gam of passions, which to his mind was a fundamental ingredient in human experience.

For Freud, the varied forms that the Oedipus complex could take pointed to a long, motley history. In *The Interpretation of Dreams*, pub-lished in November 1899, in which he first analyzed the oedipal phase in print, he placed great weight on the fact that the protagonist of *Oedipus Rex* acts out his incestuous passions while Shakespeare's Hamlet represses them. This "changed treatment of the same material," he noted, "reveals the whole difference in the mental life of these two widely separated epochs of civilization." This momentous observation makes the Oedipus episode available to the historian, for it places each exemplar of the domestic triangle within a concrete cultural context while at the same time affirming the continuity of human nature. It is not, as critics of psychoanalysis have charged, that the Oedipus com-plex holds only for Freud's Viennese patients. Rather, Victorian middle-class culture had brought intimate styles of family interaction, their passionate vagaries and indirections, close to the surface.

The high visibility of the oedipal drama in the family life of the nineteenth-century middle class reflects the mounting and spreading prosperity of the bourgeoisie, the increasing use of contraception, the more marked (though never complete) segregation of men and women in the world of work, in short the widely advertised triumph of the modern family. That kind of family served as a splendid rehearsal for life, both in its genial and its authoritarian habits. It met conscious and unconscious needs or, quite as vital, failed to meet them. Nineteenth-century bourgeois did not love their children more than had their forebears, but in their new, more secure life, they had more time and money and could devote more, and closer, attention to them. The Victorian cult of domesticity reinforced the meaning and expanded the reach of the children's hour.

▓ DETRACTORS OF THE MODERN FAMILY DEPLORED it—quite wrongly—as spreading the vice of excessive individualism, of choosing solitude over sociability. The critics taking this tack had, they thought, social science on their side. The nineteenth century, an age of avid self-scrutiny, discovered ever newer techniques for taking the mental—many preferred to say the "spiritual"—temperature of individuals and institutions. Intent on realizing the Enlightenment's program for a science of man and society, the Victorians earnestly investigated social ailments: prostitution, poverty, suicide. By midcentury, it was the family's turn.

There was much to study; the modern family was enmeshed in controversy among social observers and the better monthlies. But, unfortunately for the sociology of the family, its two founders, the French engineer Frédéric Le Play, an indefatigable fieldworker and social reformer, and the German cultural historian Wilhelm Heinrich Riehl, journalist and fluent essayist, pursued a political agenda that their researches only too conveniently confirmed. Their two key texts, the first volume of Le Play's *European Workers* and Riehl's *The Family*, the last of a trilogy he described as the "natural history" of the people, were both published in 1855 and virtually monopolized the study of the family among the Victorians. This proved a disaster for social science, for both writers traded in nostalgia for a past that existed only in their writings.

In their tendentious and influential publications, Le Play and Riehl claimed that the contemporary family had proved a destructive agent of social instability and moral decay, a poisonous substitute for the crowded, lively, affectionate household of olden times. Le Play provocatively called the modern type "unstable," while Riehl extolled the old "whole house," to his mind once the social norm, in which three generations had lived together in harmony and piety. He bemoaned that horrid modern invention in which parents and children form an antisocial unity; to his mind, it had virtually uprooted the whole house, most devastatingly among the urban middle classes.

Between them, these two sociologists offered largely overlapping diagnoses of what they criticized as the deplorable history of family life. The decay of parental authority, the flight from religion, the fading of community, the separation of home from workplace were, to them, the bitter harvest of individualism, at once its cause and its consequence. True, the modern Victorian family was in itself not new. But in earlier centuries, middle-class families had not aimed at confining themselves to a small model as they would do more and more in the nineteenth century. In earlier centuries, many infants died, and an appalling number of the children lucky enough to survive their first year were mowed down by childhood diseases for which there were then no cures. Mothers, too, were at an inordinate risk of succumbing to what the Victorians would call childbed fever, a risk that remained high through their century. It induced bereft fathers to marry again quickly: stepfathers and step-mothers, stepbrothers and stepsisters were a common phenomenon. If the seventeenth- or eighteenth-century middle-class family was generally as small as its Victorian successors, this pointed to an "unnatural" modern family, a household produced not by human will but dictated by the helplessness of physicians or the lethal effects of household nostrums. More intentional now than accidental, the nineteenth-century small family could look back on ancestors tragically decimated

▩ FOR ALL THE COMPLAINTS OF CONSERVATIVE observers, the Victorian age had not yet become what in 1909 the Swedish feminist Ellen Key called "the century of the child." There were, as usual, striking differences from family to family, status to status, and society to society. But the memoirs that throw light on the Victorian decades leave the impression that at least in the upper reaches of the middle class, notably in England and Germany, there was a wide gulf between children and their parents, particularly their fathers, wider than it was in the middling ranges. Those affluent enough to afford sizable houses included rooms for nannies, and later governesses; in any event, boarding schools loomed large in the parents' program for their sons.

As long as they were at home, though, social discipline for youngsters in well-to-do families could be very demanding. In her memoirs, Julie Kaden, born into a prosperous Jewish family in Dresden, recalled that she and her siblings would join their parents during a dinner party, "cleaned from top to toe, in white sailor blouses." During the meal, "we had to sit silently, our governess by our side, like stuffed dummies, erect, hands at the edge of the table, our elbows pressed against our sides, without rattling the silverware. If one of us violated these rules, she would meet the reproachful glance of the governess or, which was worse, of our mother." It is mainly in American autobiographies, even when they tell of a strict or ever busy father, that one finds a more companionable, more informal tone.

▩ WHAT IS MORE, THE CHARGE OF WILLFUL SELF-isolation is greatly overdrawn. Though closely knit, bourgeois households steadily threw out lines to cousins, aunts, uncles, and grandparents;

major events like christenings, bar mitzvahs, anniversaries, or wakes, to say nothing of weddings, made for festive gatherings of the clan, often from distant places. And the mails hummed with private, strictly confidential communications: the familial world was far larger than would at first appear. It was also, in a sense, smaller. Compared to the family in earlier times, the Victorian middle-class household found itself engaged in fewer tasks as the state took over most of the schooling of middle-class children. And by midcentury, industrial enterprises reduced the housewife's need to bake or to make her own clothes. Similarly, the family's role as an economic unit, paramount in preindustrial times, atrophied as bourgeois fathers, and even a number of mothers, went out to work.

None of this eroded the psychological impact of the modern family on its children. As family prayers or the observance of the Sabbath attest, certainly for devout households, the focused Victorian family retained a preeminent share in coopting children in the faith and morals of their parents. Again, even though most middle-class children left the house for school, the family continued to provide lessons, as a rule quite unceremoniously, in advocating (if not always practicing) ethical ideals, social skills, table manners, and marital strategies. Paradoxically, this shrinkage of functions kept alive, even fostered, ties between the family and its society—the school, the university, the church, the club, the political party. Devotion to domesticity did not automatically undercut gregariousness.

The paradigm of domesticity was no more of recent date than the small family, but its intensity was unprecedented and its possibilities were idealized as never before. Bourgeois culture prompted its men to treat their family as their principal motive for pursuing material success. The concurrent ideal of manliness was no obstacle: it explicitly eschewed aggressiveness and brutality, extolled consideration for others, and even found room for manly tears. Hence bourgeois—or so they told themselves—made money, gave speeches, wrote articles, ran for office, and performed in concerts in large part because as the destined breadwinner, they had a responsibility to give their wife and children as peaceful and prosperous a life as was within their power.

Naturally, like so much else, the manifestations of the ideal differed from place to place. When Hippolyte Taine visited England in the 1860s, he was struck by the widespread devotion to domestic life, with a force that seemed to him astonishing. "When it comes to marriage," he wrote, emphasizing the point by giving the word "home" in English, "every Englishman has a romantic corner in his heart: he imagines a 'home' with a woman he has chosen, a tête-à-tête, children; this is his little universe, closed, his own. When he does not have it, he is uneasy, contrary to Frenchmen, for whom marriage is ordinarily an end, a last resort." He was exaggerating the contrast for effect; that throughout the century marriages in France were complex business transactions says little about the solidity of the French middle-class home. The bourgeois who favored novels by writers of advanced views — Flaubert or Zola — no doubt relished reading about adultery, but it does not follow that they stood ready to violate the sanctity of the *foyer*.

In this atmosphere, the word "home" and its equivalents — *Heim, foyer, casa*, and the rest — acquired a magical aura beloved of poets, writers for popular periodicals, and conventional bourgeois in general. Late in the century, in 1892, the brothers George and Weedon Grossmith, prominent men of the London theatre, condensed these sentiments into an amusing, immensely popular spoof, *Diary of a Nobody*, whose hero, the clerk Charles Pooter, spoke for millions: "'Home, Sweet Home,' that's my motto." No further comment seemed necessary.

However one judges the nineteenth-century family, then, it made for an emotional intimacy that was more than merely rhetorical. Competition among siblings, tensions between parents, cheerful joint excursions, punishments harsh or lenient, affection expressive or reserved, alcoholic fathers and attractive mothers left their imprint for good or ill, whether the children were aware of it or not. No external influences, whether church or school, could wholly distract middle-class parents and children from their daily commerce. The home of the Victorian family was an echo chamber to which one could not close one's ears.

2

─────────

🏶 ONE ARRESTING EFFECT OF THESE DOMESTIC imperatives among the Victorians was a tough-minded realism about life, especially about naked physical realities, that presumably more liberated times have not approached, let alone equaled. In patronizing caricatures by their Edwardian denigrators, the Victorians had turned their back on the body and wrapped it, literally and figuratively, in modest muslin. The age, we are told, was an age of embarrassed euphemisms. It is easy to see what led to retrospective indictments of bourgeois prudery: the much-noted excision of sexual passion, say, from English novels. In fact, these charges are largely unwarranted. To discover Victorian openness, its measured candor, is one of the most astonishing rewards of studying nineteenth-century middle-class culture. If "Victorian" is a synonym for "squeamishness" or "prissiness," the Victorians were not Victorians.

A handful of examples may stand for a regular pattern of conduct. Take Isabella Beeton's classic *Book of Household Management*. Published in 1861 as a bulky encyclopedia of recipes and domestic tips after first being serialized in *The Englishwoman's Domestic Magazine*, it proved a long-lived bestseller to middle-class housewives. Evidently its readers did not balk at its tone and its frank allusion to gore on page after page. She told her public, without circumlocutions, how to make turtle soup: one must "cut off the head of the turtle the preceding day. In the morning open the turtle by leaning heavily with a knife on the shell of the animal's back."

Mrs. Beeton's prescription for engaging a wet nurse was quite as forthright. When "from illness, suppression of milk, accident, or some natural process, the mother is deprived of the pleasure of rearing her infant," she must employ a wet nurse, and inspect her carefully. "The age, if possible, should not be less than twenty nor exceed thirty years, with the health sound in every respect, and the body free from all eruptive disease or local blemish. The best evidence of a sound state of health will be found in the woman's clear open countenance, the ruddy tone of the skin, the full, round, and elastic state of the breasts, and especially the erectile, firm condition of the nipple, which in all unhealthy states of the body, is pendulous, flabby, and relaxed, in which case the milk is sure to be imperfect in its organization, and, consequently, deficient in its nutrient qualities." Not a whiff of smelling salts hovers over these pages.

What emerges quite incidentally in this little lesson is the reality of nineteenth-century class society; one would suppose that a bourgeois woman's breasts would be so unblinkingly examined only by her physician. Or, it turns out, by her husband. William Gladstone, the quintessential Victorian, watched his beloved wife Catherine with some anxiety as she bore him child after child—the numbing blessings of chloroform were still a few years away—since with her second, and again her fourth, she developed difficulties producing milk. It was a painful and, if left untreated, dangerous condition. When neither aperient medicines nor a breast pump met the emergency, it was her husband who gently and prayerfully rubbed her breasts to alleviate the stoppage.

Ill health, far from isolating the patient, was a royal road to physical intimacy. Mrs. Beeton noted that a sick nurse (mainly the wife or the eldest daughter in the family) must be good-tempered, compassionate, neat, quiet, orderly, clean, and prepared for some repulsive duty. With those qualities, she would "surmount the disgusts which some of the offices attending the sick-room are apt to create." What she had in mind was grandfather's diarrhea, vomiting, bleeding, drooling, incontinence. In the nineteenth century, only the poor went to the hospital, a virtual death sentence. Middle-class Victorians were born at home, gave birth at home, and died at home. When, late in the century, the German novelist and eminent Egyptologist Georg Ebers fell ill with a plethora of ailments, not all of them hysterical, his wife nursed him for twenty years, and conscientiously recorded her daily ministrations. She patiently stomached administering morphine injections and dealing with attacks of screaming, vomiting, and histrionic farewells to his family.

Unless the family banished them from the sickroom, children had an opportunity to witness the vagaries of bodily conditions. When, in

March 1895, Berthe Morisot lay dying, she forbade her adolescent daughter, Julie, to come to her bedside, lest she see her in her appalling condition, though Julie, suffering exquisitely in her helplessness, visited her just the same. And husbands were generally participants in the critical moments of childbirth; most of them were present at delivery and assisted the doctor, or the midwife, in whatever way they could. Gladstone found his wife "exceedingly beautiful" as she endured her labor pains "without bitterness." In 1869, Richard Wagner was unable to witness the birth of his son, Siegfried, only because his mistress, Cosima von Bülow, in excruciating labor pains, expelled him from the room because his anxiety made her nervous.

There were, no one doubts it, domestic tyrants through the age, more or less protected by the laws. It is an indictment of the time that harsh, or at least indifferent, fathers should populate its fiction. There is M. Grandet in Balzac's *Eugénie Grandet,* the very model of provincial misers; Dr. Sloper in Henry James's *Washington Square,* who coldly hates his daughter; or Charles Dickens's Mr. Dombey in *Dombey and Son,* who, until he implausibly reforms to become a loving grandfather, is villainous in his arrogance and unresponsiveness at home. Anecdotal evidence, including court records, suggests that these horrendous fictional personages had counterparts in real life. But after facing entrenched resistance and repeated setbacks, nineteenth-century bourgeois husbands and wives (and in a greater measure than ever before, children) were beginning to experience the uncertain delights of a companionate household.

🏵 IN ONE SIGNIFICANT DOMAIN, THE ANTI-authoritarian bourgeois family stopped short: it failed to bring equality with it. For the wife, the Victorian family could be prison as much as refuge. This terrain has been so thoroughly traveled by historians of women that it requires no more than a glance; in law, in custom, and much to the chagrin of feminists even in female self-appraisals, women were deemed inferior to men in intellect and in the capacity for public business. Their precinct was the home, where alone they could fulfill their God-given vocation as wife and mother. Even though some authorities, nearly all of them men, admitted that nature had endowed women with some ability to lead the human pack, their superiority was confined to the realm of feeling: aesthetic sensitivity, feminine solicitude, maternal wisdom, instinctive social graces. Women discontented with life in the doll's house did not consider this acknowledgment to be a real concession; the separation of spheres conveniently served to keep women from the vote, from the right to attend an institution of higher learning or keep an independent bank account, from equality in divorce proceedings, and from other rights understood to be men's province. That in late nineteenth-century France women tried for murdering their husbands or their lovers were regularly acquitted gave feminists no comfort; the usual ground for these exonerations was the presumed natural irrationality of the accused.

The reasoning employed to reach the conclusion of woman's inherent incapacities, a result so gratifying to many males of the species, drew on firmly held superstitions sanctified as traditions. One apologist for the status quo, the German historian Heinrich von Sybel, advanced what may have been the most original version of this thesis: women are perfectly capable of doing men's work, but men cannot possibly do women's work, hence social cohesion requires women to keep doing what they had always done so superbly. Others resorted to verses from the Bible, pronouncements from tractates by misogynistic church fathers, or sermons from contemporary preachers or moralists. Still others adduced the authoritative verdicts of physicians.

In fact, nineteenth-century medicine and anthropology, only too often touting prejudices that masqueraded as physiological information, did their bit to buttress this male-centered ideology: women's brains are smaller and less developed than men's; women's monthly "sickness"—the great French historian Jules Michelet called it "a wound"—incapacitates them for the severe tasks that study in universities imposes or for independent work outside the home; women's glands (this was the contribution of the famous German pathologist Rudolf Virchow) determined not only their lovely curves but their gift for loyalty and tenderness.

The prevalent cynical view of woman as gossip, seducer, and almost professional liar only exacerbated the situation. On this matter, Schnitzler was ambivalent. Some of his heroines are more decent, one or two even more intelligent, than their male pursuers. And he would read passages from work in progress to the two or three of his mistresses whose judgment he trusted. But casual remarks candidly immortalized in his diaries show a more conventional Victorian male. Women are untrustworthy, incapable of high imaginative flights, nearly all of them whores. The thought that lovers like him made women into whores seems not to have occurred to him.

🌸 NORMALLY, THE NINETEENTH-CENTURY LEGISLATION that governed relations between spouses was far harder on women than the practice in thoughtful bourgeois families. An abundant supply of domestic sketches suggests that wives often participated actively in making familial decisions, or in goading their husbands into greater efforts at work to better the family's financial situation. In 1905, in her informal survey *Home Life in France,* idealizing matters only a little, Miss Betham-Edwards summed up what she believed to have been the domestic situation for a century: "In most French households women reign with unchallenged sway." But by imposing crippling limitations on women's capacity to act on their own, the laws provided husbands with tempting incentives to play the lord of the manor. In 1868, the English feminist Frances Power Cobbe had bitterly, and accurately, observed that in the laws of her country, women were essentially classed with minors, criminals, and idiots, though these harsh conditions were about to change.

Indeed, in the following year, John Stuart Mill's trenchant *The Subjection of Women,* probably the most influential feminist text of the century, laid out the legal situation with its author's customary clarity: the wife is in effect her husband's slave, "the personal bond-servant of a despot." After all, "she vows a lifelong obedience to him at the altar, and is held to it all through her life by law." She needs her husband's permission, at least tacit, to perform any act whatever. "She can acquire no property but for him; the instance it becomes hers, even if by inheritance, it becomes ipso facto his." In short, the married couple being one person in law, whatever is hers is his, even though, Mill grimly noted, it is never true that what is his is hers. Even the children belong to the husband: "They are by law his children. He alone has any right over them." But the year after — Mill, who died three years later, could still delight in this — Parliament passed the Married Women's Property Act, supplemented by later acts in 1882 and 1893, giving wives some of the legal rights that single women already enjoyed.

The law in other countries was even more male-oriented than this. In Bavaria, late in the century, the husband could still legally "chastise" his wife, as long as he did so "moderately," while in Prussia, she could sue for divorce if her husband's beatings endangered her health or life — but only then. It was a matter of course that in German states all the wife's property, including her earnings, was at her husband's disposal. France, which had legalized divorce during the Revolution (a right far more important for wives than for husbands), had promptly repealed it in 1816 after the Bourbon Restoration, and did not reauthorize it until 1884, after furious battles in the legislature and the press. After all, the word "obey" that the wife was required to utter during the marriage ceremony was not an empty phrase. The most vigorous pillow talk could only go so far to rectify these inequities.

3

IN JANUARY 1896, SCHNITZLER TOLD DORA Fournier, a married acquaintance who seemed a good prospect for his catalogue of conquests, that her alleged inability to love must stem from her fear of having children. This seemed reasonable to her. The two then launched into a conversation "about the way of avoiding that danger." Two weeks later, "Dora F." sent him a letter enclosing some medication to impede conception, a "cure" the two had discussed earlier. Yet there were times — he records at least one instance — when contraceptive precautions yielded to his willfulness. One evening in May 1896, when Marie Reinhard, his greatest love, complained about his lack of tenderness "because I was cautious," Schnitzler because furious, "called her a stupid female—then I was incautious." As will emerge, when Schnitzler found himself in conflict between restraint and appetite, restraint almost always lost.

This harsh anecdote is one of the rare moments when Schnitzler chose to put on record his opinions on that vital topic. It *was* vital; the size of the bourgeois family was after all influenced in large part by whatever rights the wife enjoyed over her body. The marital conversation over birth control, however private much of it had to be, further discredits the slander of middle-class squeamishness or prudishness in the Victorian age. Schnitzler's intemperate craving for sex meant that he must have discussed contraception, or at least thought about it, a great deal. But so did countless men less compulsively womanizing than he; the nineteenth century was awash with popular pamphlets, medical treatises, and printed sermons on marriage, published to satisfy a market whose craving for intimate advice seemed inexhaustible.

The expanding assortment and easier availability of contraceptives, then, and the far-reaching implications of limiting family size must have made the topic quite inescapable to nineteenth-century bourgeois. Respectable couples could hardly avoid talking frankly to one another, with fewer self-imposed inhibitions than did the proper novelists they liked to read. One correspondence that has survived indicates nothing less. In 1864, Arthur Roe, off fighting in the American Civil War, exchanged heated letters with his wife Emma. He painted suggestive word pictures and she led him on with mock-shy replies. The Roes had two children, and wondered whether to have another. This predicament produced what Emma Roe called "our disputes" which, she was confident, the two would not have "much trouble in amicably & pleasurably settling"—she meant as they prepared to make love or were resting afterward. "I love to look forward to being pregnant again," she assured him, and added seductively: "Yes I think we shall lie many a night in sweeter intimacy than we ever yet have known body and soul in former bonds." If many bourgeois must have touched on such subjects as fleetingly as they dared, others, like the Roes, relished canvassing them. Of course, we have no statistics, but for married Victorian bourgeois, a happy sexual life must have been necessarily, and pleasantly, interwoven with talk.

VIRTUALLY NONE OF THE PUBLICATIONS THAT advertised themselves as useful to the young on matters of sex sidestepped the issue of preventing conception. Nor did they evade the moral and medical issues that birth control was bound to raise in a century still widely formed by biblical injunctions to marry and multiply. These Cicerones to marital happiness were naturally aware that clerical strictures against limiting one's offspring remained persuasive and had to be handled tactfully. Even polemicists who had no respect for church teachings liked to inject some pious phrases into their brief. "There is certainly nothing in Reason and Religion to forbid the exercise of prudence in giving existence to sentient beings," wrote an anonymous "American Physician" in 1855. Another tried to soothe his readers: "I am acquainted with many moral and religious people who think that the practice . . . is perfectly justifiable and proper, and some even consider it a duty." Such assurances were preemptive strikes against pious disapproval.

One battleground was the term "nature," and opponents of birth control tried to appropriate it: to interfere with possible pregnancy was "unnatural." But partisans of contraception met the enemy on his— and, quite as likely, on her—own ground. "It is perfectly proper that we should endeavor to rise above 'nature' and the destiny of the brutes in this matter," wrote John Humphrey Noyes in 1866. Noyes was a notorious advocate of communal families and founder of utopian communities, but on the point of elevating artifice over raw nature he spoke for an articulate party of physicians and lay reformers.

The adversaries of Malthus, who had around 1800 famously foretold a destructive glut of population if wars, pestilence—and "preventive checks" like birth control—did not rein it in, denounced contraception as "conjugal onanism." But the Malthusians were no less skilled in finding catch phrases, and nailed high-flown words to their standard: freedom, choice, common sense. Children, they argued, have a right not to be born; their non-existence preserves the health of the mother and safeguards the well-being of the entire family. Besides, to attack birth control as unnatural begged the question; virtually every activity— growing food, building houses, inventing machinery—intervenes in natural processes. Preventing the birth of unwanted children was simply designed to make life more agreeable, or even bearable.

This was, no doubt, perfectly obvious to middle-class families. As the bourgeoisie grew in numbers and disposable income, it seemed only reasonable to calculate what an added child might cost the family directly or indirectly. Even if the economic depression that beset most of Europe from the mid-1870s to the early 1890s led to lower prices on many goods, the general cost of things the middle classes particularly desired rose steadily. And that put savings, including on the number of children, on the domestic agenda. This rationalist bookkeeping could particularly appeal to highly fertile wives, for whom the nuisance, to say nothing of the danger, inherent in having baby after baby worked as an eloquent advocate for birth control. Alarmists in many countries, notably France, Germany, and the United States, pointed with horror to falling birth rates and predicted the advent of what Theodore Roosevelt liked to call "race suicide." But there is evidence, in France at least, that some Catholics, urged by their confessors to stop interfering with nature, chose instead to stay away from church. In short, unknown but certainly large numbers of bourgeois found that the arguments in behalf of limiting their family overrode ethical, political, and religious scruples. The question was how to find out about safe, reliable contraception.

Demand for such wisdom readily met, at most times exceeded, supply. Contemporary evidence indicates that rising numbers searched for birth control information and, with some difficulty, found it. Sturdy advocates of contraception braved the threat of prison for distributing their precious lore, and made the newspapers their unwitting (if not always unwilling) allies. When, in 1877, Charles Bradlaugh and Annie Besant were prosecuted in London for daring to republish and disseminate Charles Knowlton's forty-five-year-old birth control manual, *Fruits of Philosophy,* their sensational court case spread the word to quarters innocent of such impious intelligence before; by 1880, the tract had sold almost 200,000 copies.

Fortifying the pressure, scores of physicians in as many countries advised and applauded married couples intent on taking control over the size of their family. It allowed bourgeois couples to imagine that they were mastering their domestic future—always an agreeable feeling. And yet, although by late in the nineteenth century information about antidotes to pregnancy was widely available, the subject remained blanketed by discretion. Not all of this reticence was voluntary. The leagues of decency that sprang up in most industrial countries after midcentury were an ominous deterrent. Founded in panicked response to greater liberality of discussion among the respectable about remedies for pregnancy, they confiscated literally tons of birth control literature and paraphernalia, or brought court cases that led to their suppression.

It took some courage to speak up, but there were those who did. Around the turn of the century, the intrepid English student of human sexuality Havelock Ellis, probably the most celebrated casualty of the international campaign for purity, could not find respectable publishers in his own country for his monumental *Studies on the Psychology of Sex,* and those who did publish him were exposed to lengthy legal harassment. Yet he could not have written the work without witnesses willing to relate their sexual experiences to him with exemplary frankness. "I desire most heartily to thank the numerous friends and correspondents, some living in remote parts of the world," a grateful Ellis wrote in his preface, "who have freely assisted me in my work with valuable information and personal histories." The curtain of Victorian discretion grew increasingly porous with the years.

No doubt some of the work that birth control could have done for the modern family was frustrated by its adversaries. But reticence did not mean silence. Writing to an intimate woman friend in 1874, the American Mary Halleck Foote called the matter "a delicate thing to speak of in a letter," and dubbed what she had just learned "perfectly revolting": there are "shields of some kind" to be "had at some drug-gists." They are "called 'cundums' and are made of either rubber or skin." She confessed that she was shuddering to write about this dis-gusting subject. But she wrote about it.

LIKE MANY OTHER CULTURAL HABITS THAT DEFINE the Victorian bourgeoisie, birth control was not a recent invention. But it was in the nineteenth century, especially in its second half, that it produced far-reaching consequences for the middle-class family. Novel or modernized contraceptive techniques enlarged the arsenal for fend-ing off what Mary Foote called "the inevitable results of Nature's meth-ods." One preferred form of birth control, *coitus interruptus*—the Victorians called it "withdrawal"—was as old as the Old Testament. It had always been, and long remained, the method of choice because it was simplicity itself. It could be learned almost instantly; the steep price of a mistake was sufficient to make men as cautious as they could force themselves to be. It called on no outside intervention—pharma-cists or physicians—and no intimidating devices. Some enthusiasts for withdrawal proclaimed it to be infallible, which, a number of unex-pected nineteenth-century babies attest, it was not. But it was the best, it seems, that many couples had at their disposal.

Most physicians advocating withdrawal squarely addressed the cen-tral physiological and psychological issue: its effect, if any, on sexual gratification. One Dr. James Ashton in America, countering the asser-tion that such a method dulls the very ecstasy it is designed to safe-guard, declared: "it does not really diminish the pleasurable sensations of the connection." With an outspokenness that surpassed the candor of Mrs. Beeton's recipe for making turtle soup, he recommended that the man arm himself for the raptures ahead: "Always carry to bed a clean napkin, which is to be kept in the hand of the male during the nuptial act. It will then be a very easy matter to place this napkin in a proper position to receive the semen on withdrawal." This technique, Dr. Ashton assured his readers, would in no way reduce the delights of either partner, and "habit" would soon make the man an "expert in this respect." Such encouragement from so imposing a source could only be welcome to middle-class readers.

In the nineteenth-century, especially among the lettered, withdrawal faced some vigorous competition: vaginal jellies, douches, or pessaries. But the most momentous Victorian innovations to serve the modern family were the rubber condom, and, several decades later, the diaphragm, both born of industrial resourcefulness. Condoms had been in use since the eighteenth century; but, produced mainly from the intestines of sheep, they were expensive and untrustworthy. Then, in 1839, Charles Goodyear first vulcanized rubber and five years later he received a patent for his invention. By midcentury, after further refinements in the process, the time for the mass manufacture of rubber condoms had come, more reliable and less expensive than their precursors. In England, the price of a condom dropped from tenpence to a ha'penny around the 1860s.[*]

Two other birth control methods captured middle-class attention: the first, abstinence, unpopular and reliable; the second, timing intercourse, popular and unreliable. Abstinence was a practice of last resort. Highly approved by priests and parsons, it was usually imposed on men by their wives. Worn with childbearing, they dictated it by banishing their husband from the bedroom. As for calendars designed to outwit fertility, they could be devised at home or recommended by a physician, but professional guidance was little more dependable than amateurish schemes. The doctors' ignorance was massive: many drew an inappropriate analogy between women's most fertile time with that of animals in heat. Like lovers unduly trusting in withdrawal, those trusting in scheduling intercourse eventually had unforeseen and unwanted infants on their hands. There must have been untold times in the Victorian age when people were better off listening to their mothers than to their doctors. It was this kind of misplaced professional erudition that led R. Koehler, a zoologist at the University of Lyon, to note in 1892 in a well-informed article on impregnation: "Our knowledge of

---

[*]Still, the condom had its detractors. it could fail, and, numerous users judged, it all too often interfered with erotic pleasures.

the nature of the intimate phenomena of fecundation is of quite recent origin." In those decades, the Victorian family must have suffered almost as much from its allies as from its adversaries.

4

🌼 AMONG THE SILENT VICTORIAN REVOLUTIONS changing bourgeois family life out of all recognition, romantic love, or what passed for it, was perhaps the most far-reaching. Vulgarized in popular fiction, sentimental etchings, poetry, and songs, it came to make a strong case for letting affection rather than assets dictate the choice of one's life's companion. Not uniformly, to be sure: the network of roads to marriage demonstrates once again the utility of that invaluable plural, middle classes. Courting rituals, parental roles, financial considerations formed distinct amalgams that differentiated each bourgeois society from all the others. Unmarried British and American middle-class couples were far freer to converse or take unsupervised walks than their German or Italian counterparts. Taine found that "a young English girl wants to marry from inclination alone; she conjures a novel for herself, and that dream forms part of her pride, her chastity." Not that she despises practicality, Taine added; dreaming by the light of the moon hand in hand with her lover was not her way. "She wants to give herself fully and forever," to be her husband's comrade. The implication was that respectable people did things differently in France.

So they did. In France, marriage remained a businesslike affair decades after young lovers in other countries were permitted to make up their own minds—always providing, of course, that their heart's desire passed their parents' test of suitability. Repeatedly, French visitors across the Channel admired English freedom and deplored, at home, the oppressive intervention of lawyers, undignified wrangling over finances, and regal family conferences in the absence of the future bride and groom who barely got to know one another before the wedding. Evidently, these self-critical French travelers complained, we French do not take love to be a secure basis for marriage. Too much of the time, the size of a young woman's dowry, a marriage gift with which the English were notoriously skimpy, is of greater concern.

Normally, cultural outsiders like Jews in Central and Eastern Europe, even those who had been partially assimilated into the Western bourgeoisie, paid tribute to their insecure status by clinging to time-tested customs more tenaciously than less vulnerable groups. "How beautiful it is to be an Aryan," Schnitzler bitterly mused in 1904; "one's talent is so unimpaired." This sense of something unsettling held true not just for Polish, Ukrainian, or Romanian Jews but for Western Jews as well. The relative flexibility of marital choice that especially English and American "Aryans" increasingly enjoyed became available to Jews only after a significant number of them could find their way into the gentile society that surrounded them. Down to the end of the nineteenth century, Jewish parents, often calling in a marriage broker to render assistance, carried all before them.

In her autobiography, Rahel Straus, the first Jew to open a medical practice in Germany, straightforwardly describes this transition. She married a man she loved and who loved her. Their union had revolutionary overtones; her chosen partner felt compelled to reject his father's strong recommendation to marry a rich girl, and she abetted him in his defiance. This was being "modern." But the rest of her family kept faith with the old dispensation. In the 1870s, her father "came directly to Posen to look at mother," following "the custom that parents, relatives, friends of the family, or professional marriage brokers" would come to propose someone. "Then, if external conditions—family, profession, fortune, health—were appropriate, the girl's parents would give their permission to have the young man 'take a look.'" The consequence of this inspection was almost always that the couple became engaged, for to leave without that was regarded as a "powerful insult for, after all, one married 'into a family,' not the individual girl." Even Rahel Straus's oldest sister, Trude, found her husband—or he found her—in the same long-established manner. That this particular marriage turned out well was an unforeseen dividend. All too often, the bromide that a potential bride's parents usually handed out to her, "Love will come later," proved sadly specious.

The more highly placed the families involved, the more widespread the ancient aristocratic practice of fathers negotiating a marital alliance. In 1850, Samuel Bleichröder, a rich banker in Berlin whose son was to become Bismarck's financial adviser, wrote to another Jewish banker, B. H. Goldschmidt, in Frankfurt-am-Main, whom he had never met: "You have a daughter, and I a son, would you perhaps be disposed to form close family ties with me and destine your daughter to become my son's wife?" He assured Goldschmidt that the Bleichröders were in a position to provide his daughter with "all the amenities of life" and would make it their "sole endeavor to make her happy." Promptly and politely, Goldschmidt refused on the ground that he was not yet ready to give his daughter in marriage. In the middling and lower reaches of bourgeois German Jews, indeed, of most bourgeois, this exchange of letters would have seemed a quaint survival.

🌹 LATE IN THE CENTURY, THEN, AS MORE AND MORE middle-class women went out to work, were accepted at universities, even to medical school, and improved their legal status, love matches struggled to become the rule rather than the exception. It was not an easy campaign, and not wholly won before the outbreak of World War I. And a working love match came to imply sexual compatibility, for, after all, sexual satisfaction was becoming as much an ingredient in the definition of true love as affection and permanent commitment. This was an old idea now rewritten to include, at least among progressive social circles, a measure of equality between husband and wife. When in 1910 Freud defined "normal" love as the confluence of "two currents," the *"tender"* and the *"sensual,"* he was echoing long-established doctrine. Countless poets, novelists, philosophers had damned carnality without affection as lust and defined affection without carnality as friendship. At their best, Victorian bourgeois marriages resolved these tensions in family life, in bed, the nursery, and the kitchen.

At their best: the most fortunate among nineteenth-century middle-class families—we shall never even remotely know how many—seem to have risen above sheer sensuality or financial considerations to discover less brutish and less mercenary forms of marital love. For them, the bittersweet home had more sweetness in it than bitterness. Exalted spirits might look down on average couples: a character in Schnitzler's *The Fairy Tale* speaks contemptuously about ordinary folk for whom the word "family" includes the notions of "seclusion" and "trivial ease." But for many, this was good enough; the ideal of ease embraced that of affection and a sense of duty. Granted, not all Victorian middle-class families were successful. But in their successes, they stand like a deserved reproach to the generations that followed them, including our own.

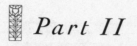

Part II

DRIVES AND DEFENSES

THREE

Eros: Rapture and Symptom

1

AT SIXTEEN, ARTHUR SCHNITZLER GAVE EVERY indication that he was growing into an expert in matters of sex; we recall Emilie, who, probably with other charmers, had starred in the diary that caused his father's anxious anger. In future years, he strenuously labored to fulfill his promise—labored: at times he engaged, with a casual mistress, in "debauchery" from sheer "willingness to oblige." Theory and practice, private history and public expression coincided for him when it came to Eros in action. No wonder that, if there was one theme on which Schnitzler's audience, even his detractors, acknowledged his expertise, it was carnality. Schnitzler said in one of his poems that he had been criticized for concentrating too much on love, play, and death. But he had no apologies to make: these "eternal three," he wrote, contain all the world, all its meaning and soul. But the first of these was love, sexual love.

Fortunately, the eternal three did not exhaust Schnitzler's subject matter. Half a dozen plays from *Casual Love* of 1894 to *The Second* of 1927, and his most brilliant novella, *Lieutenant Gustl* of 1900, his impressive stream-of-consciousness monologue, attest to his contempt for dueling. And when racial anti-Semitism grew more brazen in the 1890s, the "Jewish question" found its way into his fiction. Yet love, its ecstasy and pathos, lay at the heart of his work.

Schnitzler knew only too well what he was writing about. As we know, the literary bachelors with whom he associated in their favorite Viennese café were almost as casual about their love affairs as Schnitzler. A catalogue of his adventures with women, only three or four of them emotionally absorbing, would be long; it set him apart from the vast majority of less ardent bourgeois lovers with fewer opportunities and more moderate urges. The man whom the French call *l'homme moyen sensuel*, the quintessential bourgeois, neither could, nor would have wanted to, muster so frequent an expenditure of sexual energy. Schnitzler's conquests never silenced his ever alert appetites for long. We know so much about them because for some years he would record each orgasm and at the end of the month add up the total— unfortunately, he omitted those of his partners.

In early September 1887, on one of his walks in Vienna, he picked up an attractive young woman, Anna Heeger. She called herself "Jeanette" in a pathetic attempt to elevate her status, for in real life she did embroidery for a paltry living. She was, in Schnitzler's pitiless class society, an eminently unsuitable and hence all the more desirable target for sexual advances. Two days later, she visited his rooms and became his mistress. To his astonishment, he grew attached to her, which did not keep him from pursuing other, equally effortless triumphs. When he returned to Vienna in August 1888 after a long absence, he celebrated his reunion with Jeanette five times.

This recurrent exercise, far from exhausting the couple, barely slowed them down; Schnitzler's diary logs two further encounters the next night and four the night after that. Compiling the balance on August 31, he determined that in the eleven months since he had launched his affair with Jeanette, they had made love 326 times. When the couple parted at the end of 1889—their romance had deteriorated as she made jealous scenes—the proofs of his potency with Jeanette Heeger stood at 583. Leporello could have sung an impressive variant of the catalogue aria about this modern Don Juan.

Schnitzler had no reason to lament this farewell. Since mid-year, he had started a serious liaison with a former patient, the young, moderately gifted actress Marie Glümer, his adored "Mz." It infuriated Jeanette Heeger, who halfheartedly tried to commit suicide; the day you get married, she told Schnitzler, will be my last. But, confident that this was an empty threat, he persisted in his revels with Mz. On the day he drew up his final tally of intercourse with Jeanette Heeger, he could look back on thirty-five times of the same sort of carousal with his new flame.

For rakes with their conscience well under control, an affair with what Schnitzler taught the Viennese to call "the sweet girl—*das süsse Mädel*" provided raptures without imposing responsibilities. Some well-calculated talk of love, a few dinners in a fancy restaurant, an occasional weekend in the country struck many of these young women thirsting after life as adequate recompense for the favors they dispensed. And yet, for all the gratification they might derive from these encounters, they were victims, as Schnitzler stood ready, though only rarely, to acknowledge.

🌸 THE PRODIGIOUS RECORD THAT SCHNITZLER compiled was a symptom more than an achievement. It will emerge that his fixation—it was nothing less—did not provide him with pure delights. This becomes clear from Anatol, the protagonist of a sequence of one-acters written between 1888 and 1892 that established Schnitzler's reputation as a wit flirting with the forbidden. Like Anatol, he was "a hypochondriac of love." His meticulously registered orgasms intimate that he was driven to prove something to himself, inviting the conjecture—without more definitive evidence, it can never be more than this—that his heroic exhibitions of virility were ways of drowning out homoerotic impulses. It is awkward to make a diagnosis by an absence, yet Schnitzler's near silence about such desires, except for a handful of casual jokes, suggests a deep-seated need for denial. That perversions should seem like a taboo not to be breached, not even to be approached, would have been far from surprising in a conventional Victorian bourgeois, but it calls for comment in an indefatigable traveler across the fascinating sexual landscape of his time.

This is so particularly because students of Schnitzler have liked to think of him as the Freud of Fiction. Freud himself did so. In May 1906, thanking Schnitzler for a letter congratulating him on his fiftieth birthday, Freud replied that for years he had been impressed by "the far-reaching agreement" between his own and Schnitzler's views on important psychological, particularly erotic questions. He had often asked himself "whence you have been able to take this or that secret knowledge." This was a specimen of Freud's habitual unresentful envy, the envy of a scientist of the mind for the artist who, almost by instinct, penetrates to obscure, well-defended regions without having to do the "laborious research" imposed on the psychoanalyst. Though glad of distinguished company, Freud was no flatterer, and so extravagant a tribute was exceptional for him.

It was also overly generous. Compared to Freud's sweeping *Three Essays on the Theory of Sexuality*, first published in 1905, Schnitzler's explorations of erotic entanglements were relatively parochial in their agenda; they had nothing to say about the love of man for man and woman for woman. After all, despite prevailing genteel evasiveness among respectable people about homosexuality, the subject had been scarcely a secret, certainly not since 1869, when the Hungarian physician Karoly Maria Benkert coined this technical term. Toward the end of the century, after the sensational trials of Oscar Wilde in 1895, it was beginning to be studied and widely aired, though seldom without the fig leaf of polite-sounding circumscriptions like "inversion" or "contrary sexual feelings." Theories about its origins abounded, often disappearing as rapidly as they had arisen. Until Freud, heredity trumped environment as the leading cause: one school of thought even imagined a third sex, with a man in a woman's body, a woman in a man's body.

In those decades, a small but conspicuous company of specialists, collectively known as the sexologists, ventured into the darker reaches of love. They made the unspeakable speakable, certainly in medical circles and even beyond. In 1886, Richard Freiherr von Krafft-Ebing, soon internationally recognized as a leading authority on the perversions, published his masterpiece, forbiddingly titled *Psychopathia Sexualis,* a map to the varieties of physical love. To ward off the prurient reading public hoping for titillation rather than scientific knowledge, he lapsed into Latin (easily deciphered by anyone who had attended an elite secondary school) whenever he offered a vignette to illustrate a sensitive topic—and virtually all of his topics were sensitive—to drive home his medical point. Not long after, Havelock Ellis catalogued the array of sexual conduct in England with a sense of discovery and without moralizing.

Inescapably, some of the mushrooming literature about sexuality amounted to special pleading. The pioneering crusader for frankness about, and acceptance of, homosexuality, Magnus Hirschfeld of Berlin, was a hearty advocate of the sexual behavior he was investigating. So were others. One stylish way of lending the sheen of purity to what the devout denounced as an unforgivable violation of God-given commandments—the Old Testament had bluntly ranked it as an abomination deserving death by fire—was to liken it to Greek love. Among educated bourgeois with a classical education who had read their Plato, the prestige of antique Athenian culture had barely begun to wane, and the practice of older men loving younger men, socially acceptable under specified conditions, was anything but esoteric.

Perhaps the most prominent Victorian apologist for Greek love, writing to legitimize his own sexual passions, was John Addington Symonds, a prolific English biographer, travel writer, and historian of the Italian Renaissance. In 1883, he published *A Problem in Greek Ethics,* a brief for "manly love," that "powerful and masculine emotion in which effeminacy has no part"—witness Achilles and Petroclus. Deviating from dominant middle-class ideals was to Symonds a source of pride. Writing to his daughter in 1889, he maintained that "a large part of human life, the largest part"—he meant to say, the best part— "of human life, is involved in not being bourgeois."

Not being bourgeois doubtless gave free spirits a thrill of pleasure, but it carried risks in most nineteenth-century countries. France was a signal exception: even the Bourbons of the Restoration did not repeal the 1791 act of the Constituent Assembly that had decriminalized homosexual relations between consenting adults. It would take many years before other states followed the French lead: the Netherlands in 1886; Italy in 1889. Most other countries repealed capital punishment for sodomy in the nineteenth century, though these laws were rarely enforced—in England, even though they remained on the books to 1861, no one had been executed for that crime since 1835. On the other hand, lesser penalties, precisely because they did not compel juries to hand down a death sentence, continued a virtual, if intermittent, reign of terror. In these countries, "inverts" faced coarse ridicule, social ostracism, and professional barriers. Hence only exhibitionists among them advertised their love life outside covens of likeminded intimates. They hid in marriages of convenience, consummated their desires in faraway places, exiled themselves permanently to more tolerant climes, and lied to prying interviewers. Replying to persistent questions from Symonds, Walt Whitman, who extolled the love of comrades in his poetry, claimed that he had fathered six children—"two are dead," he added, lending his disguise of virility the authority of false specificity.

Reversing the general trend, here and there legislation against sexual deviance grew more severe in the second half of the century, demonstrating the vitality of time-honored moral ideals. The German states of Hanover and Bavaria had no criminal statutes against consensual homosexual conduct, but in the North German Federation in 1869 and the united German Reich in 1871, the more stringent Prussian law prevailed, and under its fiercely debated paragraph 175, each year some five hundred homosexuals were sent to prison for up to four years. To judge from these figures, most offenders escaped unharmed, but among the "guilty" the anxiety remained. And in Britain, in 1885, the Labouchere Amendment to the Criminal Law Amendment Act provided a life sentence for a sodomite, ten years of penal servitude for a man attempting sodomy, and two years with hard labor for "any act of gross indecency." Unfortunate as Oscar Wilde was to be sent to prison—it ruined his career and certainly shortened his life—he was lucky to be convicted only of the least of these offenses. It is interesting to note that even though that case preoccupied Europe for years, there is no sign that Schnitzler ever commented on it.

Yet as a man of the world who read widely, he could not have remained ignorant of these events and the literature that grew up around them. There are indications, too, that he learned about perversions in his wide acquaintance. To give but one instance: in March 1893, on vacation, he met a young singer, Sophie Link, who, visibly unhappy, poured out her troubles to him: "Married six weeks ago," he noted, "unloved husband, imp[otent] besides and 'unnatural.'" Schnitzler was preoccupied with sex in his life and his work alike, but of a more bourgeois sort; his specialty was infidelity.

2

SCHNITZLER'S DEALINGS WITH SWEET GIRLS LEND weight to the suspicion that he never outgrew his boyish longings and never quite sorted out his erotic identity; apparently his love affairs, so necessary to him, grew from and in turn liberated some dismaying anxieties. In his diaries and letters, and instructively if indirectly in his plays and stories, he emerges as the slave of an obsession: he desperately wanted his mistress of the moment to be a virgin and would suffer spectacular anguish when it became apparent that she was not. He must have known, especially considering the class of women he seduced, that this was a preposterous fancy, and known that most of his loves (as he would have said) had not waited for him.

Still, Schnitzler persisted in trolling for virgins among *süsse Mädel*, or married women, who had by definition already lost their "innocence" with someone else. His women's emotional—that is to say, erotic—history fascinated him; he would interrogate them, badger them, press them for the full truth about previous affairs, and then despise them when they yielded and confessed that they were no longer what he wanted them to be. "I am," he noted, perceptively enough, "a habitual tormentor." In his *Anatol* cycle, he offers (among other pleasures) a self-portrait of the roué as compulsive investigator. One of its episodes,

"Anatol's Megalomania," has Schnitzler as it were debate his predicament in public. Anatol is a well-situated bachelor with no visible need to make a living and who changes mistresses, it seems, every week. Happening to run into a former flame, he quizzes her energetically to extract every detail about her love life then and now. As Henrik Ibsen had already demonstrated in *The Wild Duck,* such uncontrollable hunts for the truth can be a kind of sadistic aggression. Questioned by a friend about his persistent interrogation, Anatol admits, "It is stupid . . . it is sick." But, he adds, he cannot help it, for he, Anatol-Schnitzler, is dragging all his memories with him. This was a dazzling bit of self-analysis.

He was quite as aware that he could not give his amours what he wanted from them. "Love," he wrote a friend in September 1893, "now belongs not to my emotional life but to my hygiene." He provided himself with an alibi for his infidelities by following a homemade prescription for mental and physical health. In 1890, he commented on his "impertinent sensuality. When I have been chaste for several days—six to nine are the maximum—I am simply an animal." Two years later, he underscored this diagnosis: "I would suffer terribly from abstinence, and whores disgust me." It was a suffering he usually managed to remedy quickly and with only occasional self-reproaches. As he sometimes admitted, his self-serving logic could not withstand a moment's scrutiny. He knew and he did not know. Try as he might, his reasoning failed to protect him from his "bad attacks" of jealousy as he pictured his mistresses in the arms of earlier lovers.

Schnitzler's hunger for absolute sexual purity was not a sporadic anxiety attack but a crippling ailment. He recalled in 1890 during his affair with Marie Glümer how the previous summer his "jealousy of the past" had almost driven him mad. One night he had lain in the woods, a favorite backdrop for his sexual episodes, next to his beloved Mz, "moaning, screaming, weeping as all those thoughts assailed me again!" He cried easily and often. In a confessional and brutal letter to his beloved little angel, he justified his refusal to marry her by the torments he undergoes when he remembers her two former lovers. The thought that others had heard her sigh during lovemaking, that others had gloried in her charms, was intolerable to him. It overwhelmed him with an "immense disgust," he told her ungraciously, and often.

Imagining for Mz's benefit a distasteful little scene, he drove his tactlessness beyond his normal bounds, wide as they were: he has married her and is taking her to a party where he encounters one of her past lovers, "a man who has held you in his arms, a man who, in your home, has thrown you on a couch and possessed you while your mother is in the kitchen, a man who, when we leave the party, can smile to himself and think, I have enjoyed her, too—before him—and even I was not the first!" He could sagely tell himself that Mz was superior to "the great majority of well-guarded virgins," but he could not get over sensing the lips of other men on the lips he was kissing.

🌼 SCHNITZLER'S JEALOUSY OF THE PAST WAS exceeded only by his jealousy of the present. When, in March 1893, he learned from anonymous letters that on tour Marie Glümer had slept with another man, he threw torrid diatribes at her, mobilizing the most hurtful epithets he could marshal. His sweet confidante, his dearest beloved child, his treasured comrade had demeaned herself to become a shameless tart, a miserable traitor, "the lowest creature under the sun." His scorn for her, he told Mz, was growing larger than his love for her had ever been. "Disgust, disgust, disgust! You have soiled me as no man has ever been soiled," unchecked hyperbole that in his calmer moments he recognized to be tasteless, childish, and egotistical. He knew that, though he felt "the most honest indignation" at the unfaithful Mz, "she has only done the same thing I have.—And I have madly loved her, while I betrayed her." He consoled himself with the thought that life is like that: inconsistent, irrational; it generates paradoxes that pervade all of human existence. "At times love is very sweet when one is not in love."

Such fated absurdities gave Schnitzler the space he needed for his escapades. For, while he was pouring out his fury at his mistress's brazen duplicity—"you would have to blush before the sincere street whore who plies her harmless trade"—he was carrying on an affair with "Fifi," another former patient, had been engaged in it since the previous November. Nor was Fifi his only consolation for Mz's absences, even though he presumably loved Marie Glümer more than he had ever loved anyone. In October 1892, some three months before he discovered his principal mistress's unspeakable treachery, he slept with Z. three times and tried to conjure up Mz. In vain. "No, no, it is not 'the same,'" he grimly concluded. "The cold hotel room. Hypochondria," his word for being depressed. He made himself believe that by betraying Mz with Fifi and with Z., he could love Mz "all the better, more beautifully, in a less tormented way." He asked himself, reasonably enough, "Sophisms?" and did not stay for an answer. His gift for casuistry served him too well as he pursued his obsession.

THAT HE SHOULD UNDERTAKE SUCH EXPLOITS fully aware just how little pleasure they gave him bears witness to their neurotic character. What made them all the more agonizing was Schnitzler's intermittent recognition that their implicit—at times explicit—contempt for women put him in a class with a large party of ordinary bourgeois attached to the traditional double standard. In a genial mood, he described Mz in the accepted misogynistic manner as being of a "wild but for a woman a comparatively truthful nature." This was the lover who could tell his mistress, the actress Adele Sandrock, to her face, "You are like all women a liar and a whore." He did not always believe that, but he believed it often enough.

For all this crudity, Schnitzler was subtle enough to satirize his all too commonplace masculine ideology by creating unlovable male protagonists: unabashed egotists, men about town who callously exploit the women they sleep with and have no thought of marrying—in short, himself. In one of his wittiest short dialogues, "The Overwrought Person" of 1894, he has an evidently middle-class married woman announce to her lover that she is pregnant. The news draws a flurry of anxious suggestions from him, growing more insensitive, and more annoying to her, as he stumbles along. He insinuates that the child must be her husband's, which she indignantly, it seems truthfully, denies. He hints that she ought to get an abortion, a solution that she firmly rejects. He whines that the two cannot run away to America since he, alas, working for his father, earns only a pittance, an opportune declaration of dependence she receives with derisive skepticism. Finally, he proposes that she have intercourse with her husband just once to provide legitimate cover for the child she is carrying. Whereupon she slaps him and leaves. The man has the last word: he mutters just before the curtain falls that this is no way to respond to sound advice. She's eccentric, she will come back! Schnitzler leaves no doubt, though, that his repellent hero is quite wrong; it is the woman's contempt for him that will reverberate in the audience's mind.

One of Schnitzler's most controversial early dramas, *The Fairy Tale*, written in 1891 and first performed two years later to widespread condemnation for its "immorality," was quite as unsparing about his own defects. The male protagonist, Fedor, is an articulate social progressive particularly scathing about the double standard. The current wisdom that a respectable man cannot marry a "fallen" woman is, he insists, canting bourgeois prudery. Fanny, an appealing actress, whom he loves and who loves him, is a perfect test for his principles: she has confessed to two previous affairs. In the end, unable to resist the pressures of his conventional crowd, Fedor drops back into the ways of the compact majority. He snidely informs Fanny that "the shame that clings to you is ineradicable." Whereupon she shows her moral superiority to her lover by dismissing him and signing a lucrative contract that will take her to Russia and greatly advance her career. Plainly, Schnitzler was inviting his audience to see Fedor as a boastful weakling and a hypocrite. In short, himself a parttime Fedor, he could only rarely muster in his life the good sense and liberal morality he mobilized more readily for his plays.

🥀 YET THERE WERE TIMES WHEN SCHNITZLER FOUND love in the full sense, merging affection with appetite. In July 1894, a new patient with a sore throat, Marie Reinhard, came to consult him—

she was twenty-three and very pretty—and he was immediately smit-
ten. During the summer and fall he wooed her as he had never wooed
before, plotting his approaches discreetly and moving far more slowly,
far more delicately, than was his inveterate habit. In October, three
months after he had met her, he confided to his diary, "I have not yet
dared anything." Soon after, there were kisses and quarrels and serious
conversations, though it took several more months before Marie
Reinhard was ready to proffer the "ultimate gift" that a proper young
middle-class woman of her time could bestow.

Her "surrender, " on March 13, 1895, was a well-pondered decision,
and once she had made it, she was all the more passionate. "It was all
wholly unforced, without pathos," Schnitzler recorded the consumma-
tion, "and she became mine quite as naturally as this whole business
has developed naturally." Of course he could not keep himself from
asking her if he was the first one, which she could honestly affirm. But
when she asked him to swear that he trusted her word, he did so with
his fingers crossed; he could hardly believe that he had found a virgin
at last! Still, some of the time at least, her initiation into Schnitzler's
erotic world was idyllic, evoking in him an unprecedented sense of
ease. On April 14, he noted, "We had supper and loved one another
tenderly and sensually."

Marie Reinhard, his "Mz II" or "Mz. Rh.," was neither an actress nor
an embroiderer, but a cultivated singing teacher from a solid bourgeois
family. This was the kind of woman that a man in Schnitzler's social
position could marry. He talked to her as an equal—almost; he read his
work to her and could make use of her suggestions. Yet his diary
entries for his liaison with the second Mz are punctuated with danger
signs: she bores him, she makes him nervous. In January 1896, just ten
months after the couple had consummated their love affair, he gave
voice to his restlessness: after spending an afternoon with Mz II in
their private hideaway, he reports: "pleasant, sweet, pretty—but I'd
like to have another mistress again." And he soon did, with beneficial
emotional side effects. "Since I have a second mistress," he decided, "I
also love Mz. Rh. more, physically, too, than before." The gratification
of his keenest wish, a mistress who "had not yet belonged to anyone,"

was no match for his imperious cravings. Having got what he wanted, he wanted something more—and someone else.

He was incorrigible. Though in a fury he had broken off his affair with Marie Glümer two years earlier, he let himself be impressed by the deluge of abject messages and flowers she sent him. He allowed her to come and see him, meetings she mainly spent literally on her knees, begging him to pardon her. Then it happened as it had to happen. On July 10, he had seen Mz II: "She was very beautiful," he noted, "and I loved her very much." Only a week later, he found himself alone with Mz I: "she wept, she was tender, and she became mine once again." He kept up this duplicitous game. Late in July he recorded receiving "tender letters from the Mz's." No wonder that in a moment of self-analysis dating from that time, he found himself "downright prostituted." As usual, this insight had no effect on his conduct.

When Marie Reinhard died in March 1899 after a botched appendectomy, Schnitzler grieved for her sincerely, with an intensity rare for him. He thought of her often, he remembered the anniversary of her death. Yet his body all too soon reminded him of his needs, at a highly inappropriate moment of mourning. On May 1, less than two months after Mz II's death, he was talking to a young acquaintance who noticed his sadness. "Wept," he noted; "she wept along with me. Later sensuality flared up, which offended her." Somewhat to his surprise, there *were* such women.

SCHNITZLER'S AMBIVALENT FEELINGS ABOUT THE nature of woman and his anxieties about the imperative of virginity were quarrels with himself, conflicts he took to the outer edges of neurosis. But, as Freud has reminded us, neurotics only give extravagant expression to normal behavior: we may read Schnitzler's inner battles, particularly over the call for a good girl to remain "pure" until marriage, as a somewhat distorted reflection of social ideals on the verge of transition. True: "However sensual he may be," Krafft-Ebing pronounced in the mid-1880s, "the man of higher feelings demands a wife in marriage who had been, and is, chaste." But during these years, some bourgeois with advanced views—Schnitzler's Fedor, at least until he retreats to safe conformity, is a good example—were beginning to question the fetish of virginity. For the cult of female purity was an integral element in the double standard, and liberal-minded spirits were finding that paradigm increasingly unconvincing, increasingly unjust. After all, few apart from severe divines called on men to make the same strenuous demands for self-abnegation; the male animal, as the cliché had it, was supposed to prepare himself for monogamy by sowing his wild oats.

The milestones of nineteenth-century feminist protest and their rare triumphs are landmarks of the mounting discontent with traditional moralistic maxims that men had established to govern women's conduct. In 1848, divines and editorial writers, scandalized and fearful, maligned the meeting of feminists at Seneca Falls, New York, for setting down a catalogue of women's demands, including the vote. They were no less alarmed by the agitation led by Josephine Butler, beginning in 1869, against Britain's Contagious Diseases Act, which penalized prostitutes but not their clients. Many of the most principled feminists were idealistic middle-class women, loyally supported by a few men of the same class, rather than bohemians or bourgeois-hating radicals. But whatever their social location, all of them chipped away at dominant cultural attitudes. And among these was the place of Eros in women's life. The call for the equality of the sexes, dreamt of but never completely achieved in the Victorian age, strongly implied the right of women to the same sexual freedom that men had claimed for centuries.

It was bound to be a hard-fought struggle, since the cult of virginity was inextricably intertwined with religious dogmas even among bourgeois for whom the Virgin Mary was a legend; devout Protestants and Jews, as much as Catholics, were committed to its enforcement and to punishing its violators. In many middle-class circles, it was just as closely intertwined with social status. Sheltered young women in the upper reaches of society, who in their convents or segregated schools were shielded from sexual temptations, had few opportunities (even if they should have had the desire) to lose their virginity before the wedding night. Their intact hymen remained a trophy worth preserving. Once "ruined," their price in the marriage market dropped precipitously.

Behind these social and economic aspects of idealizing the *virgo intacta*, psychological conflicts quietly did their subterranean work. As a rule, once a boy has unmasked the secret of adult sexual activity, he is likely to topple his mother from her pedestal and sadly conclude that she is no better than she should be. If the boy is fortunate, he will grow up to integrate these extravagant fantasies into a more realistic view, make peace with his mother, and seek out a different love in whom to invest his emotions. If he is less fortunate, though, if he is left burdened with the sense that his unfaithful mother never gave him the love he had craved and deserved, he will be tempted to replay over and over his yearning to reinstate her in her saintly guise. He will be doomed to fail, and retain a pathetic unconscious hankering for revenge.

Something like this seems to have been at work in Schnitzler. The clues he planted suggest that he remained mired in unfinished childhood business. In the affair of the little red diary, his mother seems to have been quite uninvolved, since in the Schnitzler household the discipline department was evidently in the father's hands, a division of labor that accorded with the fading, though still lively, practices of the paternalistic family. But Schnitzler's nearly unbroken silence about his mother was a clue, not an accident. In his autobiography, *Youth in Vienna,* he refers to her rarely and casually, but it does not follow that she had no emotional, if often hidden, importance for him.

As we have seen, in the tightly knit world of the modern family, children's emotional expectations from their parents, especially their mothers, were greater, or at least more visible, than they had been in past centuries. Schnitzler thought that with all their fondness, all their concern for his education, his parents had been insufficiently affectionate and had concentrated far too assiduously on securing his father's worldly position and its external trappings, a campaign to which his mother had devoted her best exertions. "All in all," Schnitzler appraised his childhood, "the character of our relationship then and through many years after could be described as cordial rather than intimate." No doubt, Frau Professor Doktor Johann Schnitzler thought herself a good mother; but for her eldest, she was simply not good enough. As late as 1891—he was almost thirty—he noted in his diary a "scandal" at home, with his parents calling him a wastrel and a fool. The clash made him muse mournfully: "I think I have a right to more understanding."

It could hardly have helped Schnitzler to reflect that the Austrian bourgeoisie, lagging behind its equals in other countries, largely shared his parents' outlook on love, work, and morality. His cousin Otto Markbreiter had to renounce all connections with his family after marrying a barmaid. And in 1897, Schnitzler discovered that his cherished Marie Reinhard, with whom he had lived in Paris for some time, could not return to the city of Vienna but had to seek shelter in a suburb because she was bearing his child. This was the atmosphere that Bertrand Russell stigmatized in 1902, the year after Queen Victoria's death, when he exploded to his friend, the classicist Gilbert Murray, about "Black-Coated Respectability; the living God." Playing variations on this theme, all of them scathing and none of them appreciative of the changes in bourgeois attitudes, bourgeoisophobes accused the middle classes of cant, prudery, sanctimoniousness.

3

THE HATERS OF THE BOURGEOISIE, BOTH THEN and later, reserved their particular scorn for middle-class sexuality, to their mind a physical and moral disaster decked out as a model of civility and reticence. To support their anti-bourgeois propaganda, they invented preposterous tales, allowed themselves rude jokes, and wildly generalized from a limited number of instances. These fabrications, jests, and global verdicts acquired international circulation and almost unquestioned authority. They permitted twentieth-century denigrators of the Victorians to feel superior to their ancestors, and left traces among professedly scholarly texts in print today. They liked to tell of Victorian guests who at a dinner asked for the "bosom" of the chicken, or Victorian families who covered the "limbs" of their grand piano with modest little paper skirts. And they endlessly recycled a favorite, the imaginary Victorian mother who informs her trembling daughter on the eve of her wedding that once he is alone with her, her husband will coarsely assault her, and advises her to meet this terrifying moment by closing her eyes and thinking of England.

The facts were quite different, and the erotic options far more varied than this, including pleasant ones. Many in the Victorian middle classes felt a good deal of hesitation about Eros, tugged one way by the teachings of the churches and cultural tradition and another by the attractions of skepticism about time-honored social habits and of natural urges. Perhaps the eternal verities that had guided their parents — or at least their parents' pronouncements —were time-bound after all! Perhaps the ideal of the bourgeois girl as sexless angel was driven not by high standards but by unacknowledged anxiety! Perhaps it was only a gross extension of the reasonable boundaries that any civilized society must impose on exigent human needs!

The documents the Victorians left to their historians have invited incompatible interpretations. Dickens, the most widely read and most beloved novelist in the English-speaking world, at once lampooned prudery and practiced it. Mr. Podsnap in *Our Mutual Friend* worries that someone might bring up a subject that would "bring a blush to the cheek of the young person." But the same novelist who had so much pleasure at the expense of this prissy gentleman could also touch on Dora Copperfield's miscarriage so fleetingly that most readers of *David Copperfield* missed the source of her pallor. Again, in the same novel he has the prostitute Martha speak like a well-educated young lady. Dickens's inconsistent responses to sexual love are so many intimations of characteristic and in the end unstable Victorian compromises.

Yet, despite their bad reputation, these compromises did not exclude the opportunities of deep sensual gratification for middle-class couples. For over a century, historians disdainful of the Victorians have handed down the slander that the bourgeois husband of that time regularly felt compelled to resort to brothels, chorus girls, or kept women to make up for inescapable sexual frustration at home. But this is another of those spiteful, largely unfounded legends that does violence to the abundant possibilities that marked the middle-class life of the age. The unsatisfied middle-class husband straying was of course not unknown to the nineteenth century. But the most reliable remedy was often more and better sex within the marriage bond.

More and better sex, but always in moderation. This requirement was a vital element in virtuous Victorian agendas that envisioned emotional well-being for wives as much as for husbands. It was understood that raw instincts, even women's instincts, are uninhibited and insatiable in their pristine state; hence moral training for proper bourgeois must include shaping inborn savage desire into civilized, loving satisfaction. For most contemporary educators, restraint and celibacy were not synonyms or even allies but adversaries. The Victorians believed strongly in what psychoanalysts call sublimation, the conversion of the erotic drive into artistic, intellectual, and craftsmanlike activity. Far more than most of their later detractors have allowed, nineteenth-century bourgeois put over their marriage bed not the motto of abstinence but that of temperance.

The more "progressive" nineteenth-century marriage manuals did much for the cause by spreading word that sexual appetites, being natural, are not in themselves sinful. This was the principal theme of *Mysteries of Females or the Secrets of Nature* by the German physician J. F. Albrecht, published around 1830. His concise tract on sexual psychology and physiology proved a notable publishing success in its time: by 1851 it had gone into six ever enlarged editions, reworked after the author's death to satisfy a steady demand. It is a particularly valuable text, since Dr. Albrecht was a paragon of discretion and piety, intent on affronting as few readers as possible and straining for decent language with blushing circumlocutions. Inoffensive as he tried to be, he found it possible to recommend to wives that they should not deny their husband's desire for "marital tenderness," let alone express disgust for it even if at the moment they were less interested in intercourse than he seemed to be. For, failing such cooperation cheerfully offered, the husband may "seek to indemnify himself outside marriage for the lack of gratification." This was the warning that, many decades later, anti-bourgeois publicists would mistake for common reality.

In advocating sexual gratification for both spouses, Dr. Albrecht politely noted that he was permitting himself to disagree with the theologians: if wife and husband feel the urge to copulate during her pregnancy, let them proceed, though considerately and more sparingly as the months go by. He asked why nature should have equipped human beings with a drive if it did not want it to be gratified. It seemed to him a reasonable rhetorical question. Such a liberal, sympathetic viewpoint, which Dr. Albrecht was among the first to proffer in the nineteenth century, is a reminder that the earliest and most constructive publicists reflecting about middle-class sexual morality were bourgeois writing for bourgeois, intent on remedying the ignorance that diffident husbands and wives often brought into marriage.

Of course, as this genial physician knew well, there were thousands of married couples who did not need any exhortations to shared pleasures. They discovered on their own the level of gratification that suited them both. It is instructive that on the many occasions that Schnitzler dealt with lovemaking in his work, he apparently took it for granted that the one thing his women characters did not have to worry about was frigidity. His most conspicuous failure in bed, presented humorously, is a man: in *Reigen,* a lover is too nervous to perform with a married woman until she soothes him down to bring their coupling to a satisfactory climax. In short, for every episode of ill-advised reticence about the facts of copulation and of disabling repression or psychological impotence among the Victorians, there must have been an episode—perhaps several—of sexual truthfulness and sexual satisfaction for the wife as well as the husband.

This momentous reality of Victorian middle-class life has been obscured not just by the sarcasms of later generations but also by the allegations of contemporaries, derisive self-assessments that later generations were only too happy to exploit. The best—that is, the worst—representative of Victorian testimony about a woman's natural incapacity for sexual gratification was a treatise by the English gynecologist William Acton, *The Functions and Disorders of the Reproductive Organs,* first published in 1857. What would the detractors of the Victorian bourgeoisie do without him? Acton notoriously pronounced the well-brought-up woman to be sexually anesthetic: "The majority of women (happily for them) are not very much troubled with sexual feelings of any kind. What men are habitually, women are only exceptionally." A nervous or feeble young man need not hesitate to get married on the ground that his bride would make excessive demands on him. Quite the contrary: the welfare of her husband, her household, and her children were bound to absorb all her emotional force. "The married woman has no wish to be treated on the footing of a mistress." A large number of middle-class Victorian wives would have astonished Acton with their comments on such sentiments, had he taken the trouble to ask them.

In any event, Acton's inability to differentiate between biological pre-conditions and social pressures invalidate his conclusions. But his views, proffered in an accessible and assertive style, enlisted a certain following, especially outside Britain. Nor was he the most extreme among physicians to deny that normal respectable women are endowed with powerful erotic appetites. Dr. H. Newell Martin, professor of biology and physiology at The Johns Hopkins University, discovered that middle-class, especially upper-middle-class, women actually find inter-course painful. She will consent to it only to give her man the thrills he craves: "A loving woman, finding her highest happiness in suffering for those dear to her," he wrote, "is very unlikely to let her husband know this, so long as she can bear it." Like Acton, Martin allowed that some women's sensuality can be aroused, and permanently. But he dismissed such females as abnormal, bound to be bad wives and mothers, at heart prostitutes by profession or avocation.

The great Krafft-Ebing agreed. In 1890, summarizing his latest find-ings, he maintained that woman's notably shallow interest in sexual activity is the consequence not of cultural constraints but of bodily processes. "If she is normally developed mentally and well brought up, her sensual desire is small." Were she not passive, not submissive, "the whole world would be a bordello, and marriage and the family unthink-able." In his classic *Psychopathia Sexualis*, heavily relying on the Italian sexologist Paolo Mantegazza, he had taken a somewhat different tack, admitting that woman is like man in craving the gratification of her sensual drives; but unlike him, she also hungers after "protection and support for herself and her children." Whatever the nuances of his shifting views, Krafft-Ebing never doubted that while woman may become an expert on love, sexual aggression is the man's part.

Naturally these were the witnesses whom twentieth-century critics of Victorian culture chose to remember. Had the mid-Victorian poet Coventry Patmore not written a long adoring poem about woman, the angel in the house? The caricature depicting woman as divinely appointed to find carnal coupling a matter of indifference if not outright repugnance was too deeply etched into the nineteenth-century mind to yield easily to evidence that contradicted it. There were physicians, even those specializing in women's ailments, for whom received stereotypes trumped the unmistakable record. The prize for disregarding evidence that literally lay before them on the table must go to the German specialist, Dr. Otto Adler, who in 1904 published *The Defective Sexual Feelings of Women*, trying to substantiate his thesis with case reports. They include patients he had brought to orgasm during an examination, and others whom every open-eyed observer would have qualified as beset by potent, if frustrated or somewhat specialized, erotic longings. It may be a platitude that those who will not see will remain blind, but it is true.

Despite Acton, Adler, and their allies, the obstinate vitality of this dogma of anesthetic woman was hardly the sole responsibility of specialists in women's diseases. In fact, the majority of these authorities denied what the prevailing mystique asserted. This mainstream of medical opinion included Dr. Albrecht, who, with all his prudence, arrived at his verdict on grounds of a higher logic rather than of clinical encounters: "It cannot be settled which of the two genders has a greater stimulus and consequently the stronger gratification in the fulfillment of the drive for procreation; but one may conclude that the beautiful gender, which has to endure the greatest sufferings from it, enjoys the greatest pleasure. And who will blame the Creator of this institution?"

Certainly not the majority of specialists, who preferred evidence from their practice to speculation. They knew, and clinical examinations confirmed, that when a woman consulted them about an absence of sexual responsiveness, she did so because she thought that there was something wrong with her, or her situation. And there were women who entrusted their diaries (or, more rarely, their letters) with sheer delight in their sexual experience. Inescapably, the evidence is skimpy but it crosses borders. In the nineteenth century, a woman's frank avowal of sexual appetites was bound to be exceptional, even among the Romantics. Too many barriers of discretion and delicacy had to be breached before it could become the acceptable coin of open discussion. Most women seeking to convey remembered or anticipated sexual bliss largely confined their disclosures to suggestive little sketches of hot kisses or sleeping in their husband's arms.

More earthy communications have proved hard to come by, partly because many of them must have been destroyed. But they exist. Here is a Parisian petty bourgeoise, a dressmaker, name and age unknown, writing to her lover in 1892: "I am compelled to acknowledge to myself, 'I love you,' and I won't forget the night of love I spent with you. Dear friend, you must have noticed with what freedom I abandoned myself. I was not at all embarrassed by your presence for the first time. It must be that I am greatly taken with you, and that I'm almost convinced that I will experience happiness in your arms under your hot caresses."

Recalling to Schnitzler an equally glorious night, a breathless Adele Sandrock was even more articulate: "I felt upon awakening as though I were still within the magic circle of your love, as though I lay still in your arms. . . . I felt how your mouth sucked in my breath—I felt not love, happiness—and like all these words, words hounded to death, abused until they are caricatures, it was far more certainly something different—it is a new birth—an unknown world disclosing its splendors to me, a marriage of body and soul filled with unending yearning—and more blissful self-dissolution—a blissful dreaming over into another world, a half-conscious dying came over me," and much more of the same.

Sandrock, one may object, was a promiscuous actress, a "liberated" and in every way histrionic woman. But more ordinary bourgeoises could sound quite like her. In the mid-1860s, Laura Lyman, an educated American, was corresponding with her husband, Joseph, then in New York, from their home in Easthampton, Massachusetts. He let her know that he yearned for her. "I anticipate unspeakable delights in your embrace," he wrote her on March 11, 1865. Two days later, he redoubled his ardor; he wished he could "feel close around me the caressing hands & be soothed by the voluptuous touch! But soon we will have it—all—full measure." He had no intention of staying away long. Her replies show that though Laura Lyman enjoyed, she did not require, this epistolary seduction. She presented herself, if anything, as more tempting than he did. On March 13, she passionately declared her love for him and added, "How I long to feel the contact of my mind with yours." True, the couple occasionally collaborated writing articles for phrenological journals, but obviously on this occasion she meant "body" when she wrote "mind." Ten days later, she made that perfectly plain: "I'll drain your coffers dry next Saturday I assure you." By that time, she had already tormented him with a luscious image of herself, naked and aromatic: "I have just bathed in warm water here before the fire and am just as sweet as a rosebud. Don't you wish you were here?"

When he complained that she was stirring him up too much—"you *will* talk about those baths of yours and how ravishingly sweet you make yourself"—she raised the ante, quite unapologetically, and made herself more provocative still: "I am not bathed," she told him on March 24, "the sheets are not clean—my undergarments are not fresh—you shall not be tantalized any longer," knowing full well that she was tantalizing him all the more. The Lymans conducted this lubricious exchange not just after their honeymoon, but after they had been married for seven years. Had Laura Lyman, to say nothing about Adele Sandrock, read Dr. Acton on the natural frigidity of bourgeois wives, they would merely have smiled.

4

ALL THIS IS IMPRESSIONISTIC. BUT WITH THE conspicuous exception of conservatives who feared the loss of a world not yet ridden by statistics, nineteenth-century bourgeois were enamored of science and devoted to the probative power of facts. Virtually impossible though it was to quantify sexual felicity—or misery—they looked for numbers. Dickens's appalling Mr. Gradgrind in *Hard Times,* an unbending, unimaginative teacher who has only contempt for feelings and insists on facts, facts, facts, was a malicious burlesque of social and political reformers who sought precision rather than vague cogitation. And in that time, when scientists of society had grown impatient with sheer anecdotes, some of them felt inspired to compile figures that might illuminate, though not possibly settle, the question how interested, or how uninterested, middle-class women were in copulation.

None of the nineteenth-century surveys conducted in a physician's office or with a questionnaire could even remotely approach the sophisticated sampling techniques of our time. But these small-scale, inescapably subjective studies are not useless, and they buttress the case that middle-class women are endowed with the same, or almost the same, sensuality as middle-class men. In 1883, Dr. Matthews Duncan, a distinguished Scottish obstetrician, reported to the Royal College of Physicians that he had interviewed 504 sterile women about their sexual desire and their sexual pleasure—the experience of orgasm. Only some 40 percent of his population had chosen to answer. The results, always assuming that the respondents were not bragging, were heartening to partisans of a woman's right to, and capacity for, erotic activity. One hundred and fifty-two women admitted to feeling desire; 134 to orgasm. It seems probable that if those who refused to be drawn had been persuaded to testify, their answers would have lowered the percentage of sensual women in Dr. Duncan's sample. But the responses he did obtain supported what he called the "almost universal opinion" that "in women desire and pleasure are in every case present, or are in every case called forth by the proper stimulants." So much for Dr. Acton!

The much-discussed Mosher Survey of female middle-class sexuality in the United States offers further support to these cheering figures. In 1892, Dr. Clelia Duel Mosher, a zoologist and physician, herself intensely reserved and "Victorian," launched a series of interviews with American women about their sexual experience. The forty-five respondents who filled out usable replies, all of them married, were anything but a true sample of the country, not even of the American middle class.

They were well educated, having in the main attended college or normal school, at a time when gaining access to higher learning was still a tribute to a young woman's spirit. They had seen something of the world outside the confines of the home, most of them working as teachers. They had married educated men, which was almost certainly an aid, and in no way a barrier, to sexual felicity. They were not "new women," but of and in the Victorian century, good bourgeoises all. However unrepresentative, their replies remain immensely revealing.

Three conclusions emerge: Dr. Mosher's respondents attested to an affectionate and relatively active sexual life, ranging from gratifying their appetites rarely to once or several times a week. Many of them linked their erotic enjoyments to the matrimonial obligation to produce children. And most of them paid earnest tribute to their husband's tact and sensitivity. Just about a quarter of them were altogether indifferent to intercourse or unable to enjoy it. One fifth reported that they reached a "venereal orgasm" all the time and another fifth did so "usually" or "sometimes"—figures that approach the results in late twentieth-century surveys. A few among them who expected to reach orgasm every time lamented the occasional failure as "depressing and revolting." There were those—a good number—who continued intercourse during their pregnancy, and one who explicitly wanted to make love during her menstrual period and in the daytime, though this adventurer in the realms of carnal gratification thought that once a month was about right. Praise of intercourse ranged from resigned to pleased to ecstatic; it was, one of these women said, "usually very delightful," and another, that she "would have hated to have omitted the experience." It all spoke of relatively guilt-free legitimate pleasure.

It was legitimate pleasure for legitimate purposes. Some of the respondents sounded a little apologetic about finding so much enjoyment in lovemaking, as though a priest or a strict mother were listening in on their confessions to Dr. Mosher. One of them, to be sure, explicitly discounted procreation as a good reason for intercourse: "I think women as well as men need this relation during middle life," she wrote. "It makes more normal people. Even if there are no children, men love their wives more if they continue this relation, and the highest devotion is based upon it, a very beautiful thing, and I am glad nature gave it to us." A substantial minority, though, offered a defense of intercourse for the reason most earnestly urged by clergymen and moralists: "I cannot recognize as true marriage that relation unaccompanied by a strong desire for children," one wrote. Without that desire, she added, marriage is simply "so-called legalized prostitution." Still, her own gratifications—being very much in love with her husband, she noted, she had "rather cultivated the passion"—undercut her stern reiteration of traditional ideals. The replies to Dr. Mosher's indiscreet probing inquiries, normally laconic and seldom lyrical, must be read with some caution.

God put in an appearance in many of the answers, but respondents invoking religion also used it to support secular feelings. "I think the man and woman married from love, it may be used *temperately* as one of the highest manifestations of love, granted to us by our Creator." Not surprisingly, the word "spiritual" was much in use. "It seems to me," wrote one, "to be a natural and physical sign of a spiritual union, a renewal of the marriage vows." In the minds of these middle-class women, mutual fondness was essential before they could fully enjoy their sexual experience. This was the love that Schnitzler craved and so rarely got.

This points to the last conclusion, prominent in most of these earnest little sexual autobiographies: it was the thoughtful husband, alert to his wife's needs and perhaps still unawakened appetites, who made marriage a true success in bed. Intercourse, one of Dr. Mosher's witnesses put it, "is the expression of love between man and woman"; it is "frequently simply the extreme caress of love's passion." One respondent who had been divorced and remarried put it best: "My husband is an unusually considerate man; during the earlier months of marriage"—she was then fifty-three—"intercourse was frequent, two or three times a week and as much desired by me as by him." It was this sense of "oneness" that made sexual congress serve "a higher purpose, as uplifting as music." There is no evidence that Schnitzler ever heard of the Mosher Survey; had he read it, he might have been a little astonished by its stress on spirituality, but not at the woman's sexual pleasure.

———

TO DENY THAT THE VICTORIANS' SEXUAL LIFE WAS an unrelieved catastrophe is not to assert that it was a uniform orgasmic paradise. It suffered abundant casualties; often enough, the cultivated evasion of erotic matters by shamefaced middle-class parents had deleterious long-range effects. In a short paper of 1907 on the sexual enlightenment of children, Freud vehemently reproached parents for refusing to answer the burning questions a child is bound to ask about the distinction between the sexes and the origin of babies. He blamed the childrens' later failures on their parents' "habitual prudery and their bad conscience about sexual matters." The story of the stork, no doubt well meant but a sorry instance of bad faith, did children no favors. In short, the intimate knowledge of the body which, I have claimed, was characteristic in proper Victorian households did not necessarily extend to the physiology of sex.

But since the early decades of the nineteenth century, writers of vademecums for parents had taken up the cause of candor. When it came to telling children the truth, Dr. Albrecht, that devout radical, did not hesitate: "Father and mother should try to establish a trusting friendship with their son and daughter, and acquaint them, as friends, with their desires and urges. Or, if the parents for some reason cannot manage this, they should secure a friend for their children who shall, decently, try to get them to confess their feelings." On the whole, retailers of advice concurred: it was impossible to keep an intensely curious child wholly in the dark about sex; parental self-censorship only tempted it to resort to obscene books or more experienced schoolmates, both agents of corruption rather than of knowledge.

Still, openness about these delicate matters was far from unknown in the Victorian bourgeoisie. In May 1888, Marcel Proust, then seventeen, asked his grandfather for thirteen francs. "This is why," he wrote. "I needed to see a prostitute so badly to put an end to my bad habit of masturbating, that my father gave me ten francs to visit a brothel. But, in my excitement I broke a chamber pot: three francs. Moreover, flustered as I was, I was unable to screw." The letter, whether a truthful report of the adolescent Proust's real sentiments or not, attests to an impressive measure of frankness and cordiality. A grandfather taken into an adolescent's full confidence, and a father, anything but censorious about the boy's "self-abuse," prescribes an extreme remedy—"healthy" sex to drive out "unhealthy" sex.

Proust's contretemps recalls Schnitzler's confrontation with his father. The two young men were almost of an age—one seventeen, the other sixteen; their fathers were eminent physicians; both incidents bespeak a refreshing honesty about presumably forbidden topics, an honesty that bourgeoisophobes considered unthinkable in middle-class families. True, the fathers' tone and their remedies contrasted instructively: the Frenchman, kindly and understanding, recommends frequenting a whorehouse; the Austrian, enraged, worried, and just a touch sadistic, warns his son *away* from a whorehouse. The difference may have resulted from a disparity in the fathers' characters, in national styles, or both. But plainly the invariably tight-lipped, uncommunicative, and authoritarian parent of the anti-Victorian legend deserves to be replaced by more realistic models.

Still, the casualties of bourgeois evasiveness deserve their day in court. Annie Besant, who in a career of many turnings moved from Christian ritualism to Theosophy, with atheism, socialism, and other ideologies in between, is a particularly cogent witness with her candor and her intelligence. In her autobiography of 1893, she testified to her own experience and generalized from it to issue level-headed instructions to Victorian parents. If there is one duty they must above all fulfill, it is to enlighten their children about the facts of life. She had been tethered in 1867 to a clergyman she hardly knew and unduly idealized, "with no more idea of the marriage relation than if I had been four years old instead of twenty. My dreamy life, kept innocent on all questions of sex, was no preparation for married existence, and left as defenceless to face a rude awakening."

Essentially, she wrote, her marital initiation was the sacrifice of an innocent. Looking back, she sturdily drew the consequences: "no more fatal blunder can be made to train a girl to womanhood in ignorance of all life's duties and burdens and then to let her face them for the first time away from all the associations, the old helps, the old refuge on the mother's breast." Indeed, "many an unhappy marriage," she was sure, had started from "its very beginning, from the terrible shock to a young girl's sensitive modesty and pride, her helpless bewilderment and fear." In short, "Eve should have the knowledge of good and evil ere she wanders forth from the paradise of a mother's love."

Although the available material suggests that middle-class young women were more likely to be "protected" from the facts of gender differences and their implications than were young men, these, too, often had to find their way through the maze without a map. Take the history of Emily Lytton, later Lady Lutyens, an English Victorian who persuasively stigmatized the well-meant conspiracies of silence that made marital trauma a real threat. In 1893, at eighteen, not long after falling in love with the handsome explorer, poet, and unscrupulous womanizer Wilfrid Scawen Blunt, then fifty-three and trying to seduce a girl a third his age, she had barely kept her virginity intact. Bitingly, she delivered a little lecture on "the folly of the conventional protection which is relied on for shielding women from corruption. A particular passion is the cause, directly or indirectly, of perhaps half the vice and misery of the world. This passion is implanted for beneficent purposes in the constitution of man, and with this indwelling informer, besides the thousand hints, or more than hints, that are continually cropping up, it is assumed that innocence will be preserved by an impossible ignorance." Yoked to the contrived "purity" of well-bred girls, the sexual passion can only produce catastrophes.

A girlish near affair was bad enough, but Emily Lutyens's marriage four years later brought greater shocks. Her husband, on his way to becoming a famous architect, was as ignorant as his wife. Hence, as she reminded him years later, their honeymoon had been "a nightmare of physical pain and mental disappointment." Utterly inexperienced yet irresistibly importunate, Lutyens initiated intercourse without a thought for his wife, leaving her "night after night unappeased and resentful"—resentful of the man she loved and had married. "Remember," she told Lutyens, looking back, "that I married you loving you and wanting you physically as much as you wanted me. I don't reproach you one instant for what happened after because you were just selfish and did not think and I was silly too." The couple's shared ignorance did not just double the marital calamity but multiplied it.

That the wedding night could be a trial became a cliché among the Victorians, the butt of heartless jokes and irreverent cartoons. Let a French lithograph of 1832 stand for a small library of commentary. We see a young bride the morning after, propped up on large satin pillows and wearing an alluring nightgown that reveals her breast. "Well," a young woman visitor asks the newlywed, "how are you?" "Oh! My dear friend," is the answer, "never get married, it's a horror!" A sly smile seems to be lurking on her face as she purportedly discloses the price of female naïveté and male brutality. The bride's lounging posture, her body fetchingly on show, suggests that viewers should not take her conventional protestations literally.

The principal message lurking behind the surface of this ambiguous lithograph is that innocence about the mechanics of sex was not always irreparable. The first exposure to intercourse could be unnerving, and lastingly so. But it could also be, quite literally, an educational experience, the opening move toward training the sufferer, or sufferers, for joys ahead. Many nineteenth-century physicians and novelists shared that optimism. Dr. J. Matthews Duncan spoke for most colleagues when he observed in 1884: "Pleasure is frequently absent in marriage, and gradually developed during the continuance of that state." A German physician, Dr. Friedrich Siebert, echoed this prognosis in 1901: wives often come into marriage sadly unprepared, but after all they do not run away or scream for help! They may find the first night horrendous, but they "know how to adjust themselves" without fleeing from their husbands "and discover the cheerful side."*

Discovering the cheerful side of sex in marriage was a theme of fiction as well as of medical science. One splendid instance is Gustave Droz's *Monsieur, Madame et Bébé,* a vastly popular lighthearted essay, first published in 1866 and enjoying 121 printings in fifteen years. It traces the

---

*On February 10, 1999, a story in *The New York Times* reported that a survey of Americans from ages eighteen to fifty-nine found "over forty percent of women and thirty percent of men regularly have no interest in sex, cannot have an orgasm, or suffer from sexual dysfunctions" (p. A16). It is quite possible that married Victorian bourgeois did better than this.

happy history of a bachelor to marriage and fatherhood. His wedding night occupies a central place in Monsieur's humble history. The long wedding feast is finally done with, aunts have shed their last tears, cousins have run through their wishes for future happiness, and the bride's mother has conveyed her last instructions to her daughter, whispering of "sacrifice, the future, necessity, obedience," and piously expressing hope for "celestial patronage and the intercession of a dove or two, hidden in the curtains." The advice—remember—is a piece of fiction.

Once the couple is alone at last, the bride, the "poor child," slips into bed, crouching under the blankets, "her head lost in the pillow," her eyes closed as though she were asleep. Her husband approaches her, speaking to her as gently as he knows how—*"eh bien, mon amie, eh bien?"* But she shudders every time he touches her, even her fingertips. When he murmurs into her ear that he loves her, she replies, her eyes filled with tears, that she loves him, too—she addresses him with the formal *vous*—and begs him to let her sleep.

He wraps her up in the covers "as one would a child" and prepares to spend the night in an easy chair. But the room is freezing and so Madame, worried lest he catch cold, invites him to bed. His teeth chattering, he joins her to discover happily that he no longer frightens her. "You want to be my wife, then," he tenderly asks Madame; "tell me, my Louise, do you want me to teach you to love me as I love you?" He can barely hear her answer, but he takes courage from it; the time is ripe for the comedy to reach its climactic scene. Droz suppresses all further detail, but the encounter must have been a success for Madame as much as for Monsieur, if not the first time, then soon after. *"Mon Dieu,"* says Droz as he drops the curtain, "how many times have we laughed as we recalled such memories, now so distant."

🌸 I HAVE CALLED THIS ACCOUNT PART OF A HUMBLE history. Even so, even if we have no statistics to lend it the persuasiveness of large and dependable numbers, we have much evidence—I have cited only a few fragments—to declare the love life of Monsieur and Madame typical for many unsung bourgeois in the Victorian decades. For them, as for countless others, nature had a way of asserting itself. And not nature untouched, but nature civilized. And middle-class love—I cannot say that enough—was more than sex or rational calculation. "Love never goes hand in hand with reason," wrote Dr. Louis Berlioz to his wife, Joséphine, with sincere affection, and there were many nineteenth-century husbands and many wives, even in France, who loved their spouse for themselves. It was Schnitzler's tragedy that much of the time his rapture *was* his symptom. But it was not a price that unknown thousands of other bourgeois were compelled to pay. And if this is so, as I believe it to be, we will have to rewrite the accepted history of Eros in the Victorian bourgeoisie to make it more lifelike, and in gratifying ways far less desolate than we have been led to expect.

T. WILLIAMS. SC.

FOUR

Alibis for Aggression

1

IN ONE OF HIS APHORISMS, SCHNITZLER CALLED hate "quite as divine as love." Certainly the characters he invented attest that he took this agonistic opinion seriously. And his hunt for complaisant women gave real meaning to the banal phrase "sexual conquest," which implies an intimate bond between sexuality and aggression. Not that most of his "victims" were likely to resist his overtures. But that did not make them any the less predatory.* In any event, he was far from alone in this view of human nature; few Victorians ever doubted that mankind is endowed with dynamic aggressive impulses. If any uncertainty lingered about the central role of its basic contentiousness, it was silenced after Charles Darwin published his epochmaking

---

*On July 4, 1897, alone on vacation in a resort, he recorded in his diary: "In the early morning, I passed her room, whistling. The second time she appeared—I, quickly into the room, lock the door and take her."

Origin of Species in 1859. The classic argument of his treatise seemed to enshrine warlike drives in nature, including human nature. Survival in his godless world was the outcome of feral struggles for existence, all the more harrowing for being beyond human planning. The Christian injunction to love one's neighbor now had some severe competition.

Almost inevitably, the scientific theory of evolution spawned some crude, though exceedingly popular, alibis for pugnacity. His views, Darwin noted in some irritation, were being read as alibis for selfishness and cruelty. Buccaneers of business welcomed this new dispensation, and it served the Social Darwinists, Darwin's most tendentious acolytes, to validate ruthlessness in politics, business, diplomacy, and social policy. Philanthropic assistance to the poor, the diseased, the mad, the aged, a sentimental humanitarian delusion! Stern ideologues read Darwinian evolution as support for the proposition that wars among great powers or distinct races are preordained. In sharp contrast, Darwin's less bellicose and more sophisticated followers interpreted his teachings as an urgent reminder that evolutionary rivalries required determined resistance, lest organized societies lapse into barbarism. Whatever his readers inferred from Darwin's writings, the nature of aggression, its proper extent, its limits and consequences were on the agenda of the nineteenth century.

The Victorians, then, saw conflict built into the human condition. "Ancestral evolution," wrote William James in 1902, encapsulating the post-Darwinian consensus in a phrase, "has made us all potential warriors." The history of persecutions, he thought, demonstrated that human beings still carried traces of "neophobia," and this hatred for the new had survived even into the enlightened nineteenth century. The hold of this biological dogma on intelligent opinion seemed unshakeable. In their voluminous journal, the brothers Goncourt, realistic novelists and disillusioned observers of Parisian society, put it aphoristically: "The sentiment of destruction is innate in man." Just after 1900, Georg Simmel, the subtlest student of the human tragicomedy that German sociology produced, maintained just as tersely that human beings share what he called "the inborn need to hate and fight." He saw the "fighting instinct" to be universal.

It is easier, though, to assert the ubiquity of aggressiveness than to define it, for aggression speaks in many voices, few of them in tune with one another. Nor is all of it cold-blooded vindictiveness or sadistic cruelty; a sly piece of gossip or a mean-spirited book review, a boast about one's sexual prowess or the obsessive public display of self-pity, too, have their aggressive dimensions. Humor can be a deadly weapon. But even though many alibis for aggression turn out to be self-serving, they are not automatically unjust or immoral. They may serve social needs; the most humane of lawgivers must permit some aggressive behavior, whether in the law courts or on the battlefield.

In fact, robust forms of aggression, like the energy that fuels the purposeful pursuit of a rational goal, are essential ingredients in productive efforts. Nor is the same quantity of ferocity implanted in all humans, or unalterable like an instinct. Patently there have always been individual and collective variations in the strength and pressure of assertive urges. Pacific societies may depreciate the verbal or physical combat that their neighbors relish without paralyzing them. Bourgeois ideologues may, in the course of time, redefine what they mean by manliness. Aggression, in short, has not only its psychology but its geography and its history.

An alibi, as I use the term, is not a cause of events but a rationalization of behavior, a license that authorizes aggressive conduct by supplying it with high-sounding legal, ethical, biological, even religious justifications. Context matters: a civilian who shoots someone to death will be indicted for murder; put him into a uniform in wartime and the same act will earn him a medal. One did not embrace bellicose nationalism or imperialism, two of the most effective ideas to prompt Victorians into action, in order to find a home for aggressive desires. Rather, one put the sheer joy of legitimacy over appetites whether holy or unholy. A French chauvinist of midcentury derived solace from the thought that he may harbor destructive sentiments against the "natural enemy" across the Rhine without apologies. That is why Fedor, the unattractive protagonist of Schnitzler's *The Fairy Tale*, has no compunction in heartlessly maligning Fanny, the woman he presumably loves and who admits to two previous affairs, after he has succumbed to the conventional worship of virginity

———

IT HAS BEEN NO SECRET SINCE THE ANCIENT Greeks that if humans were to act out all their fantasies of triumph, of revenge, of erotic dominance or pleasure in inflicting pain—if in short there were alibis for all conduct—nothing could last for more than a moment: no love, no family life, no group acting in concert, no settled community. Plato had already conjured up a striking metaphor, the horses of reason and passion straining to go their separate ways, and in the seventeenth century, Thomas Hobbes painted the dread scenario of individuals raging out of control in the state of nature, generating the war of all against all that left life solitary, poor, nasty, brutish, and short.

Beyond diagnosing the cardinal problem for human society, the desolation that the unchecked will leaves in its wake, these thinkers prescribed an external authority as the sole remedy. Plato envisioned an energetic charioteer who yokes the untamed horses to serve a common purpose; Hobbes called for an overarching sovereign, the great Leviathan, to suppress the ravages of lawless ferocity. And from the beginnings of orderly societies, subjective means, not all of them conscious, have served as props of order. A full list of these curbs on aggressive action would be very long; what they share is that they internalize fears and feelings of guilt, and these invisible policemen could be more persuasive than men in uniform wielding night sticks. They amount to self-censorship assembled from the commands and prohibitions of adult authorities. It is too harsh to say with Hamlet that conscience makes cowards of us all; it makes us human.

Like all collective habits, inhibitions on aggression are seeded at home, most manifestly in the modern family that habitually enacts emotional encounters on its minuscule stage. The nineteenth century knew the family as a school for love. It was also a school for hatred—or, less melodramatically, a school for aggression and its management. Weaning, toilet training, family prayers, parental rewards and punishments, demands for obedience, good manners, and satisfactory performance in lessons are so many cultural interventions against raw nature. Small children, who want every gratification and who want it now, must learn to wait and to accept frustrations as an essential part of their routine. Such pressures may be onerous, but they are indispensable ways of training future members of society by molding their aggressive impulses into acceptable forms. Alibis, in short, offer privileged exceptions to self-control, safety valves without which overly repressed individuals and societies would wither or explode.

Like other ages, other societies, other classes, nineteenth-century bourgeois constructed their own rationalizations that permitted them to strike out at others—to criticize and ridicule, to police and exclude, to exploit and at times kill them. And for all their perception of a world perpetually at odds, compared to other bourgeoisies the Victorians were markedly restrained in their domestic and their social demeanor. None of the liberating alibis they constructed went uncontested. Even justifications most firmly supported had to count on opponents who, in the contentious atmosphere of the age, did not go unheard. In sum, bourgeois preferred self-control to self-expression, even though they sought, and often found, legitimate channels for letting themselves go.

🪷 DR. SCHNITZLER LECTURING HIS ADOLESCENT SON about his hazardous explorations with his "goddesses" fits the expected pattern, especially among affluent bourgeois families. He made no threats of physical punishment, only loosened a kind of benign terrorism, a verbal ambush fortified by visual props, undertaken of course for the sinner's own good. Young Arthur Schnitzler, we know, bowed passively under the paternal storm. He was unable to contest the tirade; the incriminating facts were beyond dispute. All he objected to, and timidly, was his father breaking into his desk. His feelings and his behavior were radically opposed to each other: rage within, subdued mannerliness on the surface. Later, after his father's death in 1893, the more independent he felt himself to be, the more successful his attempts at settling domestic conflicts. When his mother voiced some objections to the women he was seeing, he brusquely cut her off: he was an adult and could tolerate no interference in his affairs. This did not lead to a breach between them; on the contrary, from then on, he spent many an hour playing arrangements of the classics for four hands with his mother. There was nothing unusual about this inner tumult and its resolution; every human being has experienced the like many times. We have a name for that struggle with one's aggression: civilization.

Politics has been called the art of the possible, but it may be more to the point to call it the art that makes society possible. Schnitzler at once recognized its importance and detested it. "It is always politics, not science and culture," he acknowledged, "that determines a country's atmosphere." His attitude bears directly on the issue of aggression permissible and impermissible. As I have noted, he put himself at odds with tone-setting middle-class circles by condemning the duel, an illegal but tolerated blood sport that preoccupied military men and upper-bourgeois society in the Austro-Hungarian Empire. To slash or shoot at one another, at times with lethal outcome, thus to avenge an insult real or imagined struck him as obsolete and literally inhuman bravado. When, in 1896, his friend, the writer Felix Salten, engaged in a formal duel with sabers, he declared the swordfight "stupid and bestial."

Consistent with this antagonism to personal aggression, Schnitzler had a pacifist's contempt for the cult of heroism, and denounced World War I as a quarrel contrived and foisted on the world by diplomats. In a tart unpublished note, he said: "Only real and permitted basis of militarism: idea of kings. We don't always have money at our disposal, but we have power; so we invent something new: general conscription. That's cheaper for us. Let the citizens pay us for the soldiers, the fathers pay for the sons we send to their death. We don't have a right to do that? So we invent the divine right of kings. Our soldiers don't know what they go to their death for? So we invent dynastic sentiment." Could he have done so, Schnitzler would have outlawed duels, and wars as well.

2

ONE OF THE MOST DEPENDABLE BAROMETERS FOR approved aggression in any culture is how severely it chastises its children. Among Victorian bourgeois, as the episode of Schnitzler's diary attests, it was in retreat. As so often, in this matter too the nineteenth century was the heir of the eighteenth. Early in that century, in their *Spectator*, Richard Addison and Joseph Steele — the essayists, we recall, who had good words to say about stockbrokers — had preached to their middle-class audiences the merits of kindliness; their secular sermons called for a (literally) light hand with dependents of all sorts, notably women, children, and servants. The moral weeklies that imitated this English model on the Continent followed it in that respect as well. And around 1800, the Romantics, with their poet's worship of the child, carried the Enlightenment's pedagogical liberalism into the age of Victoria.

By the time of her reign, then, the partisans of the *Spectator*'s brand of gentle dealings with subordinates had secured a sizable following, largely among better-educated and better-off bourgeois. At midcentury, in his best-selling *History of England*, a treasure trove of invidious comparisons with times gone by, Thomas Babington Macaulay proudly concluded that "the more we study the annals of the past, the more shall we rejoice that we live in a merciful age, in an age in which cruelty is abhorred, and in which pain, even when deserved, is inflicted reluctantly and from a sense of duty."

Macaulay's patented optimism pressed him beyond the evidence; there were still respectable parents and highly regarded pedagogues in his time, who, far from abhorring brutality, inflicted pain with all too much pleasure. If the harshness that had governed the raising of children in earlier times, including regular beatings, was fading among nineteenth-century bourgeois, it was far from extinct. So loving a father as William Gladstone whipped his eldest child, the seven-year-old Willy, for being unruly and inattentive to his tutor. He found it a "painful office" but a necessary one. Many fathers, fixated on the paternalistic model with military trimmings, agreed that such physical chastisement was perfectly appropriate: boys are headstrong, they would say, far more than girls, and it is imperative to "break their will" before it hardens into a character trait. "Ungoverned, unrestrained, willful boys become turbulent, violent, and vicious men," maintained Henry A. Drake, chairman of the Boston School Committee, in 1867.

It seems right somehow that this dictum should come out of an

English-speaking country. Naturally, the practice of spanking children at home or at school for offenses real or trumped-up varied widely, following family traditions, individual neuroses, or plausible-sounding lessons imparted by tracts on the art of education. But certain national styles differentiated one Victorian bourgeoisie from the others, and in Britain and the United Sates licensed aggression against youngsters seems to have flourished most and longest. In the 1840s and after, reforming pedagogues like the eloquent Horace Mann in Massachusetts objected vehemently to corporal punishment in the schools. Rather than nurturing "Duty, Affection, Love of Knowledge and Love of Truth," Mann charged a quarter century before the Boston School Board decided to uphold the traditional ways, local teachers were freely resorting to sheer physical cruelty, relying on all they knew: "Power, Violence, Terror, Suffering!" It was one battle he would lose.

Some carefully calibrated school discipline persisted through blind conservatism—had it not always been that way? had it ever harmed a single boy?—some of it was a war over turf. Teachers did not welcome thin-skinned physicians, anxious parents, sentimental public officials invading the territory that had belonged to them alone. But the bastions of flogging were that dozen or so elite private institutions known as the English public schools. In these worlds apart, pupils and masters constructed for themselves an odd compound of absolute monarchy and anarchic democracy, the whole presided over by the headmaster in whose likeness the school had its being. It governed itself by arcane rules; it spawned intimate membership in, or wounding exclusion from, cliques; it reveled in sports that resembled nothing so much as outright warfare. Worse, it bedeviled barely grown boys with crushes that could last, or be recapitulated, through a lifetime. With perverse pride, the little community professed the cult of manliness: victims of a flogging were to endure, stoically, the bleeding wounds left by the liberal application of the birch.

Foreign observers were appalled. Two French educators, reporting on their tour of British public schools in 1867, called the beatings they had witnessed an "old and degrading custom," a social habit "scarcely proper and scarcely decent." Since striking schoolboys was forbidden

in France by law, even if there were occasional reports of corporal punishment, these visitors condemned British headmasters, who often liked
to administer the chastisement themselves, as sheer sadists. Their diagnosis was a little sweeping but much to the point: a number of these
local authoritarians were only gratifying their barely suppressed sexual
needs in the guise of penalizing absentmindedness, poor study habits, a
missed lesson, an insubordinate look—or reached for the rod for no
discernible reason at all. Sometimes there were scandals; a few headmasters, whose homoerotic leanings were becoming too blatant or who
were too indiscriminate in their beating rituals, received discreet invitations to retire. They left behind casualties, like Algernon Swinburne,
who never outgrew their taste for being whipped. No wonder that on
the Continent masochism was called the English vice—which does not
mean that sanctioned cruelty to children was unknown outside Britain.

Yet even the Germans, whose primary schools had long employed
retired soldiers with no desire to "mollycoddle and effeminize" the
young, and who would have scored high in any international contest
for manliness, gradually turned against the physical punishment of
pupils as a favored weapon for enforcing conformity. At least the country opened the matter for debate. By the 1870s, progressive educators
and likeminded politicians, the idealists whose "misunderstood humanistic principles" traditionalists deplored, counterattacked by charging
that the "flogging pedagogues" possessed but one skill: to beat Latin or
mathematics into the hides of their miserable charges. And after 1900,
German states like Bavaria or Prussia laid down progressively restric-
tive rules against the kind of discipline that might physically injure its
victims. This reiterated recourse to legislation and administrative rules
suggests, though, that the old ways—bringing up by hand, Dickens
called it in *Great Expectations*—were dying slowly. It was a sign that
many German parents, much like their British counterparts, were only
too pleased to have their sons' spirits broken. Though steadily shrinking, the satisfactions inherent in inflicting pain kept a certain place in
Victorian culture.

Yet, as I have suggested, it *was* steadily shrinking; the compassionate
countertradition had recruited influential advocates among parents,

teachers, and imaginative writers. When, in *David Copperfield*, Dickens has David's stepfather beat him "as if he would have beaten me to death," the reader is expected to detest Mr. Murdstone as a cold-blooded brute. By then—the novel was published in 1850—as the thoroughly un-Christian celebration of inherent childish innocence had gained support even among Christians, the argument that boys need to be beaten for their own good had lost much of its luster. If in the past, the playwright Andrew Halliday noted in 1865, "almost every father in Great Britain kept a strap, or a cane, for the special purpose of correcting his children," this was no longer prevalent: "He has relaxed his old severity of aspect, and become more human." Idealizing children was taking the place of demonizing them, and one was beginning to hear complaints about the tyranny of His Majesty the Child.

As before, the eighteenth century furnished texts for the nineteenth: Rousseau's doctrine that human beings are born pure and that it is society that corrupts them, was to find pervasive resonance across the decades in the writings of educators, and in gushy depictions of children in paintings, sculptures, and stories. It became a commonplace that, as Rousseau had made plain and Wordsworth famously confirmed, the child lives in a world of its own and must be treated with love and indulgence rather than as a sinful little adult.

Once again, Gustave Droz may serve, this time as a representative of a school of nineteenth-century Rousseaus. The last part of *Monsieur, Madame et Bébé* is a paean to a father's love for his son. Not a word about punishment. "Conceal your paternal sovereignty as a police inspector hides his sash." Unmanageable children are not vicious from birth; they are only responding to an adult's "maladroit pressures." A century, though generally committed to the supposedly dominant influence of heredity, was making room for an environmentalism that echoed John Locke, holding that the infant's mind is a blank slate on which the world gradually inscribes character. Significantly, Droz firmly refused to believe in "inborn vice." So much for fallen man whom good Christians had taken over from the Old Testament!

3

IF, DURING THE VICTORIAN DECADES, DOMESTIC aggression declined for all its surviving appeal, the same held true of forcible tactics designed to preserve the social order. The fate of politicians fallen from royal grace has a particularly instructive history. In the sixteenth and seventeenth centuries, most of them had gone to the scaffold; in the eighteenth century, they were "exiled" to their provincial estates, bored and impotent onlookers at the political game; in the nineteenth century, they profited from that modern invention, a recognized opposition, which preserved its life and fortune even out of office. More, they retained much of their political visibility, enjoying the realistic expectation of returning to office in the future. In earlier times, political dissent had been treated as equivalent to treason; as recently as the first decades of the United States, the founding fathers denounced opposition as sheer factionalism, at the least irresponsible, at worst subversive. But during the Victorian decades, advanced societies established the cardinal right of opposition candidates to sit in legislatures, debate, and vote on the gravest matters.

Yet on dramatic occasions, rumblings from what Edmund Burke had called the swinish multitude seemed to call for regressive measures by the military or the constabulary, and then bourgeois would likely approve the furious, panic-stricken mayhem that governments visited on the "mob." In an age when energetic, self-confident bourgeois increasingly shaped public responses, many of them allied themselves with the powers that be when they thought their basic interests imperiled. Demonstrators shouting slogans or erecting barricades threatened the stability that ruling circles, and with them most bourgeois, prized so highly. As I have said before, respectable citizens seemed unable to exorcise the specter of the French Revolution, which made them see bloodthirsty Jacobins running every public gathering.

One long-remembered sanguinary incident occurred on August 16, 1819, at St. Peter's Field in Manchester. A massive rally called to protest hard times was broken up by drunken militiamen and cavalry;

they charged into the peaceful crowd, leaving eleven demonstrators dead and hundreds injured. That was the infamous "Peterloo Massacre," christened in sardonic allusion to the Allies' splendid victory over Napoleon at Waterloo four years earlier. Learning of the massacre soon after—he was then in Italy—Shelley poured out a long poem boiling over with indignation, "The Mask of Anarchy," in which he indicted what he called "hired Murderers"—leading government officials, lawyers, bankers, bishops. Political reformers, who had counted on the middle class to denounce the outrage, were shocked by its silence. In stinging words, the political pamphleteer John Wade reproved those who had remained neutral. But those who had shown their support of the troops were, he added, "still more deplorably wicked and fatuous. They have taken arms to defend a plundering Oligarchy, and with tiger ferocity, lent their aid to stifle the complaints of misery and famine, by the sabre, the bayonet, and the dungeon!" Thrust into the maelstrom of politics more than ever before, bourgeois were under assault from both extremes. The very class that Metternich feared as a subversive element bent on destroying the God-given order of society, English radicals accused of being toadies to a reactionary state. In either case, they were seen as aggressors.

THE EVENT THAT SHELLEY STIGMATIZED WITH ALL the poetic force at his command shared with other instances of governmental repression the ferocity of official vengeance. If any corroboration should be needed for inborn human aggressiveness, these excesses supply it. The instances of disproportionate retribution—really rampages ordained, or insufficiently controlled, by the authorities—came to enjoy the dubious immortality of having names bestowed on them. Britain, we just saw, had its "Peterloo Massacre." France had its "June Days" of 1848 in Paris, when workers and their sympathizers, publicly expressing their rage at having been cheated of the benefits of a revolution they had done much to win four months earlier, were unmercifully shot down by troops at the cost of some fifteen hundred dead.

For its part, the United States had its "Nat Turner's Rebellion," which occasioned a particularly savage instance of bloodthirsty revenge by the forces of order. In August 1831, in two days of sudden slaughter in Southampton County, Virginia, Nat Turner and a small band of fellow slaves murdered every white they could find—men, women, and children—with any primitive weapon that came to hand. Fatalities numbered fifty-seven. The rebels were soon subdued, and then, before a few survivors could be brought to trial, white planters settled scores with blacks, guilty and innocent alike, mutilating their victims, often, as one eyewitness put it, "under circumstances of great barbarity." This bloodbath was more than a rational attempt to restore order; a tribute to the pleasures of aggressiveness, it loosened common restraints and turned the most vicious fantasies into reality. The exact number of blacks killed in this counter-riot will never been known, but observers estimated it at several hundred.

Yet these figures, dismaying as they are, pale before the reprisals French troops took against the Paris Commune in the late spring of 1871. Early that year, after France's defeat by Prussian forces at Sedan the previous September and the merciless siege of Paris, a hastily assembled French government, sitting in Versailles, had made peace. Then, in February 1871, national elections gave royalists a sizable majority, and radicals in the capital, fearing a restoration of the monarchy, refused to go along. Socialists of all stripes, allied with patriots who rejected the humiliating peace treaty and populists who hated the Versailles régime, took over Paris in March and instituted a number of left-wing measures. The government took them as an invitation to civil war. Frenchmen fought Frenchmen until, on May 28, the last resistance in Paris ceased.

Then it was time for retaliation. The Communards had eighty-four hostages, including the archbishop of Paris, on their conscience, but the victors outdid them beyond measure. In Paris they shot hundreds on sight, bayoneted women and children, and sent thousands to Versailles to be dealt with there. Many of these were selected for execution without trial and often for peculiar reasons: shot because they had a watch, shot because they had white hair, shot because their looks displeased the marquis de Gallifet, in charge of selecting Communards for the ultimate punishment. More than twenty-five thousand Parisians were "legally" murdered this way. The days after May 28 were dubbed "the bloody week — *la semaine sanglante*"; but the orgy of revenge continued much longer, as special courts sentenced perhaps thirty thousand more to death, weeks and months that would live in infamy.

The totals, including the Parisians killed or deported to New Caledonia — really a slow kind of death sentence — amounted to nearly a hundred thousand. The fate of the Commune was a triumph for vindictive monarchists made all the more ferocious after France's mortifying military defeat. But it was also a class war in which all too many bourgeois rejoiced. The bitter eloquence of French men of letters after the event, for once speaking for rather than against the bourgeoisie, is hair-raising. Théophile Gautier, prolific poet, critic, and novelist, called the Communards "wild animals" and "gorillas"; Maxime du Camp, Flaubert's friend, liberal editor, pioneering photographer, and chronicler of Paris, denounced them as wholly indifferent to politics, as "ambitious men in love with themselves and drunk with power"; the playwright Ernest Feydeau thought that "it is no longer barbarism that threatens us, no longer every savagery that surrounds us; it is bestiality pure and simple." Scarcely a word against the barbaric "saviors of civilization."

4

IT SHOULD BE APPARENT BY NOW THAT IN Victorian days, the alibi best calculated to acquit aggressors in action — diplomats, politicians, entrepreneurs, fathers, citizen militias — from any cause for regret was the certainty of their indelible superiority over lesser beings. Schnitzler saw through this convenient alibi. "How does one serve one's nation?" he asked in an unpublished fragment. "How does one show one's love? By screaming: I am a good German! We are the first nation! By portraying others as inferior!" This arrogance was easy to adopt and hard to shake off; it borrowed prestige from superstitions common among Victorian social scientists and biologists. That some human beings—laborers, heretics, Jews, Asians, African tribesmen—apparently cannot measure up to the white man provided gratifying elbow room for Americans facing Indian tribes, mill owners facing their workforce, husbands facing wives, conquerors facing the defeated.

Commonly accepted stereotypes left indelible marks. With illustrations in the popular press more easily accessible than ever, they served as substitutes for reasoned argument. Victorians were fed, and only too eagerly consumed, caricatures of the drunken Irishman, the deceitful Jew, the uncouth peasant, the lazy black man. When, at midcentury, Thomas Carlyle sneered at Caribbean natives, "sitting yonder with their beautiful muzzles up the ears in pumpkins, imbibing sweet pulps and juices," John Stuart Mill broke with his mentor in disgust, but Carlyle had a good portion of the reading public on his side.

As Mill's furious response to Carlyle shows, the conviction that white men are chosen, by God or by evolution, to dominate the world and to save lesser people from themselves was not universally held. In the contentious Victorian era, what view was? The progressive impulses released by the American Declaration of Independence were not erased by half a century of failure to redeem its pledges, the ideals of the French Revolution had not been forgotten despite decades of conservative reaction. On the contrary, the history of abolitionism and of social legislation in the Victorian era leaves no doubt that setbacks inspired liberal spirits to talk, and even to act, in the service of humane reforms. By midcentury untold numbers of bourgeois campaigned for, or at least praised, the ten-hour work day, the banning of child labor, the fostering of universal literacy, and—a brave minority—the enfranchisement of women.

Fortunately, the pleasing sense of one's innate excellence did not necessarily generate exploitation and oppression; even abolitionists who did not really consider the black man their brother kept up their fraternal campaigns. But the comfortable conviction that one's race, one's nationality, one's religion was in the human vanguard, occupying the highest branch on the tree of evolution, was almost too seductive to resist. When compelling interests, whether economic or territorial, were at stake, the invidious ranking of races dulled many a sensitive conscience.

The ascent of race as a biological entity and, for many, the supreme agent of historical change was the contribution of so-called science to nineteenth-century attempts at making aggression respectable. In 1870, looking back, Benjamin Disraeli could assert that "the general influence of race on human action" had been "universally recognized as the key to history." In singling out race as the key to history, Disraeli was an archetypal Victorian; in climbing to the top of the political ladder as Britain's prime minister and to an earldom, he was an emblem of the absorptive capacity of his society: the baptized son of a Jewish family—a fact that his enemies never let him forget—he did not find his "race" a serious impediment. And, just like the loosely employed, largely useless term "race," the inappropriate metaphor of "blood" as the carrier of mental and moral qualities lent a veneer of uprightness to the coarsest prejudices. "The blood one brings along in one's veins upon birth one keeps all one's life," wrote the self-styled French "anthropo-sociologist" Georges Vacher de Lapouge, one of the most influential racial theorists of this time, in 1899.

By that time, this peculiar notion had been current for half a century. And the invention of the Aryan race at midcentury—it *was* an invention—came to be hallowed as demonstrated dogma. No "scientific" student of culture who used race as a significant category was in the least troubled by the fact that the criteria for defining race, let alone comparing one race with others, were exceedingly hazy and could be manipulated at will. Anyone could play the race game and nearly everyone did: the British against the French, the French against the Germans, the Germans against everyone. And whatever the real or ostensible reasons for the great powers to divide up Africa and Asia among them late in the century—economic, strategic, religious, or the *mission civilisatrice*— the alibi that eased the imperialists' conscience and that of their supporters was the conviction of their own racial superiority.

The sins of imperialism have been amply pilloried in the last few decades, but a sampling of how atrocities abroad were received at home may display the apologetic power of racist sentiments—and their limits. The African venture of King Leopold II of Belgium is a case in point. The Congo Free State, his personal property, was rich in ivory and rubber, and from the mid-1880s, on his explicit instructions, his agents squeezed the highest productivity out of the indigenous population they virtually enslaved. They flogged them, often to death; they mutilated them; they engaged in "disciplinary" shootings. J. A. Hobson, whose *Imperialism* of 1902 was the most withering and most effective anti-imperialist polemic of the age, quoted King Leopold: "Our only programme is that of the moral and material regeneration of the country." Hobson's cool comment: "It is difficult to set any limit upon the capacity of men to deceive themselves as to the relative strength and worth of the motives which affect them." It was not until 1908, after more than two decades of his savage regime, and after years of mounting international protests, that the Belgian state took over the central African territory from its king.

The response in Belgium to this history was mixed. Socialists, radicals, left-wing liberals objected to Leopold's imperialist venture on principle, and denounced the king's greed. But the country was deeply divided over the issue whether the country should take over his monopoly. Religious and political agendas complicated matters and hence slowed the resolution. They did so quite as much in Germany, where imperialist policy became a central campaign issue in the national elections of 1907. Germany had come to the scramble for overseas territory late, but once it did, its colonial governors quickly learned to exploit their territories, which is to say their peoples. In 1904, the tribe of the Hereros in German Southwest Africa rose up against their alien masters. As one army officer on the scene put it, the "hatred of the natives against German domination naturally grew and grew as German influence spread and, with that, the native element was pushed back."

This was a euphemistic explanation typical of conquerors. "German influence" meant that the invading troops had dispossessed the Hereros, an agricultural people, of their cattle, driving them from their grazing land. In their rebellion, the Hereros killed some one hundred settlers, although—more humane than the forces of order against the Paris Commune in 1871—they spared women and children. In retaliation, the German forces virtually annihilated the Hereros: by 1906, some three quarters of them were dead or reduced to wretched beggary. As in Belgium, German left-wingers protested while the right defended the triumphant troops as heroic patriots. The consequence: the conservatives gained seats in the Reichstag. The appeal of patriotism, manliness, and racism combined was still hard to discredit.

The same degree of often embittered division bedeviled middle-class voters elsewhere, whether in response to revelations of the misconduct by the Dutch East India Company in Java or of Cecil Rhodes's brutality in South Africa. Aggressive imperialism was under unremitting assault by humanitarians of all stripes: social scientists suspicious of unprovable statements about differential racial endowment; Socialists, by the turn of the century a powerful political force; even some missionaries who were less eager to impose Christianity on so-called benighted peoples than to protect the way of life of its presumed beneficiaries. Race was a powerful alibi, but not omnipotent. But it played a particularly pernicious role in the emergence of modern anti-Semitism.

JEW-HATRED IS AN OLD AND FAMILIAR DISEASE. Only the word "anti-Semitism," a mid-nineteenth-century coinage, was new. Through the ages, Christians had scorned, or at least isolated, Jews as the killers of Christ, desecrators of holy objects, and (in the muddled minds of fanatics including some princes of the church) slaughterers of Christian babies to draw their blood for making the Passover matzoh. Though these primitive slanders continued to have some appeal among the unlettered in the nineteenth century, they were losing support in the light of increased worldliness, fading piety, and the assimilationist ideals of the Enlightenment. Losing support but not disappearing: the dismal history of pogroms continued into Victorian days, though no longer (as Western commentators observed with no little self-satisfaction) in "advanced" countries like Britain, France, the Low Countries, or Scandinavia. The deadly pogroms of 1881, of which these countries' newspapers were full, could, they said, only have happened in Russia, a backward country with an underdeveloped political culture. That this complacent analysis was a delusion was exhibited for all to see in the France of the 1890s, with the notorious Dreyfus affair. A divisive scandal graduated from the widely accepted and obviously unjust conviction of a Jewish officer's supposed treason to rise to a critical national referendum in which the very survival of the republic was at stake. With the mobilization of French anti-Semites, the depth of anti-Jewish bigotry in a civilized country stood revealed. It is hardly astonishing that Schnitzler followed the case closely and was a vigorous Dreyfusard.

By that time, the brew of religious anti-Semitism had been enriched with an even deadlier antagonism: the racial variety. In earlier times, conversion to Christianity—promoted, at times extorted, by enthusiastic proselytizers—was the recognized way for a Jew to shed the centuries-old burden of his people's collective sins. Now, presumably cursed with indelible racial stains, a Jew, anti-Semites argued, could never find a true home. If he persisted in his traditional piety, perhaps even his traditional garb, he was only making a highly visible statement about his incurable otherness; if he tried to assimilate by changing his name or being baptized, he was only making a transparent attempt at camouflage, unwittingly revealing his characteristic Jewish cleverness. Once a Jew always a Jew, the racists proclaimed, always alien, always dangerous. On this showing, hating Jews was a legitimate exercise of aggression. How far this hatred would be permitted to go was a question that different countries would answer in their own way.

In Austria, the precipitous acceleration of racial anti-Semitism dominated Schnitzler's young adult years. We recall that for Austria's Jews, the decades following 1848 had been a time of abundant, reasonable hope, and that in his Gymnasium, the lone anti-Semite in his class was despised by his classmates. But to Schnitzler's mounting dismay, anti-Semitism became a force in politics and even invaded his social circles. His diaries record the contretemps to which he was increasingly exposed. In 1898, he had to be defended against the reproach that he, as a Jew, could not possibly know what goes on in the mind of a Viennese woman. Schnitzler could not decide what was worse: the viciousness of such bigotry or its stupidity. "Ninety-nine percent of Christians in Vienna," he commented, "think this way."

He was exaggerating, of course, but his hyperbole is a measure of Schnitzler's irritation and growing sense of alienation. He, the lover and discriminating connoisseur of German literature, had to endure being told by a Germanophile Austrian writer that he, Schnitzler, could not hope to understand a German classic like Goethe. And in an unpublished and undated jotting, he reproduced a conversation about Mahler: "How wonderful the popular tunes in the scherzo of the Fifth, [I said]; aroma of native forests, smell of knowledge and flowers. A whole German landscape rises up. The other: Impossible. Mahler is a Jew, hence in no way capable of comprehending Germanness." There was a moment in 1895 when he was touched by a historic vision and casually set it aside. In April, he had a visit from Theodor Herzl, journalist, playwright, who virtually single-handedly invented Zionism, driven to that radical solution of the "Jewish Question," he later claimed, by the Dreyfus case. Schnitzler knew Herzl well, especially as a playwright, and did not really like him very much. "Conversation, Jewish question," he recorded. "His idea for a solution in which he seriously believes." Schnitzler, the cosmopolitan, did not.

In his autobiography, Schnitzler comments sagely on the mixture of fanaticism and political opportunism that together made up the racist alibi in the Vienna of his maturity. In May 1873, there had been a spectacular crash on the stock exchange, with baneful consequences for banks and for investors all across Europe, Schnitzler's father among many others. This gave anti-Semites the right, or so it seemed to them, to blame Jewish speculators for the vagaries of the Austrian money market, to call for the ouster of Jews from university fraternities and public employment, and for an end to their "domination" of the press. A small self-selected group of Viennese bourgeois intent on uprooting political corruption, which had initially included Jews, was transformed into an anti-Semitic party by the clever demagogue Karl Lueger, who, we recall, would rise to the mayoralty in 1897, on an anti-Semitic platform.

This disheartening sequence of events was, Schnitzler thought, a perfect demonstration of how far modern mass politics could sink by appealing to the "lowest instincts of the masses." Rather than exposing the individuals responsible for the economic slump or for government scandals one by one, no matter what their religious allegiance, politicians with an ear for bigoted undercurrents discovered that it was easier to simplify the intricate network of business fluctuations and political malfeasance by singling out Jews, and Jews alone, as the villains. Schnitzler did not use the term, but his analysis is a shrewd diagnosis just how an alibi for aggression works. It needs an easily recognizable enemy, even if—at times especially if—the aggressors grossly distort or even invent that enemy's vices. A century earlier, William Blake had exclaimed that to generalize is to be an idiot. It was also a way of coopting idiots for one's political ambitions.

5

AMONG ALL THE DEBATES OVER PERMISSIBLE aggression, those over capital punishment are perhaps the most illuminating. They reveal, too, the agonized doubts that swirl around the issue. Surely, there is no aggressive act quite so emphatic as the state, solemnly acting in the name of society, judicially killing one of its own. Except possibly for the clashes over slavery and over prison reform, no question aroused greater effusions of rhetoric and larger avalanches of print among the Victorians than the death penalty. The abolitionists saw only its inhumanity, the defenders only its necessity. Editors editorialized, preachers preached, legislators legislated on the subject, citizens wrote letters to the editor and immortalized their opinion in ephemeral brochures. Name-calling was the standard weapon of the contestants: abolitionists disparaged their adversaries as nothing better than barbarians; believers in capital punishment in turn called the abolitionists sickly sentimentalists lacking in virility. Bismarck and other apologists for the noose and the blade did not hesitate to play the manliness card.

The vast and varied controversial literature does not permit a social or political profile of the contenders. Not surprisingly, more opponents of capital punishment took up the pen than did its backers: those who called for change were all the more determined to make themselves heard than those intent on keeping things as they were. Nor does the vocation of polemicists permit predictions. Men of the cloth urged an end to un-Christian murder, but they confronted clerical opponents who resorted, just as they did, to scriptures.

In 1842, Joseph P. Thompson, pastor of the Chapel Street Congregational Church in New Haven, Connecticut, delivered three sermons on the text, "Whoso sheddeth man's blood, by man shall his blood be shed." He thought this biblical pronouncement "an absolute, unequivocal, unconditional command," one that "*has not been repealed.*" In the opposing camp, Reverend Milo D. Codding of Rochester, New York, also turned to the Bible to show that human government, "which should coincide with the divine government," must interpret God's commands from the heights the nineteenth century had reached. His adversaries, "taking their cue from the developments of a barbarous age," have overlooked the glorious progress "so plainly manifested by the records of the Past, and the tendencies of the Present." Historical understanding was to assist the reading of sacred texts to reach humane verdicts. These publications were at times dialogues across time. In 1863, the Italian philosopher A. Vera, who held chairs in philosophy in Italy and France, called for the abolition of capital punishment in all cases, including political and military offenses. In the following year, attempting an explicit and detailed refutation of Vera's arguments, another Italian, Raffaele Mariano, concluded that "the abolition of the death penalty is a utopia."

THE ARMY OF REFORMERS DEMANDING AN END TO executions had many valiant foot soldiers. One of the most conspicuous among them was Charles Jean-Marie Lucas, economist and lawyer. In 1830, he had been appointed General Inspector of France's prisons; three years later, he founded a society to care for young convicts recently released from jail. Almost to his death in 1889 at eighty-six, he petitioned ministries, wrote pleas against "the abnormal condition" of capital punishment, and supported committees and associations to carry on his lifelong crusade. Such associations covered the map. The

Society for the Diffusion of Knowledge Respecting the Punishment of Death and the Improvement of Prison Discipline, launched in 1809 in England by the Quaker William Allen, a public-spirited scientist, was apparently the first. There were similar societies in Paris and London, in Berlin and New York. Responding to their pressure, governments formed commissions to study the matter; at times, it seemed, less to prepare the way for abolition than to obstruct any change for which reformers were clamoring.

Around the 1860s, virtually all the arguments on both sides had been thoroughly ventilated; the polemics that appeared after that only added pseudo-scientific glosses and statistics to a quarrel that never grew stale. "The Capital Punishment controversy," wrote the English pamphleteer Francis Bishop, an abolitionist, in 1882, "is one that can lay no claim to any charm of novelty." It stayed alive largely because the gains of the abolitionists were so gradual and because determined lobbies of officials, judges, lawyers, and conservative citizens put up vigorous resistance. At times, too, successes proved evanescent, as legislators rescinded their abolition of the death penalty, only demonstrating the need for undiminished vigilance. In 1863, a congress of German jurists had voted that future legal codes should omit capital punishment, but in 1910, a majority at a successor congress took it all back.

Yet some developments cheered the abolitionists, including the presence of specialists in mental disease in courtrooms. In France, from 1811 on, an expert witness was admitted to court proceedings to determine a murderer's moral responsibility for his acts, an example of medical jurisprudence that other countries would follow. The trial that brought the alienist in the courtroom to the attention of a larger public took place in England in 1843 with the celebrated M'Naghten case. The accused had murdered Edward Drummond, the private secretary of the prime minister, Sir Robert Peel, under the delusion that Drummond was Peel, and the jury found M'Naghten not guilty on grounds of insanity. Responding to this consequential ruling, the Lord Chancellor formed a panel of judges to revisit the case, which confirmed the verdict: accused persons are not responsible for their acts if they cannot tell right from wrong.

Such advances were accompanied by the acts of numerous countries eliminating the death penalty entirely, or, as in Belgium, ceasing to enforce it even though it was still on the books. Few criminals condemned to die were actually executed: in 1887 in France, 210 of 240 offenders sentenced to the guillotine were officially spared, and of the remaining 30, only 6 went to their death. By the second half of Queen Victoria's reign, public opinion had visibly shifted away from the conviction that it was necessary to take a life to avenge the loss of another.

THE DEATH PENALTY HAD BEEN PART OF THE arsenal of legal revenge since the most ancient codes to have survived, but it took its modern form only with the rise of the state from the sixteenth century on. Before then, murders and like offenses were usually avenged in blood feuds among warring families and clans. But once states began to abolish private retaliation in their efforts to establish a monopoly over the exercise of violence, the right to deprive a criminal of life was transferred to public agencies, the only authorities delegated to try, convict, and punish malefactors.

In the eighteenth century, this concentrated visibility of capital punishment called for humane responses from the Enlightenment, though slowly, almost hesitantly; to support the death penalty was the way good citizens, even philosophes, thought about crime and punishments. In the 1760s, when his efforts in behalf of legal reform came to consume his attention, Voltaire spoke out eloquently for the most sparing employment of capital punishment. The only malefactor whose fate — being drawn and quartered — he could support was that of Ravaillac, who had murdered Henri IV, Voltaire's favorite king, in 1610. He was not a wholly consistent abolitionist.

The Italian marchese Cesare Beccaria was. In his terse treatise *Of Crimes and Punishments* (1764), he rejected all exceptions and denounced capital punishment as savagery, as violence clad in the august aura of law. His little book was promptly translated into French and English, and with its uncompromising thesis, enlisted outspoken admirers among whom Voltaire was only the best known. In the early nineteenth century, the English Utilitarian philosophers, with Jeremy Bentham taking the lead, though far more businesslike in tone and calculations, projected Beccaria's rationale into the Victorian age.

With considerable gusto, men of letters kept the debates alive in the marketplace of ideas. The awesome event of a public hanging aroused their loathing and stirred their imaginations. The most powerful artistic portrayal in the century was a short novel by Victor Hugo, *The Last Day of a Convict* (1832). Hugo was battling demons of his own; as an adolescent, he had witnessed harrowing scenes of butchery that never left him, and they turned him into a crusader against cruel justice. In *The Last Day*, he evokes the convict's day before the execution from his perspective, punctuated by nightmarish fantasies, attacks of fear and self-pity, and the pathetic visit of his three-year-old daughter who does not recognize him. About thirty years later, in 1860, Emile Zola defended Hugo's high emotional pitch: *The Last Day* had been a political statement. "He had but one aim: to render the death penalty odious; do you want him to write an idyll?"

Two much-discussed journalistic accounts of a hanging at Newgate in 1840, one by Dickens and the other by Thackeray, taught an even wider public that executions are obscene entertainments. Thackeray, who could not get the murderer's face out of his mind for two weeks, included himself among the sinful spectators and damned his own "brutal curiosity." Dickens described the crowd as ribald, drunken, and debauched. By making hangings public affairs, the modern state was unwittingly conniving with spectators to gratify the ugliest, most unsublimated of their aggressive impulses. A hanging was a carnival that diverted not merely the unemployed and the unemployable. Good bourgeois or curious aristocrats who could afford it watched from a carriage or rented a room that gave them a clear view of the proceedings. In *Bleak House,* Dickens devotes a single devastating phrase to the dandy who "goes to see all the executions." There was much to see. Itinerant peddlers hawked crudely printed broadsides about the murderer and his (on occasion, her) victim. Prostitutes plied their trade. Pickpockets gathered rewarding dividends in the tightly packed crowd.

Hundreds brought their food and drink, mainly drink. There were few occasions in modern societies in which one's pleasure in the pain of others was so blatant, an excitement in which sexual arousal seems to have been a welcome accompaniment.

THE ABOLITIONISTS' AGENDA WAS SIMPLICITY itself. But by midcentury, middle-class opinion, wanting things both ways, began to favor a compromise: to move the deadly scene to an inaccessible spot. This would deprive avid spectators with vulgar or depraved tastes of a base amusement but keep the vengeful majesty of the law intact. It seemed a desirable move toward civility, and it was. But it attracted partisans whose opposition to the death penalty had been halfhearted all along. Dickens was only one abolitionist who retreated from an unconditional endorsement to a qualified—and, to his former comrades, cowardly—support for hanging far from public view. The arrangement struck many as an irreproachable halfway house; out of sight really did seem to imply out of mind. And it had consequences. Great Britain stopped public executions in 1868. Paris moved the guillotine from the heart of the city to a distant section of town some thirty years later. Berlin did its lethal duty in some obscure prison courtyard. But these civilized arrangements placed abolitionists into a cruel dilemma; they were really defeats that only looked like victories, good reasons to keep up the struggle aiming at complete abolition. As we shall see, in the midst of the Victorian age, that struggle was to register some notable successes.

The favorite rationalization for capital punishment was that it served as a deterrent to major crimes. Enlightened reformers argued that all but the worst offenders should have an opportunity to be rehabilitated, and rejoin society after they had paid their penalty. But experimenting with various forms of imprisonment only showed that few malefactors were likely to leave prison better men than they had been when they entered. The favorite Victorian rationale, rather, was deterrence, a plea that proved to be trivially true—a criminal put to death would violate the rules of society no more—and significantly false. Dickens underscored how little this alibi amounted to when he sarcastically called the hangman "the Finishing Schoolmaster." Nineteenth-century criminologists and statisticians in fact found no reliable evidence that the abolition of capital punishment encouraged crime. Quite the contrary: after midcentury, countries like the Netherlands, Belgium, and Portugal reported no increase, and even some decrease in homicides after they had taken the brave step of punishing crimes without killing killers.

The evolution of capital punishment in Victorian Great Britain reads like a test of the deterrence argument for students of crime. From the early eighteenth century on, Parliament had swelled the catalogue of capital crimes to over two hundred, most of them aimed at thieves and forgers, including children of the slums. The pettiest offenses—stealing an object worth a mere couple of shillings—threatened their perpetrators with the noose. But such wholesale efforts to enforce law and order in behalf of the propertied proved to be self-canceling: juries refused to convict, judges contrived to have the accused tried on a lesser charge, death sentences were commuted to transportation. In 1830, in an act of delicious irony, more than a thousand British bankers petitioned Sir Robert Peel, then home secretary, to eliminate most forgeries from the list of capital crimes because savage penal laws were working for criminals. Whatever the motives of these solid citizens—as usual, they were mixed, looking to their economic self-interest and their humane discomfort with hangings—by the time Victoria ascended the throne, executions had begun to diminish. Looking back in 1880, in introducing a new English translation of Beccaria's immortal treatise, James Anson Farrer noted that in 1832, the year of the great Reform Act, "it ceased to be capital to steal a horse or a sheep, in 1833 to break into a house, in 1834 to return prematurely from transportation, in 1835 to commit sacrilege or to steal a letter." This trend continued inexorably, so that by 1914 only four felonies remained capital crimes. Yet Britain was not inundated by crime waves.

Even so, there remained legions of upright citizens for whom abundant proofs that the death penalty is ineffective seemed written in water. And this denial of overwhelming evidence is of central import

for the student of the aggressive drive in public life, and not in
Victorian times alone. However irrational and unproductive the punishment, advocates of the death penalty found its enactment emotionally satisfying, virtually indispensable to their well-being. Their
grandiose rationalizations covered a simple emotion: the craving for
revenge. They would speak of the necessity to preserve, or restore, the
sacred contract of the social order, a contract that the criminal had
wantonly torn up, an order that he had despoiled. They would insist
that there is only one way to make the body politic whole again: to
cleanse it of the violator's presence forever. His death is the only adequate price to pay. They were, they assured their listeners, also thinking of the victim's family and closest friends: to these victims in their
own right, a killer who lives must haunt them as unfinished psychological business. But they were also thinking of themselves, of the pleasure
they would derive from the demise of the malefactor.

There is something to the advertised disinterested respect for the victim's nearest and dearest. Those who mourned him most sincerely
looked for what the twentieth century has made into a cant phrase:
"closure." That is why some of them petitioned to be present at the execution, to free themselves from a burden that did not grow lighter with
the passage of time. But some frank and intelligent Victorians broke
through to the heart of the matter, and called a raw passion a raw passion. "The notion of desert in punishment," wrote James Farrer, himself an abolitionist, is based entirely on "the justice of resentment." Late
in the century, this discovery was becoming something of a commonplace. Louis Günther, a "modern" German expert, acknowledged a
decade later that even "in our enlightened and humane time, the first
impulse to punish an injustice springs from the characteristic of human
nature to take revenge for wrongs and injuries undergone." Self-
control could restrain human urges only so far.

This sober recognition that the understanding of aggression, notably
aggression against an aggressor, makes a statement about human
nature belongs among the most penetrating psychological insights of
the Victorians. In 1860, the French psychologist and philosopher
Claude-Joseph Tissot, though convinced that his enlightened century,

rising above the primitive need for retaliation, had established "justice tempered by compassion and kindness," felt compelled to acknowledge that the "thirst for vengeance" is a fundamental human characteristic. For the English jurist, historian, and conservative James Fitzjames Stephen, a sturdy Hobbesian for whom society was essentially a war zone, all this was perfectly self-evident. Criminals are punished, and should be punished, he wrote in 1873, mainly because that gratifies "the feeling of hatred—call it revenge, resentment, or what you will— which the contemplation of such conduct excites in healthily constituted minds." Society cannot survive without outlawing certain forms of aggressiveness, but the desire for revenge is a quality, this eminent Victorian thought, of healthily constituted minds.

THERE ARE MANY PEOPLE WHO THINK THEY HAVE grasped the Victorian mentality when they have smiled at gushy keepsakes, maudlin poems, shy euphemisms, silences about matters that matter. True, the Victorians seem in so many ways distant from us. But there was more to them than sentimentality or hypocrisy. Victorian bourgeois, whether liberals or conservatives, had a tough-minded realistic streak in them, a gift for seeing life as it is. To repeat: within their limits, they lived with eyes wide open. It should astonish no one that perplexing issues which engaged them engage us still; current debates over capital punishment have hardly advanced over their Victorian predecessors. Today's vehement defenses of the death penalty as a deterrent to crime are being proffered in the teeth of proofs well over a century old, a sure sign that its principal function is to provide mourners with a sense of relief.

This vitality across many decades—I could cite many other instances— only underscores the Victorians' modernity. With all their evasiveness, all their taste for circumlocutions, the Victorians' widespread—though far from unanimous—self-congratulatory conviction that they were living in a time of progress had solid grounding in reality. Acting out their aggressive impulses was becoming less and less attractive to them. In the course of years, fewer of them beat children, fewer of them maltreated servants, fewer of them exploited workers or lorded it over their wives. And they executed fewer convicted criminals. This is not to say that by the death of Queen Victoria, bourgeois had no outlets for their aggressive urges. For those who needed to gratify them, they always had Social Democrats, feminists, Jews, and neighboring nations to hate. As long as their acts of aggression remained within the officially licensed limits and were privately approved by the bourgeois conscience, the only consequence they brought in their train was pleasure. But in an age when these limits were blurred, persistently in dispute, and steadily narrowing, especially for the middle classes, the psychological results were more complicated and less agreeable than they liked, leading to self-doubt and (another experience typical of Victorian bourgeois) to sheer anxiety.

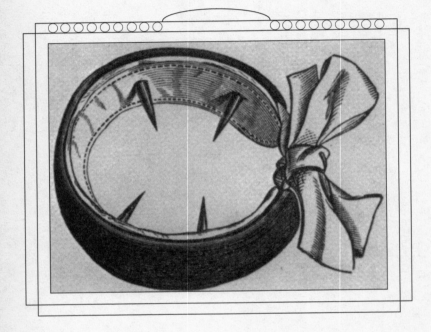

FIVE

Grounds for Anxiety

1

WHEN IT CAME TO ANXIETY, FEW BOURGEOIS could rival Arthur Schnitzler. His diary is punctuated by references to his "nervous condition," his intermittent, tormenting worries over his writing, his moral stature, and, as we have seen, his love life. In short, if he wore his nervousness much like most of his contemporaries, he was more intense about it than most of them. But he certainly was in good company: Victorian bourgeois seem to have been more alert to symptoms of apprehensiveness than their fellows in other epochs. All ages are ages of anxiety, but it seemed appropriate somehow for the Victorians to diagnose anxiety as a modern disease and to give it a technical name: neurasthenia. That was in 1880. Several decades before that, popular usage had already converted a familiar epithet for high spirits and energy—nervousness—into an ailment, a timid, tremulous sense of agitation.

It was not a secret to the nineteenth century that there was more than one kind of anxiety; it could be irrational or realistic, produced by inner stresses or by objective warning signals. From that perspective, the Victorians' manly ideal of complete fearlessness proved to be a poor preparation for life: there were things—people, situations, ideas, wishes—that a sensible person had every right to fear. That is why a child's socialization always included inculcating anxiety: watch out for a friendly stranger in the street! beware the hot stove! The eighteen-year-old Schnitzler speaks in his diary of "praiseworthy resignation." This is one of the lessons that judicious anxiety teaches: it is reasonable to sacrifice tempting problematic pleasures for the sake of avoiding later pain. Attending warily to looming, often ill-defined dangers is another.

I have said that Arthur Schnitzler had good company in his anxiety. When his father rifled through his desk, he did not commit this glaring violation of propriety casually, on a whim. Dr. Schnitzler was anxious, as a physician all the more anxious, about his son's health. What company might the boy be keeping, to what infections might he be exposed? These were not frivolous question, nor tokens of paternal overprotection. Venereal infection was a real menace of the age, and middle-class adolescents, thousands of Arthur Schnitzler's contemporaries, armed with a lighthearted sense of their immortality and given to nocturnal escapades with ladies of dubious reputations, were particularly susceptible to the hazards of gonorrhea and syphilis.

The statistics were public, abundant, and shocking, spreading out from medical research to troubled discussion in technical journals and the more open-minded popular journals. Let one example stand for many: in a comprehensive study of modern marriage, the German philosopher Otto Caspari noted that in Paris between 1872 and 1888, the number of venereal cases treated in local hospitals added up to 118,223, with roughly half of them syphilitic. In England, he added, the figures showed that from 1861 to 1884, deaths from syphilis had increased by 84 percent. Although physicians had made some progress during the century in diagnosing sexually transmitted diseases, much remained obscure, and knowing what he did not know, far from lessening Dr. Schnitzler's disquiet only enhanced it.

Worse, much that seemed to be known about syphilis in 1879, the year that Schnitzler tangled with his father over his diary, was simply wrong. The most consequential medical misconception (one that cost many faithful wives and many innocent children their looks, their health, even their lives) held that the disease was cured after a single bout. Reputable physicians believed that the very attack their patients had overcome acted as a prophylactic against later outbreaks. Hence an unknowable, surely sizable number of syphilitics reassured by ignorant doctors thought themselves safe to keep up their wild pursuit of sexual pleasure, safe to marry after one episode of "the pox." In 1860, Charles Baudelaire expressed a majority opinion when he wrote that "no one is healthier than the man who has had the pox and has been fully cured." He would soon know better.

Other men of the world sharing Baudelaire's situation also congratulated themselves. In an exuberant letter of 1877, Guy de Maupassant informed a friend that a physician had attributed his loss of hair and related symptoms to syphilis and put him on a regimen of mercury and potassium iodine. Then a twenty-seven-year-old writer acquiring a reputation for brilliant, worldly—many said obscene—short stories and a libertine of almost legendary capacities, he was glad to hear it. His hair, he reported, was growing back and he was feeling very well. "I've got the pox! At last! The real thing! Not the contemptible clap," or any other minor venereal ailment, "no—no—the great pox, the one which Francis I died of. The majestic pox, pure and simple, the elegant syphilis." He was "proud of it, by thunder, and to hell with the bourgeoisie." In his exhilaration he repeated himself. "Allelulia, I've got the pox, so I don't have to worry about catching it any more, and I screw the street whores and trollops, and afterwards I say to them, 'I've got the pox.' They are afraid and I just laugh." Some years after this eruption, he entered what physicians were beginning to recognize as the tertiary stage of the disease, went mad tortured by horrifying delusions, and died. He was forty-three.

It would have been better for Maupassant if he had been more of a bourgeois, like the young Schnitzler; in his unquenchable appetites Schnitzler resembled Maupassant, whose novellas he greatly admired; in his prudence he was, luckily for him, very different. Whenever in his bachelor years he was tempted to pick up attractive and available young things, his fear of infection nearly always kept him from obeying his impulse. This was, we know, a wisdom his father had so rudely taught him. However one judges Dr. Schnitzler's pedagogical tactics, his concern for his son was perfectly justified. His anxiety became even more justified in retrospect, once researchers discovered that one cannot cure syphilis with syphilis.

2

IT WAS DR. GEORGE M. BEARD, BORN IN Connecticut in 1839, who coined the clinical term "neurasthenia." The name was something of a latecomer: a pervasive, imprecise inner tension had been canvassed for half a century and more. Poets, moralists, preachers had censured their age as deficient in the vitality and imperturbability that is the signature of a robust mind. As early as 1813, linking debility to excessive self-indulgence, the London *Examiner* charged that the "present luxurious age is remarkable for its nervousness." A quarter of a century later, in 1840, the American physician William Alcott, author of widely read manuals of advice to the young, considered women especially susceptible to "those indefinable feelings of ennui," which "for want of a better name, are called, in their various forms, 'nervousness.'"

To single out women as more vulnerable to nervousness than men, not unexpected in the male style of the time, grew to be a topos in the literature, while poets like Matthew Arnold generalized nervous trouble to his times in a much-quoted passage from *The Scholar Gypsy*, which speaks of

> this strange disease of modern life,
> With its sick hurry, its divided aims.

That was in 1853. By the 1860s, some psychiatrists stood ready to advance the extreme position that modern civilization, by its very existence, makes for nervousness.

The English-speaking world had no corner on such anxieties. Not long after 1800, French novelists had detected and bemoaned what they called the *mal du siècle,* a blend of melancholy with a crippling sense of disorientation. Benjamin Constant, referring to the eponymous hero of his novel, *Adolphe,* noted that he had intended to lay bare "one of the principal maladies of our century: that fatigue, that uncertainty, that lack of strength, that perpetual analysis which puts an afterthought against all feelings and corrupts them at birth." Decades after that fashion had faded—it had been the creation of a few select spirits for select spirits—talk about nervousness had spread to the reading public. We encounter the phrase "our century of nerves" among novelists, cultural critics, and playwrights. In this as in so much else, Schnitzler's leading characters in his plays and stories, like Schnitzler himself, fit perfectly into his class and time. His men and women are nothing if not agitated, given to unexpected outbursts, disquieting regrets, sudden shifts of sentiments from ecstasy to disgust, attacks of violence including violence against themselves. To recall Schnitzler's line from his play *Paracelsus*: safety is nowhere, which is to say: anxiety is everywhere.

Nervousness was not just wholly modern, it seemed to be growing exponentially. In 1895, the authoritative Krafft-Ebing laid down that "nervousness is rising fatally." No one could have been astonished. In 1890, one C. Falkenhorst had already made current medical wisdom available to a petty bourgeois readership in the *Gartenlaube,* Germany's favorite family weekly: "Our age suffers from nervous weakness; it is the malady of the nineteenth century." Meanwhile in Italy, in 1886, the well-regarded sexologist Paolo Mantegazza labeled his whole century neurotic in his study entitled *Il secolo nevrosico.* The book appeared in a German version two years later, documenting the international free trade in anxiety during the Victorian age. In fact, before the turn of the century, the prevalence of nervousness was so widely accepted that copywriters felt free to make the most of it. In 1895, the *New Haven Leader* carried an advertisement for "Paine's Celery Compound," which guaranteed to alleviate "nervous exhaustion in children" to which their parents, experiencing "a constantly increasing strain," were also exposed. Cultural anxiety had become a fad inviting commercial exploitation.

———

THE ROOTS OF THIS VOGUE WERE SHALLOW, BUT the notion of a melancholic temperament had a long history; it went back to Hippocrates, and he had followers through the ages. In the early seventeenth century, Robert Burton published his enormous scholarly compendium, *The Anatomy of Melancholy*, in England, which was still quoted as an authority two centuries after his death. The nineteenth century, then, had little new to say about melancholia, and long compounded the general confusion. It called what today we diagnose as depression or severe anxiety "low spirits" or "shattered nerves," and identified its sources as the most diverse individual endowments or experiences: a business failure, a religious doubt, an unrequited love, an inborn trait.

For decades, until psychological and sociological explanations carried the day, the favored etiology of nervousness was "bad" heredity. Brooding over his nervousness, in which, he noted, his sister shared, Schnitzler took the old-fashioned view and concluded that it probably came from his mother. And the origins, the very definition of anxiety remained controversial until Freud, years later, persuasively argued that anxiety is a signal of trouble waiting in the wings. In short, the Victorians' preoccupation with anxiety—itself a symptom of the ailment they were trying to understand—explored every possible avenue. Reaching back to the late eighteenth century for light, they compiled a catalogue of warning signs that emerged from the fertile soils of cultural habits or institutional arrangements. Though these seemed to be capable of victimizing whole populations, it was obvious that not everyone suffered alike; the sturdiest could resist, perhaps find ways to shake off, whatever had infected the rest. But the polluted atmosphere seemed ever present and originated in society itself.

The culprit first suspected as a leading cause for this diffuse ailment was the specialization indelibly linked to the dawning industrial age. Pale one-sidedness rather than the wealth of possible human activities was, these critics reasoned, a direct consequence of the demands that the factory system made on the workforce caught in its toils. At first, then, the principal victims seemed to be the working poor. In 1776, in his masterly *Wealth of Nations*, when the modern division of labor was still largely in the future, Adam Smith had presciently analyzed its Janus face: new, efficient methods that would enormously enhance productivity would at the same time cripple workmen's minds and spirits. Toiling in factories to perform monotonous tasks day after day, year after year, would deprive factory hands of the capacity to realize potentialities essential to their humanity. They would drop into a virtually subhuman existence, degraded into slaves drudging in a pitiless mechanism with no prospect of release.

It did not take long to broaden this grim prognosis and include the bourgeoisie among the victims of contemporary society. In the early 1790s, in a long, brilliant essay, *Letters on the Aesthetic Education of Mankind*, Friedrich Schiller denounced specialization as the dismal fate of modern humanity. His contemporaries, he charged, in this as in all else hopelessly inferior to the ancient Greeks, had fractured into pitiful fragments. At best, they might do one thing well, but nothing else. The increasing distance of one science from all the others, the widening gulf between classes, the separation of reason and emotion, had "torn apart the inner bond of human nature." And, Schiller concluded gravely, "it was culture itself that has dealt modern man this wound."

Nineteenth-century students of society employed portentous names to account for these fatal flaws. The term "alienation," first rediscovered by Hegel and used as a weapon for his critique of capitalism by Marx, served the purpose that "fragmentation" had done for Schiller. The Victorian worker, as Marx put it, whether toiling in a factory or at a desk, had been compelled to become a stranger to his fellows, to his work, and to himself. Wholeness was forever beyond him. And under capitalism, he contended, other classes, the bourgeoisie in the lead, were similarly demoralized—in every sense of that word. Finally, around 1900, Emile Durkheim secularized the theological term "anomie" to stigmatize contemporary individualism in the pernicious sense of that term: a self-centeredness that kept Western societies from forging the sturdy collective bonds that made for intact communities. Such sociological and historical assessments provided free-floating social anxiety with compelling foundations. Dr. Beard, and the readers who borrowed his "neurasthenia," had no doubt that they were describing a disease distinctive of the Victorian decades. When, in 1890, the German philosopher Bartholomäus von Carneri wrote, "Nervousness is the disease of our time," he was telling no one anything new.

THE TITLE OF DR. BEARD'S PRINCIPAL PUBLICATION, *A Practical Treatise on Nervous Exhaustion (Neurasthenia), Its Symptoms, Nature, Sequences, Treatment*, discloses the scope of his aspirations. His life's purpose was to civilize the wilderness of diagnoses of, and remedies for, current mental distress until it resembled a neat French garden. "Order," he copied into his journal as a young man, "is Heaven's first law." It was evidently a maxim he cherished. But his inventory of indications for neurasthenia was far too indiscriminate to clarify the workings of the disease he thought he was putting on the map, and far too miscellaneous to identify a single ailment. "Insomnia, flushing, drowsiness, bad dreams, cerebral irritation, dilated pupils, pain, pressure and heaviness in the head . . . noises in the ear . . . mental irritability, tenderness of the teeth and gum . . . sweating hands and feet with redness, fear of lightning, or fear of responsibilities, of open places or of closed places, fear of society, fear of being alone, fear of fears, fear of contamination, fear of everything," and more.

This compilation was preposterous enough, but Beard's observations on national types, closely interwoven with his "discovery" of neurasthenia, were if anything even more so. He was ambivalent about this collection of symptoms, since it seemed somehow linked to high culture and physical beauty. Nervousness, in short, had its compensations. As one who had seen the world—that is, mainly the principal European capitals—he vouched for the "phenomenal beauty of the American girl," unsurpassed, indeed unmatched, in any country or at any time in history. In his besotted vision, the "American girl" splendidly combined her highly developed mental faculties with the finesse of her "physical organization." He allowed that one might see beauties "here and there" in Britain, "rarely" in Germany; one might meet them more frequently in France and Austria. But none of these could ever measure up to their American sisters. A self-

taught art critic, Beard was persuaded that the "almost universal homeli-
ness of female faces" in European art stemmed from the distressing fact
that painters on the Continent "never saw a handsome woman." And he
speculated that if Raphael had been fortunate enough to live in the United
States, he would never have painted the Sistine Madonna as "the neuras-
thenic and anemic type that is there represented."

These excursions into the comparative study of women's looks were
unique to Beard; his analysis of how neurasthenia originates was
supremely unoriginal. The "chief and primary cause" of the "very rapid
increase of nervousness" was, for Beard, quite simply, *"modern civilization."* Five characteristics, he noted, distinguish it from its predecessors:
"steam power, the periodical press, the telegraph, the sciences, and the
mental activity of women." Then, finding his list not exhaustive
enough, he added religious excitement, political machines, technical
education, fragmenting specialization, rigid schedules, demanding
clocks, enforced punctuality, excessive noise, incessant travel, stock
speculation, repressed emotions—in a word, just about everything.

Nearly all Victorian students of nervousness considered this catchall
to be practically self-evident: surely the "hustle and bustle" of modern
urban life was responsible for the evident and rapidly increasing nervousness that dominated the age. The literature on this subject was vast,
and texts, substantially agreeing in their conclusions, differed only in
their rhetoric. "Our time is quick, stormy, and frivolous," wrote the
German physician Ernst Freiherr von Feuchtersleben in a little tract,
Dietetic of the Soul, in 1838. This book of good counsel went through
dozens of printings, and as late as 1910, Bruno Walter recommended it
to Gustav Mahler. Obviously the world had greatly changed since the
1830s, but not enough to make Feuchtersleben dated or irrelevant.

This diagnosis dominated the Victorian age and beyond. In *North and
South*, of 1855, Elizabeth Gaskell has her protagonist, Margaret Hale,
compare the hardiness of the countryside with the restlessness of urban
existence that makes for labor unrest. "'It is the town life,' said she.
'Their nerves are quickened by the haste and bustle and speed of everything around them.'" Forty years later, the *New Haven Leader* agreed,
making "the hurry and bustle of modern life" the culprit that rendered

modern men and women nervous. The number of texts reiterating this belief is almost limitless.

The hustle-and-bustle theory did not weaken significantly until World War I. In 1911, Dr. Wilhelm Bergmann, a German psychiatrist who owned and ran a clinic using the "cold water cure," gratefully referred to Feuchtersleben and described the contemporary bourgeoisie with similar intent, if more garrulously: "it knows only the flight from the land and life in the metropolis filled with excitement, worry and anxiety, the unleashing of the wildest passions in the chase after happiness and the dance around the golden calf; it knows only puniness and the struggle for advancement and reputation, an unbridled craving to the point of exhaustion, a craving for pleasure that throws off all moral shackles, places itself beyond good and evil, and boasts of its decadence as an absurd counterpart to [Nietzsche's] superman." This heated indictment of bourgeois existence reads like an expression of, far more than a report on, neurasthenia.

IN THE MID-1890S, DURING HIS FIRST YEARS OF psychoanalytic theorizing and clinical experimentation, Freud read Beard closely and concluded that his work, like that of his many followers, was too vague and inclusive to be trustworthy. That was putting it too politely: Beard knew too little and the wrong things, and for all his claims to being a meticulous empiricist, he generalized indiscriminately from casual impressions and ingrained prejudices. That Freud, a physician specializing in mental suffering, should join the discussion of neurasthenia was foreordained. In one respect, his first comments were conventional: he shared the prevalent verdict that nervousness was indeed on the rise in the contemporary world. It was, in short, a historical phenomenon, which raised the fundamental question that others, in Freud's view, had failed to answer correctly. And here his medical orthodoxy ended. Nervousness, as he saw it, was the consequence of excessive sexual repression in the Victorian middle classes.

This thesis amounted to a thoroughgoing critique of bourgeois morality, which, Freud believed, had pushed the frustration of biological urges beyond sustainable limits and generated anxiety neuroses among other ailments. It is a theory not without value but dubious in its sweeping formulation, since it goes beyond the evidence. Freud took the neuroses of his female patients as representative of respectable Victorian sexuality; one reason I have written this book has been to refute, or at least to complicate, this all-encompassing judgment. We have seen plentiful and sound evidence that frigidity among middle-class women was not so prevalent as Freud believed; he was on more solid ground as a theorist and a clinician than as a critic of the bourgeoisie.

In directing attention to the causal importance of sexual frustration in emotional distress, Freud was not wholly alone. Dr. Beard had been working on a book about "sexual neurasthenia," but died prematurely in 1883 before completing it. Freud's increasingly confident, utterly subversive publications touching on the central role of sexuality in human functioning, and malfunctioning, remained exceptional. Even though Freud's inferences about bourgeois culture need to be amended, his fundamental reorientation of psychology, in which his theories on sexuality were of crucial importance, was a historic moment in the study of the human mind. It delved beneath the surfaces of nervousness that had contented other specialists.

The logic informing the psychoanalytic theory of mind that Freud built may be stated simply. He treated the mind as part of nature, and thus subject to laws like all other natural phenomena. There are, in a word, no uncaused events in mental life. It must follow that peculiar, apparently nonsensical mental acts—slips of the tongue or pen, unaccountable lapses of memory, inexplicable symptoms, absurd dreams, the incoherent speech of schizophrenics—must have a natural explanation, however hard they may be to interpret. Such acts point to the subterranean activity of a dynamic unconscious whose needs manifest themselves in these distorted, virtually illegible forms that had baffled other scientists of the mind.* The

---

*To be sure, not all this activity is problematic enough to merit analytic attention. Freud, to the best of my knowledge, never said, "Sometimes a cigar is just a cigar." But the statement, whoever made it, fits perfectly into the psychoanalytic way of thinking.

raw drives, notably sexuality and aggressiveness, bulk large in the unconscious, as do the defenses that disguise and battle hidden but exigent
needs, whether blasphemous, obscene, or aggressive. Freud's human
species is the wishing animal that fits uneasily into the constraints of civilization. It is the wishing animal in conflict.

Freud's psychoanalytic system of thought was a call for human modesty: much remains unknown about motives, and reason is not master
in its own house. This dethroning of sovereign reason helps to account
for the resistance to Freud's ideas in the psychiatric profession and in
public attitudes. His emphasis on the power of sexuality and of the
unconscious were simply too radical in assailing the very foundations
of respectable talk—or silence—about matters deemed beyond public
utterance in the Victorian age. Yet he never had the slightest use for the
party of irrationality; to study the dark forces of mind did not entail
joining them. The idea that one can deal rationally with the irrational
appeared hard to absorb, but it was fundamental to Freud's sense of his
work. To him—to put it tersely—science must be master and religion is
superstition. However un-Victorian Freud's conclusions turned out to
be, then, however critical he was of middle-class morality, he remained
in his essential orientation a Victorian bourgeois unbeliever, a disciple
of Darwin and Huxley.

And it was the bourgeoisie whom he and other students of nervousness had mainly in their sights. They agreed that the middling orders
were far more susceptible to this malaise that the working classes in
town and country, to say nothing of the aristocracy. These, too, had
their worries and their grounds for despair. But the poor were so heavily occupied scratching a living from day to day that they could scarcely
afford the luxury of neurasthenia. And the nobility, as it were, floated
above such middle-class pastimes. But the bourgeoisie, with a modicum
of leisure, with exacting domestic and social duties, and a rigorous conscience to plague them as they pursued their economic interests, was
most likely to succumb to hysteria, to sickly lassitude and dreary imag-
inings—in short, to neurosis. The most affluent men and women with
time on their hands were the most conspicuous casualties of nervous
diseases. But the malady of the century could afflict impecunious petty

bourgeois; nervousness had pervaded the age so thoroughly that one could work and be nervous at the same time.

3

THE TESTIMONY ASSERTING A RAPID GROWTH OF nervousness and its increasing sway over the middling strata was, though largely anecdotal, extensive and seemed persuasive. But why of all centuries did it assert its power in the nineteenth? Perhaps the unprecedented attention that physicians were paying to female complaints had made neurasthenia more eye-catching than before. It certainly reflected what has been called the medicalization of the age, the tendency to refer inappropriate moods and eccentric behavior to mental states rather than to instances of demonic possession or divine punishment.

By its very nature, the answer to this question must elude certainty. This much, though, seems plain: the detailed documentation showing the potent presence of anxiety in nineteenth-century bourgeois life had a subtext as elemental as it sounds banal—change. It is a commonplace among historians that the past is a duel between persistence and change. On a ground of persistence, change, whether individual or cultural, engraves its marks. But the vast majority of humanity in the past must have experienced persistence as their overwhelming reality. This is not to say that the poor were not deeply anxious, often about the basic question of sheer survival; or that they did not confront sudden shifts and dramatic upheavals as they went through wars, epidemics, threats of starvation, peasant uprisings, economic crises, natural catastrophes, new religions and new masters. But the basic facts of life around which they organized their existence—their unremitting toil, their persistent duties—remained entrenched, usually for centuries.

Then, around the fifteenth century, and chiefly in cities, the tempo of change seemed to accelerate. A series of highly complex events that we sum up all too simply as the Renaissance, the Reformation, the invention of printing, the discovery of America, the rise of the modern state, the scientific revolution, the Enlightenment, the beginnings of industrialization rattled the sense of permanence that had governed so much of the past. By the Victorian age, change was in the saddle, and Victorians knew it; late in the century, it became a platitude that if someone born three generations after the rule of Napoleon could return to around 1800, he would hardly recognize his surroundings.

ALL CHANGE HAS ITS TRAUMATIC SIDE, INCLUDING change for the better. The appetite for adventure, the pursuit of the untested, the eagerness for experimentation, increasingly tone-setting since the age of the Enlightenment, defied the conservatism that is as inherent in human nature as is the pleasure in the new. The dizzying inventions and discoveries, the unsettling ideas that invaded every domain of Victorian life gave its bourgeois culture an air of tension, of hopeful enterprise with anxiety following it like a shadow. It is not surprising that the vision of continual improvement, the theory of progress (wrongly attributed to the eighteenth-century philosophes) should have been a nineteenth-century ideology.

Few contemporary observers were unaware of this supreme fact of their lives, and they responded in wonder, delight, or dismay. In 1831, John Stuart Mill called his time "an age of transition." There were few to disagree with him. Several decades later, Zola wrote a friend, "our century is a century of transition." These observations sound hackneyed today; some anonymous wit has joked that leaving Paradise after their expulsion, Adam tried to console a weeping Eve by telling her, "Be of good cheer, my dear, we are living in an age of transition." But in the Victorian age, this was a measured judgment: the time markedly differed from its predecessors and continually called for new responses. The railroad, the transatlantic cable, the germ theory of disease, the evolutionary theories of Darwin, the advent of mass politics were only the most memorable innovations of a time that reshaped human life everywhere and forever.

Not everyone welcomed living in this bewildering time. In 1829, as so often anticipating other Cassandras, Thomas Carlyle, a sensitive barometer of emerging tendencies, wrote: "That great outward changes are in progress, can be doubtful to no one. The time is sick and out of joint." For his part, Jacob Burckhardt, the great Swiss historian of the Renaissance, writing in 1843, observed (and regretted) that "everybody wants to be *new*, but nothing else." And in 1874, in its lordly way, the London *Saturday Review* lamented "these days of tumultuous revolt from all fixed conditions." It was a heady time, and these laconic pronouncements smack of rhetorical overkill. But they recalled to their readers' minds realities that many of them confronted every day.

These realities have become the staple of history textbooks. I have briefly mentioned some of them in previous pages. There were more, a great many more: the European population rose from about 150 million in 1750 to about 260 million a century later. The total of emigrants to the United States from Eastern Europe, Germany, and Ireland fleeing pogroms, starvation, or anti-Catholic persecution numbered in many millions. A massive number of migrant workers deserted the countryside and settled in cities: Paris, with fewer than 600,000 inhabitants in 1801, counted over 1 million fifty years later; Vienna and Berlin, both with 120,000 inhabitants in 1815, had to accommodate more than three times that number in 1848. Urbanization drew population from villages and hamlets in unprecedented numbers: at midcentury, England and Wales, and Belgium, reported more urban than rural dwellers for the first time. Modern forms of commercial and industrial organization permitted hitherto unheard of accumulations of capital.

These are all well-known statements that have lost their freshness with sheer familiarity. Concretely all of them touched individual lives, whether a poverty-stricken Irishman being swallowed up in an English slum, a German investor losing his all in the crash of a bank, a Jew fleeing to Vienna from the East to escape being murdered in a Russian shtetl, a trade union organizer arrested for his activities. Their anxieties were often keen and usually rational, and the troubles of the poor inescapably impinged on the lives of nineteenth-century bourgeois.

Destabilizing shifts, then, pervaded the century; its explosive innovations were more far-reaching and irreversible, downright breathtaking, than shocks in earlier times. Movement was the rule, a promise or a menace, in science, technology, and medicine, in economics, politics, and government, in religion, taste, and mores, and in sexual expressiveness. Matthew Arnold articulated a broad consensus when he observed, "There is not a creed which is not shaken, not an accredited dogma which is not shown to be questioned, not a received tradition which does not threaten to dissolve." With its ubiquity and its rapidity, indeed, there was change in change itself. The "fury of innovation" of which Samuel Johnson had complained in 1783 grew more extreme in decades after. And it is this extraordinary linked pair of qualities—the universality of change and its speed—that, more than anything, more even than bourgeois sexual fiascos, made Victorians nervous.

IT ALSO MADE VICTORIANS HAPPY. PESSIMISTS about what they disparaged as the ravages of progress were on the whole more quotable than their sanguine counterparts, and thus have garnered more than their deserved share of notice among historians. Actually, the balance between hope for, and fear of, innovation had been shifting in favor of hope since the early days of the Enlightenment. The argument from tradition, which conservatives had once mobilized with uniform success in earlier days, gradually lost its power to persuade. In 1850, speaking at the Lord Mayor's banquet in London, Prince Albert gave voice to the optimists. "Nobody who has paid any attention to the peculiar features of the present era," he said, "will doubt for a moment that we are living in a period of most wonderful transition, which tends rapidly to accomplish that great end, to which, indeed, all history points—the realization of the unity of mankind." He reminded his listeners that the Great Exhibition, which would serve as a graphic confirmation of the Prince Consort's words, was soon to open, and with it, "knowledge acquired becomes at once the property of the community at large." And thus, "man is approaching a more complete fulfillment of that great and sacred mission he has to perform in this world." To him, as to others disposed to see the cheerful side of change, it seemed almost self-evident that their century was one of continuous and triumphant progress.

And it is true: inventors, engineers, natural scientists made the old fantasy of power over nature, articulated as an ideal by Francis Bacon over two centuries earlier, appear more realistic than ever. The organization of, and striking increase in, the number and functions of governmental institutions, though at first often clumsy and inefficient, aimed at the same goal: to underwrite human control over many of the new problems triggered by urbanization and industrialization. Private entrepreneurs—bankers, merchants, factory owners—built international companies, financed railroad networks, opened that glittering bazaar of Victorian life, the department store. So-called ordinary citizens—at least many of them—also benefited from all this activity. Certainly the impressive improvement in the speed, reliability, and inexpensiveness of communication after the great reform of the mails in the 1840s delighted them as much as it did merchant princes.

All this is easily said: it is necessary to enter the minds of those experiencing these changes. Let one major development of the Victorian age stand for the rest. No nineteenth-century invention can convey more impressively than the railroad the Victorians' vertiginous sense of living through a hailstorm of prodigious transformations in their accustomed ways. Early in 1848, just before the fall of his master, Comte Duchâtel, Louis Philippe's minister of the interior, described his age as one when "things move more quickly than they did sixty years ago. Events, like travelers, move by steam." The railroad proved a triumphant metaphor for this enveloping sense of surprise and insecurity I have mentioned—did it not literally speed up life almost beyond belief? And not just a metaphor; for more and more bourgeois, and for working people as well, it uprooted them from where they lived and how they lived. It radically modernized the transport of goods and people. It ruined some market towns and boosted others. The feeling of having to take in more stimuli than one could readily assimilate—in short, nervousness—was generated as much by that stunning novelty, traveling by train, as anything else.

The humorous hyperbole of Thackeray trying to convey the feeling of just what it was like before the railroad provides a graphic clue to the distance the civilized world had come since the years of Napoleon I. "We who have lived before railways were made," he wrote in 1861, "belong to another world." He granted that gunpowder and printing had "tended to modernize" civilization. But no less a shock, the railroad now "starts the new era." Those who had lived before its advent were antediluvians, "like Father Noah and his family out of the Ark. The children will gather round and say to us patriarchs, 'Tell us, grandpa, about the old world.' And we shall mumble our old stories, and we shall drop off one by one, and there will be fewer and fewer of us, and these very old and feeble." Thackeray is joking, of course, but not only joking.

It is not surprising, in fact characteristic of the time, that the railroad should invade the literary imagination. Anthropomorphism was rampant; the locomotive in particular became a potent, humanlike force. It was a quick and thundering lightning in a poem, "On the Railroad" (1844), by the minor German poet Luise von Plönnies, or a "Fierce-throated beauty" in Walt Whitman's "To a Locomotive in Winter" (1876). Both poets hint, and more than hint, at the erotic energies of the locomotive, energies spelled out more overtly in Jules Claretie's *Le train 17* (1905) whose protagonist, a married man who drives this beauty, is really in love with his engine.

More often, though, and quite as appropriate what with frequent and spectacular lethal accidents on which the press liked to dwell in detail, writers saw the locomotive as a demonic menace. More than one fictional character loses his, or her, life under its wheels. Anna Karenina is only the best known among them; Carker, the villain of Dickens's *Dombey and Son,* is run down and dismembered by a train; and in Zola's *La bête humaine,* a train decapitates two battling characters at the climax of the novel. This is only a small selection. For a massive majority of Victorians, of course, the mundane realities of the railroad—the ease of communication, the glamour of grand terminals, the chance at speculation, the irritations attached to travel, the realities of traveling in first-, second-, or third-class carriages—were closer to their hearts. But the prominence of the railroad in fiction attests that it had come to occupy a dominant place in the Victorian mind. For some decades, in fact, it even claimed its own disease, "railway spine," a disorder causing severe back pains after accidents. One can hardly imagine a tribute to the cultural importance of the railroad greater than this. It made people cheerful much of the time, but anxious no less.

4

WHAT GIVES THE ANXIETIES OF VICTORIAN bourgeois their distinct flavor was their susceptibility to non-rational, indeed far-fetched fears. Among the most striking of these was the hysteria over masturbation, which deserves detailed treatment. For, with its omnipresence and its tenacious popularity, its imperviousness to disconfirming evidence, it documents a superstition of educated nineteenth-century bourgeois they were reluctant to do without. Not surprisingly, Victorian generations did not like to call masturbation, that virtually universal habit, by its name. Rather, they bestowed on it harsh, moralistic labels like "solitary vice" or "self-pollution" or "self-abuse." It seemed somehow right to its small army of "experts" to denounce this largely adolescent entertainment rather than to analyze it.

The Victorians' anxiety over this "impious," "immoral," "filthy" path to solitary pleasures cast a deep shadow over pedagogues and parents alike. By midcentury, a French provincial physician and avid specialist in self-abuse, Dr. J.-B.-D. Demeaux, could report that it afflicted the future French "elite of political, moral, industrial society." Late in the century, German researchers investigating Gymnasium pupils, a student body that in effect excluded the lower orders, estimated the percentage of masturbators among them to be anywhere between 71 and 100 percent—a statistic as alarming in its size as it is amusing in its unwarranted precision.

Like so much else, this nineteenth-century display of anxiety was a legacy from the eighteenth, a disease not so much of the youngsters under fire but of those who fired on them. That highly respected philosophe, Dr. Samuel-Auguste-André-David Tissot, lent his considerable prestige to the demonization of "self-pollution," wresting this imaginary disease from obscure quacks and making it a matter worth being anxious about. Tissot was an enlightened physician, the friend of

Voltaire, and his eminence made his Latin treatise of 1758, which he translated into French the following year—*L'Onanisme*—a notable publishing success. Other translations followed and later editions took its alarmist message into the Victorian era. There was yet another and enlarged edition as late as 1832.

The anti-masturbation crusade hit its stride around this time. A triple alliance—preachers, educators, and doctors—spread the alarming forecast that if self-pollution were not eradicated, a medical and cultural catastrophe was inescapable. Seconded by phrenologists and charlatans, the guardians of social morality wrote monitory manuals, so that by the 1850s and 1860s, the bibliography of righteous publications denouncing self-abuse had swollen into the hundreds across the civilized world. They included, though less frequently, warnings to young women, for they too, it seemed, could fall victim to this secret wickedness. Tracts and treatises differed in their level of dismay and their remedies. Some were literally graphic, reinforcing their message with repellent illustrations, mainly "portraits" of the depraved sinner, his face haggard, his cheeks fallen, his eyes dim, his mouth drooling. Yet, whether relatively moderate or fanatical, all anti-onanism publicists could claim membership in the Victorian family of anxiety.

Most scolders dwelled with almost sadistic relish on the afflictions the habitual masturbator must expect. Tissot's catalogue of symptoms had included boils, pains, diminished mental and physical vigor, and a trio of sexual maladjustments—gonorrhea, impotence, and premature ejaculation—these last three great favorites. His list had been intimidating enough, but it fattened with the decades. Later Jeremiahs, as though intent on outdoing their predecessors, added epilepsy, consumption, hypochondria, and, more devastating still, insanity and death. One American physician, Dr. George R. Calhoun, put it succinctly: "Self-abuse is the most certain road to the grave."

Writers engaged in the sacred mission of keeping the young from a vice only too addictive were sadly aware that mere words could hardly compete with irrepressible sexual urges. "The hopes of heaven,—the fears of hell,—and all the terrible calamities of earth," wrote the Presbyterian divine Sylvester Graham, food reformer and inventor of the cracker that bears his name, "are insufficient to deter from the excesses of sensuality, those who, from their birth, have been regularly educated in the depravity of their appetites and susceptibilities." This confession of helplessness did not keep zealots from continuing to pour out threats, reproaches, appeals to conscience, pleas for self-control. But they also resorted to more aggressive antidotes: hot baths, cold showers, hard mattresses, sensible clothing, long walks, unseasoned food. Strenuous exercise was a general favorite; it was accepted dogma that fatigue was a reliable prophylactic against self-abuse.

Pupils housed in dormitories required special control; doctors recommended, and sometimes applied, ingenious devices like trousers without pockets, toilets without doors, a wooden board placed over the boy's bed dividing his body in the middle, making it hard for itching hands to reach the executive organ of illicit gratification. The most enterprising invented mechanical auxiliaries to support the cause of purity: straitjackets, trusses, handcuffs, or penile rings with little spikes on the inside to make an erection painful. Most barbaric, there were even a few clitoridectomies to control girls who could not control themselves.

Such appalling measures were far from rare among the crusaders. Serving the holy principle of sexual purity and frustrated by their failures to reform ingrained habits, they adopted the high verbal temperature and touted the questionable panacea of extremists. Typically, seasoned campaigners like Dr. Demeaux mobilized the hyperbole that nineteenth-century readers had come to find commonplace. The "scourge" of onanism was already exercising a baleful influence on families, on society, on mankind. Indeed, this "shameful vice has never been so widespread, so deadly as at present." The "subtle libertinism" of self-abuse was producing demoralized young men, their abilities and their intelligence irreparably compromised. When masturbators marry, he concluded, "already exhausted in the prime of life," their children will be sickly, doomed to die prematurely or to a miserable, languishing existence. Onanism is a matter of private parts, but for Dr. Demeaux and his like it was not a private problem.

————

◈ THE PUZZLE WHY PRESUMABLY WELL-INFORMED and rational professional men should have yielded to this collective anxiety attack calls for explanation. The answer lies in a confluence of physiological notions, some of them harking back to Hippocrates, with the contemporary, highly unstable cultural atmosphere. Physicians and those who bowed to their authority saw the human body as endowed with a fixed amount of vital energies. True, these were renewed after some time, but not at the same rate, and the sexual fuel restored itself with worrisome uncertainty.

Tissot had made this point central to his argument. It is exceedingly hard to restore the frequent losses of men's "seminal liquor." His conclusive evidence—conclusive to him, and faithfully repeated by scores of Victorian writers—the lassitude, even exhaustion, that men, and in their own way, women, feel after coitus. This kind of imaginative physiology, which lent undeserved prestige to what was essentially a long-lived myth, afflicted most of the solemn talk about sexual matters in the Victorian era. Its mercantile rhetoric about gains, losses, and expenditures seemed natural to the age.

For those who subscribed to this argument, it followed that men must husband their precious fluid. That ruled out masturbation not only as indefensible from a moral and deplorable from a religious perspective but also physically crippling. Hence, the advisers advised, good health required continence before, and the most moderate expenditure of semen within, marriage. "MATRIMONIAL EXCESS," exclaimed O. S. Fowler in 1846, exhausts the body, enfeebles the mind, impairs the digestion, deranges the brain, causes nauseating diseases, and, if that were not enough, ruins marriage. Fowler was a phrenologist who decorated his name with an unearned medical degree, but his views did not materially differ from the prognoses of genuine physicians.

As I have suggested, the offensive against libertinism, whether practiced in solitude or with a partner, produced an unintended, in many ways unwanted, coalition between secular salesmen of anxiety and their clerical counterparts. This partnership helped to keep the campaign alive even after skeptics late in the century raised inconvenient doubts about all-encompassing assertions drawn from little evidence, dubious evidence, and no evidence at all. A few sensible physicians were beginning to object that the panicmongers had not proved their case. In 1870, the eminent English surgeon Sir James Paget denied that "self-abuse" was responsible for a variety of neurological symptoms. And eleven years later, in his article on "Onanism" published in the *Dictionnaire encyclopédique des sciences médicales*, Dr. Jules Christian declared that he had never observed the slightest ill effects caused by masturbation. But it took decades before common sense began to erase the devil that anxious Victorians had painted on the wall.

After 1900, then, after boasting a run of well over a century, the assault on masturbation began to wane. In 1912, though the panic had largely subsided, Freud could still observe that "the subject of onanism is practically inexhaustible." At the time, psychoanalysts thought "self-abuse" harmful because it induces feelings of guilt and attenuates the desire for other love objects, a mild, arguable objection free of hysteria. Even so, two years later, in the handbook that Robert Baden-Powell, the founder of the Boy Scouts, wrote for his recruits, he bluntly called masturbation "beastliness," the most unmanly of impurities. But it was a rearguard action.

🔳 THE ANTI-MASTURBATION MOVEMENT WAS, AS WE have seen, a symptom of anxiety that pervaded both the profession mainly responsible for it—physicians—and society as a whole. Nineteenth-century medicine was undergoing its own age of anxiety. In country after country, physicians were pushing ahead with the arduous process of making themselves into a profession, with all the stigmata this entails: diplomas, periodicals, conferences, specialties, teaching hospitals. Their self-transformation was of overriding importance to them, because (no less anxiety-generating than the quest for status) it gave them an opportunity to exclude competition—faith healers, sellers of nostrums, saints and holy places favored by the superstitious—by enlisting the support of the state, which would defend their privileges and license their monopoly.

At the same time, nineteenth-century physicians, more than ever, carried on their shoulders the desperate hopes of their patients. It was a time of stunning discoveries in chemistry and biology, and these raised unprecedented expectations, only to be disappointed over and over. The most candid medical practitioners conceded that in the midst of this scientific revolution, their knowledge remained inadequate, their progress uneven. Everywhere, the statistics tell a story of some successes and many failures. In France, between 1801 and 1901, mortality dropped from 27.1 per 1,000 to 20.1; during the same time span, the life expectancy of women rose from thirty-six to forty-six years. But these impressive numbers contrasted starkly with the far slighter gains in infant mortality, which decreased from 190 per 1,000 to 160. In short, French babies, like babies elsewhere, still died in appalling numbers, and so did their mothers. Much had been done for health in the age; far more remained to be done.

It took time, too, for diagnostics to advance much beyond inspired guesswork and combat over speculative theories. At least until Pasteur, France was particularly handicapped by the habit of borrowing from doctrinaire philosophy. But so were physicians in other countries. Rival schools of thought furiously struggled for dominance; hiding behind incompatible technical vocabularies, they had no way of scientifically determining which of them, if any, was right.

Flaubert, the son and brother of a physician, immortalized these bootless battles in his *Dictionary of Accepted Ideas*, sardonically commenting on doctors' ignorance that masqueraded as profound knowledge. His definition of "Stomach" tells us: "all diseases stem from the stomach." And "Humidity: cause of all diseases." To say nothing of good health: "too much health, cause of diseases." Yet, after largely overcoming centuries of distrust, the late nineteenth-century physician became a domestic hero to the bourgeoisie. We see him in amiable paintings, sturdy and bearded, sitting by his patient's bedside, thoughtfully contemplating how to cure the sufferer in his charge. It is perhaps a consequence of their newfound prestige that doctors' panic, and with that the public's panic, about self-abuse began to fade around the same time.

5

—————

▩ ANXIETY ACTIVATES DEFENSES, STRATAGEMS designed to master or to deny it. Victorian anxieties were no exception. But nineteenth-century defensive maneuvers failed as often as they succeeded, producing new anxieties in their turn. The natural response to the sense of disorientation, even chaos, that perpetual innovation is bound to plant is no doubt the reassuring security of order. But, as Victorians were to discover, and their critics liked to exploit, order driven beyond reason makes for rigidity, a stiffness of lip and attitudes, an inability to adapt to unexpected situations, a driven dependence on routine.

Much of the order that Victorians managed to establish grew out of particular needs. The vast growth of organized sports at schools and in public forums called for recognized guidelines—the size of the tennis court, the kinds of permissible blows in boxing, the number of players in a soccer team, and the rest. The work discipline that the demands of efficiency made imperative in factories and offices imposed regular hours of attendance, for managers almost as much as for secretaries or machine operators. The expansion of the railroad network required reliable schedules. In fact, the timetable became as much an emblem of the Victorian as the referee who enforced the rules of the matches he was supervising vigilantly and impartially. In the nineteenth century, as Dr. Beard had already observed, the world was subject to the ideal of punctuality, the insistent demands of schedules, the reminders sounded by clocks.

But for nineteenth-century capitalism, rule-making and rule-observing were more than simply technical devices to keep life going along smoothly. They invaded and shaped character. In *The Protestant Ethic and the Spirit of Capitalism*, a famous pair of still controversial articles published in 1904 and 1905, the great German sociologist Max Weber grimly depicted the character of contemporary entrepreneurs and financiers as dominated by a bleak asceticism. The bourgeoisie, plainly most deeply implicated in this dreary system, he wrote, was caught in an iron cage, compelled to make money not so much for the pleasures this might buy, but for its own sake, from simple internal duress. Rationality could be the most irrational of habits. In a striking phrase, John Stuart Mill damned "the sabbathless pursuit of wealth," and this phrase, more effective than any particular grievance against greedy capitalists, was a lament for their joylessness.

This portrait of the Victorian bourgeoisie took a part for the whole, casualties for the norm, just as Freud had done with his patients. If many bourgeois became victims of their success, to many others success tasted sweet, without bitter aftertaste. Yet these critiques of rationalism gone mad were not without their point. As I have said before: defenses against anxieties had ways of creating new anxieties in their place. That is why, as we turn to the Victorian bourgeois mind, it is interesting that among the maladies that specialists were called on to relieve, obsessive neurosis was the ailment of choice. But it is worth remembering that untold thousands of middle-class Victorians formed their minds without having to consult a psychiatrist.

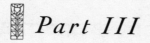

Part III

THE VICTORIAN MIND

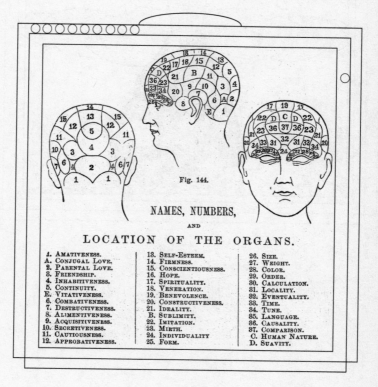

Fig. 144.

NAMES, NUMBERS,

AND

LOCATION OF THE ORGANS.

1. AMATIVENESS.	13. SELF-ESTEEM.	26. SIZE.
A. CONJUGAL LOVE.	14. FIRMNESS.	27. WEIGHT.
2. PARENTAL LOVE.	15. CONSCIENTIOUSNESS.	28. COLOR.
3. FRIENDSHIP.	16. HOPE.	29. ORDER.
4. INHABITIVENESS.	17. SPIRITUALITY.	30. CALCULATION.
5. CONTINUITY.	18. VENERATION.	31. LOCALITY.
E. VITATIVENESS.	19. BENEVOLENCE.	32. EVENTUALITY.
6. COMBATIVENESS.	20. CONSTRUCTIVENESS.	33. TIME.
7. DESTRUCTIVENESS.	21. IDEALITY.	34. TUNE.
8. ALIMENTIVENESS.	B. SUBLIMITY.	35. LANGUAGE.
9. ACQUISITIVENESS.	22. IMITATION.	36. CAUSALITY.
10. SECRETIVENESS.	23. MIRTH.	37. COMPARISON.
11. CAUTIOUSNESS.	24. INDIVIDUALITY	C. HUMAN NATURE.
12. APPROBATIVENESS.	25. FORM.	D. SUAVITY.

An die Sittlichkeitsprediger in Köln am Rheine

Six

Obituaries and Revivals

1

—————

☙ "I UNDERSTAND MURDER, BUT NOT PIETY." THUS Arthur Schnitzler in his diary on March 21, 1902. He was by then a seasoned author with a professional's sensitivity for the subtle varieties of human experience. But he had no ear for transcendence. In late adolescence, between eighteen and twenty, he brooded briefly on eternal questions, but soon graduated to a worldliness that had no need for such reflections. Soon after, he settled into agnosticism and denied that there could be a true materialist or atheist. Whoever claims to get "beyond the bounds of a thinking human being," he wrote, is simply "blathering, sanctimonious, lying, or mad." But that reservation did not imply that religion played any appreciable role in Schnitzler's life and work.

On the rare occasions when he raided the sacred precincts for metaphors, he was making a secular point. Reflecting on the aged Goethe completing the second part of *Faust* just before his death, he wondered: "How does that make you feel! I will say nothing about genius, but his ethos! What piety in the highest sense of the word! To do your daily work at eighty-two as though you were twenty!—These are the deepest contrasts: piety and hypochondria." Since being a victim of hypochondria was one of Schnitzler's most persistent self-reproaches, this was a weighty tribute to piety. But he was only showing his admiration for that most bourgeois of virtues: the gospel of work.

Schnitzler came by his irreligion honestly, at home. The little sermon his father had preached to him after going through his diary was a purely prudential lecture. There was not a hint in that homily of possible divine retribution or, for that matter, of confessional obligations. The only member in Schnitzler's sizable clan who was at all devout was his maternal grandmother. It was for her sake that the family continued to observe the Jewish high holidays even after her death. But that was a wholly non-religious piety: a way of showing respect for a favorite matriarch. Schnitzler described her with only a touch of condescension as an "educated bourgeoise," an intelligent and competent *Hausfrau*, "the most devoted and patient wife to a somewhat problematic husband and a loving and beloved mother to her numerous children."

Dr. Johann Schnitzler's formal pronouncements are drenched in this secular humanism. In 1884, when he was appointed director of the Allgemeine Polyclinic in Vienna, he laid down his profession of faith: "A physician's religion is humaneness—that is, love of humanity without regard to wealth or poverty, without distinction of nationality or confession. Therefore, wherever national chauvinism and religious fanaticism predominate, he must stand and work as an apostle of humanity—in behalf of peace among nations and human fraternity. Whoever does not think this way, whoever does not feel this way, is not a true, not an authentic physician." His son, though he doubtless would have tamed the pathos, would have endorsed these views.

SO WOULD MANY OTHERS. THE SCHNITZLERS, father and son, shared the secularism of a sizable and, it seemed, growing bourgeois faction across Europe and the United States: heirs of the ideals of French revolutionaries, scientifically disposed agnostics in Britain, disciples of such heterodox philosophers of religion as Ludwig Feuerbach in Germany, Roman Catholic members of Freemasonic lodges, doubters and scoffers everywhere—all writing off conventional faiths, no matter how modest their conduits to God, as survivals from a more credulous past. They thought religion on the defensive and, they dared to hope, dying. The spectacular, irresistible string of discoveries announced by physicists, chemists, biologists, astronomers, and geologists almost year by year which challenged the origins of mankind as laid down in scriptures, and the intense anti-clericalism of working-class radicals, left an indelible impress on Victorian culture. So did the German higher criticism, soon exported to the rest of the civilized world, a criticism that read sacred texts with a skeptical eye and picked them apart as all too human creations. No wonder that nineteenth-century secularists were bursting with confidence—for a time.

The last of these buttresses for secularism, the scientific study of the Bible, is of particular interest for a history of the Victorian bourgeoisie, for it addressed itself directly, and only, to the educated. The impious idea that Holy Scripture is a book like any other, subject to critical examination like any other, was a legacy from the two previous centuries. A handful of rigorous seventeenth-century thinkers—with Spinoza, Hobbes, and Bayle only the most eminent—led the way toward skepticism with their contention that the Bible should enjoy no special privileges when it came to examining its text. This demand, extended to all matters, became a principal ideal for the Enlightenment. "Everything must be examined," wrote Diderot, "everything must be shaken up, without exception and without circumspection." In 1879, in *Some Mistakes of Moses*, Robert Ingersoll, the celebrated American orator, the "Great Agnostic" who took his message across the country in defiant speeches and wrote emphatic sermons about his freethinking, sounded precisely like Diderot: "Until every soul is freely permitted to investigate every book, and creed, and dogma for itself, the world cannot be free." The Enlightenment was alive and well in Victorian times.

That eighteenth century had been nudged toward an anti-Christian mind-set and a more naturalistic theology—and this, too, would reach the Victorian age undimmed — by the small but widely read company of deists. Their God was a beneficent creator who had established the laws of nature and of morality, but who never interfered with his creation, stepping back to let nature and humans go their own way; hence all tales of miracles must be impostures. And they saw it as their assignment to torment Christians with impertinent commentaries. Their amusing but pointed challenges to the pious were never merely jokes; they were seditious political statements in an age when casting doubt on the doctrines of the ruling religion was no laughing matter. How was it that the Pentateuch, ostensibly written by Moses, records his death? Why does St. Matthew give a genealogy for Jesus Christ that differs from the one offered by St. Luke if the New Testament, like the Old, is divinely inspired and hence free of contradictions? I have taken these examples from Voltaire's *Dictionnaire philosophique* of 1762. His wicked little book proffered many such instances, and his spirited shafts, like his reputation as a wit and a humanitarian, survived into the Victorian era. "When the right sense of historical proportion is more fully developed in men's minds" — with this ringing sentence John Morley opened his biography of 1872 — "the name of Voltaire will stand out like the names of the great decisive movements in the European advance, like the Revival of Learning, or the Reformation."

Voltaire's attempt to discredit Christianity by making it ridiculous (as well as showing it up as the source of persecutions and wars) was supplemented in the nineteenth century by erudite efforts to make it intellectually untenable. Probably the most offensive of these was David Friedrich Strauss's *Life of Jesus, Critically Examined*, published in two volumes in 1835 and 1836. Its history and that of its author make for an instructive story. Strauss was a learned German theologian and philosopher who in 1833 resigned an academic post at the University of Tübingen to devote himself to his radical *Life*. More than a biography, it was, as one German historian has put it, an earthquake. Significantly, Strauss titled his book a life of Jesus, not of Christ. In his reading, the authors of the New Testament had been men of their time, with all its credulity, all its proclivity to substitute myths for facts. Hence, given their disregard for sober truth, their inconsistencies and contradictions—and the New Testament, Strauss showed, was rife in both—did not trouble them. The Christ that good Christians worshipped, then, was a product of collective nostalgia, nothing more.

The result: literally dozens of polemical assaults on Strauss, the author's vigorous responses to his critics, and, by 1840, a fourth edition. Four years later a brilliant young Englishwoman, Mary Ann Evans, far better known as George Eliot, began to translate the text into English. It took her two years, for it was a difficult book, even to readers whose first language was German. By that time, Strauss's career had taken a dramatic turn. In 1839, he had been appointed to a chair in theology at the University of Zurich. Yet local indignation against this disciple of Satan was so strong that the canton decided to pension him off before he had even started to lecture. But, as usually happens with such craven peace offerings, this did not appease anyone, and amidst street violence—there were fifteen dead—the liberal government was compelled to give way to its conservative rivals. Strauss went back to writing books, mainly biographies. In 1864 he returned to Jesus with a popular life, which, in four decades, went through thirteen editions. Then, in 1872, two years before his death, in his last book, *The Old and the New Faith*, he took the consequences of his apostasy: he declared himself a materialist and a follower of Darwin and announced that he was no longer a Christian. For this scholar, at least, the clash between science and religion had become clear-cut.

Another ground of optimism for unbelievers, almost of complacency, was that through the long nineteenth century, many states abandoned, or pulled back partway from, sponsoring a single denomination as the official religion. This was not in itself a secularizing policy, but it betrayed a willingness to accept members of other faiths as good citizens, a stance that could only please the anti-clerical body of opinion. Great Britain retained the Anglican Church as the state religion, but in 1829, with what was called "Catholic Emancipation," Roman Catholics could enter Parliament, and in 1858, with the passing of the Jewish Disabilities Bill, British Jews were granted the same rights. In nineteenth-century France, with its turbulent history, the relations of church and state naturally reflected whatever régime happened to be in power, and underwent repeated drastic shifts, until in 1905, republican anti-clericals scored their greatest triumph: the formal separation of church and state. Elsewhere, too, citizenship was increasingly uncoupled from religious professions, at least in law; social or economic discrimination on denominational grounds, virtually impossible to cure through legislation, retained much of its power. The United States, of course, had built the separation of church and state into its Constitution with the First Amendment, even though a few established churches survived in some states to the 1820s. But it says much about public attitudes that no Roman Catholic was elected president until 1960.

At the same time, as Schnitzler's multinational empire attests, none of these moves guaranteed religious amity, or even the most basic courtesies. Mutual acrimony among Austria-Hungary's nationalities was exacerbated by sectarian hatreds, most rancorously from the 1880s, we know, by anti-Semitism. In March 1898, Mark Twain reported in *Harper's New Monthly Magazine* on an unseemly parliamentary session in Vienna that would have embarrassed the crudest of American politicians. The deputies shouted at one another, screamed insults, refused to obey the chair's call for order, until the police entered the hall and dragged away the most vociferous of the legislators. Trying to explain this turmoil to his American readers, Mark Twain noted that the 425 members of parliament represented eleven languages, which meant "eleven distinct varieties of jealousies, hostilities and warring interests" and numerous political parties. They come from all walks of life, he added, and "are religious men; they are earnest, sincere, devoted; and they hate the Jews." But, we recall, many Austrians—including Schnitzler, then in his thirties—could remember times when confessional passions had been at a relatively low ebb. In the Victorian century, intervals of open-mindedness alternated with severe setbacks.

2

❧ THE PREDICTIONS OF ANTI-CLERICALS ABOUT THE progress of secularization naturally followed the ballot box, but not wholly. Late in 1843, Karl Marx had already stated rather too confidently, "for Germany, the *criticism of religion* has been largely completed." By the 1860s and 1870s, the theory of godless evolution was starting to persuade a mounting minority of Victorians—it long remained a minority—that they need not invoke a deity to explain the wonders of nature and the gamut of human possibilities. Around the turn of the century, as Nietzsche's fame spread with stunning rapidity even—perhaps especially—among those who knew only some quotable bits from his writings, there was much brave talk about the death of God. Around 1908, Thomas Hardy could write a solemn poem on God's funeral. But these obituaries were premature. The age of Darwin was also the age of Pope Pius IX; talk of nature red in tooth and claw coexisted, however uneasily, with pilgrimages of the faithful to places sanctified by the appearance of the Virgin Mary. The public manifestations of religion—parochial schools, church building, political action, debates over doctrines and observances—were supremely contentious presences across the Victorian cultural landscape, ranging from minor skirmishes to pitched battles.

To the most intractable partisans among contemporaries, this martial rhetoric seemed perfectly apposite; they saw these clashes as nothing less than a war to the death between science and superstition, or, as enthusiasts for the other extreme preferred to put it, between saving belief and diabolical atheism. But as usual, the situation was more complicated than the extremists would admit: one could be anti-clerical without being an outright unbeliever. In France, Léon Gambetta, a founder of the Third Republic, was hospitable to both groups when he exclaimed: "*Le cléricalisme, voilà l'ennemi.*"

There has been much wry comment about the naïveté of historians who have taken the image of the warfare between science and religion literally to describe a long-lived, straightforward social conflict, particularly heated in the nineteenth century. And in fact, the lines between the combatants were often blurred. The worship of Nature, for one, was hard to classify—was it a genuine surrogate faith, a new religion, or a tepid evasion for those brave enough to desert the denomination they had been born with but not brave enough to shed all belief? To the

few detached observers the hostile camps presented a confusing spectacle, with interweaving fronts, incongruous alliances, abrupt shifts of
doctrinal commitments, unyielding obstinacy alternating with politic
compromise. The components making up an individual's religious sentiments were often ill assorted, inconsistent, in part lodged beneath the
level of awareness. They could be a matter of habit more than of
authentic feeling, a family tradition rather than an earnest decision for
God. No summary description could hope to capture more than an inti-
mation of this ever-shifting compound of faith and doubt. In 1906, the
conservative French literary critic Emile Faguet claimed Nietzsche as
his authority for saying in the same sentence that the French are essentially religious and essentially irreligious. This is not very helpful, but it
conveys the widespread air of bafflement.

Amidst all this confusion, the party of science, the Schnitzlers' party,
seemed to be making inroads on its enemy's territory. The most articulate detractors of religion were given to quotable aphorisms that grew
into political slogans. Nietzsche made it a central theme in his work
that Judaism and Christianity were gigantic frauds successfully perpetrated by the weak upon the strong almost two thousand years before,
frauds that still haunted the nineteenth century. Freud was just as lapidary; to him all religion was essentially a collective neurosis, the product of the child's fear of the father and of its craving to propitiate him
translated onto a larger stage—a proceeding, to Freud's mind, unwor-
thy of grown men and women. Sir James Frazer, whose *Golden Bough*,
first published in 1890, did more to popularize cultural anthropology
than any other text, announced flatly that the study of religion must
lead to the conclusion that its rituals and beliefs are "false and foolish."
It should have surprised no one that the response of publishing divines
and virtuous churchgoers to such provocations was so vehement.

To confound matters further, for many Christians, the aesthetic element in piety made professions of faith agreeable and undemanding. In
1802, François-René de Chateaubriand, an aristocrat with a vast middle-class following, sought to win assent to the truths of Catholicism
with his best-selling *Genius of Christianity* by dwelling on the colorful
splendor of the church. The dramatic expressions of religion—the

mass, the liturgy, fervently intoned hymns—became so many forensic weapons in his hands. Chateaubriand maintained that the Bible is a more enjoyable as well as a more elevating text than the *Odyssey*. For him and many of his admirers, Christianity was not beautiful because it was true, but true because it was beautiful.

Half a century later, in 1857, in *Madame Bovary*, Gustave Flaubert vividly evoked the sensual self-intoxication that could pass for religion by following the imaginative flights of his young, susceptible, doomed heroine. Boarding in a convent run by kindly nuns, Emma Rouault, as she then was, "gently succumbed to the mystical languor induced by the perfumes of the altar, the coolness of the holy-water fonts, the gleaming of the candles" and the "holy pictures with their sky-blue borders." She luxuriated in her aroused senses, making suggestive pictures for herself rather than carefully listening to the religious message of the mass. "The metaphors consistently used in sermons—'betrothed,' 'spouse,' 'heavenly lover,' 'mystical marriage,'—excited her in a thrilling new way." This appeal to the emotions was not a monopoly of Roman Catholic worship, nor did it necessarily descend to a barely concealed sexual level. Wesleyan Methodists, for one, joyfully responded to visits by charismatic preachers. "The real spirit of the age," wrote the English journalist Thomas Cooper in 1837, was a "prevailing thirst for religious novelty and variety," the kind of excitement that a star among sermonizers could provide. Attendance could double or triple on a Sunday when he made his appearance.

Flaubert does not mention music, but to Dissenters in Britain, Lutherans in Germany, and Protestants elsewhere, church choirs and organs could lift the congregants' minds to higher thoughts and fortify a sense of harmony with their fellow worshippers. Hymns composed in the Victorian age, added to the rich harvest of musical offerings written earlier, attest to the sustained vigor of a religiosity in which aesthetic sentiments played a privileged role, even as this raised questions whether lustily joining in the choir necessarily had anything religious about it. Nineteenth-century anti-clerical writers like Heinrich Heine regularly berated Christianity for its asceticism, for its hostility to the body and to free sexuality. Not without good reason. Yet a good deal of religious faith had its unconscious dimension, and believers for whom feelings dictated their formal allegiances were sure enough of their piety to hold that theology was best left to theologians.

In short, as we shall see again, not all the pious were equally devout, not all the unbelievers equally irreverent. Anatole France was more than half serious when he observed that Catholicism is the most acceptable form of religious indifference. Moreover, piety was selective, varying with particular denominations, class, and location. Sincere belief was compatible with a wide range of political attitudes: most devout Lutherans were known for their passivity before authority, many devout Unitarians for their public spirit. Often, men and women responded differently to the appeal of faith: in 1897 at Lourdes, that unrivaled spa for believers suffering from diseases that only prayer could cure, a procession of people miraculously restored to health—the *miraculés*—consisted of a hundred seventeen women and only ten men among the attested cases. This striking imbalance had substantial political repercussions. Late in the century, when feminists were increasingly active in demanding the suffrage, left-wing politicians in countries with strong Catholic parties like France or Italy, who could have been expected to be sympathetic to their cause, vehemently opposed it on the ground that women were too much in thrall to their priests and thus likely to vote wrong, that is to say, conservative.

Despite all these complications, the polemical literature on all sides strongly suggests that a solid majority of Victorians suspected that, whether they liked this or not, they were witnessing a struggle with no prisoners taken. This very suspicion acted as a self-fulfilling prophecy. Alban Stolz, a prolific German Catholic controversialist who specialized in forceful tracts and almanacs, could lump together his adversaries under the convenient umbrella of "Protestant Jews." And, also in Germany, a liberal Protestant author labeled strict believers of whose rigidity he disapproved "Protestant Jesuits." In the eyes of militants, the Others were enemies, and most of them looked alike. Not all of them: toward the end of the century, the Evangelical Consistory of Westphalia commented that among the Catholics in their region, anti-Protestant sentiment was more pronounced than anti-Semitism. Students of modern Jew-hatred have often forgotten that the loathing of Christian for Christian could be even more absorbing, even more enjoyable, than that for Jews.

The most unrestrained religious detestation in the Victorian age, then, seems to have played out between Protestants and Catholics. It flared up in historic events, like the anti-Roman Catholic *Kulturkampf* that Bismarck launched in 1871 and sustained for half a decade. With this aggressive Protestant, largely Prussian move against Catholic majorities in western and southern Germany, understandable (if hardly commendable) in his fledgling Reich, he sought to cement the allegiances of Germans by proceeding against those who, he alleged, were as loyal to their pope as to their kaiser. It was a policy in which religious and political issues were wholly intertwined. In everyday life, too, dominant majorities practiced the politics of exclusion: chicanery, social ostracism, favoritism to one's own. To give but a single instance, in 1863 James Bromfield, an English Protestant who had lived in Brittany for years and written about it extensively, protested angrily against the bigoted mind-set and official regulations of local administrators. In one *département*, the Bible was not allowed to circulate at all; elsewhere its circulation was tightly controlled. Most books and pamphlets advocating Protestantism could not be published. Attempts to open Protestant schools were doomed to failure. "Romanism alone was flourishing, and its professors triumphant and smiling." This was carrying on the religious warfare of earlier centuries by less lethal means.

The proposition that the Victorian age was a period of secularization, almost universally credited at the time, therefore requires the historian to draw some careful distinctions. The road from Damascus, which could be as shattering an experience as the blinding epiphany of discovering God, did not proceed in a straight line and could not be traveled at a uniform speed. The classic autobiography of the prolific English literary critic and historian Edmund Gosse, *Father and Son*, published in 1907, is often rightly cited as a lucid, touching demonstration just how painful it could be to free oneself from one's parents' piety, in this case a stern Protestant cult, the Plymouth Brethren. And the century was rife with reversals of direction, with inner missions and revivals recapturing souls for Christ, events that expose the obituaries to God to be largely wishful thinking.

There were many sensitive and straightforward Victorians who tortured themselves for years as they wavered between what they thought equally cogent reasons for believing and for not believing. Herman Melville was one of them. In the fall of 1857, he stayed with his friend Nathaniel Hawthorne for some days; the two took long walks, smoked cigars, and canvassed intractable issues including the immortality of the soul. Melville, Hawthorne observed in his journal, "will never rest until he gets hold of a definite belief. It is strange how he persists—and has persisted ever since I knew him, and probably long before—in wandering to-and-fro over these deserts, as dismal and monotonous as the sand hills among which we were sitting. He can neither believe, nor be comfortable in his unbelief; and he is too honest and courageous not to try to do one or the other."

In short, not all unbelievers were quite so confident as Marx had been that the battle against faith had largely been won. In 1879, a French secularist, Raoul Rosières, called for scholars, who had already "*deroyalized*" the history of the church, to "*declericalize*" it, a call to arms implicitly conceding that religion still had too much power over people's hearts. Nor did Nietzsche, for all his resounding assertion that God was dead, really quite believe that; if he had, he would not have thundered against religion quite so often and so energetically. In the 1890s, by no means pleased with the esoteric beliefs that were once more growing fashionable, Abraham Kuyper, a leader of the orthodox Calvinists in the Netherlands, observed, "Hardly a century after the once glittering tinsel of Rationalism, now that materialism is sounding a retreat in the ranks of science, a kind of hollow piety is again exercising its enticing charms, and every day it is becoming more fashionable to take a plunge into the warm stream of mysticism." The census of 1899 showed that precisely 115,179 Dutch men and women confessed themselves to be either agnostics or atheists, a mere 2.25 percent of the population. The actual numbers of unbelievers was certainly larger than this, and it is true too that in twenty years they had multiplied tenfold. But the totals were scarcely impressive. This is what Emile Durkheim had in mind when he grumbled in 1895 about "these times of renascent mysticism," and included his own country in his bleak survey.

Durkheim did not toss out this observation casually. From the 1880s, a notable number of French novelists and poets, by their very vocation only too willing to share their religious pilgrimage with the public, converted, or intensified their commitment, to Catholicism. Paul Bourget, at first known for his perceptive essays on modern psychology—Schnitzler read him with interest—turned devout as he came to reject the positivism of his early career, and celebrated his newfound piety in 1889 with his best-known novel, *Le disciple*. Paul Claudel, converted as a young man, made the religious agitation of his youth followed by serene certainty the leading theme of his dramas. Léon Bloy, novelist and journalist, was another youthful convert who poured his life's experience into his fiction. And Joris-Karl Huysmans, probably still the most widely read of this group, started out worshiping Nature, moved on to aestheticism, diabolism, and spiritualism, before he too fled to the embrace of the Catholic Church. The poet Charles Péguy belongs in this catalogue. Like so many others, he came to Catholicism from atheism.

The religious history of these French writers was not an isolated phenomenon. It was shared by publicists of a conservative, royalist, often anti-Semitic cast of mind. Yet this move to the right was countered by an even stronger campaign for secularism, at least toward anti-clericalism. While poets, novelists, and political journalists celebrated their religious clarity, radical politicians steered France gradually to a break with the Vatican. On balance, the forces of unbelief, at least of anti-clericalism, seemed to have the upper hand by the last decades of the nineteenth century. Yet like that of love, the course of what Max Weber, with Durkheim the founder of modern sociology, called the disenchantment of the world—the cessation of reliance on magical powers that transcend natural laws—never ran smooth.

3

IT WAS THE GERMAN ROMANTICS WHO, EARLY IN the nineteenth century, first mounted a large-scale mission to undo that disenchantment. By their lights, the philosophes—Voltaire, Hume,

Gibbon, Diderot, and the rest of that impious gang—had taken the poetry out of life with their propaganda in behalf of amoral science, pagan notions of virtue, indefensible calls for toleration, and sly insults to church history, to saints, to God himself. To hear these re-enchanters speak, the men and women of the Enlightenment had dealt religion the gravest injustice; they held them responsible for all the evils the world had suffered since. The dire results were inscribed in recent history: the atheistic French Revolution and a calamitous retreat of true faith from the center of life to its periphery.

This hostile reading of the enlightened mind in action gave Romantics their political agenda. In the words of the influential German literary historian and theorist August Wilhelm Schlegel, the "process of depoeticization has lasted long enough; it is high time that air, fire, water, earth be poeticized once again." The Enlightenment's aggression against poetry meant, to the German Romantics, something far more severe than an assault on the pleasures of verse, though it was also that. It had meant to make life prosaic, which was to rob it of the truths, the consolations, the miraculous saving grace of religion. The German Romantic painter Philipp Otto Runge, as fluent with his pen as with his brush, thought it "a shame how many splendid human beings have had to succumb to the miserable mentality of the so-called Enlightenment and philosophy." Such laments spoke to millions seeking certainty in a world changing before their eyes. And obviously the crusade to re-enchant the world—to turn back the clock, as they said in the nineteenth century—greatly impeded whatever progress unbelief was making.

🏵 LIKE POLEMICISTS EVERYWHERE, THESE Romantics overstated their case, overstated the irreligion of their adversaries and the originality of their crusade. Many of the subversive philosophes, Voltaire and Rousseau most famous among them, were deists, with their absent god, which made them anti-clericals but not atheists. In the other camp, important eighteenth-century writers like

Alexander Pope and Jonathan Swift, far from renouncing their Christian beliefs, did the work of the Enlightenment by inveighing against religious "enthusiasm," the undisciplined expressiveness of excited churchgoers. And the critic and playwright Gotthold Ephraim Lessing, Germany's most eminent Enlightenment figure before Kant, went so far as to construct a reasonable religion of his own. The same unhistorical amnesia that made the German Romantics overlook the remnants of religion in the Enlightenment also made them neglect the roots of their movement in the eighteenth century, notably the rise of humane sensibility and the emergence of the imagination as a prized human endowment, to say nothing of the cult of poetry. Even the most notorious anti-clerical writer of the age, Voltaire, openly professed his admiration for the poetic vision. And the Unitarians, at their strongest in England, were enlightened men and women and at the same time good Christians by their lights.

These finer points were lost in the thrill of nineteenth-century cultural feuds. Again and again, the anti-religious writings of controversialists or the secularizing acts of governments brought visceral responses from the faithful. It was at such times, having been put on the defensive, that loyal Christians would rally and temporarily bury their interdenominational tensions. Yet revivals of religious passions were accompanied by sharpening frictions within or among closely related confessions. They confirm Freud's thesis about the narcissism of minor differences: to strict sectarians, those in their theological neighborhood, those closest to their own treasured commitments, were particularly open to their irritation and their suspicions. Clashes between Orthodox and liberal Jews, Calvinist and Lutheran Protestants, English High and Low churchmen, confronted one another with emotions that had flagged in more torpid periods. They produced visible displays of adherence to a faith now apparently at serious risk, demonstrations whether spontaneous or organized by clerical authorities, strenuous campaigns to save one's faithless fellow citizens, collisions in the press or the learned literature that generated public attention and brought more of the faithful to churches than ever. In short, hostile action provoked hostile reaction on stages small and large. Though love thy neighbor—which is to say all of humanity including one's enemies—was a supreme Christian duty first enunciated by Jesus himself, hate thy neighbor remained a pervasive fact of nineteenth-century religious life.

THE CAMP OF THE UNORTHODOX WAS JUST AS crowded and just as quarrelsome. With the spread of skepticism and with mounting opportunities to construct one's own faith, the Victorian age became a paradise for imaginative individualists. In May 1868, Charles Augustin Sainte-Beuve, France's most eminent literary critic, speaking in the Senate, issued a shrewd reminder that there was "another great diocese" in addition to the Christian one, "with no fixed boundaries, extending over the whole of France and over the whole world." It was steadily enlarging its numbers and solidifying its power. Its members were "in various stages of emancipation, but all in agree-ment on one point—that above all else they must be freed from an absolute authority and a blind submission—which counts in their thou-sands deists and adherents of spiritual philosophies, disciples of natural religion, pantheists, positivists, realists, skeptics and seekers of every kind, the devotees of common sense and the followers of pure science." Like its religious counterpart, it was irreparably split into mutually dis-trustful camps, and made common cause only if its very existence seemed to be in danger.

Sainte-Beuve's other great diocese was, as he noted, a gather-all of the most diverse thoughts and fantasies, notable for its controversies and instability. But it deserves a special place in a study of bourgeois religiosity in the Victorian years because middle-class sectarians were at home, and in leading positions, in virtually every creed. Not that bourgeois deserted the dominant denominations in droves—they did not. On the other hand, outright atheists had numerous middle-class supporters, though many unbelievers, much like Schnitzler, apparently preferred the less doctrinaire, more modest stance of agnosticism. T. H. Huxley, Darwin's most dependable, most effective partisan and a dis-tinguished zoologist in his own right, coined the term, with its felicitous mixture of devotion to experience and experiment on the one hand and respect for unsolved and unsolvable mysteries on the other. It proved to be a welcome refuge for savants and intellectuals. "Understand that all the younger men of science whom I know intimately are *essentially* of my way of thinking," Huxley wrote in 1869 in a much-quoted letter to Charles Kingsley, who had attempted to convert him to the Christian doctrine of immortality, as Huxley was grieving over the death of his young son—in vain. "Sit down before fact as a little child," he replied. He could not accept Christian consolation, but he was not an atheist.

Among the prominent sects in Sainte-Beuve's other great diocese, the Saint-Simonians were, for all their unconventional, often eccentric views on love, women, and religious leadership, the most bourgeois and, in the end, the most influential. They were also the most paradoxical. Their founder and principal inspiration was the comte de Saint-Simon, who died in 1825 after an adventurous life including years in support of the French Revolution. His doctrine, expounded in a series of publications and constantly revised by his successors after his death, gratified diverse tastes with its agenda of bringing religion up to date, its radical feminism, above all its affinity for Carlyle's captains of industry. His own epitome, called *The New Christianity*, published in the year of his death, had nothing to do with Christianity; even the Saint-Simonian gospel of love, preached by his successor, Barthélemy Prosper Enfantin, was thoroughly pagan, calling as it did for the rehabilitation of the body. Enfantin, an engineer with electrifying powers over his audiences, came to see himself as a messiah divinely appointed to preside over, and reformulate, the Master's church. During his lifetime and after his death, Saint-Simon attracted an impressive and varied group of disciples: the authoritative literary critic Sainte-Beuve, the passionately political poet Heinrich Heine, the philosopher and political thinker John Stuart Mill, the sociologist Auguste Comte, who had been Saint-Simon's secretary, and other later luminaries who all went through a Saint-Simonian apprenticeship and then went their own way.

Yet Saint-Simon's advocacy of a kind of scientific capitalism left its mark on practical men, on bankers and financiers close to the seats of power, like the Péreire brothers. The Suez Canal, built by Ferdinand de Lesseps, was a Saint-Simonian legacy; many decades earlier, the founder himself had presciently proposed the construction of a canal joining the Atlantic and Pacific oceans. With all its extravagances and absurdities, the Saint-Simonian program, which incorporated economic and industrial progress in its articles of faith, was a rationalist religion—a capitalist-bourgeois Christianity without Christ.

AS THE FORCES OF MODERNITY, THEN—SCIENCE, politics, scholarship, philosophy, technology—put mounting pressure on traditional churches, the nineteenth century became a spawning ground for new paths to salvation. Few of them were as closely attached to the mundane industrializing society as Saint-Simonianism; rather, they were exceedingly bold in promising their recruits not only happiness in this world but also eternal bliss in the next. Christianity's loss was not always the unbelievers' gain. Strange faiths, like the Nordic cults fostered by Wagner's Bayreuth, found some vocal backers; Houston Stewart Chamberlain, a transplanted Englishman who became Wagner's son-in-law, propagated the notion of an Aryan Jesus. The founder of Theosophy, Madame Blavatsky, dictatorial, omniscient, believable to those inclined to believe—W. B. Yeats was her most celebrated disciple—advertised her "secret doctrine" as nothing less than a synthesis of science, religion, and philosophy. Noteworthy in her grandiose claim was the inclusion of science, a wry tribute to the prestige of physicists and biologists. The terse self-description of Mary Baker Eddy's Christian Science, a brilliant campaign slogan, was quite as clear-headed about the drift of the times toward the scientific outlook.

Pugnacious atheists like Freud regarded the name of her faith as a blatant oxymoron. But not all Victorians were so sure. Mark Twain, who had written against Mrs. Eddy, wryly admired her business acumen but nothing else; in 1909, a year before his death, he told a Scottish correspondent, obviously one of her followers: "You say you have 500 in Glasgow. Fifty years from now, your posterity will not count them by the hundred but by the thousand. I feel absolutely sure of this." He predicted better than he knew: for all the contempt of unbelievers, all the thundering anathemas of popes, Calvinist preachers, or Anglican archbishops against these so-called religions, they would flourish by the many thousands.

The reasons for this outpouring of alternatives are almost self-evident and were much discussed at the time. They are encapsulated in the name of spiritualism, the most widely disseminated of the new dispensations, evoking an ancient pedigree. Sizable numbers of Victorians who could no longer faithfully support the teachings of their churches, finding them incredible on logical, historical, or moral grounds, were quite as unwilling to substitute for them what they disparaged as the icy, literally inhuman dogmas of science. For them, materialism (which, not unjustly, they treated as synonymous with atheism) failed to provide them with consolation in times of stress and bereavement, explanations for cosmic conundrums, support in ethical dilemmas, and the emotional gratifications that had made time-honored rituals, prayers, and hymns so welcome a part of their lives.

The teachings of materialists, they charged, reduced the universe and mankind alike to a collocation of lifeless atoms with no room for the soul and the spiritual dimension that alone makes humans human. Nor could materialists provide the comforting sense of community that established denominations took for granted. Good Catholics, good Protestants, good Jews celebrated and mourned together and sanctified joyous and tragic events; materialists had nothing better than to contemplate the vast starry emptiness—alone. Surely, something spiritual must be an essential ingredient in any system of thought that does justice to legitimate human needs and longings. In 1884, S. C. Hall, a fervent Irish Protestant spiritualist who, with his equally devout wife, held séances in their house, proclaimed, speaking of his cause, "I believe that as it *now* exists, it has mainly but one purpose—TO CONFUTE AND DESTROY MATERIALISM, by supplying sure and certain and *palpable* evidence that to every human being God gives a soul which he ordains shall not perish when the body dies."

The house of spiritualism had many mansions, and the internecine

disputes of their votaries at times rose to the acrimony of family quarrels. European practitioners even turned to fashionable anti-
Americanism to differentiate their own "higher" version of the faith
from naive "history-less America." Carl Kiesewetter, a German historian of "occultism"—by which he basically meant spiritualism—noted
that spiritualists in the New World relied on the "most fatuous reflections, 'explanations,' and 'philosophies.'" And since Americans "possess
neither scientific nor any other kind of conservatism, they are open to
everything that is new." The one advantage of such mindlessness, he
thought, was that Americans were far more practical than "Germans,
who are superior to them in knowledge and conscientiousness." The
historian must grant that American spiritualists, many of whom flourished in upstate New York, home of spectacular nineteenth-century
revivals, were responsible for pamphlets of embarrassing inanity.
Andrew Jack Davis, born in Blooming Grove, New York, one of
Kiesewetter's targets, a mesmerist, somnambulist, and clairvoyant,
claimed among other accomplishments to know the contents of books
he had not read. Fellow enthusiasts expended endless hours listening
for uncanny and inexplicable noises in house after house, and presented a sympathetic public with painstaking "proofs" for the reality of
these supernatural sounds. But Americans could have countered that
snobbish Europeans had overlooked English, French, German, Italian
spiritualists and others elsewhere who credulously reported séances
about ghosts rapping out messages and tables moving with a purpose of
their own, many of them no more sophisticated than those thrown on
the marketplace of religion by their despised American colleagues.

What united the discordant and ungenerous spiritualist family was its
unquestioning belief in immortality, and in the possibility of establishing contact with those who had passed over. Séances depending on the
intercession of a medium that conveyed messages from the dead were
the signature of spiritualists whatever their position on Christian dogmas. In what appears as an involuntary parody of scientists' principled
reliance on facts, spiritualists, too, were constantly parading facts. In
her book of reminiscences about her brother, the German physician,
poet, and spiritualist Justinus Kerner, Marie Niethammer noted that

those who thought that Kerner's investigations into ghostly appearances had compelled his imagination into belief were very much mistaken. "It was pure facts that were observed and written down with clear eyes, not only by him, but by men of every social rank and age." Spiritualist publications piled up what they could swear were trustworthy corroborations, and they particularly treasured accounts by skeptics converted by the transcendent truths of spiritualism after attending a session with a medium.

🌼 IT IS WORTH REITERATING THAT, HOWEVER peculiar talking tables and disembodied voices might be to conventional Christians, in the Victorian age the warfare between science and religion, so passionately heralded by anti-clerical writers, was never simple. Those unambiguous categories—here science, there religion— that a consistent unbeliever like Schnitzler found eminently satisfactory, were repeatedly subverted by believers (and unbelievers) making their personal peculiar choices. Some liberal men of God preached sermons on the compatibility of the two supposedly irreconcilable enemies. "There is no conflict between religion and science," declared Dr. J. E. Roberts, probably a Unitarian, before the congregation of All Souls in Kansas City, Missouri, in 1895, "none between religion and reason, but there is an irrepressible and relentless conflict between the dogmas of orthodoxy on the one hand and science and reason on the other." He maintained that "history will some time place the names of Jesus and Voltaire side by side as deliverers of mankind from that worst of thralldoms, the religious thralldom." He titled another of his sermons "Jesus and Voltaire," in which he declared in ringing summation that "If Jesus came to save the world, Voltaire came to save *Christianity.*"

Some spiritualists wholly assimilated their beliefs to modern science. To Kiesewetter, "science" was the proper description of his occultism. Hence "every natural scientist and philosopher who is not a materialist, who acknowledges the law of evolution that pervades the All, and who is irresistibly pushed forward by the facts of astronomy and of Darwinism, must become an occultist, whether he likes it or not." Occultism, Kiesewetter said, is neither a Christian nor a Buddhist nor any other kind of religious doctrine. It is "as a part of anthropology, respectively of natural science as such, free of all confessions — *konfessionslos.*" That is why spiritualists with scientific pretensions treasured remarks attributed to great names like Giuseppe Garibaldi: "This religion of reason and science," the hero of Italian unification was quoted as saying, "is called spiritualism."

On the other side of the fence, there were spiritualists who saw their credo as an acceptable extension of their Christian heritage. Around 1871, S. C. Hall confessed that spiritualism had "removed all my doubts. I can and do believe all the Bible teaches me, in the efficacy and indescribable happiness of prayer, in the power of faith to save, in the perpetual superintendence of Providence, in salvation by the sacrifice of the Saviour, in the mediation of the Redeemer: in a word, I am a CHRISTIAN." One could hardly ask for more; but this was the sort of peace offering that few Christians in the mainstream, whether Catholic or Protestant, were likely to accept.

4

IN THESE FLIGHTS FROM ORTHODOXY, MIDDLE-class spiritualists, Theosophists, and their fellow explorers of the life beyond produced almost all the flood of apologetic literature seeking to gain credibility for ghostly appearances that unbelievers for their part found preposterous and probably fraudulent. Their ranks were crowded with merchants, professional men, public officials, judges. The spiritualists whom activists liked to display as witnesses to their respectability were honored names for other activities: Sir Oliver Lodge was a physicist, professor and principal of Birmingham University; Sir Arthur Conan Doyle was the creator of Sherlock Holmes; Justinus Kerner, whose poetry had a large following, was also a physician and novelist.

Professional people were everywhere in the movement. At midcentury, a French medium named Eugène Vintras aroused marked enthusiasm with his magical tricks, filling empty glasses with delicious wine and making the consecrated Host bleed. Kiesewetter, who reported on the case, acknowledged that some of these astonishing sights were manufactured miracles, but he added that even Vintras's opponents, "outstanding personages, physicians, attorneys," nobles, and priests, were won over by his performances. Other French miracle workers, adept deliverers of messages from the beyond, whether in provincial or Parisian society, attracted bourgeois supporters by the thousands.

Russia, too, underwent a middle-class wave of modern mysticism in the decades before World War I. It has been estimated that during those years, more than thirty-five occult societies flourished in the major Russian cities and even some lesser towns, their literary needs largely supplied by over thirty newspapers and periodicals. Their votaries, as one of these journals put it, included novelists, philosophers, poets, literary critics, theologians, philanthropists, translators, and other members of the intelligentsia, and their members certainly did not reach down into the proletariat or the peasant masses. Bourgeois also managed to inject themselves into moneymaking schemes developed to house and feed pilgrims who visited sacred spots with supernatural healing powers, even when the excitement about the miracles attached to the place had been generated by poverty-stricken villagers: witness the profitable enterprises built up at Lourdes after Bernadette Soubirous reported seeing the Virgin there in 1858.

The same, we have seen, holds true of spiritualism in Great Britain, though artisans and better-educated working people were also admitted to hear lecturers bringing news from the other world. *The Year-Book of Spiritualism for 1871* was pleased to report that "Among investigators we may number divines, logicians, and teachers in our schools of learning; physicians and lawyers; men of note in the arts, sciences, and literature; statesmen"—to say nothing of educated women. Leading spiritualists were editors of newspapers and periodicals, members of Parliament, and professors, all happy to accept and disseminate their modern versions of ancient wisdom. Somehow, these "investigators," to use the charitable language of the *Year-Book*, consistently found reports of spiritual experiences convincing. In short, bourgeois who could no longer conscientiously remain Anglicans or Dissenters but were not ready to plunge into the cold waters of reason, found welcome opportunities for compromises that proved psychologically satisfying—though, as skeptics would object, never rationally defensible. But, of course, these believers did not think of their faith as a compromise; for them it was simply true. They demonstrated not what William James, in a celebrated essay, called "The Will to Believe," but more urgently, the Victorian *need* to believe.

5

WILLIAM JAMES REMAINS THE NOBLEST EXEMPLAR of that need. The most widely read and highly regarded American philosopher and psychologist of the late nineteenth and early twentieth century, he was no compromiser. Far from it; he unsparingly explored his mind and that of others, and mobilized the courage to fight his bouts of depression and besetting uncertainties about the nature and destiny of man by confronting his ordinary like his esoteric experiences without regard to consequences. He was the most personal, most autobiographical of thinkers, who permitted his imperative needs to inform his philosophizing more candidly than did any of his colleagues. He believed in a god—a very individual, very heterodox god who needed human help to encompass his purposes—because he thought a world without a deity an intolerable prospect. In the conclusion to his masterly lectures, *The Varieties of Religious Experience* of 1902, speaking of his "over-belief" in divine sources of energy, he admitted frankly: "By being faithful in my poor measure to this over-belief, I seem to myself to keep more sane and true." He takes pride of place in these pages because he was, in his way, a bourgeois philosopher par excellence: his deftly chosen examples and his vigorous, informal prose (which at times concealed more problems than it resolved) attracted hundreds to his lectures and thousands to his pamphlets and books. None of the common terms of disparagement for professors—scholastic, stultifying, unreadable—applied to him. The old joke that William James wrote like a novelist, while his brother Henry wrote like a typical (which is to say barely comprehensible) philosopher, does an injustice to Henry James's genius for fine discriminations, but one can see why it might have arisen.

As a groundbreaking psychologist, William James disdained neither facts nor objectivity. On scientific grounds, he objected to the reductionist doctrine that explained the odd vagaries of the mind by physical preconditions, whether an upset stomach, a poor digestion, or a sexual perversion. But when it came to higher things, such as religion, he was a gambler, taking Pascal's wager, to which he explicitly refers, into the age of science. Pascal had argued that in debating the existence of God, one might as well affirm it, for if it turns out that he does exist, one may have a hope, however slim, of salvation; if he does not exist, one has lost nothing. This attitude greatly appealed to James since Huxley's agnosticism struck him as a comfortable stance of indifference. To believe in assertions for which there was no persuasive warrant was, to James, sheer superstition, but to believe in assertions that might possibly be true was constructive. After all, as he put it in "The Sentiment of Rationality," reflecting about the value of believing what one desires, *"There are then cases where faith creates its own verification."* He preached nothing less than giving possibilities a chance.

This commitment to the active consequences of belief made James's trek to mysticism almost inescapable. He took it in ways distinctive of him, joining scientific probity with his particular brand of higher credulity. In 1884, he joined the Society for Psychical Research, founded in Cambridge two years before by Henry Sidgwick, moralist and feminist, perhaps the most distinguished English philosopher of the period. As a fellow at Trinity College, Sidgwick was obliged to subscribe the Thirty-nine Articles, but eclectic reading and painful rumination convinced him that the defining doctrines of Christianity—miracles or the Virgin Birth—were untenable. He found himself far from isolated: his acquaintances—physicists, astronomers, poets, politicians, a notable clan of the well-educated—joined the society, and began to scrutinize reports of supernatural happenings at table rappings and other incredible doings.

Much like William James, Sidgwick did not lapse into scientific rationalism, partly because he continued to find the prospect of worlds beyond worlds intriguing, partly because he felt let down by natural scientists who declared his investigations a waste of time. Sounding like William James, he told fellow members of the society in 1888, "we believed unreservedly in the methods of modern science, and were prepared to accept submissively her reasoned conclusions, when sustained by the agreement of experts. But we were not prepared to bow with equal docility to the mere prejudices of scientific men. And it appeared to us that there was an important body of evidence—tending *prima facie* to establish the independence of soul or spirit—which modern science had simply left on one side with ignorant contempt." This easy dismissal seemed to him almost as wicked as the frauds perpetrated by spiritualists.

Ignoring the differences between them, some spiritualists became members of the society. But they soon clashed with their more open-minded fellows. Both, of course, we know, claimed to be scientific; but while Sidgwick and his associates did some admirable detective work and applied skeptical tests to implausible occurrences, the Christian members were certain that *their* investigations would confirm what they already believed. In face of these strains, investigators exposed fraudulent mediums and published a devastating report on Madame Blavatsky, her forgeries, sleights of hand, and use of confederates to encompass her effects.

Yet the Society for Psychical Research was more a symptom of a culture irrevocably torn about religion than a promise of usable knowledge. The university-bred members who ran Sidgwick's society were not representative of the mass of middle-class citizens, but their leading position illustrates the precariousness of traditional doctrines among Victorian bourgeois. Those who continued to believe in the time-honored God and those who, at the other extreme, embraced secularism, could witness all this turmoil with some ease. But in those years when change was king and doubt endemic, the middle ground was a swamp of perplexity. It is telling that spiritualists came from all the points of the religious compass: Catholicism, Calvinism, Lutheranism, Orthodox Judaism, atheism, deism. In 1906, John Maynard Keynes, six years after Sidgwick's death, defined him best in a malicious quip: "He never did anything but wonder whether Christianity was true and prove that it wasn't and hope that it was."

6

BOURGEOIS ON ALL SIDES OF THE RELIGIOUS question in the Victorian era had another burning issue to contend with: the problematic faith of the peasants and the working classes. What interested them was less lower-class beliefs than the political stance that followed from them. For the majority of the urban middle class, peasants were largely an unknown quantity, whether they had remained in their villages or had moved to town. The great fact of migration is a useful reminder: many urban workers had come from rural districts, bringing their habits and their superstitions with them. Bourgeois encountered peasants among their servants, at market stands selling fruits and vegetables, or, if they had a retreat in the countryside, in casual encounters. In consequence, they felt it necessary to construct their own legends based on fiction, casual anecdotes, or an ideology idealizing either city or rural life. German and Swiss writers developed the genre of peasant literature, stories and novels that approvingly set off the healthy simplicity of rustics, their closeness to the land, to say nothing of their heartfelt faith in God, against the insincerity and materialism of city dwellers. *Der Oberhof,* by the satirical German novelist Karl Immermann, a free-standing, vastly popular segment of his four-volume novel *Münchhausen* (1838–39), was perhaps the most successful example of this literature; his villagers appear as hardworking, honest, and devout, while his bourgeois are disingenuous or hysterical in their religiosity.

The irreligious party naturally could count on its novelists as well, most spectacularly Zola. His *La Terre* of 1887 upset even French readers accustomed to the audacious freedom of naturalistic prose. The uncivilized peasants Zola portrays—his critics would say maligns—have an overpowering passion for the soil that has something obscene about it in its sheer brutality. The men are bent on sexual pleasure at all costs or, rather, at no cost to themselves, since these barbarians care little about a woman's pain. Utter selfishness, rape, incest, murder are all instruments Zola's peasants deploy when they find it profitable. Some forty years earlier, the French physician Auguste Debay had already maintained that "where the imagination is little or not at all developed," that is, in rural areas, "the men make love brutally to satisfy a need." *La Terre* worked out this generalization in shocking fiction.

Nearly all of these authors, then, painted their rural portraits, as it were, without a sitter. About the only contemporaries really well informed about the social and religious life of the countryside were divines, whether Protestant or Catholic, men close to villagers as they superintended their morals and tried to recruit, or retain, them for Christ. Their reports are necessarily fragmentary, but nearly all of them held surprises for those who believed the nineteenth-century peasantry secure in its faith. It emerges from these documents that attending church or celebrating time-honored rituals was no guarantee of sincere piety. Pilgrimages and processions, so popular in Roman Catholic regions, raised troublesome questions in the minds of the priesthood. They had become secular, often immoral entertainments, featuring dances and drinking and all that followed from such amusements.

The dismay of clerics at all this unseemly behavior is understandable, but the meaning of these secular displays remains hard to determine. Piety and greed often coexisted in one person and were, for many, impossible to sort out. It was in part a matter of taste. In the winter of 1902, a few years before his death, the decadent novelist Joris-Karl Huysmans, the aesthete who had traveled from unbelief to faith, visited Lourdes. After the Catholic Church had officially accepted Bernadette's account of her experience as authentic, the simple little town and the obscure grotto where she had had her vision had become a focal point for international pilgrimages. With that, the place had been ruthlessly rebuilt to accommodate the thousands of visitors desperate to be freed from a variety of diseases, some of them hysterical, others incurable. By the end of the century, Lourdes had been decked out with garish commercial touches and was virtually choking in pilgrims. Huysmans was sickened. Speaking with the ardor of the convert and the refined taste of a cultivated *littérateur*, he felt moved to protest against the "appalling hodgepodge," the vulgar eclecticism he found in that world-renowned gathering place of supernatural cures. The "plethora of vileness" at Lourdes, the "haemorrhage of bad taste," the sheer kitsch, made him wonder quite seriously whether perhaps the devil himself had taken a hand. To him, villagers were no longer reliable children of their church. And it was true: bourgeois holding on, or returning, to the faith of their ancestors provided a more edifying spectacle.

🖾 IF THE DEVIL HAD INDEED SEDUCED MANY A peasant to stray from the true religion, he had accomplished far more among the working classes. And this was necessarily of more immediate concern for the middle class. Profits, social peace, and (not to be despised) the disinterested gratification of making good Christians hinged on it. How to discipline the urban poor that they might get used to regular working habits in factories and mines, accept insalubrious conditions and persistent insecurity about employment, and docilely approve of, or at least subordinate themselves to, the existing social order was a vexing, much-debated issue in Victorian society.

There was nothing new about the problem. The ancients, too, had had to devise ways of pacifying their restless populace; the cynical advice to keep the masses happy with bread and circuses goes back to Juvenal, writing in the early Roman Empire. More recently, in the Enlightenment, the question how to make the poor obey the social compact they had done nothing to forge but did much to sustain had preoccupied political discussions among the philosophes. Voltaire above all was saddled with witticisms—not all of his own making—warning that if the lower orders ever adopted their betters' deist or atheistic views, they would, no longer constrained by fear of eternal punishment, feel free to rob their masters and cut their throats. Since antiquity, then, religion had been considered to be, among other things, an internal policeman, an effective and relatively cheap agent of order.

In Victorian times, especially after midcentury, with the rise of the factory and large-scale enterprise, this issue acquired a new urgency. Critics of Victorian capitalism have insisted that inoculating the lower orders against unbelief was essentially a capitalist conspiracy. After all, a workingman who believes in God is less likely to go on strike, sabotage machinery, let alone try to organize a labor union. Hence teaching workers to read the Bible and organize Sunday Schools in which their children would be exposed to the saving message of the Word would make for a tranquil workplace and political culture.

This is the theory of social control, an invidious view of bourgeois motives first put forward by Victorians themselves. The notion that the rich and powerful would put religion to irreligious uses became familiar enough to attract the attention of popular novelists. It is a theory not without a certain plausibility. We have some sketchy indications that there were officials and employers who applied such a policy, at times with secular remedies as surrogates for religious ones. Marx had already noted in 1847 that "the social principles of Christianity," which sermonize on the need for a ruling and an oppressed class, "preach cowardice, self-contempt, abasement, submissiveness, humility, in short all the qualities of the canaille." Partially supporting his analysis, a nineteenth-century English parliamentary committee suggested that workingmen would not kick a policeman if they could kick a football instead. And in the French town of Vienne, on the Rhône, where manufacturers organized a team, local observers noted cynically: "As long as they go to rugby games, they'll keep quiet." These, the partisans of the social control thesis argued, were frank attempts to stifle, or divert, the working classes' animus to take up arms against inequality and exploitation.

But this thesis fails to address the complexity of human motives. Philanthropists who founded Bible classes, Sunday Schools, retreats for fallen women, or publishing houses that distributed elevating texts written in accessible language could be devout, disinterested Christians. If they wanted to save the great unwashed from hell, that was in part because they thought it perfectly natural to share some of one's wealth with those less fortunate, in part because they feared that they too might be doomed if they failed to do good in the world. Nineteenth-century satirists found it all too easy to lampoon lady philanthropists as bustling and autocratic idlers who condescendingly distributed charity to lesser beings, at bottom callous, publicity-hungry, and heartless. Dickens was not the only Victorian to ridicule them savagely. But in truth their intentions, conscious and unconscious, were far from simple. Had any of these affluent bourgeois been asked whether holding out to the poor the prospect of heaven was not a sly attempt to perpetuate what should not be perpetuated, or whether serving the unfortunate was not just a way of serving themselves, they would not have understood the question. In any event, the record shows that whatever efforts at social control were made, they largely failed.

They failed in more than one way. With notable exceptions, the bulk of the working classes were alienated from the churches across Europe and remained so. The proofs for this are overwhelming. Two brief examples will do. In France, priests uttered despairing *cris de coeur* from one decade to the next. "In Paris, the center, they say, of the religious movement, three quarters of the population live in indifference toward religion." That was in 1836. "Indifference is the great malady of Christians in our time." That was in 1845. "Walk into our innumerable factories and ask the workers what they think of God, of the religion of Jesus Christ. You will ascertain that for them the God of the Gospels is every time the *unknown God*." That was in 1853; all the way to 1906: "No need to run to China to find pagans and savages. They swarm in the outskirts of Paris and the large cities." Meanwhile in England and Wales, the notorious religious census of 1851 gave valuable testimony that dismayed churchgoing bourgeois no less than Anglican or Dissenting clerics. Among a population totaling almost 18 million, only slightly more than 7 million were counted to have attended services on Census Sunday. Even exempting children, the sick, and others unable to be present, some 5.25 million could have gone and failed to do so. Contemporaries were horrified: plainly it was the lower orders, notably the working classes, who were the great absentees.

To Victorians, the reasons for this chasm between the workers and the churches were all too palpable. There was the shortage of ministers and priests to cater adequately to their parishioners and to ward off unacceptable entertainments. There was the much-lamented failure to educate the young in the truths of religion which philanthropists could do only little to remedy: many working-class youngsters grew up in ignorance of what was second nature to middle-class children, whether their parents were pious or not. There was the embarrassment of the poor about their miserable clothes, which made many ashamed to enter a church, and the expenses for marriages and burial fees that churchgoing exacted. There were powerful currents of ideas competing with traditional faiths, especially after Social Darwinists popularized, and vulgarized, Darwin's masterpiece *The Origin of Species*. There were local hatreds of clerics for their social and political positions. In short, the unchurching of the working classes was as intricate a matter as that of peasants.

Then in the second half of the century, working-class anti-clericalism became organized. Irreligious socialism grew into what was called a counter-church; rival Christian Socialist groups had at best a limited following. After agonizing vicissitudes, Robert Owen's ideas (as anti-clerical and anti-religious as any circulating in the early decades of the century) were taken over by Socialist parties everywhere. Their insistence that religion only perpetuated the slavery of the proletariat became their watchword years before Marx. In Germany, in the late 1870s, the Social Democratic Party, faced with a conservative Christian Social movement, decided to make a formal ceremony of its members' repudiation of whatever faith they had grown up with.

In a word, bourgeois and workers went separate ways. Yet with the passage of years, in some countries more than in others, the two came to engage in some cordial exchanges. As Socialist parties entered the political mainstream, though fiercely denying that they were doing any such thing, they came to look suspiciously bourgeois. They had little difficulty entering coalitions with left-liberal parties. And for their part, bourgeois liberals could cheerfully vote for the Social Democrats, the Labour Party, the Partito Laburista Italiana. They could do so even when they continued to be devout.

———

AFTER ALL THESE PROBES, WHAT REMAINS? Clearly, there was no such thing as a representative bourgeois religiosity among the Victorians. A collective portrait would look like that of a clown in motley. One may suggest, tentatively, on diverse, often anecdotal evidence, that Victorian bourgeois were more religious than workers, bourgeois husbands less religious than their wives, nineteenth-century bourgeois more religious (or more churchgoing) than their eighteenth-century grandfathers. But all generalizations about the persistence or the subversion of faith among the Victorian middle classes—about regions, social rank, family traditions—are undermined by exceptions. The rest is local history.

The Emancipator of Labor and the Honest Working-People.

SEVEN

The Problematic Gospel of Work

1

IF THERE WAS ONE GRIEVANCE THAT MORE THAN any other provoked the disputes which embittered Arthur Schnitzler's life at home, it was his supposedly incurable idleness. That charge coalesced with his parents' worry over his erotic exploits: they thought that the time and energy he wasted chasing women would have been far better spent being a diligent student, and later, a conscientious physician. Spending virtually every evening in cafés with his equally profligate bachelor friends was not work, certainly not the kind of work he should be doing. In November 1879, not long after his father had confiscated his diary, Schnitzler noted: "Grumbling at home about my social life, my sloppiness, my negligence." We remember that more than a dozen years later, in 1892, he still had "disagreeable discussions at home." By then he was already thirty. He did not have a private practice or solid prospects for his literary experiments. In short, he was continually offending against one of the commandments of the bourgeois Decalogue: the gospel of work.

This pious language is fitting: for middle-class ideologists, the ideal of work embraced more than just steady application. An ethical imperative, it embraced much that Victorian bourgeois valued, a principle to which good burghers felt compelled to subscribe. It implied honest dealings with employers, customers, and competitors, a dedication to self-discipline, a wholesome commitment to family, and an alert sense of duty. Work purified the soul. On this issue, even devout Victorians dared to revise God's word. Scriptures had treated work as the harsh punishment God had imposed on Adam and Eve and on all future generations for committing the unpardonable sin of disobedience. In contrast, according to nineteenth-century bourgeois ideologists, work was a prophylactic *against* sin. They held that laboring in the sweat of one's brow—for bourgeois, speaking metaphorically of course—was perhaps as effectual as prayer.

Since the ancients, the rewards of work had been tersely summed up in tags and proverbs, and Victorian middle-class parents had them available to teach, and probably torment, their children. Those who still remembered their school Latin could intone Virgil: "*Labor omnia vincit improbus*—Persistent labor conquers all." Germans could resort to a well-known song, "*Arbeit,*" which begins: "*Arbeit macht das Leben süss*—Work makes life sweet," and, even more to the point for the middle class, their beloved Friedrich Schiller, whose didactic ballad "The Song of the Bell," much quoted and much parodied, has the famous line: "*Arbeit ist des Bürgers Zierde*—Work is the burgher's ornament." There were those who made gentle fun of these exhortations—the English humorist Jerome K. Jerome wrote in 1889: "I like work; it fascinates me. I can sit and look at it for hours." But such mild jokes are only a tribute to the power of this strenuous idea in the Victorian days.

Perhaps no one drew out the solemn implications of work more drastically than Thomas Carlyle, from whose writings one could easily compile a little anthology on the subject. "Blessed is he who has found his work," he wrote in 1843, in *Past and Present*, "let him ask no other blessedness." Seven years earlier, in *Sartor Resartus*, he had pushed his worship to its limits: "A certain inarticulate Self-consciousness dwells dimly in us; which only our Works can render articulate and decisively discernible. Our Works are the mirror wherein the spirit first sees its natural lineaments. Hence, too, the folly of that impossible Precept, *Know thyself*; till it be translated into this partially possible one, *Know what thou canst work at*." And he shouted at his readers: "Produce! Produce!" For Carlyle, work almost literally defined the good person. Nineteenth-century bourgeois were disposed to agree with him and to turn preachments eulogizing work into commonplaces.

Commonplaces are, well, common, and though their predictability and crudeness may make the fastidious wince, they are clues to prevalent cultural styles. Among the most telling exemplars of that style is a letter that the prosperous Berlin merchant August Friedrich Hirsekorn wrote to his son Carl August, his chosen successor, upon retiring from his flourishing men's store. The date is March 31, 1833. "My dear Son: the moment has come when I am leaving my situation and you are starting on a new independent career. However, before I leave, I must follow the promptings of my heart and address a few words to you. As I thank you, deeply moved, for your loyal and prudent direction of my shop, I add at the same time the wish that after a succession of years suitably spent, you will enter retirement with the same joyfulness and satisfaction as I am doing today. However, in order to reach that point it is necessary to observe the strictest economy (without, though, being stingy), and to administer the business with the greatest diligence and activity, even by sacrificing some favorite habits. Now, as you wholly fulfill your duty, you can also strictly insist that your people do the same. Hence strictly insist on it from the start, but be equally indulgent with petty offenses, for to do wrong and go astray are human, and after all every one of us is human.

"And," Hirsekorn senior goes on, evidently enjoying the role of Polonius, "in order to be strengthened and fortified in the good resolve to fulfill your duties faithfully and honestly, and to find consolation and reassurance during life's gloomy and melancholic circumstances, I have found it reliable to turn to religion, and to attend official divine services now and then. Without being sanctimonious, I must confess with real conviction that I have found in religion consolation and reassurance in some bitter and melancholic situations that also touched me. You too should attend official divine services now and then. In that case, if you should wish it, I would be glad to spend a few hours in your store. And encourage your people to do the same, and give each of them a few hours' time for that purpose. Believe me, this is also not lost time for you, since there they too are called upon to carry out their professional duties. Take the enclosed purse and its contents as a memento for today's day. May the same remain closed to every unnecessary expenditure, yet be steadily open in support of poor, innocent casualties."

The stilted diction, the repetitiveness, the awkward effort to show affection virtually warrants that Hirsekorn had gathered his wisdom not from books but from his own resources. He stands as a good Victorian bourgeois with all his contradictions; his sermon invites mixed responses. He is the calculating employer who uses sending his people to church as a psychological device to keep them uncomplaining, relieved only by a cool personal reverence that has made his occasional religious conformity a comforting anti-depressant. He is preaching piety not only to his employees but also to himself; for him, social control, of which this letter is a vivid instance, is only the public face of private predicaments. He shows himself, too, as the rational steward of his assets, who believes in his right to establish moderate patterns of consumption: commendable thrift must not degenerate into unattractive miserliness; liberality on the other hand must be carefully measured. He shows himself, finally, as the advocate of hard work who at the same time refuses to elevate the daily treadmill into an all-consuming deity.

The gospel of work: this, for all of Hirsekorn's genial reservations, is the lesson that his quintessentially bourgeois homily purveys. This was the lesson, too, that the prosperous Lübeck merchant Thomas Johann Mann, the father of Thomas Mann, wanted to leave for his heirs in the will he wrote in 1891: "Tommy will weep for me. He must never neglect prayer, respect for his mother, and diligent work." Interestingly enough, in his first novel, *Buddenbrooks*, published in 1901, Thomas Mann made use of this paternal prescription in a scene depicting a furious quarrel between two brothers as Thomas Buddenbrook, a respectable businessman, shouts at Christian, a neurotic ne'er-do-well, "work!"—which says curtly: occupy yourself with something useful instead of indulging in your hypochondria. It was the attitude toward work, we recall, that Freud believed to be one of the defining differences between the middle classes and the "people." And we recall, too, that it was the "incessant work" that Count Paul Vasili celebrated as the distinctive quality of Vienna's bourgeoisie.

Naturally, as critics of the modern bourgeoisie did not fail to point out, to extol the virtues of work included exhortations to make money—surely a vulgar ideal. But in defense, its champions could reply they were not exalting moneymaking for its own sake. After all, François Guizot's much-quoted slogan, "*Enrichissez vous,*" uttered in the Chamber of Deputies while he was prime minister, should not be read as an invitation to fellow Frenchmen to enrich themselves at any price. Rather, the rest of his sentence qualified his injunction: "*par le travail et l'épargne.*" He was urging them to pursue wealth through work and savings, appealing to another, related bourgeois ideal: self-control.

In an ironic twist, some of the most impassioned haters of the Victorian bourgeoisie found themselves in thrall to the bourgeois work ethic, without saying so, without even noticing it. As dependable manufacturers of fiction, Thackeray and Zola, Ibsen and Hofmannsthal, and other devotees of advanced artistic and literary positions, devoted long, concentrated hours to their vocation. Schnitzler, we have come to see, was no exception. For all his sexual explorations that included time-consuming daytime dalliances, for all his rueful entries in his diary deploring yet another unproductive day, he poured out impressive quantities of stories, novels, plays, poems, to say nothing of a vast correspondence and even vaster numbers of notebook entries.

🖾 NECESSARILY, AS THE VICTORIANS IDEALIZED work, they deplored, like Schnitzler's parents, its counterpart: the mortal sin of sloth. The sons of prosperous parents seemed particularly susceptible, and they needed stern warnings. Moralists were only too happy to oblige. There was, for one, Theodore H. Munger, whose *On the Threshold*, first published in the United States in 1880, was in its fifteenth printing five years later: "When a young man comes to feel that because his father has wealth he has no need of personal exertion, he is doomed. Only the rarest natural gifts and the most exceptional training can save the sons of the rich from failure of the true ends of life." The conviction that idleness is not just morally vicious but physically debilitating to boot was widespread. In 1873, A. Magendi, director of a French school, voiced a wide consensus when he observed that these consequences showed themselves early: "Inactive, the child becomes vicious." The twig thus bent is ready for breaking once the boy grows to manhood: "Young men of vigorous constitution but disposed to physical idleness soon lose, with their bodily inaction, their muscular energy. Robust in appearance, they grow increasingly feeble at the slightest effort." An idler's likeliest fate is a short life.

In other words, work and character, another Victorian ideal, were inseparable companions. Work was the royal road to good character. Crusaders in the cause of manliness, like Theodore Roosevelt, worried over what they bewailed as the decadent traits among the late Victorians. He did not use the term "castration," which psychoanalysts would make familiar, but in essence what he deplored was the grave danger that idleness presented to virility. Strenuous work was the only cure for the sickness of the age. "One of the prime dangers of civilization," he said in 1910, in a speech at the University of Berlin, "has always been its tendency to cause the loss of virile fighting virtues, of the fighting edge. When men get too comfortable and lead too luxurious lives, there is always danger that the softness eats like an acid into their manliness of fibre." The American president liked to amuse himself at the expense of "men of cultivated taste and easy life." Apparently collecting paintings or writing poetry was not work.

There was nothing new in T.R.'s strictures. To satirize or to censure drones had long accompanied exhortations to work. At midcentury, in 1850, the eminent American educator Horace Mann, offering the Boston Mercantile Library Association "A Few Thoughts for a Young Man," had told his audience: "No matter what may be the fortune or the expectations of a young man, he has no right to live a life of idleness. In a world so full as this of incitements to exertion and of rewards for achievement, idleness is the most absurd of absurdities and the most shameful of shames." A few years later, in 1863, the Italian painter Michele Cammarano exhibited a canvas, *Idleness and Work*, that shows a bourgeois, in top hat and tail coat, hands in his pockets, strolling along a field in which peasants are diligently harvesting wheat. The message could not be more apparent: the lazy, who reap without sowing, will harvest nothing of value. In the same vein, in 1883, the article "A Proper Use of Time," in *Gay's Standard Encyclopaedia and Self Educator*, a popular American work addressed to the lower middle class avid for self-improvement, threatened its readers: "If habits of listless idleness are once formed they rivet their fetters about the mind, and it requires the most gigantic effort to throw them off. Wealth once gone may be recovered by patient industry. Forgotten knowledge will return by application, but lost time has fled forever."

This is the ominous tone so typical for the advice literature of the age: calamities loom in the wings, good things are bound to deteriorate, the grip of evil on the soul is tenacious. In an expansive age celebrated for its progress in all departments of life, professional providers of advice sought to inoculate their audience against the disease of easy optimism. Only the most concentrated application to whatever work has been ordained for the individual can serve as a dam against disaster.

⬛ AS WE HAVE SEEN, PUBLICISTS IN THE BUSINESS of exhortation found the virtues of work an irresistible topic. They repeated themselves as diligently as they repeated others. In 1850, Samuel Smiles, then thirty-eight, the most widely read and frequently cited preacher of character in the English-speaking world during the Victorian era, put work at the core of what he was pleased to call his philosophy. He was an English publicist almost as popular in the United States as at home. After a varied career, he discovered the righteousness of free enterprise and began to exploit his undeniable talent for spreading his credo. His method was simple: to explore the persuasive power of exemplary anecdotes. *Self-Help* (1859), in which he applied that technique with gratifying results, made him famous, and he never stopped. Before his death in 1904 at the age of ninety-two, he had published extremely popular little treatises like *Character* (1872), *Thrift* (1875), and *Duty* (1880), all homages to hardworking individuals.

His lives of outstanding engineers were anecdotes writ large. These biographies, he hoped, would serve his readers as models worthy of emulation. Not everyone could be a great designer of railroads like George Stephenson, but everyone could work faithfully at his post. Work, he wrote in *Character,* "is the law of our being—the living principle that carries men and nations forward." More candid than most other professional cheerleaders of capitalism, he acknowledged that "labor may be a burden and a chastisement, but," he quickly added, "it is also an honor and a glory. Without it nothing can be accomplished. All that is great in man comes through work, and civilization is its product." In short, work does not merely produce tangible things; it keeps people from being dishonest, spendthrift, irreverent, sensual, and irresponsible. Hirsekorn, could he have read Smiles's books, would have appreciated them.

2

THE GOSPEL OF WORK WAS EMPHATICALLY AND almost exclusively a bourgeois ideal. By and large, aristocrats did not value it and the working poor did not need it. These qualifying terms— "almost" and "by and large"—are necessary hedges against simplistic generalizations. There were aristocrats who conducted business like so many bourgeois, even in France where such activity supposedly offended against their status. And there were workingmen, notably highly skilled artisans, who in their striving for respectability took the ideal of work for granted. Not themselves bourgeois, nor interested in turning themselves into carbon copies of their "betters," they at least shared this credo with the middling orders. In the words of a Newcastle journalist who, in 1854, walked through a local ironworks: "The stern duty of WORK—hard, sweating, energetic work—presides over the whole." These craftsmen, and thousands of others like them, were proud of work well done. They took respectability to mean a sober, decent, conscientious way of life on the job as much as at home; they took it to mean that they wanted their superiors to treat them with respect. The evidence is overwhelming across countries and the most diverse crafts and industries that artisans sought a life with dignity, an ingredient in their existence they valued as much as a living wage.

Not unexpectedly in this century of innovations and uncertainties, the gospel of work did not find unanimous support. Thriving parvenus across Europe enjoying recently acquired wealth, maneuvered, at times shamelessly, even desperately, to translate their money into genteel or noble status. To their minds, only the highest, most visible level of idleness could wash off the stain of trade. Having worked hard most of their life, they wanted to escape the world of commerce, industry, or banking so that they, or at least their children, could enter the exalted regions of society in which leisure, or a dilettante's expensive diversions, was king.

At the end of the nineteenth century, in his classic *Theory of the Leisure Class*, the maverick economist Thorstein Veblen traced this disdain for work to survivals from feudal times, when labor had been essentially the province of the common folk. He maintained that nineteenth-century moguls showed off their wealth by what in famous phrases he called "conspicuous consumption" and "conspicuous waste." With their estates, their clothing, their jewelry, their avocations, their expensive wives, they threw money at useless, unproductive things. And these activities and these choices permitted them to compare themselves invidiously to those less fortunate than they. "Abstention from labour," Veblen wrote, "is the conventional evidence of wealth and is therefore the conventional mark of social standing; and this insistence on the meritoriousness of wealth leads to a more strenuous insistence on leisure." It was precisely this contempt for work that made the Theodore Roosevelts of the Victorian age so uneasy.

All these qualifications raise the question just how wide a range the gospel of work could legitimately claim among the Victorians. There is something problematic about an ideal that allows for so many exceptions. It is obvious that for the lower strata of the middle classes as well as for the working poor in town and country, all this hectoring must have seemed unnecessary, irrelevant to their own situation, downright insulting. There is little support for the notion that those with modest incomes ever read Samuel Smiles and his friends; had they done so, they would have been wryly amused, if not irritated, by the presumption of the preachers. They did not have to be told to work and how much it did for their character; they worked because they wanted to survive.

3

PUBLICISTS SERMONIZING ON WORK EXPLICITLY directed their stern message at the male of the species, at boys, youngsters, and men, but tacitly they included women in their purview. I have canvassed the dramatic evolution of the legal status and public visibility of women in some detail, and need not repeat what I said there. Both changed, too quickly for nervous traditionalists, too slowly for impatient feminists. But no one doubted that women had work to do; after all, Eve had been Adam's full-fledged companion in the crime of disobedience, and the doom of hard labor had been her punishment as much as his. To be sure, through the centuries beginning with the church fathers, many good and learned Christians had regarded woman as the true vessel of perdition in Eden; yet even those who held Adam equally responsible for original sin found it plausible that men and women were destined to preside over different provinces of life. Making use of this ever-repeated argument, the nineteenth-century doctrine of the separation of spheres neatly divided the sexes and dictated the proper territory of work for middle-class women: the family.

Managing the middle-class household meant buying provisions, supervising servants, prudently staying within the domestic budget, taking the principal role in bringing up children, with whom they normally spent far more time than did their husbands, gracefully presiding over what contemporaries liked to call the groaning board, making, as hostesses, as good an impression as was within their nature. There were Victorian husbands who recognized, more or less sensitively, that the home was a demanding task; looking back from our age of electrified, mechanized—and servantless—housekeeping, historians find Victorian domestic chores even more formidable than they were acknowledged to be at the time.

A home had to be kept sparkling without vacuum cleaners, clothes had to be washed without washing machines, food had to be kept fresh without refrigerators, meals had to be cooked without electric stoves, bread had to be kneaded without mixers, the air had to kept tolerable without electric fans, let alone air conditioners. Ingenious inventors did bring to market mechanical contrivances that would later ease the housewife's labor, but for decades they were too expensive or too large and clumsy to be promptly introduced into domestic use. Washing machines were first installed in commercial laundries; mixing machines served bakeries for decades before they eased domestic baking; electric lights were tried out in theatres and opera houses before they became the lighting of choice in apartments and private houses.

Dirt was the great enemy that Victorian housewives were detailed to fight relentlessly no matter how distasteful the physical labor involved might be. They had to make sure that bed linens, kerosene lamps, fireplaces, stoves, and toilets were kept clean, chores that for the most part had to be repeated daily. In its substantial appendix on household management, the *Kiehnle-Kochbuch* (1912), an enormously successful vademecum for the German housewife, the author, Hermine Kiehnle, deals with only two subjects: folding napkins and keeping the house immaculate. She considers both topics in meticulous detail, but the second easily dwarfs the first. "Order and cleanliness," she instructs her readers, "must be in the house everywhere and at all times: that is the first precondition for a competent housewife." This, in a sentence, was woman's work—responsible, varied, hard, and never done.

However fanatical German *Hausfrauen* might have been about cleanliness, books on housekeeping published in other countries clearly show that this preoccupation was a concern everywhere. After the germ theory of diseases was generally accepted, it was as though the housewife had been nominated as the physician's auxiliary. And how much heavy duty she was spared by her domestic help depended, quite apart from individual idiosyncrasies, on strongly differing national styles. Foreign observers often commented in astonishment just how much — or how little — married women had to do in the countries they were visiting. Englishwomen were amazed to see the physical labor their German counterparts were expected, and willing, to perform; German women for their part thought that French *maîtresses de maison* were on the whole better off than they were at home. To be sure, nearly every middle-class Victorian household, even on the petty bourgeois level, had a servant, usually more than one, to do the really grimy work. In her famous *Book of Household Management,* which I have cited before, Isabella Beeton was explicit about this division of labor. If a footman or a maid-of-all-work was the only servant a middle-class family employed, neither his nor her work was easy or pleasant. "His life," she writes, "is no sinecure." As for the female servant, she "is perhaps the only one of her class deserving of commiseration; her life is a solitary one." Both rise at dawn, she coolly observes, and are endlessly involved in cleaning, whether the master's boots, the living-room fireplace, or the kitchen stove.

But there were housewives who carried the whole burden. A fragmentary diary dated 1880 kept by an anonymous American housewife (all we know is that she was thirty-three years old and lived in Hallam, Connecticut) shows that in the land of the free and the brave, there were middle-class women who did most of their domestic labor themselves and could count on nothing more than voluntary help from members of their family. She was bored and resentful. Again and again she protested, sometimes in resignation, sometimes approaching rebelliousness, that cleaning the house was about all she had time to do. "One by one," she wrote on April 27, "the mountains diminish into molehills," and, the next day, contemplating her kitchen, "'The worst is over' now," as though, the quotation marks attest, she were reciting a formula to make herself feel better. At least twice, on September 12 and a week later, she tersely noted, "Monotonous day." The monotony did not lift even when her aunt Sophia came over on September 6 to assist her at the washtub. "Very romantic life," she commented. Her husband was of no help. "A home day," she noted on June 18. "The figure-head looked on while the slaves labored." She saw herself as being "chained" in her "cell," as she put it on August 10, when a visitor came over "to see her fellow-idiot." No wonder she had a "day of days" on June 12 that "makes one long for eternal rest." She sounds like an intelligent and dryly witty woman whose spirits were being eaten away by the hopelessly repetitive nature of her chores—and, one guesses, by the ostentatious idleness of her "figure-head." She belongs in the gallery of middle-class women in the Victorian age who worked and worked.

🪷 THERE WAS YET ANOTHER PIECE OF WORK THAT bourgeois wives had assigned to them in the nineteenth century. They were supposed to be a sturdy, reliable helpmeet to their husband. This obligation was seldom discussed freely among the Victorians, but it proved a cardinal item on the middle-class wife's domestic agenda. It called for soothing the husband upon his weary return from the exhausting, often disillusioning work in the outside world—in politics, in business, in manufacturing, in the university and the arts—supporting his ambitions and minimizing his failures. I said earlier that the most vigorous pillow talk could achieve only limited results in righting the legal inequities that victimized women. Perhaps, but tender pillow talk could go far to boost the husband's morale, clarify his mind in thorny predicaments, perhaps even save his career—and a marriage. When Victorian men, even those resigned to what they considered women's hidden power, were willing to talk about the wife's part in sustaining them, they did so hesitantly and looked for ways to keep the specter of full equality from the door.

Thomas Hughes's novel, *Tom Brown at Oxford*, published in 1861, is a good case in point. Tom, who had become one of the most famous characters in English fiction in its precursor, *Tom Brown's Schooldays*, has grown up and is happily married. But as he contemplates his future, he finds his financial prospects dim. Afraid that he will not be able to spare his wife, Mary, a life without servants and with only the scantiest amenities, he confesses his shame and terror to her. He calls her a "brave, generous, pitying angel," who should not be exposed to a life of deprivation. "It is a man's business," he tells her and asks rhetorically, "why is a woman's life to be made wretched?" To his astonishment, Mary Brown strongly objects to this conventional line of reasoning. "Why not put me on your own level?" she protests. Women, she argues, were not created to sit still, look pretty, and spend money. "Why not let me pick my way by your side?" Her spirited little speech promises to be a splendid moment in the history of woman's emancipation from the pedestal. But Hughes timidly retreats. "If a woman cannot do much herself," he has Mary say in conclusion, "she can honour and love a man who can." Hughes was a generous, liberal author, and his views of women were in the vanguard of a changing culture. But he let most of the old structure stand. "If a woman cannot do much herself"—plainly, he too was among the majority whom advanced women made nervous.

🛡 THERE WERE, WE KNOW, OTHER HUSBANDS LIKE Hughes. A sizable menu of anxious responses by Victorian males facing what appeared to them Amazons on the warpath—bluster, condescension, ridicule, appeal to the laws of human nature—were defenses in the decades when a few bold feminists advocated the extension of the suffrage to women and made unheard-of demands for a share in the workplace. Frightened editorialists and politicians likened feminists to an army of bloodthirsty harridans on a rampage. It was a time when the brothers Goncourt, prolific writers and diarists, dreamt—and faithfully recorded—dreams of castration: Jules about a man whose nose drops to the ground, Edmond seeing a woman with a *vagina dentata*.

Such anxieties survived to the end of the period this book covers, and beyond. It is striking how the nineteenth century, most conspicuously in its second half, witnessed a revival of ancient legends starring the devouring female—Eve, Delilah, Cleopatra, Messalina, Judith, Salome.

The sirens are so many reminders that the lethal woman was not an invention of the Victorian era, but they had come back in force, more malevolent than ever. The Sphinx of antiquity had been a murderous monster that Oedipus had conquered at long last. But in the nineteenth century, writers and painters experimented with reversing the traditional tale by making the Sphinx the victor. In 1839, in a versified preface to his *Book of Songs*, Heinrich Heine describes himself, the poet, wandering through a mysterious landscape and encountering a marble Sphinx in front of a silent, deserted castle. As he leans forward to kiss her lovely face, she awakens and, though she makes him happy with her kisses, wounds him almost to death with her leonine paws. It is a characteristic experience—characteristic for Heine—of erotic suffering and ecstasy intermixed, but however delicious his enjoyment, his suffering is poignant, almost beyond remedy. In the early 1860s, Gustave Moreau painted a very similar scene in which the Sphinx claws a virile Oedipus.

It was this theme, bellicose woman as triumphant, that had informed Keats's *La belle dame sans merci;* Heine's seductive siren, the *Lorelei;* Prosper Mérimée's evil gypsy Carmen (far more diabolical in his novella than in Bizet's operatic version); Swinburne's Lady of Pain, Dolores. In the hands of such artists, modern women were a castrating tribe. In reality, of course, these fiends bore no resemblance to feminists demanding access to the universities or to a bank account of their own, but the men of imagination I have cited did not aim at a reasonable portrait of their society. In their intuitive way, they displayed its neuroses. And soberer commentators did not remain far behind. Diarists, poets, essayists depicted contemporary woman in action and in the most urgent tones cautioned against her lethal appetites. To give but one instance from a large alarmist literature: the English essayist Eliza Lynn Linton, probably the most widely read anti-feminist woman journalist of the day, analyzed the phenomenon of modern woman in detail and declared her a menace: "Men are afraid of her; and with reason." Only a few wicked parodists suggested that a touch of humor might be a remedy against this hysterical fear of women.

A man did not need to be afraid of woman's secret power if she was self-abnegating enough about it—in short, the muse, the silent inspiration of great men. She is the wife who hangs back modestly as her man performs on the grand stage of the world, recognizing (even though he does not) that she is the true intelligence in the house. She makes him wake up to his full talents, she wins over influential people to his cause, she quietly improves his manners and his writings. She is the real ruler in her family who—the feeble, much-repeated anti-feminist anecdote had it—did not need the suffrage, since she told her husband and her sons how to vote.

The plainest exposition of how the muse does her work was James M. Barrie's popular comedy *What Every Woman Knows*, first performed in 1908. Maggie Wylie, in her mid-twenties, plain but lovable, self-effacing and very smart, is married off to an exceedingly ambitious younger man, whose political career she saves from his blunders by rewriting his inept speeches. Until the last moment he does not make out what his admiring and modest listener has done for him, and she rescues him (and their marriage) once again, this time from shame, by telling him that she has only done what every wife does, aware that her husband desperately needs to believe that he alone is responsible for his accomplishments. "Every woman knows that." It is not irrelevant to remember that Barrie was, of course, the author of *Peter Pan*, about a boy who never grew up, and that the one woman in his life was his mother, no doubt the original source of all myths about the strong woman.

WHATEVER THE DOMINANT IDEOLOGY IN THE Victorian world, the separation of spheres was never complete. Granted, with the expansion of prosperity among the middling orders after the Napoleonic Wars, the possibility of exempting women from the working world and confining their activities to the domestic and social fronts became increasingly plausible and increasingly prevalent. Down to the end of Queen Victoria's reign, bourgeois men, even when their income was uncertain, could preach the doctrine with conviction. In 1883, Freud, then an impecunious physician in love, writing to his fiancée Martha Bernays, took exception to John Stuart Mill's *Subjection of Women*, which he had just translated into German. Mill might plead for oppressed women, he told her, and for letting them earn their own income, but surely Mill had failed to see that women had enough work in the household and with their immediate family. Besides, Mill had forgotten chivalry. "Any girl, even without suffrage or legal competence, whose hand a man kisses and for whose love he is prepared to dare all, could have set him right." After all, "nature had determined woman's destiny through beauty, charm, and sweetness." Schnitzler was no more progressive. When Marie Reinhard, the love of his life, who was living with him, proposed to return to her profession—teaching singing—he threatened to break up the relationship. Both men, unconventional as they were, had conformist bourgeois on their side, and there is no evidence that this company troubled them.

Meanwhile, the growth of professions like medicine and the emergence of large-scale enterprises were sharply reducing the place of women in one occupation after another. The old monopoly of women attending births both normal and abnormal had already been compromised in the eighteenth century as men began to enter the profession and automatically gained greater prestige than their female competitors simply because they were men. But in the Victorian decades, the midwives, whose reputation had long been shaky, faced far more aggressive disapproval and rivalry from the medical community. In France and in Prussia, where they were under state regulation and where, by midcentury, reputable training schools were in operation, the profession survived in better shape than in Britain, where official supervision did not arrive until 1902, after decades of harsh controversy.

Again, with the rise of large department stores after midcentury, small specialty stores, usually owned and run by tradesmen and their wives, were hard put to survive. They hoped for the network of informal relationships that cordial neighbors and steady customers could provide, but often enough these hopes were disappointed, and then such women were driven into the vast pool of menial laborers. And of course in large enterprises, only a handful of women had any hope of rising to leading positions. Respectable women could become teachers, governesses, or writers—this last providing spectacular income for a few—but that, before the 1860s, was about all.

In 1893, writing in the Paris *Revue des Revues*, the highly regarded Italian criminologist Cesare Lombroso discussed the relation of women to genius and talent, which, given his great (wholly undeserved) prestige, unintentionally made plain just what women eager to enter the workforce were facing. He denied that women had failed to make their mark in the world, whether in painting, in music, in literature, or in science, just because discrimination invented by men held them back. "It is an incontestable fact that among all vertebrate animals the female is inferior to the male." And what holds true of birds and insects also holds true of the human animal. Woman weighs less and is less intelligent than man. She is more insensitive to pain and sexual desire; hence she can never be a great poet or artist. She is by nature a conservative; which is why it is a mistake to expect from her innovations of any kind.

There are, Lombroso concedes, some talented women like George Sand, Rosa Bonheur, and George Elliot (sic!), but none of these rises to the heights of Michelangelo or Newton. Moreover, even these three remarkable women are more masculine than many men. Just look at them or listen to their voices! Still, in areas in which little muscular effort is required, women can do well: they can be fine teachers, even doctors. There are, he notes, six hundred women physicians in Russia and about three thousand of them in the United States. In short, the educated woman who wants to be at work outside the home need not despair—as long as she does not aspire to genius. This was not much of a concession, but at least Lombroso did not descend to the familiar notion that young women should not be admitted to college because their menstrual period totally incapacitated them for part of every month.

In the face of all this anxious theorizing—for it was males nervous about women stepping out of their divinely appointed roles that led to such far-reaching generalizations—the very economic and social forces that extruded women from the workplace also provided employment for them, even if for the most part on a low level. The opportunities for public employment shifted, and in important regards improved. New businesses, new industries, new banks, new government institutions were requiring unprecedented numbers of employees literate and numerate, personnel with an acceptable appearance and manners. And an increasing number of these were petty bourgeois women: clerks, salespeople, and the like. Nineteenth-century inventions like the telephone and the typewriter, insatiable for operators, propelled women into the work force. The English censuses of mid-nineteenth century listed only a negligible number of women in commercial occupations. In the census of 1911, the total was 739,000, of whom 157,000 were women, an impressive increase to 21 percent. The American figures are an even more remarkable sign of this small revolution. In 1859, the executive departments of the federal government in Washington employed 1,268 clerks, all of them men; in 1903, the number had multiplied twenty-fold, to 25,675, of whom about a quarter, or 6,882, were women. One may be sure that they internalized the prescription to work hard and competently even if they had never seen it articulated. Honest supervisors—all men, of course—had to acknowledge that these female clerks were often extraordinarily competent, and not in routine, mindless procedures alone. Women, men discovered, had brains as well as superior small motor control.

Yet in country after country, these openings for lower-middle-class women were far from pure delight. They were tarnished by discrimination built into the wage structure by the men who made the rules, one that the most well intentioned superiors could do little to alleviate: women were invariably paid less than their male colleagues, in fact, usually less than men holding jobs inferior to theirs. In the United States, female government employees were nearly always assigned to the lowly category of "copyist" and paid $900 a year, even when they did the work of clerks paid $1,600. The lot of female teachers everywhere mirrored the same inequities, and quite understandably aroused the indignation of feminists, almost always in vain. One rare exception was the situation of women clerks in Parisian department stores, where, with bonuses, the pay might rise to about 3,000 francs a year, certainly enough for a modest independence. Sensible and engaged supporters of the right of women to enter the working world under evenhanded circumstances had concluded before midcentury that women ought to concentrate on access to higher education perhaps even more than to keep making futile appeals to men to grant them the suffrage. The road to careers in teaching, the practice of medicine, even to the lower ranks of management took this path.

4

FROM THE EARLY NINETEENTH CENTURY ON, THE idealization of work made well-meaning contemporaries uneasy whenever they faced the situation of the working poor. It was troubling enough, as we have seen, that this prized model of conduct proved to be a moral spur to a mere minority. For the untold thousands laboring in factories or offices, it simply enforced new habits and new pressures: their employers obliged them to adopt a rigorous work discipline over which they had no control. They had to adapt to demands for prompt and regular attendance, steady and attentive performance, unaccustomed routines that required drastic shifts from time-honored customs. In small workshops—the rule in nineteenth-century France and for decades even in highly industrialized England—employers and employees knew one another and could, often enough, keep a human relationship alive. In large factories, though, workers were reduced to "hands," largely anonymous, almost interchangeable units. The grip of the industrial order reached into thousands of working-class dwellings, in run-down suburbs or in urban slums, where domestic producers such as seamstresses and embroiderers—one thinks of Schnitzler's Jeanette—labored under unremitting strain to fulfill the quotas that their masters assigned to them.

It was just as troubling to bourgeois not blinded by an obsession with profits or traditional preconceptions about the lower orders that conditions in factories, for men, women, and children alike, were anything but idyllic. Granted, it took years, even decades, before average bourgeois had much of a clue to what went on among the laboring classes at home or during their working day. Their ignorance was not relieved by propagandists lending their pens to the cause of the employers. As late as the 1870s, Otto von Bismarck, Germany's presumably well-informed chancellor, felt compelled to launch investigations into these issues because, apart from being exposed to dubious anecdotes and self-serving proposals by industrialists, he knew so little about them. And so much of the public, in an atmosphere compounded of guilt feelings, truculent defensiveness, paternalistic condescension, and doctrinaire theorizing, was ready to absorb fanciful rationalizations, alibis that accented the positive side of the mechanization of work, and admired not just its economic utility but also its sheer pleasures.

Their texts make strange reading today, but they formed an integral part of the confusing array of perspectives on the factory system. To ignore all these uncertainties would do violence to prevalent states of mind, some vacillating, others dogmatic, many, as I have noted, uninformed. The advent of large-scale, at times astonishingly swift industrialization raised a host of awkward questions about workers' health, housing, pay, and other essentials that none of the old remedies, mainly local charity, could come near resolving. Doubtless, self-interest and class prejudices gave rhetorical force to clashing positions. But they were far from the sole motives of industrialists, preachers, and members of parliaments. Religious and philosophical convictions, at times but by no means always an alibi for callousness, could determine a legislator's vote or an editorialist's voice one way or the other.

There were good causes troubling the age, like anti-slavery, that offered the reformers nothing but spiritual profits. Despite this (or with some, because of this), impassioned ideologues gave them prominence in their political agenda. Still, when it came to the blessings and ravages of modern capitalism, the most principled observers, were they honest with themselves, had to admit to being quite unsure whether their ideas were at all realistic. Unfortunately for reformers, the theories dominant among early nineteenth-century political economists, practicing what was justly nicknamed the dismal science, seemed to reduce benevolent state interventions in the free marketplace to irrelevance at best. If government action to raise wages and support the casualties of the system only produced rising prices and the survival of the unfit, raising wages and supporting the sick and the old were signally counterproductive policies. What then was a humane soul to do?

Since Britain pioneered in building the industrial order and saw its example spreading beyond its borders, it seems reasonable to focus on that country's responses to the brave new economic world it was the first to make. The most enthusiastic apologist for what he called "the perfection of automatic industry" must have been Andrew Ure, a knowledgeable historian of the English cotton industry. In 1835, he published an ambitious book, *The Philosophy of Manufactures,* parading on the title page his medical degree, his membership in the Royal Society, and various other honors. His treatise was a survey of the industrial system with all manner of technical detail and a section on the factory's "moral economy." Ure was resolutely jolly, touting the "blessings which physico-mechanical science has bestowed on society." He could find no commendation strong enough for the benefits that machinery offered the operator: "every member of the loom is so adjusted, that the driving force leaves the attendant nearly nothing at all to do, certainly no muscular fatigue to sustain, while it procures for him good, unfailing wages, besides a healthy workshop *gratis.*"

Ure waxed even more lyrical about the children at work in cotton plants. He claimed to have made surprise visits to "many factories" and was pleased to report: "I never saw a single instance of corporal chastisement inflicted on a child, nor indeed did I ever see children in ill-humour. They seemed to be always cheerful and alert, taking pleasure in the light play of their muscles,—enjoying the mobility natural to their age." He found it "delightful to observe the nimbleness with which they pieced the broken ends, as the mule-carriage began to recede from the fixed roller beam, and to see them at leisure, after a few seconds' exercise of their tiny fingers, to amuse themselves in any attitude they chose, till the stretch and winding-on were once more completed." These "lively elves" saw their work as "a sport," and "conscious of their skill, they were delighted to show it off to any stranger." Nor were they exhausted by the day's labor, "for they immediately began to skip about" and "to commence their little amusements with the same alacrity as boys issuing from a school." The factory as playground! One wonders why the little elves did not wait in line at the factory gate begging to be taken on.

Ten years later, in *Conditions of the Working Class in England in 1844,* an exposé as bleak as Ure's hymn of praise had been ebullient, Friedrich Engels in his slashing manner quoted all of this passage and had fine sport with Ure's ignorance, his cleverly truncated quotations, and his "impudence." Such refutations, though, did not silence later publicists who shared Ure's views. Whether they had read *The Philosophy of Manufactures* or not, some of them seemed to echo it. As late as 1904, a French physician, Charles Féré, in his significantly titled *Work and Pleasure,* ridiculed radicals who wanted to limit the hours of work: "Socialism, whose ideal is the progressive reduction of a day's working hours to eight hours, to six hours (Vaillant), to four hours (Hyndman), to three hours (Lafargue), to two hours (Beinsdorf), to an hour and a half (Joire), tries to show us work as the greatest of evils." He urged his readers to keep in mind that no machine will ever relieve people of work, and endorsed Tolstoy's declaration that work is the joy of life. Man, Féré insisted, "is happy only through work," and since work personifies happiness, "it is easy to conclude from this that *non-work* represents unhappiness." Conveniently enough, Féré seems to have assumed that whether to work or not, and at what, was a purely voluntary decision. The distance between bourgeois and working-class ways of seeing the meaning of work could hardly have been greater than this.

▓ THIS DISTANCE WAS SCARCELY REDUCED BY THE technical studies about the relationship of work and rhythm that were saturating the market around the time that Féré wrote his book, studies that, for all their cool, professional tone, could not conceal that factory labor was usually boring and destructive of individuality. Adam Smith had warned of such dismal effects more than a century before. Yet in 1897, a German physician, Karl Bücher, went so far as to maintain that "precisely the monotony of work is of the greatest benefit to man," a staggering assertion he rescued from sheer farce (and destroyed whatever practical interest it might have had) by immediately adding the qualifying phrase, "as long as he can determine the tempo of his bodily movements and to stop at will."

Given such complacent publications, it was perhaps inevitable that in 1890 an American author, William Gannett, should produce a lighthearted essay, "Blessed be drudgery," in which he professed to find all work delightful, even the most tedious grind. Is work not the supreme pedagogue? "*My daily task,* whatever it be, *that is what mainly educates me. All other culture is mere luxury compared with what that gives.*" It is easy to be a great man, he declared. "Order, diligence, patience, honesty,—just what you and I must use in order to put our dollar in the savings-bank, to do our school-boy sum, to keep the farm thrifty, and the house clean, and the tables neat." Special talents and advanced knowledge matter far less than "how much I do with what I know." Hence, he buoyantly concluded, let us "sing a hallelujah unto Drudgery: *Blessed be drudgery,*—the one thing that we cannot spare!" He was quite right, of course, but not for his reasons: millions really could not afford to spare drudgery.

Without knowing the author's name, one can be sure that only a man could have written this. Yet, in a far more serious vein, toward the end of the nineteenth century, employers were beginning to take an interest in "scientific management." Frederick W. Taylor, who invented the term, had started out in the early 1880s as a foreman at the Midvale Steel Company in Philadelphia, analyzing the precise character of factory jobs and the effectiveness of machinery. Over two decades, the time and motion studies of Taylor and his followers added up to a meticulously researched program for redesigning equipment and redefining job performance, all in the name of efficiency. In some respects, the workforce profited from this quest for higher productivity as research into lighting, cleanliness, and the reasonable limits of demands on workers improved their environment. Other aspects, though, looked to trade unionists suspiciously like attempts to speed up output without accompanying raises in pay. For all the difference in tone and precision, then, very little seemed to have changed from the days that Andrew Ure discovered sprightly little factory elves.

5

IN WANDERING THROUGH FACTORIES TAKING notes, Ure was not just genially slumming among the lower orders, he was making a political point, in fact two political points. He was, in modern parlance, engaged in union bashing, and responding to what he called "the late parliamentary crusade against the factories." His distaste for big government equaled his distaste for trade unions, both to him unqualified evils. With good cause, he saw industrial turmoil and the threat of more all around him. Factory hands were organizing to fight for better pay and for the reduction of the working day to ten hours without being docked for it, and it was the Ten Hour Bill that particularly enraged Ure as a conspiracy of ingrates and malcontents.

But these ingrates and malcontents found support among radicals in Parliament. An alliance between Utilitarians and Evangelical Protestants, seconded by likeminded humanitarians secular and devout alike, constituted itself the bourgeois conscience to combat such excrescences as urban slums, child labor, and excessive hours for adult factory workers. In 1831, the Evangelical Protestant Michael Sadler introduced a Ten Hour Bill in the House of Commons, and in the following year, the Select Committee of the House he had chaired presented its report on child labor. That report, with its unrelieved recital of horror stories about the fatigue, the diseases, the neglect, the cruelty suffered by laboring children, caught the imagination of the newspaper-reading public. A subsequent Royal Commission, far more sympathetic to the manufacturers, found much to fault in Sadler's methods of investigation and his tendentious conclusions. Even Engels, looking back a dozen years later, admitted that the report was "emphatically partisan, composed by strong enemies of the factory system, for party ends." Finally, in 1833, after much parliamentary maneuvering and many amendments, a bill limiting the hours of children in factories but leaving the hours of adults untouched passed with a vote of 238 to 93. This Factory Act, then, saw to it that, in Engels's summary, "some of the most crying evils disappeared almost wholly." It was the first serious step toward demonstrating national concern about some of the effects of industrial capitalism. France followed suit with the law of 1841, which prohibited children under eight working in factories and limited the hours for older children. The French legislation, it turned out, was easily evaded, but an awareness of toiling, illiterate, Godless children mounted from country to country. The idea that "Something Must Be Done" mounted with it, though not always with tangible success.

The British Factory Act of 1833 was a defeat for the ten-hour agitation, which was not translated into law until 1847. But Ure, rather than
being pleased with the victory of his side, was bitterly disappointed in
the vote. "It will certainly appear surprising to every dispassionate
mind," he complained, "that ninety-three members of the British House
of Commons could be found capable of voting that any class of grown-
up artisans should not be suffered to labour more than ten hours a
day—an interference with the freedom of the subject which no other
legislator in Christendom would have countenanced for a moment."
Instead of being grateful for steady, well-paid, and generally pleasant
employment, Ure grumbled, factory operatives, ignorant and envious
every one of them, were all too easily seduced by "artful demagogues."
And their champions in Parliament, Ure sadly added, were no better
informed than factory workers about the marvelous industrial world
unfolding before them.

Engels, too, was disappointed, but for opposite reasons. Commenting
on the second government report that had become the basis of the legislation, he assailed "the most shameful recklessness of the manufacturing bourgeoisie towards its employees, the whole infamy of the
industrial exploiting system in its full inhumanity." The act, even
though it provided for factory inspectors for the first time, was an
adroit and obscene fraud: "Care has been taken to give the brutal
profit-greed of the bourgeoisie a hypocritical, civilized form, to restrain
the manufacturers through the arm of the law from too conspicuous vil-
lainies, and thus to give them a pretext for self-complacently parading
their sham philanthropy. That is all." It is not surprising that for Marx's
alter ego, the bourgeoisie had to be the villain of the piece: the gospel of
work was typical for the ostentatious middle-class piety behind which,
barely concealed, lay the reality of the bourgeois as the slave driver.

This conclusion begs the question just where the ethical impulse to
reduce the victimization of the working poor could have come from.
Knowing the full history of the legislation down to 1844, Engels could
hardly pretend that whatever reforms had been enacted were simply
inexplicable accidents. At the same time, convinced that the "bourgeoisie as a *class*" was doomed, he could give credit to only a few wor-

thy individuals: a handful of philanthropic Tories, self-denying manufacturers, and above all that "half-German Thomas Carlyle" who, more than anyone else, "has sounded the social disorder more deeply than any other English bourgeois." For Engels, "the diverse sections, subdivisions and parties of the bourgeoisie," a plurality that I have treated as of central importance in this book, were "of mere historical and theoretical significance."

Engels was making things easy for himself. Anyone who has read this far knows that when the temptation arises to offer global judgments, it is more serviceable to speak of the middle classes in the plural rather than to damn all bourgeois as a virtually undifferentiated mass. Nor is it generous, or psychologically persuasive, to revile all the opponents of reform as greedy, mean-spirited, and incurably vicious. The broad spectrum of opinions among those who opposed the Ten Hour Bill and those who favored it suggests a sense of deep puzzlement, which dominated the debate over the implications of capitalism that was virtually exploding across nineteenth-century England, to be followed, somewhat later, by Germany, Belgium, France, and the United States.

"Puzzlement" is the right word. There was so much to learn about investments and risks, the legal obligations of companies, and the implications of government intervention in the market—and so little was known. Not every railroad line, every new product, every department store could count on guaranteed and lasting profits. Failures were frequent, bankruptcies usually devastating. Economists could be grossly wrong, sages hopelessly unwise, statesmen in the dark. That dizzying innovations in machinery, transport, and finance opened the door to speculation and extravagant malfeasance is unquestionable. But, then, the rapidity and ubiquity of change on which I have insisted throughout these pages did not facilitate temperate or intelligent judgments. The men making the decisions for the most part had no maps to guide them through unexplored landscapes. And most of Ure's conservative countrymen found his defense of the free British subject highly congenial. The old system had left most economic decisions to the more than fifteen thousand parishes in the country, a chaotic structure that had in effect broken down long before. But it seemed a bulwark against centralism, an issue that would bedevil efforts at humane national legislation for decades, and not in Great Britain alone.

IN THE MIDST OF CONSIDERING THE CLASS struggle it is easy to miss the fact that the casualties of capitalism included a sizable number of capitalists. I speak here not of financial or social but of emotional damage. These walking wounded were the obsessive financiers, executives, managers, and storekeepers who could not stop working, could not take vacations, could not retire. In the 1830s, Hirsekorn the elder had already cautioned his son against that perversion of character. Early in the twentieth century, Max Weber, to quote him once more, saw the modern capitalist as a captive in an Iron Cage. The means—making money—had become the end. To repeat John Stuart Mill's apt phrase, such ignoble psychological malformations reflected "the sabbathless pursuit of wealth."

In one of her lesser-known novels, *Work: A Story of Experience*, Louisa May Alcott describes with eloquent simplicity the determination of a young woman to go out into the world to escape her tedious, uneventful, chore-ridden existence in rural New England: "I can't help feeling that there is a better sort of life than this dull one made up of everlasting work, with no object but money. I can't starve my soul for the sake of my body." This was a young idealist speaking, looking for work that would free her from her iron cage. But it is instructive to note that among the most passionate critics of single-minded materialism was none other than Samuel Smiles. In *Self-Help*, he warned that it was against the "habit of inordinate saving that the wise man needs most carefully to guard himself, else, what in youth was simple economy, may in old age grow into avarice, and what was a duty in the one case may become a vice in the other." He thought it "one of the defects of business too exclusively followed, that it insensibly tends to a mechanism of character, the businessman gets into a rut and often does not look beyond it." Smiles maintained it was easy to recognize the type. "Take a leaf from such men's ledgers and you have their life." Such people may get on well enough, even though they lack elevation of mind and goodness of character. But one must beware of taking such a disastrous turn. "Money is power after its sort, it is true, but intelligence, public spirit and moral virtues are powers, too, and far nobler ones."

If even the prophet of self-help felt it necessary to caution his readers about the wrong kinds of success, it was bound to be a serious matter. In short, success had its failures, the gospel of work its limitations. As more and more Victorian bourgeois had more and more disposable income and free hours, they found increasing opportunities to attend to Smiles's words. In their century, the ideal of work was supplemented by the ideal of leisure. More than ever before, the middle classes could spend money and time in pursuits more elevated than chasing wealth and make room in their daily schedules for listening to music, looking at art, and attending the theatre.

Chez Aubert Pl. de la Bourse, 29.

Imp. d'Aubert & Cⁱᵉ.

_ Mais si, ma femme, je t'assure que monsieur dessine un paysage... n'est-ce pas, monsieur, que vous dessinez un paysage ?....

Matters of Taste

1

IN DECEMBER 1908, ARTHUR SCHNITZLER WENT TO hear the Rosé Quartet play Arnold Schoenberg's new second quartet, opus 10, a revolutionary experiment in atonality. Earlier that year, in his program notes for *Book of the Hanging Gardens*, his setting of poems by Stefan George, Schoenberg had announced that he had "broken through all the limitations of a past aesthetic," and his quartet was no less subversive of tonality. In his diary, Schnitzler noted that there had been an "uproar—*Skandal*" during the performance, and commented, "I do not believe in Schoenberg. I immediately understood Bruckner, Mahler—should I fail now?" With his openness to the avant-garde, Schnitzler was willing to consider that his own taste might somehow have fallen short. But he soon transferred the responsibility for his failure to appreciate atonal music to the composer. In 1912, entertaining the Rosé Quartet, Bruno Walter, and Walter's wife at dinner, there was, he recorded laconically, an "animated conversation about musical questions; Schoenberg, all kinds of swindle." The man, Schnitzler concluded, was not an authentic Modernist composer but a fraud.

His response to provocative painting in that stirring time of cultural innovation was equally definite and is equally instructive. In January 1913, he recorded a two-hour conversation about "the tasks of modern art," and in the following month, on a short visit to Munich, he enjoyed an opportunity to judge it directly. He visited the Modern Gallery to see an exhibition of Picassos. "The earlier paintings extraordinary," he noted, but quickly added, "Vehement resistance to his current Cubism." Schnitzler's resistance was not strong enough, though, to keep him from attending another Picasso exhibition in Vienna two years later. Austrian and German Modernists generated reactions from him no less discriminating. At Christmastime, 1913, he attended an exhibition and found "lovely things: Klimt, Liebermann," and others. But among the "pretentious swindlers" at the show—Schnitzler evidently liked to charge artists he did not understand with charlatanry—was Egon Schiele, that exceptional draftsman and unforgiving student of the human body. Schnitzler was ready to widen his aesthetic horizons, but not to infinity.

▓ IT IS TEMPTING TO READ SCHNITZLER'S BALKING at Schoenberg, the Cubist Picasso, and Schiele as documenting a historic confrontation: the resistance of the nineteenth century to the twentieth. So it was everywhere in the restless, quarrelsome worlds of all the arts—in painting and sculpture, poetry and the drama, in the novel no less than in music, and in architecture. Everyone but a fanatical devotee of the new somewhere got off the train racing toward Modernism—witness Schnitzler's inability to absorb the latest manifestations of Picasso's art. After mid-nineteenth century, a collector of paintings bored by routine academic canvases might take pleasure in the Barbizon School of landscapists but reject the Impressionist style as too casual, even sloppy; a devotee of the Impressionists might disparage the Post-Impressionists as primitive and chaotic; an enthusiast for

Van Gogh might denigrate Kandinsky's abstractions as a speculation on a gullible public, just as Schnitzler found Schoenberg's new music an imposition on serious music lovers like himself. For their part, avant-garde artists and their supporters mobilized a united front only if the hated bourgeoisie was to be put in its place. Apart from such opportunities to lay into the philistine, they fiercely insisted on their individuality. Gauguin faulted the Impressionists for remaining shackled to visual probabilities; Mondrian criticized Picasso for failing to "progress" to complete abstraction. One artist's imaginative bravery was another artist's bourgeois spinelessness.

Slighting these complexities, historians have all too conveniently summarized the course of Victorian taste as an unending conflict between consumers of conventional offerings on one side and mutinous Modernists on the other, as though the strains roiling the arts could be understood as a straightforward duel over the heart of high culture. The front lines in the Victorian culture wars, though, were anything but clear-cut; much of the time controversies over an emerging style of painting or composition amounted to a confused, and confusing, debate among three and even more parties. And there were advanced artists, secret bourgeois, who wanted nothing better than to join the company of the respectable. Edouard Manet, the great pioneer of Modernism in painting, craved nothing so much as the ribbon of the Legion of Honor; Max Liebermann, Germany's most eminent semi-Impressionist, who headed the Berlin Secession in the 1890s and after, was a solid upper bourgeois living the most regular life. In the end, what remains particularly striking about the Victorian cultural situation with all its venomous disputes is the proliferation of tastes compelled by the art market into tense, unstable coexistence.

In short, the lines between sedentary bourgeois and audacious explorers were porous. The catalogue of Victorian middle-class collectors is long; these modern heirs of Maecenas were for the most part rich men and a few rich women—for the most part but not all. The first to collect Cézanne were anything but affluent men and, each in his own manner, was an unconventional bourgeois. Julien François Tanguy, affectionately known as père Tanguy, the kind-hearted Parisian dealer in art supplies, himself a poor man who took canvases in place of payment and let Impressionists and Post-Impressionists owe him money for years, was the first to display Cézannes in his shop. It seems that he sold just one of them, even though he priced the paintings on his walls modestly at 100 francs for the large, 40 francs for the small canvases.

That sole customer for Tanguy's Cézannes appears to have been Victor Chocquet, a clerk in the customhouse in Paris. His private means were modest, his collector's yearning beyond those means, his unbounded worship of Cézanne, well known: he wearied his friends, art critics, and collectors, anyone who would listen, by talking Cézanne to them. Compelled to conserve his resources, he haunted auction houses and regularly dropped out around 300 francs, patiently waiting for another occasion when his bids for a longed-for picture might not exceed his limits. Chocquet the collector was a maniac as all collectors are to a degree, but not a monomaniac: he also bought Delacroix, Pissarros, Monets, and Renoirs. But when he died in 1891, he had thirty-two Cézannes in his possession.

Dr. Paul Gachet, who like Chocquet accumulated some thirty Cézannes, was a specialist in mental disorders and women's diseases with a practice in Paris, the friend of painters and himself a talented amateur. A political left-winger with philanthropic inclinations, he announced on his stationery that he would treat the poor free of charge. Van Gogh, who painted his portrait, called Gachet an eccentric, and perhaps he was. Hydrotherapy and homeopathy were among the medical fads he took an interest in, but his true eccentricity was Cézanne. These three collectors—Tanguy, Chocquet, and Gachet—stand for scores of other Victorian bourgeois endowed not with great wealth but with a passion for true art.

Yet, by the nature of things, most serious collecting was in the hands of upper bourgeois with sizable budgets at their disposal. Monied German and Russian businessmen, thriving merchants in Manchester, Paris, Amsterdam, New York, and Chicago championed artists and did so in the most practical manner. "There is only one way of proving that you like a man's paintings when you have the material means to do it," wrote the playwright Alexandre Dumas fils in the 1880s; "buy them." And that is what they did. In 1853, Alexandre Bruyas, a rich banker's son with time on his hands and infatuated with amassing portraits of himself, discovered Gustave Courbet at the Salon, commissioned three likenesses from him, bought several paintings, and invited Courbet to make him his confidant. Around the end of the century, the Moscow merchant Sergei Shchukin, who had started collecting commonplace contemporary Russian painters, found his true vocation in Paris, and came home with Van Goghs, Gauguins, Cézannes. Once back in Moscow, he started to assemble an impressive collection of Matisses; exchanging the role of customer for that of patron, he sought Matisse's friendship and commissioned him to paint large canvases for his mansion.

To cite one more modern Maecenas: in 1910, the Berlin industrialist Bernhard Koehler financed the impecunious young painter Franz Marc with a monthly stipend of 200 Mark and accepted Marc's paintings in trade, thus easing the lot of an important artist whose career was cruelly cut short in 1916 by his death in the war. This is only a small sampling of a far larger population of opulent bourgeois patrons, which should put paid to the familiar stereotype of the capitalist as the incurably philistine captain of industry, banking, and commerce. In matters of taste, good bourgeois could defy powerful fashions and venture capitalists could be more adventurous in their taste for art than in their ruthlessness with competitors.

▨ A LOOK AT THE MOTIVATIONS OF RICH COLLECTORS and patrons should further discredit this stereotype; their aims were diverse and complicated. The hunt for social prestige was one, but only one, impulse for heading the list of subscribers to an opera or joining the board of directors of a museum. Playwrights and novelists from Alexandre Dumas fils to Henry James created parvenus grasping at the arts to prove their cultivation. Maupassant, in *Bel-Ami* (1885), has the speculator and corrupt publisher Walter, a Jewish social climber, display his acquisitions carefully labeled to shine at his pretentious receptions. His real taste is for sexually suggestive or coarsely humorous canvases; yet having taken advice what a man in good society must hang on his walls, he also owns some faultlessly academic paintings by the likes of Bouguereau.

But this bourgeois barbarian posing as a connoisseur is a two-dimensional caricature. Like many caricatures it contains a kernel of truth, but no more. In the last quarter of the nineteenth century, a handful of wealthy German Jews, notably James Simon and Eduard Arnhold, acquired a reputation for their philanthropies and their art collections. On good terms with Wilhelm II, they were dubbed, a little invidiously, *Kaiserjuden*, and their desire to make themselves truly at home in Berlin's upper bourgeoisie may have been one incentive for their patronage of artists and their conspicuous donations to museums. Living in a country where Jews had only recently been granted political and legal equality but were still largely excluded from most polite society, they may have had the struggle for acceptance at the back of their minds. But what we know of them suggests that the hunt for status was at most secondary for them. They collected art because they loved art. Whatever anti-Semites said, not all social climbers were Jews; not all Jews were social climbers.

In short, Simon and Arnhold, like their counterparts throughout the upper bourgeoisie, were collectors, and collectors are, as I have said, a species of madmen; they were men and women possessed more passionately with acquiring the objects of their desire than almost anything else. They obeyed their private promptings, searching the world for the things they fancied—not just paintings but rare books or manuscripts, period furniture or stamps. In 1868, an anonymous writer in the *Musical Times* of London spoke of "the prevailing 'collecting' mania." He was right, particularly since the kinds of stuff that attracted avid hunters and gatherers multiplied during the Victorian years—yet another proof of the growing availability of leisure time and disposable income among the bourgeoisies.

To call collecting a "mania" is to use strong language, but the compulsiveness of the activity is only too evident. Musing before a canvas by the highly regarded French Orientalist painter Alexandre Decamps at the Paris Salon of 1846, Théophile Thoré, the great art critic who was to discover the forgotten master Vermeer for the world, noted: "One could not start a collection without a Decamps, and everyone who has a Decamps is lost; he starts to love painting; he must collect paintings and *voilà*, he's a collector." *Il lui faut collectionner des tableaux* — a brilliant insight that points to the sheer helplessness of the collector facing up to his imperative needs. Half a century later, in 1898, in a book anatomizing collecting, an American victim of this disease, Edwin C. Bolles, aptly described the psychological predicament that is also a delight — his own and that of all his fellows — "Among the keenest pleasures of life in hope, in acquisition, memory, there is hardly one to surpass the Collector's joy. His field is the world; the objects of his desire range indifferently from blackened postage stamps to Greek vases and diamonds." Middle-class taste in Schnitzler's century was not just a confrontation between the future and the past, whatever the great simplifiers of the press said, but of a daunting diversity and unplumbed depth, differing from rank to rank, country to country, individual to individual.

The enormous miscellany of paintings and sculptures displayed at the Exposition Décennale of 1900 in Paris attests to the almost unlimited array and refreshing unpredictability of bourgeois tastes in the late Victorian decades. An integral part of the Exposition Universelle, the Décennale featured art done in the previous decade chosen by committees in participating countries. Since there was no uniformity in the selection process, the resulting feast for the eyes showed some idiosyncratic features; but in sum it displayed art presumably representative of the best, or most highly appreciated, recent work. Nearly every type of painting and sculpture was abundantly on view: landscapes, still-lifes, portraits, self-portraits, nudes, a dizzying assortment of genre scenes secular and religious, portrait busts, Amazons on horseback, peasants at the harvest, statuettes of women after a bath.

A substantial number of the artists at the Décennale unmistakably, at times obtrusively, aimed at making a didactic point. They showed landscapes to remonstrate against reckless urbanization, crucifixions to remind viewers of the august Christian faith, workingmen to generate sympathy for the exploited and downtrodden. Others were candidly ornamental or, showing naked bodies in an ingenious assortment of poses, quite frankly titillating. Still others, painters doing their self-portrait, posed as nobly serious or, showing handsome mustaches, cheerfully advertised themselves. And a few—Cézanne, Matisse, Degas, Picasso, Munch—visibly rejoiced in the sheer expressive possibilities of modern painting. The level of competence was high, the level of taste somewhat less so. If one were to use the Exposition Décennale as an index to what kind of art late Victorian bourgeois responded most enthusiastically, one would be compelled to reply: all of it. Their tastes in art were as catholic as their opinions on politics.

2

THE EXPOSITION DECENNALE WAS ONLY THE latest representative of that proliferating Victorian invention, the world's fair. These vast, crowded bazaars, exhibiting the latest novelties in machinery, gadgets, household wares, furniture, and art, were among Victorian cultural institutions like concert halls and museums largely set up for, if not always by, bourgeois. We have seen that royalty inspired and essentially paid for such establishments in Bavaria; and the leading advocate of the archetypal world's fair, the Great Exhibition of 1851 in London, was Prince Albert. Elsewhere, too, crowned heads of state translated their most ambitious cultural intentions, whether indirectly aiming at demonstrating political power or slyly struggling for economic hegemony, into splendid and expensive reality. But increasingly, reigning princes who made it their business to foster the arts coopted bourgeois magnates, bankers and brewers, to build new museums or to fill older ones with their treasures. Whoever originated these new houses of high culture, their principal beneficiaries were the audiences, spectators and listeners alike. The international fairs were companions to other Victorian cultural inventions of which there had been only rudiments before the French Revolution.

To be sure, gathering places like theatres and opera houses were not a Victorian creation. But they too would flourish in unprecedented size and numbers in the nineteenth century. High culture was reaching for democracy before politics did so. What had been to the end of the previous century the monopoly of noblemen or wealthy patricians became in the Victorian decades a public stand-in for home, showing objects that bourgeois families could not afford to buy but could afford to visit. These homes away from home mainly served the middling and affluent strata in society, though, it will emerge, visitors and audiences often included the petty bourgeoisie as well.

In 1870, looking back three decades and more, Lady Eastlake, wife of Sir Charles Eastlake, the director of the National Gallery in London, and an able critic of the contemporary art scene in her own right, noted that social forces had reshaped the production and consumption of British art: "The patronage which had been almost exclusively the privilege of the nobility and higher gentry, was now shared (to be subsequently almost engrossed) by a wealthy and intelligent class, chiefly enriched by commerce and trade." This shift, she added, had measurably benefited living artists, since the good sense of the *nouveaux riches* made them aware of their "ignorance upon matters of connoisseurship." And this in turn induced parvenus to buy contemporary art rather than older paintings of which they knew little. In other countries, this change was taking place more slowly, but it was irresistible everywhere.

In musical capitals like Vienna or Amsterdam, intimate recitals in aristocratic drawing rooms for the privileged few and occasional access to collections of pictures in lordly mansions did not come to an end, but public concerts and public exhibitions grew into favorite meeting places for the increasingly prosperous middle classes. The age of the virtuoso, culminating between the 1830s and 1860s in recitals by triumphant performers like Niccolò Paganini, Franz Liszt, and Jenny Lind, would have been unthinkable in the old régime, where music was largely performed in private aristocratic circles, in churches, and at raucous plebeian festivals. Recently founded symphony orchestras developed subscription seasons for sizable audiences. As the century progressed, even middle-sized towns across Europe and the United States such as Hartford or Rouen opened art museums, the first in 1844 and the second in 1880. Free public libraries, seconded by private subscription libraries, gratified mounting appetites for books, even for high literature. And even those cultural institutions that demanded entrance fees became affordable for substantial numbers of bourgeois; for the first time in history, plebeian lovers of art, theatre, music, and fiction enjoyed ample opportunities for enlarging their pleasures in the finer things of life.

Enlarging did not necessarily mean elevating them; governed by old-fashioned boards of directors or equally unadventurous authorities, a museum could degenerate into a mausoleum featuring forged master-pieces or derivative sculpture and keeping out the fresh breezes of orig-inal talents. They could artificially keep alive what was already dying. There were years in the nineteenth century when the Salons in Paris, normally held annually, were under the oppressive management of offi-cials too timid to give houseroom to art not taught in traditional studios and academies. This is not to maintain that all academic art was hope-lessly mediocre; faultless draftsmen like Jean-Louis Meissonier or Alexandre Cabanel amazed Salon goers with their anecdotal inventive-ness and technical facility. But the road to the future lay elsewhere.

Not content to resign themselves to these unpromising conditions, artists, and not only the outsiders among them, responded with sarcas-tic, even angry objections. In 1849, Ingres, the greatest and most hon-ored of French neo-classicist painters, castigated the "overflow of mediocrity" that was dominating the Salons at midcentury, the "banal-ity" that had grown into a "public misfortune," sickened taste, and wasted the resources of the state. "It is true that exhibitions have become a part of our lives. It is therefore impossible to suppress them. But they must not be encouraged. They destroy art, by making it a trade which artists no longer respect." These were powerful words, but others put their discontent even more sharply. The Impressionist Camille Pissarro, whose work came to prominence in the 1880s, was not the first, and not the last, to propose in some seriousness that muse-ums, those "necropolises of art," be burned to the ground. He was con-vinced that their uncritical devotion to what directors deemed the classics made for stony soil, stifling the growth of new art.

Impatient with mere derision and futile polemics, artists conscious of their superiority over what they called official mediocrity formed counter-institutions. The influence of dealers as midwives at the birth of new taste grew measurably; in Paris their one-man shows, provocatively opening at the very time the Salon was being held, rivaled in interest the offerings of state-sponsored exhibitions, at times surpassed them. It was also in Paris, in 1874, that the Impressionists organized their first Independent Salon; by 1886, when they staged their eighth and last exhibition, its principal participants—Monet, Renoir, Morisot, Pissarro, Caillebotte—were well known, if not all of them well paid, for their work. In London, the short-lived Grosvenor Gallery (1877–90), a large and luxurious setting, enlivened the artistic scene by showing Whistler, Watts, and Tissot, and invited invidious comparisons with established painting. This "palace of art" specialized in painters who fared less well in the exhibitions of the dignified Royal Academy, and was particularly sympathetic to the plight of women artists. In Germany and Austria during the 1890s, moving more ponderously than their competitors to the west, painters discontented with the tastes favored by imperial or royal academies formed what they significantly called "Secessions." Inevitably in a century dominated by dramatic transformations, these associations of rebels, often rather mild in their departure from accepted norms, spawned secessions from the Secessions as the subversives of one generation became the establishment of the next.

3

NINETEENTH-CENTURY BOURGEOIS VISITED OPERA houses, concert halls, theatres, and exhibitions public or private to satisfy a diversity of needs. They saw these as places to relax or to flirt, to be seen or to spend time in the company of business acquaintances. Would-be painters worked for days in museums to copy masterpieces. Apprentice soloists flocked to hear the masters perform. In the great halls, some interested more in physical than in spiritual enjoyment sought out prostitutes in the shadows of the upper balconies. But in the largest sense these public structures, whether built by the state or by entrepreneurs, were educational institutions. As David Hume had already recognized in the eighteenth century, tastes are made, not inborn. They require the refining of crude, quick, defiantly uninformed opinions—"I know what I like"—through repeated and prolonged exposure. But that kind of schooling entailed a substantial expenditure of time, and this in turn called for leisure, hours not devoted to making a living or superintending a household. In short, when it came to the acquisition of high culture, money was time.

It is worth repeating that work, which had been a necessity for bourgeois since time out of mind, no longer monopolized the attention of the middle classes; the attainment of good taste became a possible aspiration for many of them only in the Victorian century. Reading, whether poetry or fiction or religious tracts, had of course become feasible for ordinary burghers since printing spread in the sixteenth century, and theatres had begun to satisfy popular demand by the time of Shakespeare. But other forms of leisure spent in instructing oneself in the arts and the more demanding literature, in absorbing their collective messages in quest of something better than merely entertaining or edifying fare, obviously had to wait until they became affordable. Free days apart, most museums and art exhibitions charged entrance fees; concerts and operas could be a financial drain if the whole family wanted to attend; books and sheet music were another source of expenditure. Money bought more than time for the Victorians.

❧ HOW MUCH MONEY? HOW MUCH TIME? I HAVE visualized the Victorian bourgeoisie as an economic pyramid, rising steeply from a very wide bottom to a very narrow top. What John Ruskin called the political economy of art could not evade this fact of life. Obviously, the civilizing objects one could afford to see and hear and buy were crucial determinants in the making of taste. Just as obviously, especially if he was a married man, an English clerk earning some £60 or £70 a year—Anthony Trollope started in the Post Office with a munificent £90—enjoyed cultural opportunities substantially more constrained than those for a prosperous family sure of about £300 a year. Similarly, a German petty bourgeois shopkeeper who made about 1,800 Mark a year with long hours and hard work inhabited a universe almost unrecognizable from that of a public servant in the upper middle ranges between 5,000 and 6,000 Mark, to say nothing of the income of successful professionals, bankers, and merchants. Again, an Austrian earning between 600 and 1,200 Kronen annually must have seemed culturally underprivileged from the vantage point of a Schnitzler, who, drawing royalties for plays performed and honoraria for stories published, counted on roughly 3,000 Kronen a year and still found himself repeatedly short of cash. His earnest resolutions to live more thriftily would not have won sympathy from the majority of the middle-class population of Vienna.

The merchants of culture and the public servants in charge of such matters quickly learned to accommodate themselves to these pyramids. A Sheffield teapot manufactured by James Dixon & Sons after designs by the painter Richard Redgrave could be had in silver for 20 guineas, in silver plate for £2, and in a tin alloy called "Britannia-metal" cunningly made to look like silver for a mere 16 shillings. The Hallé Orchestra in Manchester slightly adjusted its prices to its offerings. In January 1860, with Mendelssohn's *Midsummer Night's Dream* on the program, featuring an "orchestra of seventy instrumentalists, and full chorus," the reserved seats (cushioned) cost 3s; the gallery, 1s 6d; and "the body of the hall" 1s. A month later, when the orchestra performed Gluck's *Iphigenia in Tauris*, proudly promising a "Band and Chorus of 250 Performers," the reserved seats had risen to 4s and the gallery to 2s, while the body of the hall remained at an inexpensive shilling. The price of reserved seats soon went up: by 1864, they cost 7s 6d, but the groundlings were still admitted for a shilling, which, even if the poorly paid clerk took his wife along, was perhaps three hours' worth of work.

German bourgeois well off enough to travel spent 3 Mark for a Baedeker guidebook to Berlin and environs, 5 Mark for one of southern Germany, and 12 Mark for guides to more exotic places like Spain, Egypt, and Palestine. It was as though the publisher of these celebrated guides could calculate that a German who had enough money to go the Holy Land would not cavil at a mere 12 Mark, more than two days' work for a small tradesman. Publishers in general sought to widen their market by making allowances for their prospective customers. In 1880, the essayist and editor Otto von Leixner brought out a book of studies on aesthetics: its frontispiece was a collotype of Angelica Kauffmann's painting of a vestal virgin, of which he offered engravings ranging from 150 down to 25 Mark, each of them advertised as "a masterpiece which does justice to the beauty of the original in every respect." In these and numberless other instances, high culture was permitted to trickle down to the impecunious, even to the most respectable among the working classes.

In some locations like the opera or the theatre, prices were finely calibrated, revealing layers upon layers of affluence and penury in the middling orders. Performances of Schnitzler's plays offer vivid evidence. On October 9, 1895, the Vienna Hofburgtheater performed his *Liebelei*, one of the most successful versions of a favorite Schnitzler subject: the affair between Christine, a young, loving petty bourgoise, and Fritz, an upper-class student. Fritz, who had been carrying on an affair with a married woman at the same time, is killed in a duel by the wronged husband. Soon after, Christine discovers that he died for another love. She has been, as it were, widowed twice. Tickets for this piquant drama ranged from standing room in the fourth gallery for 0.40 and 1.00 Kronen for standing room in the parterre to 25 Kronen for a loge in the first gallery; from 3.50 to 6.00 for a single seat in a loge; from 3.00 to 4.50 in the parquet. Prices carefully distinguished between a seat in the middle of the fourth gallery to one at the side. Schnitzler could have written a witty one-acter about such differentiations.

None of these distinct opportunities for culture guaranteed that all, or even most, bourgeois used their free hours to improve their powers of discrimination. The vehement denunciations by avant-garde artists, writers, and cultural critics of the uncomprehending, vulgar bourgeoisie were grossly overstated; their withering contempt for what Robert Louis Stevenson once called "the Philistines perspiring after wealth" the kind of sweeping statement that defies complex historical realities. All too often, bourgeoisophobes were slapping the hands that had fostered their careers. But if their scorn had a solid basis in reality, the pathetic tale about the true artist starving in his garret poignantly illustrated by a famous painting by Spitzweg was a romantic legend with few counterparts in real life.

It does remain true that until late in the century, advanced tastes in the arts and literature were less sought after among respectable circles, and less well rewarded, than defenders of the bourgeoisie liked to see. It is true, too, that after midcentury, one of Meissonier's canvases of massed troops with all the glittering buttons on the soldiers' uniforms correctly painted could fetch 20,000 francs and far more, while in the early 1880s a Pissarro, a glowing moment of the countryside shimmering in the sun, sold for 200 francs. But no unmeasured condemnation of bourgeois taste any more than an unmeasured defense can capture the diversity of middle-class preferences and its history in the Victorian era. This much, though, is undeniable: for long decades, for most bourgeois, easy aesthetic pleasures first formed in early youth would win out over more sophisticated satisfactions.

It is in fact enticing to describe the likes and dislikes of average bourgeois as almost literally childlike. The choices of children are unhesitating and categorical. And many middle-class adults in the Victorian age, educated men and women among them, never wholly discarded this decisiveness as they satisfied their cravings for high culture. For them, sentimental, storytelling fiction, music one could remember and sing at first hearing, and the engravings featured in the family weeklies of all civilized Western countries were quite enough. Virginia Woolf once called George Eliot's *Middlemarch* the only Victorian novel written for grownups. This pitiless aperçu is as unjust as it is brilliant. But reduced to moderate dimensions, her remark points at an important truth about nineteenth-century culture. Most Victorian bourgeois, like most people before and after them, seeing a play or reading a story wanted to be sure which side they were on, listening to a symphony or looking at a painting, which emotions they were supposed to feel. In novels, they enjoyed what E. M. Forster once called "flat" characters, personages they could identify at first meeting as heroes, clowns, or villains.

The masterly nineteenth-century fiction that presented "round" characters required precisely the cultivation of taste that it took time and effort, often tutelage, to acquire. An unsophisticated reading of *Anna Karenina* makes Karenin, Anna's husband, into an inflexible, odious bureaucratic type; a just as shallow reading of *A Doll's House* makes Torvald Helmer, Nora's husband, into an insensitive domestic dictator. Read more closely, though, it turns out that Tolstoy and Ibsen had brought to life suffering men as much victimized by the pressure of the mores governing their society as are their disobedient wives. It is hardly astonishing that Henry James's late novels, with their subtle personages analyzed to their very bones, took years to find their public.

The same incomprehension confronted painters with a penchant for listening to their inner demons rather than the lure of exalted patronage. As the pictures at the Exposition Décennale attest, most art lovers prized professional skill, a quality that almost by definition characterized all academic canvases. Through most of the century, bourgeois collectors had voted with their money and governments with their medals for artists who touched their hearts with dogs mourning their masters, made them smile at a handsome Italian youth shyly asking a local beauty to dance, gave them a patriotic thrill by displaying a conquering Napoleon riding at the head of his troops, let them gaze raptly at a repentant yet scantily clothed Mary Magdalene, or profess pious aesthetic comprehension as they stared at naked young women decorously cavorting in a Roman bath.

The bulk of the nineteenth-century public thronging exhibitions seems to have observed quite unreflectively certain rules that governed proper appreciation: a painting must be thoroughly finished rather than thrown on canvas like a preliminary sketch—this excluded the Impressionists. The shapes and colors on a canvas must aim at rendering reality as faithfully as artistic skill could make them—this put a Gauguin, a Van Gogh, a Munch, to say nothing of a Picasso, beyond the circle of acceptable artists. And when it came to nudes, which never lost the public's favor and were copiously represented in any show, the painter was obliged to obey what I have called the doctrine of distance: the naked form had to be idealized rather than portrayed as a real person, and placed by its attributes, at times only by its title, into a far-off country, a remote age, or a sacred context. To remove her to antiquity or mythology, to assign her a symbolic name that carried its own dignity was like veiling the sensual youthful model in decency. This rule explains why Manet's *Olympia*, shown at the Paris Salon of 1865, aroused so much vocal disapproval. Here was a naked model, a recognizable Parisienne posing as a courtesan almost aggressively individualized and indisputably contemporary. Far better to call a seductive unclothed young woman on canvas or in marble "Spring," or "Helen of Troy," or even "Electricity"!

4

IF INSTITUTIONS SERVED AS PEDAGOGUES TO THE Victorian bourgeoisie, so did such exceptional intermediaries in the arts as civilized literary commentators and knowledgeable music critics. At rare moments, a strategically placed personage could acquire an astonishing influence over the history of taste. The most successful propagandist for the new French painting was Mary Cassatt. From a wealthy upper-middle-class Pittsburgh family, she traveled widely in Western Europe, painting and meeting painters. By 1874 she was settled in Paris, welcomed by the Impressionists and exhibiting with them. She grew to be as close to Degas as one could with that incurable misanthrope; her paintings and pastels show her debt to him. But it was Cassatt's irresistible championship of French anti-academic painters that made her into a historic force. Her American visitors starved for culture, the rich women whose eyes she opened to Courbet, Manet, and other seditious artists, went home and began to assemble major collections. One of them was Louisine Elder, Cassatt's close friend, soon to marry the wealthy Henry O. Havemeyer. She started with a Degas, and moved on to other important subversives, notably Courbet, Manet, Monet, even Cézanne, whom most late nineteenth-century museum goers considered an untalented dauber who could not even paint a table correctly. Her splendid collection would greatly enrich the Metropolitan Museum of Art.

The names Cassatt and Havemeyer are necessary reminders that the nineteenth-century United States, though still a young and in many ways a raw country, had every right to claim that at least some of its citizens loved and fostered high culture. Americans were more cultivated, less hopelessly philistine, than the caricatures drawn by European visitors led their readers to expect. Contrary to pervasive European condescension in Victorian times—still enjoying a certain support today—not all American taste was low and vulgar. Rich Americans formed symphony orchestras and well-supported public libraries, established and munificently endowed local museums. A small elite patronized contemporary artists: Daniel Wadsworth of Hartford, who founded the Hartford Atheneum in 1844 and supported the American painters Thomas Cole and Frederic Church; William T. Walters of Baltimore, who backed the productive French animal sculptor Louis Barye. Henry Clay Frick bought the best old masters—Halses and Gainsboroughs—he could find, and Henry Havemeyer acquired a substantial number of Rembrandts, some of which actually were Rembrandts. Both collectors eventually made their booty available to the public, the one in the Frick mansion, the other in the Metropolitan Museum.

I could extend this list almost at will: Charles L. Freer amassed a major collection of Asian art, and after starting a close friendship with James Whistler, the most impressive hoard of Whistler's work anywhere; Isabella Stewart Gardner an eclectic, highly personal accumulation of paintings including Titian and Manet. Both left splendid showplaces to let the general public take pleasure in their acquisitions. It is worth noting that some of these wellsprings of American culture were severely denounced, not always unjustly, as monopolists and robber barons: Havemeyer virtually engrossed the sugar supply in the United States, as did Freer the manufacture of railroad cars, while Frick was Andrew Carnegie's ruthless associate in the steel industry. In a country in which neither the states nor the federal government set aside funds for concert halls, theatres, or picture galleries, there was no alternative to private philanthropy no matter how tainted its source.

The diversity of tastes was transatlantic. Like their European counterparts, American millionaires prized seventeenth-century masterpieces and American music lovers greeted new music with skepticism. Around the turn of the century, fear of Brahms, in his time considered a difficult composer, was acute in Berlin no less than in New York. The tale of a sign—"In case of Brahms, exit here"—presumably put up by musically conservative workmen, gained intercontinental currency: sightings were reported in Boston's Symphony Hall and in the concert hall of Vienna's *Gesellschaft der Musikfreunde*. The sensational Armory Show that opened in February 1913 in New York, organized by a handful of individualists including the photographer Alfred Stieglitz and the collector John Quinn, was another bridge between two continents. Purposeful in their aesthetic radicalism, the makers of the show displayed the latest, most unconventional work of European Modernists for the delectation—or the derision—of an avalanche of visitors.

Some 130,000 art lovers came to the Armory Show, many of them to be shocked—and they were. Picasso the Cubist, Matisse the Fauve, Brancusi the Cubist sculptor of *The Kiss*, gave rise to outraged editorials, to cartoons, to jokes—and, for some, a delighted recognition that modern art opened new vistas. The favorite import was Marcel Duchamps's ingenious *Nude Descending a Staircase*, which baffled most viewers who could not, try as they might, find the nude that the title promised. The show was an unintended farewell to the Victorian century: World War I, which abruptly ended the Victorian century, was only a year and a half away. But with the noisy publicity it garnered, the Armory Show further cemented international bourgeois tastes in which Americans, whether patrons, collectors, or only listeners and viewers, played their part.

✿ MARY CASSATT, A PIONEER IN BRINGING Americans and Europeans together, was a much-loved and authoritative promoter who earned only gratitude for her indefatigable enthusiasms. But critics, by the nature of their mission, faced lazy indifference or determined opposition whenever they flouted comfortable tastes. It became a commonplace among them to take a dim view of the public they were trying to educate. In 1840, the English magazine *Musical World* charged that opera goers were less interested in the quality of performances than in the emotional thrill the singers could induce: "In the broadest meaning of the term, they are Sensualists—gratify but their eyes and ears." Again, as late as 1889, the *Musical Times* condescended to these deprived bourgeois: "There is a certain portion of the reading public whose minds are of so invertebrate an order that they are either unwilling or unable to form an opinion for themselves. To them any statement proceeding from an authoritative source appeals with convincing force." Quite incidentally, the passage calls attention to the authority that writers telling readers what to think and what to admire acquired among the Victorians. Although their superior derision for the general public in search of culture was overdone, those readers who were sure they knew what they liked were a greater menace to originality in the arts than those who feared they did not know, and it was the latter who most welcomed the critics' confident advice.

In fact, they were needed, often even wanted. At the very least, tirelessly championing their discoveries and turning their back on mediocrity with frank disdain, the critics enlivened the debates so characteristic of the Victorian age. More, for all their somewhat pathetic conviction that their words were scattered in the wind, they made converts in larger numbers than they dared to hope. Critics, then, were significant actors on the Victorian cultural stage. The most effective among them acquired a loyal following among readers eager to be informed about the arts and literature, and parched for verdicts persuasively expressed and firmly defended.

LOOKING BACK FROM THE DISTANCE OF A CENTURY and more, it becomes clear that Victorian readers of reviews were both fortunate and unfortunate. It was an age of major writers knowledgeably judging the work of fellow authors. They were critics who, as writers having been reviewed themselves, quite literally knew what they were talking about. We think of Charles Baudelaire, the most important French poet at midcentury; William Dean Howells, Emile Zola, Theodor Fontane, Henry James, all of them novelists of stature.

Several of them, notably Baudelaire and Zola, also wrote interesting reviews of Salons. And in the 1890s, George Bernard Shaw was better known as a music critic than as a playwright.

Theirs was a formidable assignment. Nineteenth-century critics were at once sustained and hampered by the democratization of reading with the daily and the periodical press that had started in England in the previous century and virtually exploded over Europe and the United States from the 1830s on. It gave them regular employment and a sizable audience, but they were surrounded, at times swamped, by less gifted and less scrupulous colleagues. In an age of ferocious competition for readers, publishers often limited, at times nullified, the pedagogic value of the reviewers they employed. Circulation wars or political hatreds seeped into the *feuilleton*, where they had no legitimate place. French readers were particularly vulnerable: many reviewers, often young men from the provinces seeking to make their fortune in Paris—they could have come out of a novel by Balzac—were notoriously dishonest, praising or belittling novels or concerts on their editor's orders or in return for a bribe. And they were as uninformed as they were corrupt. Bourgeois who read them could never be at all sure that such critics were refining their taste.

By the second half of the century, venality had become less of a menace to bourgeois eager to learn than the sheer number of journalists paid to have opinions. Their casual, slipshod observations about books, plays, or concerts could only lower the standards of their craft. In 1891, in a short, gloomy article, "Criticism," Henry James surveyed the dismal scene. The criticism of literature, he complained, was flowing "through the periodical press like a river that has burst its dykes." Its very success had made it into a failure. The price paid for "the diffusion of penmanship and opportunity" has proved nothing less than a "catastrophe," generating "the failure of distinction, the failure of style, the failure of knowledge, the failure of thought." Criticism had degenerated into *reviewing*—the word was, for Henry James, a sneer.

He was being excessively caustic. His own published literary opinions amply attest that all was not deceit or superficiality in the fraternity of Victorian critics. In his characteristic way of turning accepted truths on their head, Oscar Wilde went so far as to assert that the critic's task is harder and more distinguished than that of the novelist or poet. Others were not quite so self-assured. But some of them, quite apart from the lustrous names I have mentioned, were distinguished in their intellect, their diligence, their verbal felicity, their scrupulousness. Charles Augustin Sainte-Beuve must figure prominently in any account of this honorable company. Born in 1804 at Boulogne-sur-Mer to a petty bourgeois family in straitened circumstances, he became a lifelong liberal though not an activist; like others of his stripe, he made his peace with the empire of Napoleon III. But he never fundamentally tarnished his ideals. When in 1857 he reviewed Flaubert's new novel, *Madame Bovary*, just after the author, his publisher, and the printer had been tried for obscenity and blasphemy—tried and acquitted—Sainte-Beuve courageously praised the novel and resolutely maintained that it must be judged on its literary merits alone. In an essay on the marquis d'Argenson, a high-ranking minister during the reign of Louis XV, Sainte-Beuve praised him for his "bourgeois simplicity and incorruptible even temper," and those values, solid middle-class values, were his own. Literary criticism and scholarship were his life, with occasional interruptions for public lectures and private dinners of gossip and literary talk with writing friends like the Goncourts and Flaubert. He had started his career as a Romantic poet in the circle of Victor Hugo, and in 1834 published a well-regarded, heavily autobiographical novel, *Volupté*. In the same decade he undertook a massive five-volume study of Pascal and the seventeenth-century Jansenists, *Port-Royal*, which took him twenty years to complete and which still repays reading. Literature, in his words, became his religion.

As Sainte-Beuve shed his confessional frame of mind and his Romantic posture, he discovered his vocation. From 1824, the year it was founded, he had been contributing reviews to *Le Globe*, a liberal voice for French Romantics. Then, around 1830, he settled down to writing well-pondered and well-researched essays on French literature past and present. From 1849 to 1869, the year of his death, he published an essay every Monday, collected in volume after volume in the authoritative *Causeries du Lundi* and his *Portraits littéraires*. They bear the stamp of his basic principle that a work of literature, whether a novel, a memoir, or a work of history, must be understood as the product of a mind embedded in its culture, a position that later critics of this critic (most notably Marcel Proust) thought excessively rationalistic and insufficiently literary. But he never wavered. "I analyze," he described his work in 1846, "I botanize, I am a naturalist of minds—what I want to create is *literary natural history.*" To do justice to his rich palette of doing literary natural history, Sainte-Beuve made himself into one of the most learned of writers in nineteenth-century France. One reason he singled out Goethe as "the king of critics" was that Goethe had spent a lifetime intelligently studying the world around him.

With his passion for history and scholarship, Sainte-Beuve was better equipped to celebrate and rediscover past greatness and to defend high literary standards than to appreciate emerging genius. His failure to give Balzac and Baudelaire their due would earn him posthumous censure. But he made up for this blind spot with the seriousness and solidity of his essays and the ruthless honesty of his published verdicts. When he lamented "the wretched occupation of critic," he meant not just to deplore the mediocrity rampant in his profession, but to note sadly that his candor lost him friends who had tried to exploit his influence to gain a stature that he thought they did not deserve. If incorruptibility had been his only outstanding quality as a critic, he would have remained a highly appreciated pedagogue to his bourgeois public. But he had far more to offer than that: energy, scope, clarity, erudition.

▓ IN THE BREADTH OF HIS INFLUENCE, HIS learning, his conscientiousness, and his wit, the Austrian music critic Eduard Hanslick strongly resembles Sainte-Beuve. He was so powerful a figure in Vienna's musical life that the Viennese nicknamed him "Czar." Anton Bruckner tried to have his Seventh Symphony printed before it was premiered in Vienna because, he worried, Hanslick was bound to ruin its reception. Granted, Bruckner was unworldly and servile, but his pitiable plea conveys an idea of Hanslick's power. Yet in one crucial respect, the two critics differed. Sainte-Beuve's sympathies were wide-ranging; a high level of accomplishment was all he sought in the works he analyzed. Hanslick for his part was deeply preoccupied with a controversy that raged in the second half of the nineteenth century across musical Europe and the United States, as the partisans of Wagner and of Brahms called each other names. Hanslick made no secret of where he stood: he was a Brahmsian first and last.

The Wagner wars—no less emphatic a word will do—were far from trivial or evanescent. They led to demonstrations in concert halls, fostered ill-tempered debates, divided families and destroyed friendships. Brahmsians denounced the Wagner festivals at Bayreuth as morbid tributes to an egomaniac, the sickly and perverted worship of an idol, and *Tristan und Isolde* as an obscene sexual debauch. Wagnerians in return dismissed Brahms's music as traditionalist, empty, in a word, worthless; Wagner himself, never generous with the competition, called it mediocre, arid, and repulsive.

Hanslick intervened in this struggle over Wagner with the vigor that was his signature. As he put it in 1894 in his autobiography, his credo was "Criticism does not exist to praise everything, but to tell the truth." This did not mean that, especially in the beginning, Hanslick was unable to find merits in Wagner—his was a more liberal spirit than Wagner's by far. But as time went by, he became convinced that only the strongest language could exorcise the menace that Wagnerian music drama and its implications for other composers represented for the world of music. It was from this bellicose standpoint that he could dismiss Bruckner as a mere acolyte of Wagner, and a madman to boot.

There was a personal element in Hanslick's detestation of Wagner: when Wagner came to Vienna in 1862 to give readings of his libretto for *Meistersinger,* Hanslick was invited and easily recognized Beckmesser, the foolish, self-important critic in the opera, as a coarse (and thoroughly unfair) lampoon of himself. At one point, Wagner had considered calling Beckmesser "Hans Lick." Whether the fact that Hanslick's mother was Jewish called forth Wagner's cruellest strain remains a matter of dispute. But the issue went deeper than this. Wagner's declared aim was to make a profound political, cultural, spiritual statement with his libretti and his compositions and he saw himself as the chosen prophet of the Music of the Future; Hanslick in sharp contrast looked for what he called "a world of pure beauty," and to his mind Brahms embodied that beauty, especially in his chamber music. With some justice, he saw the issues raised by Wagner as political ones. Wagnerians were winning converts among the educated public and adoring composers, taking over editorial chairs in professional periodicals and engrossing conversations about music. If the Holy Spirit were to come down to earth, Hanslick wrote in an amusing little essay, the first thing he would ask is, What do you think of Wagner? Should Wagnerism succeed, there was danger that music would be subordinated to words, beauty to ideology, "formlessness raised to a principle, opium intoxication sung and fiddled, a cult, to which, as we know, a special temple has been raised at Bayreuth." For Hanslick, this was a baleful specter he must mobilize his forces to exorcise.

With all his scholarship, diligence, and self-proclaimed receptivity to a variety of musical styles, Hanslick was relatively narrow in his sympathies. He quoted Scripture: "In my father's house are many mansions." But he had great difficulties assimilating unconventional composers like Berlioz, and he placed relatively few statues into his pantheon, ranging from Handel and Gluck to Brahms. He had his doubts whether Johann Sebastian Bach was of more than historical interest, and he had nothing good to say about earlier music: he would, he said, "rather see all of Heinrich Schütz go up in flames than [Brahms's] 'German Requiem.'" Looking back a century later when catholicity in musical tastes is the watchword, this casual pronouncement verges on the philistine. Yet for his readers, Hanslick was a dependable teacher in large part because he was so frank about his tastes, and intelligently justified them in scores of literate reviews.

▓ VICTORIAN BOURGEOIS RELIED ON MUSEUMS and progressive galleries for their aesthetic education as much as they did on the printed page. Museums, of course, were not abstract entities but all too human institutions. Their directors, new men of influence, were surrogate collectors appointed to assist the art-loving public, using its money, the authorities hoped, to inform and purify its preferences in the arts. But when these cultivated bureaucrats had any original ideas at all, they could do their pedagogic work only if they managed to withstand the pressure exerted by their superiors, whether king or cabinet minister, city council or board of trustees. If the supreme authority was someone like Wilhelm II, Germany's omniscient emperor who had strong opinions about everything including painting and sculpture, the director had to master the skills of a diplomat, fashion astute accommodations, and navigate among those who had final control and his own aesthetic passions, or his tenure would be short.

An opinionated but well-liked administrator might survive to prod his public to tolerate, perhaps even approve of, his acquisition of unconventional works of art even though he irritated some of his superiors. "Some" is the operative word here: to divide was to conquer. Alfred Lichtwark at the Kunsthalle in Hamburg, appointed in 1886, managed to discount conformist middle-class tastes and stay in office until his death in 1914. He was of petty bourgeois origins but climbed up the social ladder on the strength of his sheer talents until Hamburg's patricians accepted him as one of their own. A man of striking contradictions, he was a suave society lion and a forceful fighter for his artistic convictions, a patriot who loved his city-state and a cosmopolitan in his grasp of the arts. He was possessed by a mission: to restore the taste of Hamburg—and, more ambitiously, of Germany—debased through the centuries of German disunion, he thought, and still in want of repair after the creation of the German Reich in 1871. For too long, he wrote in 1905, his fellow citizens had neglected their *Bildung*; for too long "they had lived for intelligence. It is time now for ethical-religious and artistic energies to develop fully."

This was more than simply a matter of reminding his fellow Germans of beauty and aesthetic discrimination; to his mind, good taste was a necessary ingredient in sound morals. That is why Lichtwark made himself into an indefatigable lecturer and prolific pamphleteer: talking and writing about neglected local architecture, unjustly forgotten German painters, and the applied arts in general—interior design, furniture, photography, and much else. He thought himself a physician to his culture. The German middle class, he believed, had degenerated from a respect-worthy *Bürgertum* into a shallow, modern bourgeoisie; some more highly civilized citizen—why not Lichtwark himself?—must take them in hand. "Whoever looks at the bourgeoisie from the standpoint of art and the artist will not be fond of it," he wrote in 1898. "A parvenu with all the disagreeable traits of the type, it is swellheaded with its successes, opinionated, arrogant, the born and sworn enemy of all artistic independence, the patron and protector of all those who flatter its vanity and its narrow outlook. Fundamentally quite without artistic interests, the bourgeoisie as owner, client, and buyer has reduced architecture, the decorative arts, and painting to its level. It wants to contribute nothing and believes it may demand everything," a severe indictment of a class of Germans who thought themselves in the vanguard of their country's modernization.

Though he secured a national forum with his talks and a succession of slender volumes, Lichtwark's principal schoolroom was, of course, the Kunsthalle, which he made into a place for discoveries and rediscoveries. He gave space to then little known early nineteenth-century German painters like Philipp Otto Runge and Caspar David Friedrich, and introduced French Impressionists like Monet and Renoir to Hamburg's museum goers. His supreme test, though, came in 1891, when he commissioned Max Liebermann to paint a life-size portrait of the city's eighty-three-year-old mayor, Carl Petersen. Celebrated and execrated, Liebermann, who had been deeply influenced by the seventeenth-century Dutch Golden Age and the French Impressionists, was probably Germany's most controversial painter at the time, though a true Impressionist would have found his version of his school's patented traits—free brushstrokes, mundane subject matter, and luminous coloration—rather tame. The committee to which Lichtwark had to submit his proposal at first refused to endorse it; Liebermann, with his so-called partiality for ugliness, was too anti-academic to suit conservative tastes. But it relented once Lichtwark found a private donor to back the portrait; as long as it would be no burden on their budget, these honorable and prudent Hamburgers reasoned, the painter's notoriety was bearable. Money bought not only time but, when necessary, a certain flexibility.

Liebermann chose to show the venerable *Bürgermeister* in his official attire, complete with a white ruff that beautifully framed his handsome face. Petersen detested the portrait, and had much of the patriciate on his side; he called it tasteless and a failed experiment. Lichtwark, realizing that he could not win this battle, was determined not to lose the war. He devised a compromise: he did not dare show the painting until 1894, and then only behind a curtain, an undignified concession that it took him eleven years to undo. But he kept his post and continued to pursue his self-assigned mission to tutor the German middle class. As he saw it, the cultural situation of the middling orders might be desperate but it was not hopeless.

BY 1870, THE YEAR THAT THE TROOPS OF Napoleon III were decisively defeated by the Prussians and the Second Empire limped toward its inglorious end, there were more than a hundred art dealers in Paris, both small and large. The only thing new about this number was its size; there had been many dealers in paintings in the seventeenth-century Netherlands. But it was a mark of increasing wealth among French bourgeois. Nor were these purely commercial ventures; those dealers who were well mannered, well educated, well informed—and honest into the bargain—were pedagogues to their clients almost as much as were their contemporaries, the museum directors and art critics.

The foremost figure among these Parisian educators to Modernism was Paul Durand-Ruel. Born in 1831, the son of a dealer in artists' supplies and graphics, he took over from his father after 1860 and made paintings and watercolors the sole business of his gallery. He had vertiginous financial ups and downs, profiting from the rapidly rising prices of certain painters and facing ruin with the bankruptcy of a financial backer and the slow sales of artists to whose output he had committed himself. A man of flamboyant gestures, he sometimes bought up the whole production of a painter he liked and in whose future he believed. In 1873, he acquired twenty-three Manets he had seen in Manet's studio for 35,000 francs—it would prove an immense bargain as he promptly sold these paintings for 4,000 to 20,000 francs or more each. In January 1881, he took all that Pissarro had to show him, offering to take everything Pissarro would produce in the future, and did the same for Eugène Boudin a month later. As American millionaires flooded in, he repurchased some of the canvases he had sold to French collectors to resell them for vast sums like 100,000 francs apiece.

As historians of the art market have pointed out, it was the Americans who tided over Durand-Ruel until the gratifying success of his one-man shows of Monet and Renoir in the early 1890s finally established his prosperity. The Monets he had bought for under 300 francs and sold at a modest mark-up a decade earlier now went for ten times that price. Yet, his reputation as a single-minded advocate of French Impressionists to the contrary, Durand-Ruel was quite eclectic in the stock he acquired over the years. In a letter to *L'Evénement* in 1885, he called attention to his admiration for such Salon painters as Bouguereau and Cabanel, Barbizon artists like Théodore Rousseau, and others across the spectrum of French taste. But the Impressionists were plainly his favorites. He had helped them out financially in the days they needed it, and now he expected them to be appreciated for their worth as artists. "For a long time I have bought and greatly admired works by very original and skillful painters, many of whom are men of genius, and I seek to make them known to collectors. I consider that works by Degas, by Puvis de Chavannes, by Monet, by Renoir, by Pissarro, and by Sisley are worthy of being included in the most beautiful collections." So they were, partly because of Durand-Ruel's persistent advocacy; many of them, much like the canvases that Mary Cassatt had recommended to her friends, ended up in American museums.

For all of Durand-Ruel's commitment to avant-garde painters, he was a devout Catholic and an impassioned reactionary. In 1873, in a letter to *Le Figaro,* he publicly lamented the quandaries of dealers like himself in these uncertain times and suggested an intriguing political solution: "All of us," he wrote, "as Frenchmen and as tradesmen, long for the restoration of the hereditary monarchy, which alone can put an end to our troubles." This was not inconsistency. Radicalism in tastes did not automatically carry with it radicalism in politics, any more than radicalism in politics necessarily made for radicalism in the arts. Two of the painters Durand-Ruel represented illustrate the breadth of this spectrum: Pissarro was a Socialist and a Jew, Degas an anti-Dreyfusard and an anti-Semite.

Durand-Ruel's simultaneous partisanship for the artists of the future and a restored monarchy only underscores the point I have been making from the beginning of this study: the extraordinary diversity of the nineteenth-century middle-class mind. But in matters of taste, its ability to admire and support the new should be, in view of its reputation, ground for astonishment. Bourgeois predilection for aesthetic mediocrity, even for kitsch, or, in affluent circles, reliance on interior decorators who put conventional pictures on their walls, was only to be expected. But that middle-class lovers of the arts should have been patrons of avant-garde artists, donated advanced art to museums, supported (even founded) symphony orchestras, all this must force us to rethink our common notions about the Victorian middle classes. Schnitzler, we know, thought "bourgeois" and "boring" synonymous. He was wrong.

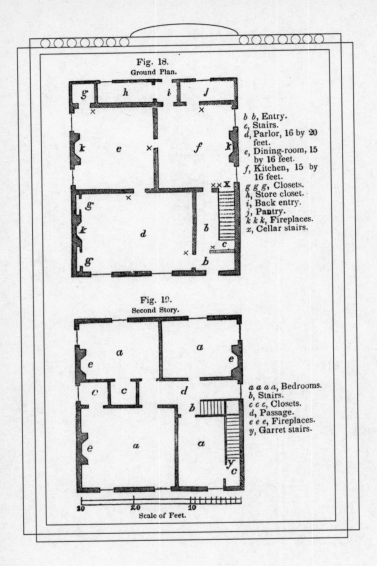

Fig. 18.
Ground Plan.

b b, Entry.
c, Stairs.
d, Parlor, 16 by 20
  feet.
e, Dining-room, 15
  by 16 feet.
f, Kitchen, 15 by
  16 feet.
g g g, Closets.
h, Store closet.
i, Back entry.
j, Pantry.
k k k, Fireplaces.
x, Cellar stairs.

Fig. 19.
Second Story.

a a a a, Bedrooms.
b, Stairs.
c c c, Closets.
d, Passage.
e e e, Fireplaces.
y, Garret stairs.

10   20   10
Scale of Feet.

NINE

A Room of One's Own

1

THE EPISODE OF DR. JOHANN SCHNITZLER burglarizing his son's desk has, I believe, served to introduce varied perspectives for the influence of middle-class culture on nineteenth-century values. But I have saved its principal implication to the last. What infuriated Arthur Schnitzler enough to destroy all trust in his father as he saw him holding that little red notebook, enough to recall this confrontation with barely controlled emotion three decades later, was Dr. Schnitzler's trespass on his privacy. It was *his* space his father had desecrated, space carefully guarded, evidently not carefully enough. This act of thievery, though certainly well meant, was an assault on his young manhood, unforgivable and unforgiven.

This incident and its long-range consequences are of special interest to the historian defining the nineteenth-century middle classes, high or low, self-satisfied or anxious. Bourgeois idealized their commitment to privacy and treated its infraction as a grave offense. Confidential letters and intimate diaries, which their writers regarded as nothing less than sacrosanct, attest that young Schnitzler's experience was anything but unique. In April 1822, "Nanci" Berlioz, three years younger than her beloved brother, the composer Hector Berlioz, noted angrily in her diary that her mother had unsealed a letter she had written to him, "which vexed me exceedingly." A month later Madame Berlioz repeated her transgression by opening another letter of Nanci's to her older brother, something, the spirited adolescent believed, her mother had no right to do: "Mama again read it, greatly to my annoyance." Nanci was sixteen, old enough to her mind to deserve some privacy. And near the end of the century, in 1898 in Vienna, the nineteen-year-old Alma Schindler was enraged to discover that "breaking her word of honor," solemn promises to the contrary, her mother had "studied my diary's stammering," an accounting intended for her own eyes alone. In resenting her mother's attempt to relegate her to the role of a child, she was characteristic of her time and class.

ALTHOUGH THE IDEOLOGY OF PRIVACY IS MODERN, its sources reach into the distant past. The ancient Athenians had already drawn a clear distinction between public and private domains, extolling the former and denigrating the latter. In their culture, the private person lacked the most highly valued of human privileges, the right to participate in the affairs of the *polis*. Little wonder that, from the Middle Ages on, the Greek word for "private," *idios*, unflattering as it had been to begin with, came to designate a mental defective. In fact, for centuries before the Victorians, some usages stood guard over a certain untouchable preserve. Painters and sculptors saw to it that men's and women's well-named "private parts" remained private. With some rare exceptions—and these were literally covered over during the Counter-Reformation with its passion for fig leaves—artists concealed the organs of generation behind a veil, a piece of drapery, a strategically placed hand. That they should have depicted putti and the infant Jesus with their little penises in full view did not violate this reticence. It elicited no protests from the pious, since artists and audiences alike found this display perfectly proper: it attested to their undisputed conviction that there is no such thing as infant sexuality.

Still, in the centuries before the eighteenth, most people led their lives largely in the open, though in a number of societies (as in ancient Athens) respectable women had been forced into the silence of the domestic sphere. The urban middling orders of merchants and craftsmen were woven into a tight tapestry of personal relations; their community was all the less inescapable for being so small. True, the few aristocrats who owned vast acres managed as early as the twelfth and thirteenth centuries to have festivities restricted to select guests and even bedrooms of their own. But this hint at deliberate self-segregation was even rarer than wealth itself.

Before the age of the Enlightenment, then, life on a public stage was generally the accepted human condition. As in villages, so in towns, encounters were mainly face to face. In Plymouth Colony, about which we are fairly well informed, families lived in small one-room, or at best not much larger two-room houses, with parents and children tumbling all about one another. The two-room houses might provide a bedchamber that could allow couples to enjoy lovemaking in a slightly protected atmosphere; and some better-off Puritans owned a curtained bed that allowed them to be alone—more or less. Since most people were illiterate, letters were treated as public texts and shame lived itself out in the engrossed presence and callous inquisitiveness of one's neighbors. To report miscreants to the authorities, especially those caught in illicit sexual adventures, was virtually a civic duty; the community, in short, made each individual's business its business. The scarlet letter "A" on the adulterer's breast was a token, in no way unexceptional or unwelcome—except, of course, to the wearer—that documented society's right to know about, and to judge, the most intimate acts in one's circle.

Even if privacy had been desirable and conceivable, then, it would have been physically impossible. Ideology was reinforced by the open plan of family quarters. Early seventeenth-century Dutch genre paintings contemporary with Plymouth Colony show that rooms furnished with a bed were also used for dining and for entertaining guests. Privacy meant closing doors, but well into the middle of the eighteenth century, as gradually more and more of those doors were being closed, the body and its functions remained something of a communal spectacle. In fact, for most people down to recent times, privacy was not an issue at all. By mid-nineteenth century, as government investigators, crusading journalists, and intrusive philanthropists went into the slums, they reported that among the poor, carving out a domain of their own was not expected, not even thinkable. We recall that Mrs. Beeton counseled mothers who could not nurse their infants to inspect the wet nurse engaged to perform that duty. As I have noted, the gulf of class between two women could not be more blatant as the bourgeois mother scrutinized the nipples of her prospective lower-class employee.

❦ FOR ALL THE ADVANCES OF PRIVACY, ITS boundaries remained shifting and fluid right through the nineteenth century. They differed, as usual, across time and place, though the core of its terrain was fairly uncontested. "To define the province of privacy distinctly is impossible," wrote James Fitzjames Stephen in 1873, "but it can be described in general terms." To his mind, these terms included "all the more intimate and delicate relations of life," like "the internal affairs of family, the relations of love or friendship, or many other things of the same sort." Stephen's imprecision suggests some of the impediments to drawing a sketch of Victorian privacy that everyone could heartily accept. It was not until 1890 that two American jurists, Samuel D. Warren and Louis D. Brandeis, in a much-cited article, proposed that the law protect "the right to be let alone."

Believers in that right could defend it with some heat. In 1888, in *Our Home: Or, the Key to a Nobler Life*, C. E. Sargent, an American divine and college president, put the case resolutely: "Secrecy is one of the first duties that the domestic relation imposes. It is one of the cardinal necessities to the existence of the family. Every family has its secrets and must have them while it is a family. To publish the secrets of any family would be to dissipate that family." The children, too, have "certain private rights," such as not to be punished in the presence of outsiders. To Sargent, privacy was also indispensable to good manners.

Not that he wished to foster coldness; after all, "the family is the out-growth of love." But married couples that "display their affections" on public occasions behave "in a most sickening manner." After all, "the sentiment of love in all its phases seeks instinctively the haunts of privacy." Nor was Sargent alone to draw a sharp line between the private and public domains, though the reserve he so passionately advocated was more at home in Northern than in Mediterranean cultures.

Yet in that contentious time, not only the legitimate bounds of privacy were subject to debate; the very claim had its adversaries. Scandalized moralists opposed the viewpoint that heterodox opinions and behavior could claim to be "merely private" and should go unpunished. We recall that in 1895 Oscar Wilde was convicted for committing the felony of "gross indecency" to noisy public approval. We recall, too, that across the Western world, energetic organizations set themselves to purifying literature and the arts. Well-meaning censors were busy everywhere and dismissed the liberal argument that people have a right to look and read and talk without interference as the alibi of libertines in behalf of wickedness.

Nor were these crusades led by inoffensive eccentrics; they often succeeded in recruiting the law in their cause. In 1868, Anthony Comstock, the most influential and most hated of American sanitary policemen, enlisted the New York state legislature, and five years later the Congress, in legislating against obscenity. For several decades, Comstock's New York Society for the Suppression of Vice, with judges enthusiastically supporting its campaigns, managed to bankrupt and imprison purveyors of birth control information and printers of nude photographs, to say nothing of some real pornographers. In 1881, after his society had been active for only eight years, it had, Comstock proudly reported, destroyed precisely 27,384 pounds of books and confiscated 203,238 "obscene" pictures as well as 1,376,939 songs, circulars, poems, and catalogues—impressive breaches in the fortifications of privacy. Libertarians, liberals, librarians, art dealers, and irritated avant-garde polemicists ridiculed these "Puritans" and protested against their ravages, but for years in vain.

2

ONE BLESSING OF PRIVACY, THAT OF THE MAILS, was always hoped for and never secure. On August 10, 1790, the National Assembly in Paris declared the secret of letters to be inviolable, and the French penal code incorporated this sweeping declaration. After Sir Rowland Hill radically reformed the British postal system in 1840, unifying postage rates and drastically reducing the costs and uncertainties of delivering letters, other countries rapidly imitated his innovations, and the habit of letterwriting took hold in the middle classes. Correspondence became a valued part of the emotional economy of bourgeois everywhere. And letterwriters, like recipients, tacitly assumed that what the Germans call the "secret of letters— *Briefgeheimnis*"—would be preserved, and that they could rest assured their missives would be delivered unopened, their seals unbroken. Country after country passed legislation promising—a promise, we shall see, not always kept—that the privacy of the mails must be respected and its violation punished. Schnitzler's Austria-Hungary enacted such a law in 1870. With the rapid rise of the telegraph, states sheltered telegrams under the same umbrella of sacrosanct privacy. As early as 1861, Bavaria for example explicitly provided a one-year jail term for a telegrapher who illegally violated the secrecy of a telegram by showing it to a third person.

Trust, in short, became an essential ingredient in the conduct of correspondence. Letters often contained information that no unauthorized reader should see: letters between lovers, invitations to a tryst; letters between sisters, clandestine contraceptive advice the sender had wormed out of her physician; letters between business partners, illegal or at least covert strategies. Under relatively liberal regimes, letterwriters felt secure; but if they thought they could count on state and church to leave correspondence undisturbed, families were not always so honorable. That is why archives contain piles of nineteenth-century letters bearing the writer's stern command: "Don't read this aloud, and burn it!" The historian can sense the inner struggle of recipients: on the one hand, they had the sender's instructions; on the other, they wished to preserve cherished signs of life. But whatever the decision, it was one taken in private.

Not all addressees were prudent or inventive enough. The number of love letters intercepted and torn up by angry parents will never be known, but it must have been sizable. And sometimes the breach of confidentiality was spectacular. In the early 1840s, Giuseppe Mazzini, the pioneer of Italian unity, lived in England as a political exile, and in 1844 he learned that the Home Office had been opening his letters. Worse: it had forwarded them to the Austrians, who at the time were occupying most of northern Italy and were keenly interested in uncovering subversive nationalist activities. In consequence of this betrayal, two of Mazzini's idealistic young Venetian lieutenants were caught and executed.

Irate, Mazzini denounced this "disgracefully un-English behavior." His outrage found immediate and vociferous echoes. Macaulay accused the British government of turning "the Post Office into an engine of the police," a practice he condemned as "utterly abhorrent to the public feeling." Carlyle wrote an indignant letter to *The Times* that reads like a manifesto in support of privacy: "It is a question vital to us that sealed letters in an English post-office be, as we all fancied they were, respected as things sacred." He likened opening mail to picking people's pockets and to other "still viler and far fataler forms of scoundrelism." Members asked uncomfortable questions in the House of Commons, and ministers, aware that they had stepped on a taboo, lied in self-justification as ministers will and buttressed their sordid spying with the appeal that they were safeguarding national interest in revolutionary times.

❦ THE PIVOTAL PLACE OF PRIVATE LETTERS GAVE nineteenth-century dramatists and novelists some attractive intrigues to play with: incriminating documents falling into the wrong hands. The fiction that immediately comes to mind is Theodor Fontane's finest novel, *Effi Briest*. In his young wife's absence, Effi's husband, the middle-aged aristocrat von Instetten, happens upon some love letters which disclose her brief infidelity some years ago—letters he has, of course, no business reading. The consequences are literally fatal: Instetten challenges his "rival," kills him with his first shot, and then, indirectly, his wife, who cannot survive the disgrace and having her daughter taken from her. She gently fades away.

What makes Instetten's unreasoning response all the more poignant is that he no longer believes in the cleansing ritual of duels, but cannot shake off the traditions of his caste. He lives out the conflict between aristocratic and middle-class standards. A bourgeois, one imagines, might have shared Instetten's outrage, but not his anachronistic way of settling his grievance. He might have leveled bitter reproaches against his wife, even sought a divorce, but not resorted to tacitly licensed murder. Whatever one's response to these divergent conceptions of honor, what matters here is the impetus that set Fontane's drama in motion: a breach of privacy. Had she burned these love letters, her marriage would have remained unshaken. But who burned letters in those years, even when the writer had asked to have them destroyed?

With the emergence of the modern gutter press, privacy found yet another antagonist. The peccadilloes of the rich and powerful were welcome fodder for them. In order to boost the circulation of their unscrupulous rags, reporters working for them pried into conduct best kept from the world; a few of them, hinting that they had embarrassing information about marital lapses in their possession, joined the trade of blackmailer to that of journalist. At times, when they had no news to report, they invented it. In the Dreyfus affair, to mention just one example, some dailies shamelessly made up reports of Dreyfus's confession to treason and other "facts." They had discovered that allegations sell newspapers, and that denials, however sincere and accurate, never quite erase the impression left behind by the original canard.

3

PRIVACY—A DESK WITH A LOCKED DRAWER, unsupervised correspondence, a diary kept inviolate, or, best of all, a room of one's own—was not a birthright but a license granted the young by adults. Children, in other words, could begin to assert their private space only after they developed into adolescents. And the concept of adolescence, a transitional stage that psychologists were beginning to take seriously only in the last years of the nineteenth century, covered a broad, not always closely defined region of years between childhood, which demanded control, and adulthood, which demanded its termination. It was at this turning point both physiological and psychological that parents were well advised to exercise self-restraint and to respect their children's privacy.

But it was precisely when pubertal youngsters wrestling with potent biological stimuli and cultural pressures were especially vulnerable that parents often resisted yielding control. In his classic study, *Adolescence,* published in 1904 in two substantial volumes, the American psychologist G. Stanley Hall warned that modern civilization, with its "accumulated mass of cultures and skills, its artifacts, its necessity of longer and severer apprenticeship and specialization, is ever harder on adolescents." In that situation, "many if not most young people should be encouraged to learn enough of the confessional private journalism to teach them self-knowledge, for the art of self-expression usually begins now if ever, when it has a wealth of subjective material and needs forms of expression peculiar to itself." Keeping a diary seemed to Hall, as to other students of the young, a royal road to maturity.

THE STRUGGLE OVER THE SANCTITY OF DIARIES seems to have been carried on in innumerable families. Middle-class youngsters often started their daily entries at the prodding of teachers, abetted by parents who bought their six- or seven-year-old, just starting on the adventure of writing, little notebooks faintly lined to make it easy to use them. Then, with a benevolent smile and a correcting hand, parents would peruse their children's productions, making encouraging noises and offering didactic comments. But children have a way of growing up, and as adolescence looms, they normally replace their laboriously traced entries about rabbits at the Zoo or visits to Grandma with accounts of school, sports, and dawning puppy love. When, in August 1893, Julie Manet, cherished daughter of Berthe Morisot and niece of Edouard Manet, started her personal record, she noted on the first page: "I have often had a mind to keep a journal, I expect to start now," and wondered at her tardiness. "It seems to me this is a little late, but the more I wait, the later it will be, and anyhow I am only fourteen years old." Her eagerness to start at long last suggests that at least in her civilized and affluent circles, her friends had all been keeping diaries for some time. But it was not too late, for in her journal, adolescence has made its appearance.

Returning to one's entries years after could be as emotional an experience as writing them in the first place. "Read old diaries, and was incredibly moved." Thus Arthur Schnitzler on June 18, 1897. A year later he noted laconically: "Diary reading afternoon. Agitated me greatly." He was, we know, an inveterate practitioner of what Hall called confessional private journalism, and on rare—extremely rare—occasions he would entrust his day-to-day entries to a particularly intimate friend or a particularly privileged lover. In 1880, the year after his father had lectured him on the perils of sexual adventurism, he planned to show his entries to his beloved Fännchen. And in 1898, he read passages touching on his early days with "Mz I" to Hugo von Hofmannsthal. Once or twice he managed to get a look at the journal of a mistress, and found the reading quite interesting. But when in 1902 the singer Olga Grossmann, whom he was to marry that year, pressed him to let her see his diaries, he energetically refused "once and for all." Knowing what was in them, we can see why. Certainly the best audience for Schnitzler's private entries was Schnitzler himself.

This was true of most diarists but by no means all of them. Some wrote for one other person or for posterity. Cosima Wagner kept adding to her enormous domestic accounting day after day, intending to have her husband as her only reader. On the day he died, February 13, 1883, she abandoned her diary and never touched it again. Marie Bashkirtseff, the talented Russian-born French painter and diarist, better known for her private writings than her public art, faithfully and courageously kept at her daily entries though she had good reasons to fear that she would die of tuberculosis before long. "Yes," she wrote, "it is clear that I have the desire, if not the hope, to *remain* on this earth in some form or other. If I do not die young, I should like to have my diary published—it cannot be anything but interesting." She was right; late-Victorian readers, touched by her bravery and her craving for immortality, gave her what physicians could not give her: a long life.

As the mirrors of their authors, journals were naturally as varied as the writers themselves, but all these writers, breathlessly or calmly, made them a friend. The American travel author Mabel Loomis Todd, that most candid of historians when it came to her sexual life, spoke of her "dear journal." She sometimes spoke *to* it: "I will tell you something, old journal." When she completed her second volume, she said a fond farewell: "Good bye little book—your loving and grateful friend, Mabel Loomis." Some went even further, not writing a diary in order to live but (almost literally) living in order to keep a diary. In 1864, the Genevan literary critic and professor Henri-Frédéric Amiel, after more than sixteen years of obsessively carrying out his self-imposed assignment—the 16,840 tightly packed and methodically counted pages must add up to the longest diary in the nineteenth century—asked himself, "For what reason keep up this journal?" The incurable bachelor knew the answer and put it down a little pathetically, investing his daily escort with the choicest human qualities: "Because I am alone. It is my dialogue, my society, my companion, my confidant. It is also my consolation, my memory, my scapegoat, my echo, the reservoir of my intimate experiences, my psychological itinerary, my protection against the mildew of thought, my excuse for living, almost the only useful thing I can leave behind." Like Marie Bashkirtseff, he was all too accurate with his prediction.

There were diarists, then, who, much like Amiel, hoped that their jottings would bring them the notice they craved. In 1833, the young German playwright Friedrich Hebbel—he was twenty—started his journal, which would grow into a massive, multivolume outpouring, with a confident prediction: "I am starting this booklet not just as a favor to my future biographer, although with my prospects for immortality I can be sure I shall have one. It will be a notebook of my heart, which, true to the tones my heart sets, will preserve them for my delight in future years." The second sentence was a striking retreat from the first: what he had proclaimed as an aid to his biographer he reformulated more modestly to say that he would be the one to enjoy most—in strict privacy.

One of the motives for documenting one's days and years lay plainly on the surface and yields the psychologically disposed historian few dividends: an account of observations on the spot, probably for later use. Scientists like Charles Darwin kept diaries on their expeditions, and were not particularly informative about their inner life. Darwin's friend and champion T. H. Huxley, scrupulously recording his scientific work on his four-year-long voyage on HMS *Rattlesnake*, regretted his inability to "tell of the wider and stranger wanderings of a human soul," as he prepared to hand the manuscript over to his fiancée in early 1850. He was sorry that he lacked all talent for writing about his moods and feelings. "Could the history of the soul be written for that time it would be fuller of change and struggle than that of the outward man, but who shall write it? I, the only possible historian, am too much implicated, too interested, to tell a story fairly." Huxley underestimated his ability to be intimate with himself: his text is flecked with humor and intriguing asides. But, a good citizen of his age, he felt the need for more revelations than he could muster for the sole intended reader of his observations. Others discovered that a diary could be a valuable *aide-mémoire*. In 1839, Asa Fitch, an eminent American entomologist, who had kept a diary as a young man and given it up, decided to return to it after a rewarding conversation with a close friend. The cordial exchange had led him "to review some of the times we have spent together, by reference to my old diaries," and thus "the value of these records is brought with redoubled force to my mind."

Whatever the reasons for compiling these spates of silent words, one thing no Victorian diarist was inclined to doubt: their friend would never disappoint them. The model of patience, it was always available, to be trusted like nothing or no one else on earth—in exceptional cases none but a single intimate. A diary did not criticize, it did not bully, it did not complain, it did not betray secrets. The Victorians had not invented the genre; great diarists of earlier times—Evelyn, Pepys, Boswell, the duc de Saint-Simon, whose fascinating memoirs reflected the notes he had taken on the spot, readily come to mind, to say nothing of Puritans or Pietists anxiously measuring their accomplishments, or more often their short-comings, in piety. What was distinctively Victorian about diary keeping was its ubiquity, its sheer democratic mass.

A veritable explosion of confessions, more often artless than artful, added up to an unprecedented determination among vast numbers of bourgeois to endow their experiences and their feelings with a tenuous permanence. Writing and reading diaries was a special form of privacy, an ingredient in the quest of respectable burghers to reach, to under-stand, and with that to enrich, their inner resources.

FOR ALL THE EVIDENT LIMITATIONS OF DIARIES, the historian of Victorian culture is bound to find them more instructive than an autobiography. They are more spontaneous and less calculated, more graphic and less literary, than a published memoir is likely to be. At a time when a measure of reticence still governed public disclosures of confidential particulars, the private quality that set diaries apart from other confessions was likely to make them fairly candid witnesses. It is true that the mind is quicker than the hand and that a self-aware diarist may write, even under time pressure, what he or she thinks an audience might want to read. Still, for the historian in search of secret emotions, especially with a witness writing in a century like the nineteenth in which privacy loomed large, a diary is the document of choice.

Some of the solemnity of Victorian journal keepers invited parody, and got it, famously, from Oscar Wilde. In his *Importance of Being Earnest,* he has a delicious scene in which the Honorable Gwendolyn Fairfax tells Miss Cecily Cardew, "I never travel without my diary. One should always have something sensational to read on a train." But the vast majority of diarists apparently took their self-examinations far more seriously. Alma Schindler's expressive self-documentation splen-didly illustrates how these confessions provide access to the emotions of an articulate and expressive young woman of the age. Her entries are scarcely of historical importance; many of them are trivial and self-absorbed gossip. But they show how revealing such a document can be; the evidence it affords about the erotic domain, of which we still know too little, adds a few essential stones for a mosaic that remains incomplete and hard to interpret. Granted, one must read her with care: she was melodramatic and hysterical, and would acquire fame mainly for marrying in succession a noted composer (Gustav Mahler), a noted architect (Walter Gropius), a noted novelist (Franz Werfel), and carrying on a passionate affair with a noted painter (Oskar Kokoschka). Still, what she thought important enough to write down at the time is far more authentic than her sentimental, characteristically titled autobiography, *And the Bridge Is Love*. And since her mother had invaded her privacy, her mother—"oh horrors!"—had "read that Klimt had kissed me!"

Actually, as her diary shows, he had kissed her twice. Alma Schindler's mother had some reason for concern: her daughter was impulsive and unpredictable, and her would-be lover Klimt notorious for being an indiscriminate and indefatigable collector of women, including the society ladies whose portraits he painted. His line of seduction, which he tried out evidently with fair success, was that only "complete physical union" turned affectionate relations into true love. Yet Frau Schindler perhaps worried too much. Tempted as her daughter was by the handsome painter, as a well-brought-up young lady, she still hesitated to endorse his self-serving doctrine. She documents that young, middle-class Victorian women found it at times harder to lose their virginity than to keep it.

Alma Schindler's gushing reportage celebrates towering instant enthusiasms and sudden, poorly motivated changes of mind. Her pages are strewn with exclamation marks. She was willowy, round-faced, with regular if somewhat indeterminate features. Yet since she attracted experienced men of the world, she must have exuded an erotic energy that made men notice, and more than notice her. What made her all the more alluring is that she apparently scattered intimations that keeping her virginity, after all still the reigning bourgeois convention in her circles, was increasingly at odds with her appetite for sexual gratification. When Max Burckhard, director of the Vienna Opera, sends her a love letter, she confesses to her diary that she finds it an aphrodisiac: "When B.'s letter arrived today, I blushed from head to foot. I was alone, I knew it. As I read it, I grew hugely excited, I kissed it. I dream of giving my body to him, even if it's only a kiss." Her imagination was working overtime. In the throes of her improbable love for the composer Alex von Zemlinsky—poor, short, ugly, and Jewish, a catalogue of powerful deterrents for her—she notes: "How I long for him. Sometimes I lay my head between my arms on the table and think about us for hours at a time. . . . I must say I can't imagine giving myself to anyone but him,—*not even Klimt!!*"

As her frustrations grew more intense, her fantasies grew more lubricious. "I *long* for *rape.* Whoever it might be." Then, not long before marrying Mahler, she is finally determined to set aside her bourgeois principles. "What I have to write today is terribly sad," she notes on New Year's Day, 1902. "I called on Gustav—in the afternoon we were alone in his room. He gave me his body & I let him touch me with his hand. Stiff and upright stood his vigor. He carried me to the sofa, laid me gently down and swung himself over me. Then—just as I had felt him penetrate, he lost all strength. He laid his head on my breast, shattered—and almost wept for shame. Distraught as I was, I comforted him." When he grew more cheerful, she collapsed on his breast. "What," she worried, "if he were to lose—that! My poor, poor husband!"

The next two encounters seem to have gone better. All her diary reveals is "Bliss and rapture" on January 3, and "rapture without end" the day after. In the late Victorian days, no public autobiographies would have been nearly so explicit—certainly not hers. The virtual razing of boundaries between private and public was to be the work of a later age. But even if the information the historian is seeking in Alma Schindler's confessions is tantalizingly incomplete, he is left after reading her excited pages with yet one more piece of evidence that not all respectable women of Schnitzler's day were frigid.

———

4

IT WAS ONE THING TO IDEALIZE PRIVACY, QUITE another to translate the ideal into reality. The most mundane concerns, like housing, could be decisive. With spreading prosperity among the middling orders in the century, many bourgeois could afford to move into spacious sanctuaries. Money could buy distance. Dwellings could detach the family from the outside world and members of a family from one another. Walls, curtains, shades, solid front doors, cunningly placed shrubs and fences were symbols and more, warning strangers, even neighbors, to keep away. They could literally ensure the privacy of the dwellers within, a freedom from intrusive others that many bourgeois particularly valued. In 1869, an American writing for a British audience observed that "respectable folk are not fond of finding themselves the neighbours of opera singers and negro minstrels, of adventurous gentlemen and retired roués." The principle of privacy had its snobbish side, an aspect of contemporary bourgeois life that Schnitzler particularly disliked.

In the mid-1860s, the well-known English architect Robert Kerr, fellow of the Royal Institute of Architecture and professor of the Arts of Construction in King's College London, firmly laid down that principle in his treatise, *The Gentleman's House*. "The test of A GENTLEMAN'S HOUSE," he wrote, consists of a dozen qualities, including salubrity, comfort, light, and air. But the most important of them all was privacy, "a first principle with the better classes of English people." Privacy meant segregation from the children and, more fundamental, from the household help. "The family constitutes one community; the servants another." This clear separation served both: "as dwellers under the same roof, each class is entitled to shut its door upon the other and be alone." The realities of nineteenth-century class society could not be exhibited more clearly than this.

A sizable nineteenth-century literature advising a public hungry for instruction about the practicalities of privacy had a good deal to say, quite literally, about bricks and mortar. In a long-selling treatise on good manners which reached its twenty-third enlarged edition in 1900, the German writer Konstanze von Franken cautioned her readers not to move into "those modern houses which represent themselves externally as stylish and splendid buildings, but which have walls so thin, so poorly constructed, that every word from the neighbor's apartment, every sound of a piano above you, reaches you." Another way of avoiding unwelcome noise was to "choose an apartment that is as segregated as possible from all the other apartments in the house." Privacy, in short, required the closest attention to detail; it had to be conquered and defended on many fronts. No wonder Victorian bourgeois were an anxious lot.

THE MOST ELEMENTARY REQUIREMENT FOR domestic privacy was, of course, a room of one's own, something that, we have noted, the poor could never afford. This distinction was a vital defining characteristic separating the nineteenth-century bourgeoisie from the working classes. "Houses for the middle class," wrote the English architect G. A. T. Middleton in 1906, summing up decades of social observation, "differ from those of the working community in so marked an extent that an entirely different system of planning is required for each." A separate bedroom for the parents obviously came first. It was a place for getting dressed, for naps and confidential talks, and, naturally, for using the bed for activities other than sleep. Legitimate sexual intercourse was made all the more agreeable for being unobserved. Many bourgeois parents, especially in the lower ranks, kept infants in their bedroom for a while, but as soon as it was financially feasible, they looked for housing that gave their children, and themselves, some privacy as well.

This is one reason why, especially after midcentury, growing numbers of bourgeois families found renting so convenient: a rise in disposable income often coincided with the birth of children, so that, as their number increased, their parents could look for suitable larger accommodations. The emergence of the apartment house in most cities assisted this mobility. And the first step in including children in the gratifications of privacy was to separate sons from daughters—an arrangement that, studies of shelter for the lower classes showed, was the utmost that even the most highly paid married artisans could realistically expect. Builders specializing in working-class housing, always intent on "extreme economy," designed the children's rooms large enough to accommodate one, or even two double beds. The middle classes rarely faced such constraints. Except in France, where the birth rate was notoriously low, particularly after midcentury, upper-bourgeois houses or apartments often boasted more than half a dozen bedrooms. The Dakota, one of Manhattan's first apartment houses, was built on this lavish scale. Amply supplied with nannies and nurses, there were rich families, who, fruitful in their business, multiplied at home. Victorian bourgeois, we know, discovered the dividends of contraception, but the town houses built after the 1850s in England, Germany, amd Austria attest to the persistence of large families. Beatrice Potter, more famous as Beatrice Webb, had eight sisters—admittedly a large family, but not one considered abnormal in her time. Nor, certainly, were the Freuds, with six children.

To be sure, the considerate allocation of private space, though widespread, was not a uniform practice. There is anecdotal evidence that well-to-do bourgeois frantic for social acceptance discovered their quest for prestige interfering with their children's desire for privacy. A memoir by Hedwig Wachenheim, an upper-class German woman growing up around 1900 in Mannheim, tells of living with her sister and her mother, a Jewish banker's widow, in a six-room apartment. Three of the rooms—a salon used twice a year for grand receptions, a living-dining room, and her mother's sitting room—were suitable for public display, while the two girls shared a tiny cubicle in the rear that oozed with rising damp.

This memoir, an exceptionally unattractive portrait of a well-to-do widow revenging herself on the world by cosseting herself, was atypical. It remains true, though, that affluent bourgeois built their villas for more than just familial privacy. In the Westend of Frankfurt-am-Main, a major German commercial center where entrepreneurs, merchants, and bankers planted themselves, houses usually featured a billiard room and a smoking room, both for men, and a room for dancing—

Tanzsaal—or perhaps all three together. In 1900, at least one architect, the brilliant Viennese designer Josef Hoffmann, was more considerate of Frau Henneberg's needs: his Henneberg house, large enough to accommodate two guest rooms, had a smoking room and a room for the wife. Still, real music lovers could arrange a relatively diminutive space to accommodate their tastes: in one of the modest floor plans for a middle-class family shown in Catharine Beecher's *The American Woman's Home* of 1869, we see an upright piano.

These variations remind us that the question just how to apportion space appropriately, including how many rooms to allot to the servants, remained controversial through the century. Many builders and their clients responded to the new generous appreciation of privacy; others did not. In 1864, *The Builder* noted with some satisfaction that Englishmen raising their little castles no longer ridiculed Parisians for building four- and five-story houses, even if Londoners never adopted the Parisian model of five-story apartment houses in which each level accommodated a different rank of income, "All private residences in the endless new streets, terraces of Belgravia, Tyburnia, and Westbournia are provided with extra floors of bedrooms; thus affording sleeping accommodations more in accordance with our present ideas of comfort, propriety, and health." But that was only one side of the story. Thirteen years later, the *Building News* complained that refurbished and newly built houses in the Russell and Bedford Square neighborhoods, scarcely London's slumland, were sadly inadequate in their "domestic conveniences." Particularly the "bedroom accommodation is in many of them deficient in proportion to the size of the house; everything is sacrificed to the sitting rooms."

In his idiosyncratic tour de force that I have quoted before, Thorstein Veblen called attention to this domestic imbalance. Conspicuous consumption meant that the living quarters of affluent bourgeois were enlarged and decorated at the expense of necessary shelter, like bedrooms, that visitors would never see. "Through this discrimination in favour of visible consumption it has come about that the domestic life of most classes is relatively shabby, as compared with the éclat of that overt portion of their life that is carried on before the eyes of observers." The "exclusiveness of people, as regards their domestic life, in most of the industrially developed communities," follows, and so does "the habit of privacy and reserve that is so large a feature in the code of proprieties of the better classes in all communities." In short, no fashionable accommodation without representation—but then, in their ideals as in their aversions, Victorian bourgeois neither strove for, nor ever attained, unanimity.

IN TRACING THE VAGARIES OF PRIVACY AMONG the Victorian middle classes, we come upon moments when custom required that it be expanded by including a few designated, privileged persons. Giving birth at home was one of them, an occasion when the father was the most natural witness. In *Monsieur, Madame et Bébé*, Gustave Droz dwells on the child's arrival in almost painful detail. Only the physician, the wife's mother, and the husband, whose arm his beloved Louise clutches as she heroically suffers the torments of birth pangs, are allowed into the room. Only after the child is safely born— *"en vérité, un garçon!"*—are a few other relatives permitted to see the newborn, as Madame whispers to her husband under her breath, not for anyone else to hear: "Are you satisfied with me? *Mon ami,* I did the best I could."

Conventions about modesty varied as usual across place and time. At midcentury, good manners prescribed that a middle-class mother could breast-feed her infant in the presence of her husband and family, including the children and servants, but not of others. There is a Daumier watercolor of a third-class railroad carriage that shows a coarse-looking mother nursing, an oblique reminder that one would not expect a passenger in a first-class carriage to bare her breast to suckle her child. But the act seemed so natural and decorous that Dickens, whose regard for the proprieties rarely faltered, could describe it and have his celebrated illustrator, Hablot Browne ("Phiz"), capture the tender moment. David Copperfield's mother is thus engaged with his little half brother as the boy looks on. Indeed, with Mrs. Micawber in the same novel, a woman who seems to be perpetually busy nursing her infants, Dickens could even joke about it, gently. "I must remark here that I hardly ever, in all my experience of the family, saw both the twins detached from Mrs. Micawber at the same time. One of them was always taking refreshment." So much for middle-class prissiness.

5

WE MUST DIG DEEPER STILL. THE VALUE OF privacy seemed obvious enough, but it required certain preconditions—no privacy without a measure of affluence—and encapsulated a wide array of feelings. True, adolescents had no difficulty visualizing its meaning to them: it was an assertion of youthful dignity, a pubertal craving to be treated as an adult. But for all others, it was an umbrella covering varied emotions and convictions: rebelliousness, misanthropy, modesty, a hankering for self-determination. In turn, a willingness to grant privacy to others presupposed a relative freedom from suspiciousness and a capacity to respect people with ideas and ideals at odds with one's own; in short, a liberality of temper.

For the psychological stance that made the cause of privacy so congenial, the Victorians were once more indebted to the philosophes. In 1784, Immanuel Kant published a popular essay, "Answer to the Question: What Is Enlightenment?" that has been interminably quoted. His reply: Enlightenment requires mankind coming of age, shedding the immaturity, the legal dependency, in which its laziness and cowardice had so long kept it. Any submissiveness to the authority of others is a symptom that humanity had not yet reached that supremely desirable state. In the characteristic eighteenth-century manner, Kant turned to the pagan classics, this time to Horace, and exclaimed, "*Sapere aude*—Dare to know!" Enlightenment, in other words, was a synonym for human autonomy. Probably the most dramatic effort to achieve this self-rule during the reign of Victoria, hard fought and far from wholly triumphant at its end, was the feminists' struggle to have women treated as men's equals, to gain, among other advantages, the same privacy that men enjoyed with all the privileges that this condition entailed. This is the meaning of the slogan that Virginia Woolf was to make famous decades later: a room of one's own.

Kant's definition followed nearly a century of Enlightened polemics against the current legal codes, a campaign aimed at rescuing problematic words and actions from the heavy hand of public authorities. Drawing practical consequences from their ideal of toleration, the philosophes argued that blasphemous and impolitic speech or homosexual tastes were private matters. I should think little of a god thin-skinned enough, Montesquieu said, to resent some foolish mortal calling me names. This sounds like a flippant remark, but it was nothing less than a program for rethinking the individual's right against higher powers, whether state, church, the family, or public opinion. To demand that blasphemy, obscenity, political grousing, and whatever adults did in bed be removed from the grasp of the censor, the police, the courts, let alone the executioner, was to propose an impressive private sphere. The most aggressive among nineteenth-century liberals called for nothing less, though the more timid—or more realistic—progressives professed to be content with weakening the shackles of authority without calling for their abolition.

THE MIDDLE-CLASS CONCEPTION OF PRIVACY WAS closely associated with a modern attitude that the Victorians called "individualism." In 1840, in *Democracy in America*, Alexis de Tocqueville described individualism as a term "recently coined to express a new idea. Our fathers knew only about egoism." He defined it as "a calm and considered feeling which disposes each citizen to isolate himself from the mass of his fellows and withdraw into the circle of family and friends; with this little society formed to his taste, he gladly leaves the greater society to look after itself." The issue this "withdrawal" raised was just how to balance the claims of the "little society" against those of society as a whole, a task at which, Tocqueville thought, the individualistic Americans were failing. But quite apart from the democrats of the

New World, he had serious doubts about the intrinsic merits of this recent coinage. He saw it as an outgrowth of the egalitarianism he had observed during his historic visit and predicted that it would spread as equality became more acceptable in European society.

Individualism (a stance against public power) might have been a current invention; individuality (an expression of private distinctiveness) was older. In 1860, in his masterpiece, *The Civilization of the Renaissance in Italy*, the Swiss historian Jacob Burckhardt argued that prominent among the hallmarks of the Renaissance, a period that he put on the map of historical awareness almost single-handedly, was the formation of the individual, "the first-born among the sons of contemporary Europe." In the Middle Ages, "both sides of consciousness—that turned toward the world and that turned inward—lay dreaming or half awake as under a common veil," a veil woven of religious faith, childlike shyness, and delusions. "Man recognized himself only as a [member of a] race, people, part, corporation and family."

Burckhardt does not dwell on the issue, but his exposition leaves no doubt that, to his mind, the medieval conception of the individual as a mere element in some larger whole had no place for privacy. But then, he adds, in Italy the veil first vanished, and an objective treatment of the state and the world, accompanied by a powerful sense of subjectivity, of inwardness, became possible. Man grew into a "spiritual *individual*"; the modern personality arose in full flower. So did its concrete forms of expression; biography, autobiography, the portrait, all first achieved the expressiveness that nineteenth-century bourgeois had learned to take for granted.

Singling out the Renaissance as the mother of nineteenth-century man did not make it, for Burckhardt, a ground for celebration. Individuality was the prerequisite for what came to be called "Renaissance man," unbound by tradition and conventions, but also, much of the time, by religion and morality. And just as in the fourteenth and fifteenth centuries the exquisitely developed individual could degenerate into such an amoral monster as Cesare Borgia, so in the nineteenth century, the bold assertion of individuality was attended by grave hazards. Often enough, young men and women who moved to the city from the countryside or a small town to escape the attentions of their stifling family and prying neighbors discovered that the independence they so ardently sought had degenerated into an unwanted anonymity, a disheartening lack of friends and appreciative community—too heavy a price, some thought, for deserting the collective nest. These lost souls had exchanged provincialism for alienation.

For these people, victimized by disorienting loneliness, the glittering slogan of privacy acquired an ironic ring, and students of contemporary society, philosophers and sociologists alike, developed technical terms— "alienation," "anomie," "fragmentation"—to characterize this tendency of nineteenth-century urban existence. We have seen it before: the division of labor, an increasingly potent driving force for modern industry, business, bureaucracy, the liberal professions, created races of specialists with all too few and all too brittle contacts with the rest of the world. It would be self-deceptive to deny the dark sides of individualism; those who suffered under them recognized them easily enough. But individualism also had another, more positive implication. Private space meant space for genuine choices, which is another word for freedom.

During the Victorian era, one solid instance of replacing sham freedom with the real thing in the political process was the introduction of the ballot. It was apparent to everyone that open voting was highly susceptible to corrupt influence, to bribery, harassment, and manipulation. That is why rulers hung on to it as long as they could. At several times, French revolutionaries legislated secret voting but never rigidly enforced it, and there were some countries that obstinately retained the old open ways. But Britain introduced the secret ballot in 1872. To vote, alone and unobserved: nothing could be a stronger exemplar of privacy in action.

The end of the century also saw the advent of an original, highly controversial exploration of the most private human recesses, psychoanalysis—privacy for two. Since the early nineties, Freud had been refining his techniques of depth-psychological therapy. The analysand lies on a plain couch, recumbent; the analyst sits behind, out of sight, in an ambiance deliberately bland and conducive to regression: no family photographs, no bright lights, the world emphatically shut out from the consulting room with its double doors. True, the patient is not alone, but the largely silent listener is pledged to secrecy and serves mainly to interpret what the patient is really saying. Moral judgments and religious reproofs are notably absent—facile comparisons of the analytic hour with the Catholic confession are wholly inappropriate—and the ultimate aim is to assist the sufferer to discover his or her true self. In later years, Freud would define the purpose of psychoanalytic therapy in terms that the student of privacy will find familiar: "Analysis does not set out to make pathological reactions impossible, but to give the patient *freedom* to decide one way or the other."

6

THE UNFORESEEN, ASTONISHING INNOVATIONS that marked nineteenth-century bourgeois life, including the rising possibilities for privacy, were intimately linked to a widespread fascination with the self. This preoccupation, we know, goes back to Socrates, Athens' great gadfly, who, differentiating himself from his predecessors' efforts to discover the stuff of which the world is made, turned to human concerns. Other remorseless voyagers into their innermost experiences from St. Augustine to Montaigne, Pascal to Rousseau, attest that the Victorians' absorbed interest in the self had a long and honored tradition behind it. Then, too, through the centuries, political theorists beginning with Plato had built their systems on their theory of human nature. In his masterpiece, *Leviathan* of 1651, Thomas Hobbes had made introspection the key to rulership: "He that is to govern a whole nation, must read in himself, not this or that particular man, but mankind." What happened in the nineteenth century to self-analysis was that it became available to men and women with a modicum of schooling. In *Beyond Good and Evil*, published in 1886, one of his fundamental and most accessible texts, Friedrich Nietzsche put it plainly: it was time, he wrote, that psychology should once again be recognized as "the queen of the sciences, for whose service and preparation the other sciences exist. For psychology is now again the path to fundamental problems."

An uncannily penetrating student of the human animal including himself, Nietzsche ran counter to the almost irresistible nineteenth-century urge toward specialization: in his thought, philosophy and psychology are inseparable. He had a remarkable fellow investigator in William James, equally impressive in both these fields. This is not the place to canvass the history of nineteenth-century psychology, except to note that well before the end of Victoria's reign, the unemotional study of emotions had become a lively possibility. In 1824–25, the German educator and philosopher Johann Friedrich Herbart, having already published a "textbook" on psychology, brought out an immensely influential two-volume treatise significantly titled *Psychology as Science, Newly Founded on Experience, Metaphysics and Mathematics*. With his stress on experience and his Realist metaphysics, Herbart established psychology as an autonomous discipline. By the 1870s, it had managed to enter the universities, most notably with Wilhelm Wundt's psychological laboratory at the University of Leipzig.

The Victorians were active in their puzzlement about the self, and pursued the question with their much-praised (and much-lamented) earnestness. That is one reason why keeping a diary was so great a favorite in the nineteenth century; innumerable daily scribblers were more or less articulate about their expectation that their words would, like a magic mirror, explain themselves to themselves. William Gladstone kept a diary not just to record the prodigious quantity of reading he did every day, but also to monitor what he called "the delusions of Selflove," a most unwelcome feature of his Christian self. It was the inquiry after "the only absolute *self*" that Samuel Taylor Coleridge, garrulous, egotistical, sodden with drugs, pursued for the last decades of his life. Stendhal, far less pathetic, was no less eager. "What is the *self—Qu'est-ce que le* moi?" he asked in passing, and conceded that he knew nothing about it. Less articulate bourgeois Victorians followed several alternate routes for acquiring the inner knowledge they craved, with the sermon, the novel, the poem, the philosophical treatise, the psychological laboratory, above all their self-scrutiny. A diary was simply the most egalitarian method for securing psychological insights.

Many diarists failed to describe their introspection as a quest. Not surprisingly, Schnitzler did so. He took much satisfaction in reaching down to his mind's bedrock with his plays and stories—and with his diary, in which he dissected himself pitilessly. His aim in these crowded jottings was quite simply, he said, "self-knowledge." That was in 1895. Five years later, after he had been taking his mental pulse for two decades, he wrote: "I have decided not to conceal from myself any of my acts of meanness and stupidity." He thought that he might not be truly deep, but felt sure that he understood the deepest things. It was a subtle distinction, not without interest; he recognized his faults better than did anyone else, but his self-knowledge rarely resulted in inward reformation. In Freud's classic formulation, he knew and he did not know.

No doubt, as usual, the majority of Victorian bourgeois, even educated ones, did less self-questioning than Schnitzler, and lived quite well without it. We have seen that for the middle classes beleaguered by change, the Victorian age was an age of anxiety. That was a good reason why many of them found the unexamined life eminently worth living. Had they been asked just how closely they monitored their religious beliefs, their political convictions, and their moral stature, how many of them considered their inner world in any way problematic, most would surely have replied that they gladly let their poets and priests, their editorial writers and personal physicians do that work for them. But for growing numbers of bourgeois living in Schnitzler's century, it must have been reassuring to feel that maps showing the ways to self-knowledge, as to prosperity, beauty, and conjugal happiness, seemed to be getting more and more dependable.

Coda

 "THE HISTORY OF THE VICTORIAN AGE WILL never be written," Lytton Strachey asserted in 1918, in the opening sentence of *Eminent Victorians*; "we know too much about it." The formulation is a characteristic Stracheyan paradox, which helps to account for the enormous and lasting popularity of his work of demolition. But, though amusing, it is dead wrong. For all the wealth of information that the nineteenth century left to its successors, we have only begun to acquire the knowledge we need, or learned to evaluate the knowledge we have long had, to permit us to judge the age fairly. The eminent Victorians whom Strachey skewered on his poisoned pen— Cardinal Manning, Florence Nightingale, Doctor Arnold, and General Gordon—were no doubt severely flawed human beings. But there was more to them, and to the minor characters that Strachey caricatured along the way, than *Eminent Victorians* would lead its audience to believe. And it is precisely this book, with its many lesser companions, that has stood in the way of discovering the truth about the Victorian middle class. That truth, to put it bluntly, does not lie halfway between greatness and wretchedness, but near the positive end of the scale.

I have no intention of idealizing the nineteenth-century past. Unlike some conservative commentators, I am not trading in nostalgia, wishing that we could restore what they like to call "Victorian values." As one might expect in human affairs, the record is mixed. There were, in country after country, mine owners and manufacturers who callously exploited their labor force until state action stayed their hand. There were bourgeois couples whose sexual pleasure was compromised, or ruined, by frigidity and other neurotic inhibitions. There were husbands who patronized their wives and fought the emancipation of women in public and private life alike. There were votaries of manliness who preached the gospel of national self-assertion and imperialistic expansion. But the grip of these men and their ideologies weakened as the century went on; virtually all the progressive causes that eventually succeeded in the twentieth century had eloquent and increasingly effective advocates in the nineteenth. More: as I noted at the beginning, the Modernist achievements in the arts and literature—in architecture, painting, sculpture, the novel, the drama, and the rest—that we associate with the twentieth century had all been anticipated well before the outbreak of World War I. It almost seems as though the Victorians left all that was best about them to the ungrateful generations that followed them, and that the evils of our times are our own invention.

I do not offer this verdict lightly. In the last quarter of the nineteenth century, a clan of gadflies uncovered the shabbier aspects of middle-class society, and there is much merit in their barbed fault-finding; the faults they found were there. These political and moral critics of the Victorian world took up where cultural critics of bourgeois philistinism like Flaubert or Zola left off. With this difference: while the artists and novelists I have called the bourgeoisophobes mounted an unsparing assault on the whole of middle-class culture, taking no prisoners, most critics of capitalism were far more precise in their choice of targets. For all their prosecutor's mind-set, they made a respectable team assailing the respectable. President Theodore Roosevelt famously called them muckrakers, but the muck they raked often yielded the pure gold of politicians' dishonesty and the abuse of economic power. One of them, Upton Sinclair, even helped to generate reform legislation, the Pure Food and Drug Act of 1906, with his grisly novel about the Chicago meatpacking industry, *The Jungle*, in which he has a worker fall into a vat and be ground into sausage.

In the United States, gifted journalists working for periodicals like *McClure's* wrote honest, searching, though far from malicious exposés. Ida Tarbell did a substantial and revealing history of Standard Oil, the company that made John D. Rockefeller into a multimillionaire with irregular, at times criminal business practices; Lincoln Steffens traveled across the country investigating city after city to find them more or less like Philadelphia, in his immortal phrase, "corrupt and contented." In Great Britain, the economist J. A. Hobson, a self-described "heretic," brilliantly exposed the demagogic campaign of the British gutter press to mobilize public opinion in support of the Boer War. In those same years, playwrights like Henrik Ibsen and Bernard Shaw put the hidden defects of self-satisfied society on the stage, exhibiting them with a clarity and power that political pamphleteers could only envy.

Theodore Roosevelt thought he could discredit the revelations of the muckrakers as being the work of socialist malcontents. But name-calling could not invalidate their objections to the unchecked entrepreneurial spirit. Upton Sinclair was a Socialist, and on the Continent, articulate Socialist politicians like Jean Jaurès in France and Wilhelm Liebknecht in Germany made their attacks on the bourgeoisie a centerpiece of their polemics. But most of the so-called muckrakers were not radicals. One of *McClure's* ablest contributors, Ray Stannard Baker, made that plain: "We 'muckraked' not because we hated our world but because we loved it. We were not hopeless, we were not cynical, we were not bitter." And Hobson for his part was a determined, almost a defiant, bourgeois. In his autobiography, he declared proudly that he was "born and bred in the middle stratum of the middle class of a middle-sized industrial town in the Midlands." Much of the bluntest castigation of the Victorian middle classes was self-criticism, another point, I believe, in their favor.

▧ THIS ABILITY TO TAKE DISTANCE FROM THEIR social and economic system attests to a certain political maturity in the intelligent and socially engaged sectors of the nineteenth-century middle class. The muckrakers were not forlorn voices in the wilderness; the untold thousands of good bourgeois who voted for the liberal or social democratic parties in their country attest to that. It was such bourgeois who participated in, at times led, movements for reform that made nineteenth-century society more humane and more equitable, whether they fought for the abolition of slavery or the introduction of the secret ballot.

Their leading roles in making the great political, economic, and social revolutions of the nineteenth century were larger even than this. Metternich had been right to warn against the bourgeoisie, for all its bouts of conservative panic, as a radical force for instability. It moved toward completing the work of burying the Old Régime that the French Revolution had so violently begun. Yet the pre-revolutionary order of distinct estates and of rulers obeying mainly their own whim did not wholly fade away—it survived into the German Reich that Bismarck founded in 1871, in which the cabinet reported not to the legislature but to the emperor; politically minded *Bürger* had chosen national unity over liberal institutions. But traditional rule was undermined across the Western world. The nineteenth century was an age of constitution making and, in states already blessed with a fundamental law, of drastic liberalization. And it was bourgeois, assisted by a few aristocratic mavericks, who presided over these moves toward democratizing governmental systems. In Britain and Belgium, France and Italy and Sweden, to say nothing about the United States, the political public was substantially enlarged.

In the economic sectors of Victorian society—mining, industry, banking, insurance, trade local and international, transformed beyond recognition during a few short decades—the share of enterprising bourgeois was necessarily even more dominant, and after strenuous conflicts more beneficial, than in politics. It is not a question of comparing Samaritans with Scrooges and finding more humanitarians than exploiters. What mattered was liberated energies at work, energies of inventors, engineers, financiers making a new world. "Historically," wrote Marx and Engels in their wry, almost lyrical tribute in the *Communist Manifesto,* "the bourgeoisie has played a most revolutionary part." Few capitalists were philanthropists, but many of them builded better than they knew.

These energies required, and generated, a striking measure of flexibility to recognize, and if possible to meet, the unprecedented problems raised by the new urban, industrialized society: the necessity for efficiency at work, the blight of urban overcrowding, the palpable inadequacy of traditional charity, the alienation of the working class from Christianity. Men of power, capitalists, industrialists, legislators, were groping in the dark as they confronted new needs and new demands—and new opportunities. They, and governing bodies, first had to define when a consolidation of companies had become an illegal monopoly, when speculating in shares smacked of criminal inside trading, before they could authoritatively pronounce and legislate on such matters. They had to improvise to determine what kind and degree of government interference in the free market, that shibboleth of mid-nineteenth-century capitalism, would harm the working class or help it. That political economists gave conflicting answers only made such matters harder to resolve.

Compared to these intractable uncertainties in the public arena, the middle-class Victorians' private ideal was relatively plain: the close-knit, harmonious family intent on absorbing high culture in its leisure hours. As the more socially conscious of them acquainted themselves with the lot of those less well situated than they, they sought to generalize this model. With their drives for universal literacy, their educational associations, their inexpensive editions of the classics, they devised prescriptions for the hardworking lower orders. The working poor, too, should be equipped to aspire to, and realize as much as they could, such domestic felicity.

That such an attitude informed wide circles in the middle class should not astonish the open-minded student of the Victorians, even if this liberality has not received the appreciation it deserves. It has been swamped by the charge, largely unmerited, that bourgeois social liberalism was merely a cloak for self-interest. Things are no different with the middle-class reception of unconventional art and literature: that impressive numbers of Victorian bourgeois enjoyed and fostered both is best known to specialists alone. Nor, as I have shown, was it only millionaires with good taste who collected contemporary paintings and supported museums; the first to buy Impressionists were modestly situated bourgeois, and it was lowly clerks, often with their wives, who faithfully attended symphony concerts. We know that not all philistines were bourgeois; we need to discover that not all bourgeois were philistines.

But it is in that most secluded of domains, the sexual life of the married Victorian bourgeoisie, that the gap between legend and truth yawns most widely. Given the Victorians' passion for privacy, the door to their bedroom remained firmly closed, and historians must make do with whatever hints private letters, diaries, small surveys, and physicians' reports have left them to analyze. But after all, even in our age of publicity, we are only marginally better informed. What we do know—and I have devoted a long chapter to it—should leave little doubt that respectable middle-class couples often shared their erotic pleasures in passionate gratification, and wanted nothing better than more of the same. The surviving mail between Victorian spouses offers few gems. But we are learning that what Laura Lyman wrote to her husband— "I'll drain your coffers dry next Saturday I assure you"—was what many bourgeois couples felt.

CRITICS WHO HAVE NOT GONE SO FAR AS TO DAMN the Victorian bourgeoisie as wholly vicious, vulgar, or frigid have denounced it as dull, as thoroughly unheroic, with its prudence, its calculations, its compromises. But that is to define heroism by the anachronistic standards of feudal society. I have mentioned their all too familiar implements before: their galoshes and their umbrellas. But the middling orders, too, had their heroes, celebrated by Baudelaire, painted by Manet, and set to music by Brahms; energetic, black-coated Saint-Simonian innovators in railroad construction, canal digging, office organization, and competence in public service. And they had other, less mundane heroes, men—and a few extraordinary women—who solved mysteries in science, tackled the scourge of epidemics, and presided over drastic reforms in education. In general, they were more pacific than bellicose, more temperate than intoxicated, whether by alcohol or by ideas.

They had convictions, though only a small minority was ready to kill for them. In short, they prized sobriety both literally and figuratively, they valued the commonplace permanence of family life. The most impecunious middle-class families, moored in some backwater, tried to look sure of one thing, even when they were not so sure: there was something distinctive about being bourgeois, even for them.

Of course there were conspicuous exceptions to this flattering middle-class self-portrait, bourgeois who drank, acted impulsively, corrupted politicians, those who moved irresponsibly from love affair to love affair—certainly the young Schnitzler did so. Confident or insecure, capable of mastering, even initiating, the fundamental transformations that were the hallmark of the Victorian age, or paralyzed by the power of the new, bourgeois recognized one another without exchanging a word. Except perhaps in moments of chauvinistic excitement, their idols were quite unlike the idols of the lower orders and of aristocrats. Their speech, their dress, their reading matter, their fantasies, their essential attitudes to work and love and beauty, not to forget privacy, marked them as members of a class thoroughly aware of itself as a class.

This self-recognition survived political conflicts, if at times barely, as in the Dreyfus affair. Throughout the nineteenth and early twentieth centuries industrial countries were agitated by unsettling domestic tensions, as organized trade unions and increasingly self-assertive labor parties mobilized their membership to work toward a new, post-bourgeois society. But, anxiety-producing as these oppositions were, in the end the struggles appeared manageable, as institutions slowly adapted themselves to the unparalleled realities of the time. As a historian, I hesitate to make invidious comparisons, but in view of the century that followed the nineteenth, I can only reiterate that the Victorian age was an admirable century, and that the bourgeoisie may take much of the credit for that.

One thinks back on the twentieth century with horror. Stunning advances in medicine, the delights of Modernism in the arts and literature, reassuring measures that mitigated the costs of capitalism through the welfare state—all this deserves acknowledgment. But these achievements pale before the barbarity of the age that would have made Genghis Khan blanch with jealousy: cowardly collusion with totalitarians, mass murders committed in the name of socialism, scientifically organized genocide originated and largely carried out by one of Europe's renowned bastions of culture. It was a century of dystopias; the Victorian age, for all its bloodthirsty episodes at Manchester in 1819, Paris in 1871, Kishinev in 1903, never sank so low as this.

The chances for continued peace seemed promising. Whatever monarchs, diplomats, military men might plot, a vast tribe of bourgeois—industrialists, bankers, merchants, art dealers, travel agents, publishers, scholars—was profitably woven into a network of a thriving world economy, which, it seemed, was a solid guarantee against war. Surely there was no reason why bourgeois should not continue to live in a world they were increasingly shaping.

▩ THEN CAME AUGUST 4, 1914. EARLIER THAT YEAR, in March, Baroness Bertha von Suttner, who had won the Nobel Peace Prize six years earlier, came to have tea at the Schnitzlers, and they talked about "new threats of war." Schnitzler was not overly impressed. "She is a good, though doubtless fundamentally banal person," he commented in his diary, "like people who 'have to believe something,' even in 'the triumph of reason.'" Schnitzler, deeply skeptical about the chances of reason ever triumphing, did not appreciate that Suttner was being prophetic. Not even the following three months alerted him to the trick that Clio was about to play on the world, using his own empire and that of its German neighbor as her principal agents for deadly mischief. Since early summer, he, his wife, and their children had been vacationing in St. Moritz. After June 28, the day that Archduke Franz Ferdinand and his consort were assassinated at Sarajevo, he succinctly recorded the major developments, the diplomatic maneuverings, and the ultimatums. But like nearly everybody else he was unprepared for what would happen.

"In the hotel," Schnitzler noted on August 5, in shock. "News of

England's declaration of war on Germany. World war. World ruin. Dreadful and monstrous news — *Ungeheure und ungeheuerliche Nachrichten.*" And, later that day, "we are going through a dreadful moment in world history. In a few days, our world picture has been completely changed. One thinks one is dreaming! Everybody is at a loss." So everybody would remain. Schnitzler's century was over. History would not hold bourgeois responsible for this catastrophe. But, whoever brought this fate on humanity, the world — and with that the middle classes — would never be the same.

NOTES

Notes

ABBREVIATIONS

A.S.—Arthur Schnitzler

P.G.—Peter Gay

Tagebuch—Arthur Schnitzler, *Tagebücher*, ed. Peter Michael Braunwarth et al., 10 vols. (Vienna, 1987–2000)

(See the Bibliography for A.S.'s other works)

Peter Gay, *The Bourgeois Experience: Victoria to Freud*, 5 vols. (New York):

        ES—*Education of the Senses* (1984)

        TP—*The Tender Passion* (1986)

        CH—*The Cultivation of Hatred* (1993)

        NH—*The Naked Heart* (1995)

        PW—*Pleasure Wars* (1998)

OVERTURE

[p. xxix] *"scenes with my father"*: A.S., March 19, 1879, *Tagebuch 1879–1892* [I], 9.

[p. xxx] *"terrible reprimand"*: A.S., *Jugend in Wien. Eine Autobiographie*, ed. Therese Nickl and Heinrich Schnitzler (1968; Fischer Taschenbuch, 1971), 86.

[p. xxx] *"in part responsible for it"*: ibid., 87.

[p. xxxi] *but to shoot himself*: ibid., 88.

[p. xxxi] *"blather about frictions at home"*: A.S. [written July 1882], *Tagebuch 1879–1892*, 10.

[p. xxxi] *"Safety is nowhere"*: A.S., *Paracelsus* (1897), scene 11. *Dramatische Werke*, I, 498.

Part I FUNDAMENTALS

ONE *Bourgeoisie(s)*

In several studies, David Cannadine has brilliantly explored social stratification in modern Britain and significantly contributed to the comparative study of class. I single out *The Decline and Fall of the British Aristocracy* (1990), *Class in Britain* (1998), and *The Rise and Fall of Class in Britain* (1999). For France, see still, Adeline Daumard, *La bourgeoisie parisienne de 1815 à 1848* (1963), and her comprehensive synthesis, *Les bourgeois et la bourgeoisie en France depuis 1815* (1987). The most authoritative survey of the German *Bürgertum* remains the relevant chapters in Thomas Nipperdey, *Deutsche Geschichte, 1800–1866. Bürgerwelt und starker Staat* (1983); *Deutsche Geschichte, 1866–1918*, vol. I, *Arbeitswelt und Bürgergeist* (1990), and vol. II, *Machtstaat vor der Demokratie* (1992). *Bürgertum im 19. Jahrhundert. Deutschland im europäischen Vergleich*, ed. Jürgen Kocka, 3 vols. (1988), contains informative essays on individual countries. Richard Hofstadter's classic *The Age of Reform, Bryant to F.D.R.* (1955), remains a joy to read and a stimulus to thinking. And see, for the United States: Stow Persons, *The Decline of American Gentility* (1973); Karen Halttunen, *Confidence Men and Painted Women: A Study of Middle-Class Culture in America, 1830–1870* (1982); Kenneth T. Jackson, *Crabgrass Frontier: The Suburbanization of the United States* (1985).

[p. 3] *"still genteel and respectable,"* . . . *"good Jewish middle-class circles"*: A.S., *Jugend in Wien*, 20, 172.

[p. 4] *"bourgeoisie, people and plebs"*: See John A. Davis, *Conflict and Control: Law and Order in Nineteenth-Century Italy* (1988), 113 [*PW,* 5].

[p. 6] *proletarians in stand-up collars*: See P.G., *ES,* 29.

[p. 7] *"the last among knights"*: Tilmann Buddensieg, "Einleitung," *Villa Hügel. Das Wohnhaus Krupp in Essen*, ed. Buddensieg (1984), 7.

[p. 7] *scattered titles by the thousands*: See Ernst Bruckmüller and Hannes Stekl, "Zur Geschichte des Bürgertums in Österreich," *Bürgertum im 19. Jahrhundert.* I, 173; Ilsa Barea, *Vienna* (1966), 290–93.

[p. 8] *perhaps some $50 million in today's currency*: For Boucicaut, see Véronique Bourienne, "Boucicaut, Chauchard et les autres, fondateurs et fondation des premiers grands magasins parisiens, Paris et Ile-de-France," *Mémoires publiés par la Fédération des sociétés historiques et archéologiques de Paris et de l'Ile-de-France*, XL (1989), 257–335. For Peabody, see Jean Strouse, *Morgan: American Financier* (1999), 49–50.

[p. 8] *"indigent, indeed shabby circumstances"*: A.S., *Jugend in Wien*, 11.

[pp. 9–12] *Dependency in the Victorian age*: See P.G., *PW,* 75–191.

[p. 12] *"The middle class must govern"*: Albert Tannes, "Bürgertum und Bürgerlichkeit in der Schweiz," *Bürgertum im 19. Jahrhundert,* I, 198.

[p. 12] *"his place in the government"*: Stendhal, *Rome, Naples et Florence* (1826; ed., 1987), 289–90.

[p. 13] *"indolence becomes honourable"*: Hippolyte Taine, *Italy: Rome and Naples* (1866; trans. J. Durand, 3d ed., 1870), 272–74. In 1868, a German visitor, Heinrich Börnstein, contrasted Italian superficiality with German thoroughness. Though

Italian unification had finally cast aside despotic regimes, "Italian *épiciers et bourgeois* had not developed a will of their own, nor how to act confidently in public business." See Martin Clark, *Modern Italy 1871–1995* (1984; 2d ed., 1996), 29.

[p. 14] *"the middle class rules in France"*: Michel Chevalier, *Society, Manners, and Politics in the United States: Letters on North America* (1836; 3d ed., 1838; ed. John William Ward, 1961), 382.

[p. 14] *"an industrial, bourgeois age"*: Heinrich Heine, *Lutetia*, part I, letter 29 (January 11, 1841). *Sämtliche Schriften*, ed. Klaus Briegleb, 6 vols. (1969–76), V, 341.

[p. 14] *"as from its own efforts"*: Alexis de Tocqueville, *Souvenirs* (1893; ed. Luc Monnier, 1943), 26.

[p. 16] *A troop of censors . . . its rulers, and its actions*: Recent scholarship has stressed that the number of secret policemen was far smaller than liberal politicians and historians believed at the time. Yet their very presence inhibited free expression.

[p. 17] *"the liberal bourgeois classes"*: Lothar Gall, *Bismarck. Der weisse Revolutionär* (1980; ed., 1983), 352.

[p. 18] *an outlet in political action*: My good friend, the historian R. K. Webb, has rightly called attention to the "difficulty of pinpointing middle-class interests." *Modern England: From the Eighteenth Century to the Present* (1969; 2d ed., 1980), 224.

[p. 19] *bourgeois interests faded into the background*: "An analysis of the last Chamber of Deputies of the Restoration [from 1827 to 1830] gives 38.5 per cent higher officials, 14.8 per cent engaged in trade, finance, or industry, 5.2 per cent belonging to the liberal professions, and 41.5 per cent large landowners, apart from such members of the previous categories who were also landowners, and probably most of them were." Alfred Cobban, *A History of Modern France.* vol. 2, *1799–1871* (1961; 2d ed., 1965), 78.

[p. 20] *largely concentrated in the northern regions*: In 1881, "there were about 200,000 'independent' landowners, rentiers and entrepreneurs, and about another 100,000 professional men—doctors, lawyers, engineers and the like. . . . There were 100,000 Italians holding respectable white-collar jobs in he private sector, and there were also 200,000 in non-manual public employment, including around 750,000 teachers." Clark, *Modern Italy*, 29.

[p. 21] *"civilized countries, the bourgeoisie"*: Friedrich Engels, *The Condition of the Working Class in England in 1844*, 95n.

[p. 21] *"all the leading government offices"*: Friedrich Engels, "On Historical Materialism," in Karl Marx and Friedrich Engels, *Basic Writings on Politics and Philosophy*, ed. Lewis S. Feuer (1959), 63.

[p. 22] *despised this boy as snobbish and stupid*: A.S., *Jugend in Wien*, 77.

[p. 22] *"even we talked politics"*: A.S., November 30, 1897, *Tagebuch*, II, 272.

[pp. 22–23] *"great gamblers with human beings"*: A.S., May 10, 1896, ibid., 190.

[p. 23] *"the music-loving middle class"*: Eduard Hanslick, *Geschichte des Concertwesens in Wien*, 2 vols. (1869–70), I, 164.

[p. 23] *"political affairs of Austria"*: Count Paul Vasili (pseud.) *La Société de Vienne* (7th enlarged ed., 1885), 347–48.

[p. 24] *"the moral gangrene" of "presumption"*: "Confession of Faith: Metternich's Secret Memorandum to the Emperor Alexander" [December 15, 1820], *Memoirs of Prince*

Metternich, 1815–1829, ed. Prince Richard Metternich, trans. Mrs. Alexander Napier, 5 vols. (1881), III, 467.

[p. 26] *"rather different from ours"*: Freud to Martha Bernays, August 29, 1883. Sigmund Freud, *Briefe, 1873–1939,* ed. Ernst L. Freud (1960), 48–49.

[p. 28] *"what is more, provincial bourgeois!"*: Emile Zola, "Le Catholique hystérique," *Mes haines. Causeries littéraires et artistiques* (1866), *Oeuvres complètes,* ed. Henri Mitterand, 15 vols. (1962–69), X, 47.

[p. 29] *"the beginning of all virtue"*: Gustave Flaubert to George Sand (May 17, 1867). *Correspondance,* ed. Jean Bruneau, currently 4 vols. (1973–), III, 642.

[p. 29] *"Bourgeoisophobus,"*: Flaubert to Louis Bouilhet, December 26, 1852, ibid., II, 217.

[p. 29] *"bourgeois and dull"*: A.S., January 1, 1893, *Tagebuch,* II, 10.

[p. 29] *"stupid bourgeois views"*: A.S., January 28, 1896, ibid., 171.

[p. 30] *"loyalty of Vienna's bourgeoisie to the Kaiser"*: *Jugend in Wien. Literatur um 1900,* ed. Bernhard Zeller (1974), 44.

[p. 30] *"the value of . . . glory of England"*: James Mill. Harold Perkin, *The Origins of Modern English Society, 1780–1880* (1969), 230.

[p. 31] *"the idiocy of rural life"*: Karl Marx and Friedrich Engels, *Communist Manifesto* (1848; introduction, A. J. P. Taylor, 1967), 85, 84.

[p. 33] *"is the best index of its character"*: Anon., *The Leisure Hour,* XVIII (1869), 109.

TWO *Home, Bittersweet Home*

See chiefly Michael Mitterauer and Reinhard Sieder, *The European Family: Patriarchy to Partnership from the Middle Ages to the Present* (1977; trans. and rev., Karla Oosterveen and Manfred Hörzinger, 1982). For the emergence and triumph of the modern (nuclear) family, I have used two general histories: Jean-Louis Flandrin, *Families in Former Times: Kinship, Household and Sexuality* (1976; trans. Richard Southern, 1979); and Jack Goody, *The Development of the Family and Marriage in Europe* (1983). Edmund S. Morgan's fine essay, *The Puritan Family: Religion and Domestic Relations in Seventeenth-Century New England* (1944; rev. ed., 1966), provides essential background. See also Jonas Frykman and Orvar Löfgren, *Culture Builders: A Historical Anthropology of Middle-Class Life* (1979; trans. Alan Crozier, 1987), which deals with Sweden; and *The Family in Imperial Russia: New Lines of Historical Research,* ed. David L. Ransel (1978). Albrecht Koschorke, *Die Heilige Familie und ihre Folgen. Ein Versuch* (2000), is an interesting essay on the "sacralization" of the family through history.

[p. 36] *"because of my emancipation"*: A.S., June 16, 1879, *Tagebuch,* I, 9.

[p. 36] *"no prospects as far as earnings go"*: A.S., December 8, 1892, ibid., 395.

[p. 37] *"as a matter of course"*: A.S., *Jugend in Wien,* 90.

[p. 37] *and started thirteen more*: Ibid., 98.

[p. 37] *"what art already is"*: A.S., October 27, 1879, *Tagebuch,* I, 12.

[p. 37] *and at least nineteen concerts*: A.S., December 30, 1879, ibid., 17.

[p. 39] *"epochs of civilization"*: Sigmund Freud, *The Interpretation of Dreams* (1899 [1900]), Standard Edition of the Complete Psychoanalytic Works, trans. James Strachey et al., 24 vols. (1953–74), IV, 264.

[p. 41] *childhood diseases . . . there were then no cures*: For some decades, historians of early modern Europe (including myself) maintained that parents must have loved their children less than they would in Victorian times because they had lost too many to invest much emotion in those who survived. This quantitative view of love now stands largely discredited: the more to love, the more love, was far from unknown.

[p. 42] *"which was worse, of our mother"*: Julie Kaden (née Bondi), "Der erste Akt meines Lebens" (ms. 1943), *Jüdisches Leben in Deutschland. Selbstzeugnisse zur Sozialgeschichte des Kaiserreiches*, ed. Monika Richarz (1979), 328.

[p. 44] *"a last resort"*: Hippolyte Taine, *Notes sur l'Angleterre* (1871; 4th ed., 1910), 103.

[p. 44] *"that's my motto"*: George and Weedon Grossmith, *The Diary of a Nobody* (1892; ed., 1995), 19.

[p. 45] *"the shell of the animal's back"*: Mrs. Isabella Beeton, *The Book of Household Management* (1861; first serialized in monthly supplements to *Englishwoman's Magazine* from 1859), 89, 98. Sarah Freeman, *Isabella and Sam: The Story of Mrs. Beeton* (1978), is an essential biography.

[p. 46] *"deficient in its nutrient qualities"*: Beeton, *Book of Household Management*, 1022–23.

[p. 46] *"are apt to create"*: Ibid., 1017.

[p. 47] *"without bitterness"*: William Gladstone, October 18, 1842, *The Gladstone Diaries*, ed. M. R. D. Foot and H. C. G. Matthew, 14 vols. (1968–84), III, 231.

[p. 48] *the presumed natural irrationality*: On this point I am indebted to Ruth Harris's excellent *Murder and Madness: Medicine, Law and Society in the fin de siècle* (1989), esp. ch. 6.

[p. 48] *had always done so superbly*: von Sybel, in Priscilla Robertson, *An Experience of Women: Pattern and Change in Nineteenth-Century Europe* (1982), 28n.

[p. 48] *gift for loyalty and tenderness*: Virchow, in ibid., 25.

[p. 49] *nearly all of them whores*: For one instance of Schnitzler's offensive tone, see A.S., April 25, 1894, *Tagebuch*, II, 75.

[p. 49] *"women reign with unchallenged sway"*: Miss Betham-Edwards, *Home Life in France* (1905), 89.

[p.50] *"has any right over them"*: John Stuart Mill, *The Subjection of Women* (1869), 57–59. On November 15, 1883, Freud, who had translated this polemic into German, wrote his fiancée: "nature has determined woman's destiny through beauty, charm and sweetness—" Freud, *Briefe*, 74. The revolutionary as conservative bourgeois.

[p. 50] *a "cure" the two had discussed earlier*: A.S., January 4, 19, 1896, *Tagebuch*, II, 168, 170.

[p. 51] *"then I was incautious"*: A.S., May 10, 1896, ibid., 190.

[p. 51] *"body and soul in former bonds"*: Emma Roe to Arthur Roe, October 5, 1864, Roe Family Papers, Yale—Manuscripts and Archives. For more extensive passages, equally passionate, see P.G., *TP,* 127–33.

[p. 52] *"giving existence to sentient beings"*: Anon., *Reproductive Control* (1855), 12.

[p. 52] *"some even consider it a duty"*: Frederick Hollick, *The Marriage Guide or Natural History of Generation* (1850), 333.

[p. 52] *"destiny of the brutes in this matter"*: John Humphrey Noyes, *Male Continence* (1866), 6.

[p. 54] *"information and personal histories"*: Havelock Ellis, Preface to the First Edition (1898), *Studies in the Psychology of Sex*, 6 vols. in 2 (ed., 1936), I, xxxv.

[p. 55] *"made of either rubber or skin"*: Mary Hallock Foote to Helena Gilder, December 7 (1876), Mary Hallock Foote Papers, Stanford University Library. Carl N. Degler has used the same passage in *At Odds: Women and the Family in America from the Revolution to the Present* (1980), 224.

[p. 55] *"of Nature's methods"*: Foote to Gilder, December 12 (1876), ibid.

[p. 56] *"expert in this respect"*: James Ashton, *The Book of Nature; containing Information for Young People who Think of Getting Married* (1865), 38.

[p. 56] *price of a condom dropped from tenpence to a ha'penny*: Michael Mason, *The Making of Victorian Sexuality* (1994), 58.

[p. 56] *The doctors' ignorance was massive*: For one fine instance of such "disasters" caused by homemade calendars, see the experiences of Mabel Loomis Todd, P.G., *ES*, "The Bourgeois Experience."

[p. 57] *"of quite recent origin"*: R. Koehler, "Les phénomènes intimes de la fécondité," *Revue générale des sciences pures et appliqués*, III (1892), 539.

[p. 57] *almost as much from its allies as from its adversaries*: The most imaginative and most preposterous advocate of birth control (hence worth preserving) was Dr. Jean Dubois, who advised a couple with "temperate desires" to perform the sexual act "on an *inclined* plane, facing upwards," to keep the semen from reaching its target. More passionate couples should indulge just once a week, since the "mutual strength of the copulative shock so far deranges the economy of the uterus, as to prevent impregnation," a rare instance of a physician recommending simultaneous orgasm as a form of contraception. Immediately after copulation, the woman should "dance smartly for a few moments about the room." Was it an accident, Dr. Dubois asked, that women dancers "rarely have a numerous progeny"? —*Marriage Physiologically Discussed* (1839; trans. William Greenfield, 1839), 88–89.

[p. 57] *"give herself fully and forever"*: Taine, *Notes sur l'Angleterre*, 101.

[p. 58] *"one's talent is so unimpaired"*: A.S., November 4, 1904, *Tagebuch*, III, 98.

[p. 58] *"not the individual girl"*: Rahel Straus, *Wir lebten in Deutschland: Erinnerungen einer deutschen Jüdin, 1880–1933* (1961; 3d ed., 1962), 19.

[p. 59] *"You have a daughter . . . sole endeavor to make her happy"*: Samuel Bleichröder to B. H. Goldschmidt, January 21, 1850, Landesarchiv Berlin, E Rep. 200–33, no. 2.

[p. 60] *"seclusion" and "trivial ease"*: A.S., *Das Märchen* (1891), Act 2. *Die dramatischen Werke*, I, 159.

Part II DRIVES AND DEFENSES

THREE   *Eros: Rapture and Symptom*

I have discussed a number of discredited but still popular critiques of Victorian sexuality (even among some scholars) in *ES*, 466–69. Among new titles, Michael Mason, *The Making of Victorian Sexuality* (1994), bravely slays some of these dragons. Carl N. Degler, *At Odds: Women and the Family in America from the Revolution to the Present* (1980) paralleled and in some measure anticipated my researches on nineteenth-century sexuality. Roy Porter and Lesley Hall, *The Facts of Life: The Creation of Sexual Knowledge in Britain, 1650–1950* (1995), provides much relevant information.

[p. 63] *"willingness to oblige"*: A.S., October 17, 1893, *Tagebuch*, II, 55.

[p. 65] *"a hypochondriac of love"*: A.S., "Agonie," part of the *Anatol* cycle (1888–91). *Die dramatischen Werke*, I, 82.

[p. 66] *"that secret knowledge"*: Freud to A.S., May 8, 1906, Freud, *Briefe*, 249. A.S.'s diary displays his interest in Freud as early as March 26, 1900; some four months after its publication, he was reading *Traumdeutung* (see *Tagebuch*, II, 325; and November 5, 1905, and October 27, 1906, *Tagebuch*, III, 164, 229).

[p. 67] *"involved in not being bourgeois"*: John Addington Symonds to his daughter Margaret, December 6, 1889. Phyllis Grosskurth, *John Addington Symonds: A Biography* (1964), 299.

[p. 69] *"imp[otent]besides and 'unnatural.'"*: A. S, March 4, 1893, *Tagebuch*, II, 14.

[p. 69] *"a habitual tormentor"*: A.S., January 24, 1894, ibid., 72.

[p. 70] *"but to my hygiene"*: A.S., September 4, 1893, ibid., 52.

[p. 70] *"I am simply an animal"*: A.S., August 10, 1890, *Tagebuch*, I, 301.

[p. 70] *"and whores disgust me"*: A.S., December 15, 1892, ibid., 395–96.

[p. 70] *"bad attacks"*: A.S., August 10, 1890, ibid., 300.

[p. 70] *"those thoughts assailed me again!"*: A.S., ibid.

[p. 71] *"immense disgust"*: A.S. to Marie Glümer, November [18], 1890, *Briefe*, I, 102.

[p. 71] *"and even I was not the first!"*: Ibid., 100.

[p. 71] *"the great majority of well-guarded virgins"*: A.S., August 10, 1890, *Tagebuch*, I, 300.

[p. 71] *"the lowest creature under the sun"*: A.S. to Marie Glümer, April 29, 1893, *Briefe*, I, 196.

[p. 71] *"You have soiled me as no man has ever been soiled"*: A.S. to Marie Glümer, [April 4, 1893], ibid., 182.

[p. 71] *"while I betrayed her"*: A.S., March 19, 1893, *Tagebuch*, II, 17.

[p. 71] *"when one is not in love"*: A.S., December 27, 1892, *Tagebuch*, I, 397.

[p. 71] *"plies her harmless trade"*: A.S. to Marie Glümer, [April 4,] 1893, *Briefe*, I, 182.

[p. 72] *"The cold hotel room. Hypochondria."*: A.S., October 22, 1892, *Tagebuch*, I, 390.

[p. 72] *"in a less tormented way"*: A.S., December 27, 1892, ibid., 397.

[p. 72] *"Sophisms?"*: A.S., December 15, 1892, ibid., 395.

[p. 72] *"a comparatively truthful nature"*: A.S., August 10, 1890, ibid., 300.

[p. 72] *"a liar and a whore"*: A.S., April 24, 1894, *Tagebuch*, II, 75.

[p. 73] *"the shame that clings to you is ineradicable"*: A.S., *Das Märchen* (1891), *Die Dramatischen Werke*, I, 199.

[p. 74] *"I have not yet dared anything"*: A.S., October 7, 1894, *Tagebuch*, II, 93.

[p. 74] *"this whole business has developed naturally"*: A.S., March 13, 1895, ibid., 129.

[p. 74] *"tenderly and sensually"*: A.S., April 14, 1895, ibid., 135.

[p. 74] *"I'd like to have another mistress again"*: A.S., January 16, 1896, ibid., 169–170.

[p. 74] *"more, physically, too, than before"*: A.S., April 4, 1896, ibid., 182.

[p. 74] *"had not yet belonged to anyone"*: A.S., February 17, 1895, ibid., 123.

[p. 75] *"I loved her very much"*: A.S., July 10, 1895, ibid., 146.

[p. 75] *"she became mine once again"*: A.S., July 17, 1895, ibid.

[p. 75] *"tender letters from the Mz's"*: A.S., July 26, ibid., 147.

[p. 75] *"downright prostituted"*: A.S., January 6, 1895, ibid., 110.

[p. 75] *"which offended her"*: A.S., May 1, 1899, ibid., 306.

[p. 76] *"had been, and is, chaste"*: Richard von Krafft-Ebbing, *Neue Forschungen auf dem Gebiete der Psychopathia Sexualis. Eine klinische-forensische Studie* (1886), 14.

[p. 77] *"cordial rather than intimate"*: A.S., *Jugend in Wien,* 44.

[p. 78] *"a right to more understanding"*: A.S., June 21, 1891, *Tagebuch,* I, 337.

[p. 78] *"Black-Coated Respectability; the living God"*: Bertrand Russell to Gilbert Murray, December 12, 1902, *The Autobiography of Bertrand Russell, 1872–1914* (1967), 244.

[p. 80] *"for the lack of gratification"*: J. F. Albrecht, *Heimlichkeiten der Frauenzimmer oder die Geheimnisse der Natur hinsichtlich der Fortpflanzung des Menschen* (ca. 1830; 6th enlarged ed., 1851), 71.

[p. 82] *"the footing of a mistress"*: Dr. William Acton, *The Functions and Disorders of the Reproductive Organs, in Childhood, Youth, Adult Age, and Advanced Life, Considered in their Psychological, Social, and Moral Relations* (1857; slightly revised and substantially enlarged 3d ed., 1863) 133–35, 103.

[p. 82] *"so long as she can bear it"*: Dr. H. Newell Martin, *The Human Body: An Account of the Structure and the Conditions of Its Healthy Working* (8th rev. ed., 1898), 664. Note that in several editions the thirty-ninth chapter ("Reproduction") from which this passage comes, was omitted or printed as an appendix (see 3d rev. ed., 1885, separate pagination, 20). The publisher offered to sell copies without this "sexy" chapter.

[p. 82] *"and the family unthinkable"*: Krafft-Ebbing, *Psychopathia Sexualis,* 38.

[p. 83] *"support for herself and her children"*: Ibid., 14.

[p. 83] *"blame the Creator of the institution?"*: Albrecht, *Heimlichkeiten der Frauenzimmer,* 23.

[p. 84] *"under your hot caresses"*: Anne-Marie Sohn, *Du premier baiser à l'alcove. La sexualité des Français au quotidien (1850–1950)* (1996), 250.

[p. 84] *"a half conscious dying came over me"*: Adele Sandrock to A.S., April 12, 1893. *Dilly. Adele Sandrock und Arthur Schnitzler. Geschichte einer Liebe in Briefen, Bildern und Dokumenten,* ed. Renate Wagner (1953), 40.

[p. 85] *"in your embrace"*: Joseph Lyman to Laura Lyman, March 11, 1865, Lyman Family Papers, box 4, Yale — Manuscripts and Archives.

[p. 85] *"have it — all — full measure"*: Joseph Lyman to Laura Lyman, March 13, 1865, ibid.

[p. 85] *"my mind with yours"*: Laura Lyman to Joseph Lyman, March 13, 1865, ibid.

[p. 85] *"next Saturday I assure you"*: Laura Lyman to Joseph Lyman, March 23, 1865, ibid.

[p. 85] *"Don't you wish you were here?"*: Laura Lyman to Joseph Lyman, March 11, 1865, ibid.

[p. 85] *"not be tantalized any longer"*: Laura Lyman to Joseph Lyman, March 24, 1865, ibid.

[p. 86] *"the proper stimulants"*: J. Matthews Duncan, *On Sterility in Women* (1884), 96.

[pp. 86–88] *The much-discussed Mosher Survey . . . "as uplifting as music"*: *The Mosher Survey: Sexual Attitudes of Forty-Five Victorian Women,* ed. James MaHood and Kristine Wenburg (1980), passim. For a more detailed analysis, see P.G., *ES,* 135–44.

[p. 89] *"bad conscience about sexual matters"*: Sigmund Freud, "The Sexual Enlightenment of Children" (1907), Standard Edition, IX, 133 (translation modified).

[p. 89] *"get them to confess their feelings"*: Albrecht, *Heimlichkeiten der Frauenzimmer,* 63–64.

[p. 89] *"I was unable to screw"*: Marcel Proust, André Aciman, "Inversions," *The New Republic* (July 12, 1999), 39.

[p. 90] *"to face a rude awakening"*: Annie Besant, *An Autobiography* (1893), 70.

[p. 91] *"the paradise of a mother's love"*: Ibid., 71.

[p. 91] *"an impossible ignorance"*: Emily Lutyens, *A Blessed Girl: Memories of a Victorian Girlhood, 1887–1896* (1953), 10.

[p. 92] *"and I was silly too."*: See Mary Lutyens, *Edwin Lutyens* (1980), 242–44.

[p. 92] *"it's a horror!"*: Gabrielle Houbre, *La discipline de l'amour* (1997), 73.

[p. 92] *"the continuance of that state"*: Duncan, *On Sterility in Women,* 94.

[p. 92] *"and discover the cheerful side"*: Friedrich Siebert, *Sexuelle Moral und Sexuelle Hygiene* (1901), iii.

[pp. 92–93] *One splendid instance . . . "such memories, now so distant"*: Gustav Droz, *Monsieur, Madame et Bébé* (1866; 1997), 134–54. And see Gabrielle Houbre, *La discipline de l'amour: L'Education sentimentale des filles et des garçons à l'âge du romantisme* (1997).

[p. 94] *"never goes hand in hand with reason"*: Louis Berlioz to Joséphine Berlioz, April 22, 1803. David Cairns, *Berlioz,* vol. 1, *The Making of an Artist, 1802–1832* (1989; 2d ed., 1999), 11.

FOUR *Alibis for Aggression*

Richard Hofstadter's classic *Social Darwinism in American Life* (1944; rev. ed., 1955) goes beyond its title; a pioneering study, it requires some adjustments, since Social Darwinists such as Herbert Spencer were more humane and liberal than they appear here. John Chandos's atmospheric *Boys Together: English Public Schools 1800–1864* (1984) includes flogging. Ian Gibson, *The English Vice: Beating, Sex and Shame in Victorian England and After* (1978), offers a psychological analysis of masochism. R. J. White, *Waterloo to Peterloo* (1957), provides a general background for the "massacre." For Frenchmen killing Frenchmen in 1871, abundantly chronicled, Frank Jellinek, *The Paris Commune* (1937), retains considerable authority; Paul Lidsky, *Les écrivains contre la Commune* (1970) has collected the hostile (sometimes savage) comments by authors. For race, see esp. Hugh A. MacDougall, *Racial Myth in English History: Trojans, Teutons, and Anglo-Saxons* (1982). Daniel J. Kevles, *In the Name of Eugenics: Genetics and the Uses of Human Heredity* (1985), is excellent on nineteenth-century pseudo-science.

[p. 97] *"quite as divine as love"*: A.S., "Aphorismen und Betrachtungen," *Buch der Sprüche und Bedenken,* I (1927; ed., 1993), 82.

[p. 98] *"potential warriors"*: William James, *The Varieties of Religious Experience: A Study in Human Nature* (1902), 366.

[p. 98] *"innate in man"*: Edmond and Jules de Goncourt, November 16, 1859, *Journal; mémoires de la vie littéraire, 1851–1898,* ed. Robert Ricatte, 22 vols. (1956–58), III, 168.

[p. 98] *"the inborn need to hate and fight"*: Georg Simmel, *Soziologie. Untersuchungen über die Formen der Vergesellschaftung* (1908), 261.

[p. 98] *"fighting instinct"*: Ibid., 262.

[p. 102] *"determines a country's atmosphere"*: A.S., "Aphorismen und Betrachtungen," 84.

[p. 102] *"stupid and bestial"*: A.S., May 29, 1896, *Tagebuch*, II, 193.

[p. 102] *"So we invent dynastic sentiment"*: A.S., Papers, reel 1a, State University of New York at Binghamton.

[p. 103] *"from a sense of duty"*: Thomas Babington Macaulay, *The History of England from the Accession of James II*, 5 vols. (1849–61; American ed., n.d.), I, 385 [ch. 3].

[p. 103] *"painful office"*: William Ewart Gladstone, September 28, 1847, *Gladstone Diaries*, III, *1840–1847* (1974), 656.

[p. 103] *"turbulent, violent, and vicious men"*: Henry A. Drake, Chairman, Boston School Committee, *Report on Corporal Punishment in the Public Schools of the City of Boston* (1867), 22.

[p. 104] *"Power, Violence, Terror, Suffering!"*: Horace Mann, *Reply to the "Remarks" of Thirty-One Boston Schoolmasters on the Seventh Annual Report of the Secretary of the Massachusetts Board of Education* (1844), 135.

[p. 104] *"scarcely proper and scarcely decent"*: Jacques Claude Demogeot and Henri Montucci, *De l'enseignement secondaire en Angleterre et en Ecosse* (1867), 40.

[p. 105] *"misunderstood humanistic principles"*: Julius Beeger, "Die Disciplinargewalt der Schule," *Allgemeine Deutsche Lehrerzeitung*, 28 (July 9, 1876), 232.

[p. 105] *"flogging pedagogues"*: Eduard Sack, *Gegen die Prügel-Pedagogen* (1878), 13.

[p. 106] *"become more human"*: Andrew Halliday. John Tosh, *A Man's Place: Masculinity and the Middle-Class Home in Victorian England* (1999), 92.

[p. 106] *"hides his sash"*: Droz, *Monsieur, Madame et Bébé*, 342.

[p. 106] *"maladroit pressures"*: Ibid., 343.

[p. 106] *"inborn vice"*: Ibid.

[p. 108] *"the sabre, the bayonet, and the dungeon!"*: John Wade. Dror Wahrman, *Imagining the Middle Class: The Political Representation of Class, c. 1780–1840* (1995), 205.

[p. 109] *"under circumstances of great barbarity"*: Tony Horwitz, "Untrue Confessions," *The New Yorker* (December 13, 1999), 80–81.

[p. 110] *"bestiality pure and simple"*: For a catalogue of telling anti-Communard examples, see Lidsky, *Les écrivains contre la Commune*, esp. 46–53.

[p. 110] *"By portraying others as inferior!"*: A.S., Papers, reel 1a.

[p. 111] *"imbibing sweet pulps and juices"*: Thomas Carlyle, "Occasional Discourse on the Negro Question" [in the original version, reprinted as "Nigger Question"], *Fraser's Magazine*, XL (December 1849), 670–71.

[p. 112] *"the key to history"*: Benjamin Disraeli. Robert Blake, *Disraeli* (1967; ed., 1968), 186.

[p. 112] *"one keeps all one's life"*: Georges Vacher de Lapouge, *L'Aryen. Son role social* (1899), 511.

[p. 113] *"motives which affect them"*: J. A. Hobson, *Imperialism: A Study* (1902; 3d rev. ed., 1938), 198.

[p. 113] *"native element was pushed back"*: P. Leutwein, "Anhang. Die Unruhen in Deutsch-Südwest-Afrika," in "Simplex africanus," *Mit der Schutztruppe durch Deutsch-Afrika* (1905), 197.

[p. 115] *"Christians in Vienna think this way"*: A.S., February 3, 1898, *Tagebuch*, II, 277.

[p. 116] *"comprehending Germanness"*: A.S. Papers, reel 1a.

[p. 116] *"in which he seriously believes"*: A.S., November 4, 1895. *Tagebuch*, II, 159.

[p. 116] *"lowest instincts of the masses"*: A.S. , Papers, reel 1a.

[p. 118] *"unconditional command"* . . . *"repealed"*: Joseph P. Thompson, *The Right and Necessity of Inflicting the Punishment of Death for Murder* (1842), 7, 19.

[p. 118] *"coincide with the divine government"*: Milo D. Codding, *Capital Punishment, Shown to Be a Violation of the Principles of Divine Government as Developed by Nature, Recorded in History and Taught by Jesus Christ, and Proved to be* INEXPEDIENT *by its Effects upon Society, its Failure to Accomplish its Object, and the Destruction of the Rights of its Victims* (1846), 6.

[p. 118] *"tendencies of the Present"*: Ibid., 17.

[p. 118] *"is a utopia"*: Raffaele Mariano, *La Pena di Morte considerazioni in appoggio all' opusculo de prof. Vera* (1864), 19.

[p. 119] *"any charm of novelty"*: Francis Bishop, *"Thou Shalt Not Kill," A Paper upon the Law of Capital Punishment* (1882), 1.

[p. 119] *successor congress took it all back*: Some states in the U.S.A., such as Rhode Island, reinstituted the death penalty several years after doing away with it. Public opinion was precariously balanced: the state of Maine abolished the death penalty in 1876, reversed itself seven years later, only to reverse its reversal in 1887.

[p. 120] *Such advances . . . eliminating the death penalty entirely*: Venezuela did so in 1864, Portugal in 1867, the Netherlands in 1870, Italy in 1880.

[p. 121] *"do you want him to write an idyll?"*: Emile Zola to Jean-Baptistin Baille [end of August, beginning of September 1860], *Correspondance*, ed. B. H. Bakker, vol. I, *1857–1867* (1978), 231.

[p. 123] *"or to steal a letter"*: James Anson Farrer, *Crimes and Punishments, Including a New Translation of Beccaria's "Dei Delitti e Delle Pene"* (1880), 66.

[p. 124] *based entirely on "the justice of resentment"*: Ibid., 82.

[p. 124] *"wrongs and injuries undergone"*: Louis Günther, *Die Idee der Wiedervergeltung in der Geschichte und Philosophie des Strafrechts. Ein Beitrag zur universalhistorischen Entwicklung desselben*, 2 vols. (1889–91), I, 5.

[p. 125] *"justice tempered by compassion and kindness"*: Claude-Joseph Tissot, *Le Droit pénal étudié dans ses principes, dans ses usages et les lois des divers peuples du monde; ou, Introduction philosophique et historique à l'étude du droit criminel*, 2 vols. (1860; 3d ed., 1888), II, 591.

[p. 125] *"in healthily constituted minds"*: James Fitzjames Stephen, *Liberty, Equality, Fraternity* (1873; ed. Stuart D. Warner, 1993), 98.

FIVE   *Grounds for Anxiety*

For the venereal danger, there is Claude Quétet, *History of Syphilis* (1986; trans. Judith Bradcock and Brian Pike, 1980). See also the useful monograph by Terra Ziporyn, *Disease in the Popular American Press: The Case of Diphtheria, Typhoid Fever, and Syphilis* (1988). On French writers and their syphilis, Roger L. Williams's essays on Charles Baudelaire, Gustave Flaubert, Jules de Goncourt, Guy de Maupassant, and Alphonse Daudet in *The Horror of Life* (1980) are authoritative. Janet Oppenheim, *"Shattered Nerves": Doctors, Patients, and Depression in Victorian England* (1991), is an enlightening study of neurasthenia.

[p. 130] *"praiseworthy resignation"*: A.S., April 28, 1880, *Tagebuch*, I, 45.

[p. 130] *deaths from syphilis had increased by 84 percent*: Otto Caspari, *Das Problem über die Ehe! Vom philosophischen, geschichtlichen und sozialen Gesichtspunkte* (1899), 19–20. The treatise, by a German professor of philosophy, is a typical product of his age and culture, a mixture of dry figures and emotional pleading.

[p. 131] *"and has been fully cured"*: Charles Baudelaire to Auguste Poulet-Malassis, ca. February 10, 1860. Baudelaire, *Correspondance générale*, ed. Jacques Crépet, 6 vols. (1947–53), III, 22.

[p. 131] *"I just laugh"*: Quoted from an auction catalogue by Quétet, *History of Syphilis*, 129–30.

[p. 132] *"remarkable for its nervousness"*: *Examiner* (London), May 17, 1813.

[p. 132] *"in their various forms, 'nervousness'"*: Dr. William Alcott, *The Young Woman's Guide to Excellence* (1840; 13th ed., 1847), 295.

[p. 133] *"corrupts them at birth"*: Benjamin Constant. Jane Matlock, "Novels of Testimony and the 'Invention' of the Modern French Novel," in Timothy Unwin, ed., *The Cambridge Companion to the French Novel, from 1800 to the Present* (1997), 28.

[p. 133] *"nervousness is rising fatally"*: Richard Krafft-Ebing, *Nervosität und neurasthenische Zustände* (1895), 80. Emile Durkheim said the same thing in his classic study of suicide: "Neurasthenia is a sort of elementary insanity . . . but also a more widespread condition; it is becoming progressively more general"—*Suicide: A Study in Sociology* (1897; trans. John A. Spaulding and George Simpson, 1951), 68.

[p. 133] *"the malady of the nineteenth century"*: C. Falkenhorst, "Jugendspiele," *Gartenlaube*, XXXVII (1890), 219–20.

[p. 133] *"a constantly increasing strain"*: *New Haven Leader*, April 4, 1895.

[p. 135] *"dealt modern man this wound"*: Friedrich Schiller, *Über die aesthetische Erziehung des Menschen, in einer Reihe von Briefen* (1794), Sixth Letter. *Sämtliche Werke*, Säkular-Ausgabe, 16 vols. (1904–05), XII, 18.

[p. 136] *"the disease of our time"*: Bartholomäus von Carneri, *Der moderne Mensch. Versuch über Lebensführung* (1890; 5th ed., 1901), 25.

[p. 136] *"Heaven's first law"*: Dr. George M. Beard, journal, ca. June 11, 1858, Beard Papers, Yale—Manuscripts and Archives.

[p. 136] *"fear of everything"*: George M. Beard, *American Nervousness, Its Causes and Consequences. A Supplement to Nervous Exhaustion (Neurasthenia)*, (1881), 7.

[p. 137] *"that is there represented"*: Ibid., 65–67.

[p. 137] "modern civilization": Ibid., vi.

[p. 137] *"mental activity of women"*: Ibid., 96.

[p. 137] *"quick, stormy, and frivolous"*: Ernst Freiherr von Feuchtersleben, *Diätetik der Seele* (1838; 5th ed., 1848), 21.

[p. 137] *"everything around them"*: Elizabeth Gaskell, *North and South* (1855; ed. Dorothy Collins, 1970), 376 [ch. 37].

[p. 137] *"the hurry and bustle of modern life"*: *New Haven Leader*, April 4, 1895.

[p. 138] *"absurd counterpart to superman"*: Dr. Wilhelm Bergmann, *Selbstbefreiung aus nervösem Leiden* (1911; 3d ed., 1913), 7–8.

[p. 138] *too vague and inclusive to be trustworthy*: See Freud, "On the Grounds for Detaching a Particular Syndrome from Neurasthenia under the Description 'Anxiety Neurosis'" (1895), Standard Edition, III, 90.

[p. 142] *"an age of transition"*: John Stuart Mill, *The Spirit of the Age* (1831; intro. Frederick A. von Hayek, 1942), 6.

[p. 142] *"a century of transition"*: Emile Zola to Jean-Baptistin Baille, June 2, 1860, *Correspondance*, I, 169.

[p. 143] *"sick and out of joint"*: Thomas Carlyle, "Signs of the Times," *Latter-Day Pamphlets, Characteristics, etc.*, Library Edition (1885), 29.

[p. 143] *"new, but nothing else"*: Jacob Burckhardt to Johanna Kinkel, August 23, 1843. *Briefe*, ed. Max Burckhardt, 9 vols. (1949–94), II, 42.

[p. 143] *"from all fixed conditions"*: Anon., February 14, 1874, *Saturday Review*, XXXVII, 204.

[p. 144] *"threaten to dissolve"*: Matthew Arnold. David Daiches, *Some Late Victorian Attitudes* (1979), 87.

[p. 144] *"perform in this world"*: Prince Albert. Nikolaus Pevsner, *High Victorian Design: A Study in Victorian Social Theory* (1951), 16–17.

[p. 145] *"move by steam"*: Comte Duchâtel. Georges Duveau, *1848: The Making of a Revolution* (1965; trans. Anne Carter, 1967), 27.

[p. 146] *"and these very old and feeble"*: William Makepeace Thackeray, "De Juventute," *Roundabout Papers. The Works of William Makepeace Thackeray, Centenary Biographical Edition*, 26 vols. (1910–11), XX, 73.

[p. 147] *"political, moral, industrial society"*: Dr. J.-B.-D. Demeaux, "Exposé de quelques mesures hygiéniques à introduire dans les établissements destinés à l'instruction publique," inserted in Jean-Paul Aron and Roger Kempf, *Le pénis et la démoralisation de l'Occident* (1978) and separately paginated, 204.

[p. 148] *"the most certain road to the grave"*: Dr. George R. Calhoun, *Report of the Consulting Surgeon on Spermatorrhoea, or Seminal Weakness, Impotence, the Vice of Onanism, Masturbation, or Self-Abuse, and Other Diseases of the Sexual Organs* (ca. 1858), 6.

[p. 149] *"their appetites and susceptibilities"*: Sylvester Graham. *A Lecture to Young Men* (1834), 79.

[p. 149] *"exhausted in the prime of life"*: Demeaux, "Exposé . . . ," 205–07.

[p. 150] *"seminal liquor"*: Samuel-Auguste-André-David Tissot, *De l'Onanisme* (1758; ed., 1832), xiv.

[p. 150] *"MATRIMONIAL EXCESS"*: O. S. Fowler, *Amativeness: Or Evils and Remedies of Excessive and Perverted Sexuality; Including Warning and Advice to the Married and Single* (1846), 41, 43, 47.

[p. 151] *a variety of neurological symptoms*: Sir James Paget, "Sexual Hypochondriasis." Oppenheim, *"Shattered Nerves,"* 162.

[p. 151] *the slightest ill effects caused by masturbation*: Dr. Jules Christian, "Onanisme," *Dictionnaire encyclopédique des sciences médicales* (1881).

[p. 151] *"the subject of onanism is practically inexhaustible"*: Freud, "Concluding Remarks, Contributions to a Discussion on Masturbation" (1912), Standard Edition, XII, 254 (translation modified).

[p. 151] *"beastliness"*: Sir Robert Baden-Powell. John Neubauer, *The Fin-de-Siècle Culture of Adolescence* (1992), 155.

[p. 152] *"all diseases stem from the stomach"*: Gustave Flaubert, "Estomac," *Dictionnaire des idées reçues, Oeuvres*, ed. Albert Thibaudet and René Dumesnil, 2 vols. (1951–52), II, 1009.

[p. 152] *"cause of all diseases"*: "Humidité," ibid., 1013.
[p. 152] *"too much health, cause of diseases"*: "Santé," ibid., 1022.

Part III THE VICTORIAN MIND

SIX   *Obituaries and Revivals*

In recent years, historians have made outstanding contributions to the study of nine-teenth-century religion. I single out here the writings of those that impressed and taught me most. Janet Oppenheim, *The Other World: Spiritualism and Psychical Research in England, 1850–1914* (1985); Ruth Harris, *Lourdes: Body and Spirit in the Secular Age* (1999), about an apparition of the Virgin Mary that the church embraced, and David Blackbourne, *Marpingen: Apparitions of the Virgin Mary in Bismarckian Germany* (1993), about one it did not; and Helmut Walser Smith, *German Nationalism and Religious Conflict: Culture, Ideology, Politics, 1870–1914* (1995), a brilliant monograph that substantially enlarged my understanding of the conflu-ence of religion and politics in the late nineteenth century. See also Thomas A. Kselman, *Death and the Afterlife in Modern France* (1993); Pierre Pierrard, *L'Eglise et les ouvriers en France (1840–1940)* (1984), enormously informative about the "decler-icalization" of the French working class; and Michael J. Wintle, *Pillars of Piety: Religion in the Netherlands in the Nineteenth Century, 1813–1901* (1987).

[p. 157] *"but not piety"*: A.S., March 23, 1902, *Tagebuch*, I, 366.
[p. 157] *"sanctimonious, lying, or mad"*: A.S., *Jugend in Wien*, 94.
[p. 158] *"piety and hypochondria"*: A.S., October 25, 1908, *Tagebuch*, III, 362.
[p. 158] *"beloved mother to her numerous children"*: A.S., *Jugend in Wien*, 18.
[p. 158] *"not an authentic physician"*: A.S., Editors' notes to A.S., *Briefe*, 717.
[p. 159] *"and without circumspection"*: Denis Diderot, article "Encyclopédie," *Oeuvres com-plètes*, ed. Jules Assézat and Maurice Tourneux, 20 vols. (1875–77), XIV, 474.
[p. 159] *"the world cannot be free"*: Robert Ingersoll, *Some Mistakes of Moses* (1879), 14.
[p. 160] *"or the Reformation"*: John Morley, *Voltaire* (1872), 1.
[p. 160] *an earthquake*: Thomas Nipperdey, *Deutsche Geschichte 1800–1866. Bürgerwelt und starker Staat* (1983), 430.
[p. 162] *"and they hate the Jews"*: Mark Twain, "Stirring Times in Austria," *Harper's New Monthly Magazine* (March 1898). In Mark Twain, *Concerning the Jews* (1985), 4.
[p. 163] *"has been largely completed"*: Karl Marx, "Contribution to the Critique of Hegel's Philosophy of Right" (1844), in *Early Writings*, ed. and trans. T. B. Bottomore (1964), 43.
[p. 164] *essentially religious and essentially irreligious*: Emile Faguet, *L'Anticléricalisme* (1906), 2.
[p. 164] *"false and foolish"*: Sir James Frazer, "William Robertson Smith" (1894), in *The Gorgon's Head* (1927), 284.
[p. 165] *"a thrilling new way"*: Gustave Flaubert, *Madame Bovary. Moeurs de province* (1857; trans. Francis Steegmuller, 1957), 40 [part I, ch. 6].
[p. 166] *among the attested cases*: See Harris, *Lourdes*, 306.
[p. 166] *anti-Protestant sentiment was more pronounced than anti-Semitism*: See Smith, *German Nationalism and Religious Conflict*, 99n.
[p. 167] *"its professors triumphant and smiling"*: James Bromfield, *Lower Brittany and the*

Bible There. Its Priests and People. Also Notes on Religion and Civil Liberty in France (1863), 1–2.

[p. 168] *"not to try to do one or the other"*: Nathaniel Hawthorne, *English Notebooks*. James R. Mellow, *Nathaniel Hawthorne in His Times* (1980), 358.

[p. 168] *to "declericalize" it*: Raoul Rosières, *Recherches critiques sur l'histoire religieuse de la France* (1879), 12.

[p. 168] *"the warm stream of mysticism"*: Abraham Kuyper. Wintle, *Pillars of Piety*, 43.

[p. 168] *"these times of renascent mysticism"*: Emile Durkheim, Author's Preface to the First Edition, *The Rules of Sociological Method* (1895; trans. Sarah A. Solovay and John H. Mueller, ed. George E. G. Catlin, 1938), xl.

[p. 170] *"be poeticized once again"*: August Wilhelm Schlegel. Eckart Klessmann, *Die deutsche Romantik* (1979), 79.

[p. 170] *"so-called Enlightenment and philosophy"*: Philipp Otto Runge (undated letter, ca. 1801 or 1802), *Hinterlassene Schriften*, ed. by his older brother, 2 vols. (1840–41), II, 179.

[p. 172] *"followers of pure science"*: Charles Augustin Sainte-Beuve. John McManners, *Church and State in France, 1870–1914* (1972; ed., 1973), 18.

[p. 173] *"Sit down before fact as a little child"*: T. H. Huxley to Charles Kingsley, September 23, 1860. Leonard Huxley, *Life and Letters of Thomas Henry Huxley*, 2 vols. (1900), I, 218–21.

[p. 175] *"I feel absolutely sure of this"*: Mark Twain to J. Wylie Smith, August 7, 1909. *Mark Twain's Letters*, ed. Albert Bigelow Paine, 2 vols. (1917), II, 832–33.

[p. 175] *"when the body dies"*: S. C. Hall, *The Uses of Spiritualism?* (1884), 6. Janet Oppenheim, *The Other World*, 63.

[p. 176] *"most fatuous reflections" . . . "knowledge and conscientiousness"*: Carl Kiesewetter, *Geschichte des neueren Occultismus. Geheimwissenschaftliche Systeme von Agrippa von Nettesheym bis zu Carl du Prel* (1891), 455.

[p. 177] *"men of every social rank and age"*: Marie Niethammer, *Kerner's Jugendliebe*. Kiesewetter, ibid., 138.

[p. 177] *"There is no conflict" . . . "the religious thralldom"*: J. E. Roberts, *The Inevitable Surrender of Orthodoxy* (1895), 8.

[p. 177] *"Voltaire came to save Christianity"*: Ibid., 57.

[p. 178] *"free of all confessions—konfessionslos"*: Kiesewetter, *Geschichte des neueren Occultismus*, xi–xii.

[p. 178] *"I am a CHRISTIAN"*: S. C. Hall. Oppenheim, *The Other World*, 67–68.

[p. 179] *"outstanding personages, physicians, attorneys"*: Kiesewetter, *Geschichte des neueren Occultismus*, 145.

[p. 179] *"arts, sciences, and literature; statesmen"*: Hudson Tuttle and J. M. Peebles, *The Year-Book of Spiritualism for 1871* (1871). Oppenheim, *The Other World*, 29.

[p. 180] *"to keep more sane and true"*: William James, *The Varieties of Religious Experience* (1902), 509.

[p. 181] "faith creates its own verification": William James, "The Sentiment of Rationality" (1879), in *The Will to Believe and Other Essays in Popular Philosophy* (1899), 97.

[p. 182] *"with ignorant contempt"*: "Presidential Address, July 16, 1888," *Presidential Addresses to the Society for Psychical Research*, in Frank Miller Turner, *Between Science and Religion: The Reaction to Scientific Naturalism in Late Victorian England* (1974), 55.

[p. 183] *"and hope that it was"*: John Maynard Keynes. Oppenheim, *The Other World*, 111.

[p. 184] *"to satisfy a need"*: Auguste Debay, *Hygiène et physiologie du mariage* (1848), 102.

[p. 185] *"haemorrhage of bad taste"*: Joris-Karl Huysmans. Robert Baldick, *The Life of J.-K. Huysmans* (1955), 319.

[p. 186] *"all the qualities of the canaille"*: Marx, "The Communism of the Paper *Rheinischer Beobachter*" (1847), *Basic Writings on Politics and Philosophy, Marx and Engels*, ed. Lewis S. Feuer (1959), 268–69.

[p. 187] *"In Paris"* . . . *"Paris and the large cities"*: Pierre Pierrard, *L'Eglise et les ouvriers en France (1840–1940)* (1984), 16.

SEVEN   *The Problematic Gospel of Work*

The all-important historical subject of bourgeois at work needs, well, more work. *The Oxford Book of Work*, ed. Keith Thomas (1999), is an impressive anthology; and *The Historical Meaning of Work*, ed. Patrick Joyce (1987), a fine, substantial accompaniment. On working middle-class women, Priscilla Robertson, *An Experience of Women: Pattern and Change in Nineteenth-Century Europe* (1982), offers a rich comparative menu. More specialized, Lee Holcombe, *Victorian Ladies at Work: Middle-Class Working Women in England and Wales, 1850–1914* (1973), is a good start. Cindy Sondik Aron, *Ladies and Gentlemen of the Civil Service: Middle-Class Workers in Victorian America* (1987), lays bare the persistent bias against women in the working arena. For the sociology of work in industrial society, Everett C. Hughes, *Men and Their Work* (1958), has much of substance to say. Among the studies of modern professions, *Professions and the French State, 1700–1900*, ed. Gerald L. Geison (1984), has valuable essays. Rudolf Braun, *Sozialer und kultureller Wandel in einem ländlichen Industriegebiet. (Zürcher Oberland) unter Einwirkung des Maschinen- und Fabrikwesens im 19. und 20. Jahrhundert* (1965), is a classic that, though it concentrates on a factory working population, is indispensable in its depiction of the working world, including that of bourgeois.

[p. 191] *"my sloppiness, my negligence"*: A.S., November 17, 1879, *Tagebuch*, I, 13.

[p. 192] *"I can sit and look at it for hours"*: Jerome K. Jerome, *Three Men in a Boat (To Say Nothing of the Dog)* (1889; American ed., n.d.), 220.

[p. 192] *"let him ask no other blessedness"*: Thomas Carlyle, *Past and Present* (1843). *Chartism* and *Sartor Resartus* (1848), 198 [book III, ch. 11].

[p. 193] "Know what thou canst work at": Carlyle, *Sartor Resartus* (1836; ed. Kerry McSweeney and Peter Sabor, 1987), 126 [book II, ch. 7].

[p. 193] *"Produce! Produce!"*: Ibid., 149 [book II, ch. 9].

[pp. 193–94] *"My dear Son"* . . . *"support of poor, innocent casualties"*: August Friedrich Hirsekorn to Carl August Hirsekorn, March 31, 1833, "Meine Lebenserinnerungen," typescript of handwritten memoirs, Landesarchiv Berlin, E Rep. 300-20, no. 51.

[p. 194] *"respect for his mother, and diligent work"*: Thomas Johann Heinrich Mann, last will. Donald Prater, *Thomas Mann: A Life* (1995), 11.

[p. 194] *"work!"*: Thomas Mann, *Buddenbrooks* (1901), part 9, ch. 2.

[p. 195] "par le travail et l'épargne": François Guizot, to the Chamber of Deputies,

March 1, 1843. A. Jardin and A. J. Tudesq, *La France des notables. L'Evolution générale, 1815–1848* (1973), 161.

[p. 196] *"the true ends of life"*: Theodore H. Munger, *On the Threshold* (1880; 15th printing, 1885), 4.

[p. 196] *"feeble at the slightest effort"*: A. Magendi, *Les effets moraux de l'exercice physique* (1873), 209, 211.

[p. 196] *"their manliness of fibre"*: Theodore Roosevelt, "The World Movement" (1910), in *The Works of Theodore Roosevelt*, ed. Hermann Hagedorn, 20 vols. (1926), XIV, 275.

[p. 196] *"men of cultivated taste and easy life"*: Theodore Roosevelt, *An Autobiography* (1913), 57.

[p. 197] *"the most shameful of shames"*: Horace Mann, *A Few Thoughts for a Young Man. A Lecture, Delivered Before the Boston Mercantile Library Association, on Its 29th Anniversary* (1850), 48–49.

[p. 197] *will harvest nothing of value*: Michele Cammarano, *Idleness and Work*, illustrated in Robert J. M. Olson et al., *Ottocento: Romanticism and Revolution in 19th-Century Italian Painting* (1992), 174.

[p. 197] *"lost time has fled forever"*: "A Proper Use of Time," *Gay's Standard Encyclopaedia and Self Educator Forming a Household Library*, vol. I (1883), 39.

[p. 198] *"and civilization is its product"*: Samuel Smiles, *Character* (1872), 97.

[pp. 198–99] *"presides over the whole"*: Keith McClelland, "Time to Work, Time to Live: Some Aspects of Work and the Re-formation of Class in Britain, 1850–1880," in *The Historical Meaning of Work*, ed. Patrick Joyce (1987), 184.

[p. 199] *"strenuous insistence on leisure"*: Thorstein Veblen, *The Theory of the Leisure Class* (1899; Modern Library ed., 1934), 40.

[p. 201] *"for a competent housewife"*: Hermine Kiehnle, *Kiehnle-Kochbuch* (1912; ed., 1951), 637.

[p. 202] *"His life is no sinecure"*: Beeton, *Book of Household Management*, 964.

[p. 202] *"her life is a solitary one"*: Ibid., 1001.

[pp. 202–03] *"One by one"* . . . *"makes one long for eternal rest"*: Anon., fragment of a diary (1880), Vol. 12, box 1, Diaries, Miscellaneous, Yale — Manuscripts and Archives.

[p. 204] *"brave, generous, pitying angel"* . . . *"love a man who can"*: Thomas Hughes, *Tom Brown at Oxford* (1861; ed., 1889), 478.

[p. 205] *"and with reason"*: E. Lynn Linton, "The Girl of the Period" (1868), in Linton, *Modern Women* (1888), 30.

[p. 207] *"beauty, charm, and sweetness"*: Freud to Martha Bernays, November 3, 1883. Ernest Jones, *The Life and Work of Sigmund Freud*. vol. I, *1856–1900: The Formative Years and the Great Discoveries* (1953), 176.

[p. 208] *"inferior to the male"*: Cesare Lombroso, "Le Génie et le Talent chez les Femmes," *Revue des Revues*, VIII (1893), 561.

[p. 209] *a quarter, or 6,882, were women*: Aron, *Ladies and Gentlemen of the Civil Service*, 5.

[p. 209] *clerks paid $1,600*: Ibid., 74–75.

[p. 212] *"has bestowed on society"* . . . *"a healthy workshop gratis"*: Andrew Ure, *The Philosophy of Manufactures: or, An Exposition of the Scientific, Moral, and Commercial Economy of the Factory System of Great Britain* (1835), 7.

[p. 212] *"I never saw"*... *"boys issuing from a school"*: Ibid., 301.

[p. 213] *"impudence"*: Engels, *Condition of the Working Class in England in 1844*, 169.

[p. 213] *"non-work represents unhappiness"*: Charles Féré, *Travail et plaisir, Nouvelles etudes expérimentales et psychoméchaniques* (1904), 2, 3, 15.

[p. 213] *"and to stop at will"*: Karl Bücher, *Arbeit und Rhythmus* (1897; 2d ed., 1899), 366.

[p. 214] *"the one thing that we cannot spare!"*: William C. Gannett, "Blessed be Drudgery," *Blessed be Drudgery; and other Papers* (1890), 8, 11, 12.

[p. 215] *"crusade against the factories"*: Ure, *Philosophy of Manufactures*, 305.

[p. 215] *"for party ends"*: Engels, *Condition of the Working Class in England in 1844*, 170.

[p. 215] *"disappeared almost wholly"*: Ibid., 173.

[p. 216] *"countenanced for a moment"*: Ure, *Philosophy of Manufactures*, 297.

[p. 216] *"artful demagogues"*: Ibid., 279.

[p. 216] *"in its full inhumanity"*: Engels, *Condition of the Working Class in England in 1844*, 172.

[p. 216] *"That is all"*: Ibid., 173.

[p. 217] *"and theoretical significance"*: Ibid., 293–94n.

[p. 218] *"for the sake of my body"*: Louisa May Alcott, *Work: A Story of Experience* (1873). 10.

[pp. 218–19] *"habit of inordinate saving"*... *"far nobler ones"*: Samuel Smiles, *Self-Help* (1859; 1860), 289.

EIGHT   *Matters of Taste*

In this chapter more than any other, I refer the reader to the substantial bibliographical essay in the most recently published of my five-volume essay on the Victorian bourgeoisie, *PW* (1998). I would add Robert Jensen, *Marketing Modernism in Fin-de-Siècle Europe* (1994), which canvasses the art market—dealers, exhibitions, etc.—to be read as a companion to Dianne Sachko Macleod, *Art and the Victorian Middle Class: Money and the Making of Cultural Identity* (1996). Sarah Burns, *Inventing the Modern Artist: Art and Culture in Gilded Age America* (1996), is a good instance of the social history of art; Roberta J. M. Olson et al., *Ottocento: Romanticism and Revolution in 19th-Century Italian Painting* (1992), a good survey of a much-neglected field; and a wonderful catalogue for an exhibition at the Guggenheim Museum in New York, by Robert Rosenblum, Maryanne Stevens, and Ann Dumas, *1900: Art at the Crossroads* (2000), illuminates the immense variety of middle-class taste around the turn of the century. Wolf Lepenies's intellectual biography, *Sainte-Beuve: Auf der Schwelle zur Moderne* (1997), is brilliant. See also Jeffrey A. Auerbach, *The Great Exhibition of 1851: A Nation on Display* (1999), and, for international bourgeois taste, including the Americans, Robert M. Crunden, *American Salons: Encounters with European Modernism 1885–1917* (1993).

[p. 221] *"should I fail now?"*: A.S., December 21, 1908, *Tagebuch*, III, 375.

[p. 222] *"all kinds of swindle"*: A.S., April 24, 1912, *Tagebuch*, IV, 321.

[p. 222] *"the tasks of modern art"*: A.S., June 28, 1913, *Tagebuch*, V, 15.

[p. 222] *"to his current Cubism"*: A.S., February 8, 1913, ibid., 17.

[p. 222] *"pretentious swindlers"*: A.S., December 24, 1913, ibid., 86.

[p. 224] *"buy them"*: Alexandre Dumas fils. Preface to Bernard Prost, *Octave Tassaert, Notice sur la vie et catalogue de son oeuvre* (1886), 1.

[p. 226] *"the prevailing 'collecting' mania"*: *Musical Times*, XIII (January 1, 1868), 249.

[p. 227] *"he's a collector"*: Théophile Thoré, "Salon de 1846," *Salons de Théophile Thoré, 1844, 1845, 1846, 1847, 1848* (1868; ed., 1879), 279.

[p. 227] *"Greek vases and diamonds"*: Edwin C. Bolles, *Collectors and Collecting: An Essay* (1898), 1.

[p. 228] *their opinions on politics*: See Rosenblum et al., *1900: Art at the Crossroads*.

[p. 229] *"matters of connoisseurship"*: Lady Elizabeth Eastlake, "Memoir of Sir Charles Eastlake." Charles Locke Eastlake, *Contributions to the Literature of the Fine Arts*, 2nd series (1870), 147.

[p. 230] *"artists no longer respect"*: Ingres, letter to the Commission Permanente des Beaux-Arts. Jensen, *Marketing Modernism in Fin-de-Siècle Europe*, 29.

[p. 230] *"necropolises of art"*: Camille Pissarro. Theodore Reff, "Copyists in the Louvre, 1850–1870," *Art Bulletin*, XLVI (December 1964), 553n.

[p. 234] *"original in every respect"*: Otto von Leixner, *Aesthetische Studien für die Frauenwelt* (1880), separate page following the frontispiece (not paginated).

[p. 234] *"the Philistines perspiring after wealth"*: Robert Louis Stevenson, "Walking Tours" (1876), *Essays by Robert Louis Stevenson*, ed. William Lyon Phelps (1918), 32.

[p. 240] *"but their eyes and ears"*: *Musical World* (April 2, 1840), 208.

[p. 240] *"with convincing force"*: "The Ethics of Art," *Musical Times and Singing-Class Circular*, XXX (May 1, 1889), 265.

[p. 241] *"the failure of thought"*: Henry James, "Criticism" (1891), *Selected Literary Criticism*, ed. Morris Shapira (1963), 167–71.

[p. 242] *"incorruptible even temper"*: Charles Augustin Sainte-Beuve, "Mémoires du marquis d'Argenson, ministre sous Louis XV, publiés par René d'Argenson," *Le Globe* (July 16, 1825). *Oeuvres*, ed. Maxime Leroy, currently 2 vols. (1956–), I, 109.

[p. 243] "literary natural history": Sainte-Beuve, Pensée no. 20, "Pensées," *Portraits littéraires*, 3 vols. (1862–64), III, 546.

[p. 243] *"the king of critics"*: Sainte-Beuve, "Qu'est ce qu'un classique?" (October 21, 1850). *Causeries du Lundi*, III, 40.

[p. 243] *"the wretched occupation of critic"*: Sainte-Beuve to Charles Didier [June 8, 1834], *Correspondance générale*, ed. Jean Bonnerot and Alain Bonnerot, 19 vols. (1935–83), I, 440.

[p. 244] *"but to tell the truth"*: Eduard Hanslick, *Aus meinem Leben*, 2 vols. (1894), II, 49.

[p. 245] *"a world of pure beauty"*: See Eduard Hanslick, *Vom Musikalisch-Schönen* (1854; 10th enlarged ed., 1902), passim.

[p. 245] *"has been raised at Bayreuth"*: Ibid., vi–vii.

[p. 245] *"are many mansions"*: Hanslick, *Aus meinem Leben*, II, 305.

[p. 245] *"'German Requiem'"*: Ibid., 304.

[p. 246] *"to develop fully"*: Alfred Lichtwark, "Der Deutsche der Zukunft," *Der Deutsche der Zukunft* (1903), 24.

[p. 247] *"believes it may demand everything"*: Alfred Lichtwark, *Das Bildniss in Hamburg*, 2 vols. (1898), I, 51–52.

[p. 249] *"in the most beautiful collections"*: Paul Durand-Ruel, letter to *L'Evénement,* November 5, 1885. *Les Archives de l'Impressionisme,* ed. Lionello Venturi, 2 vols. (1939), II, 251.

[p. 249] *"put an end to our troubles"*: Durand-Ruel, letter to *Le Figaro,* October 31, 1873. Anne Distel, *Impressionism: The First Collectors* (1989; trans. Barbara Perroud-Benson, 1990), 25.

NINE   *A Room of One's Own*

Until a few decades ago, the subject of privacy lay largely neglected. As recently as 1939, the celebrated defense attorney Louis Nizer could publish a book with the title *The Right of Privacy: A New Brand of Law.* Now, with threats to privacy from intrusive government agencies, insurance companies, investigative journalists, the Internet, and other twentieth-century technical blessings, the literature is burgeoning, though the historian could well use more empirical and theoretical work. One stimulating exception was the treatise by the sensitive, imaginative German sociologist Georg Simmel, *Soziologie, Untersuchungen über die Formen der Vergesellschaftung* (1908), relevant portions of which (particularly the sizable section on "The Secret and the Secret Society") have been made available in *The Sociology of Georg Simmel* (trans. and ed. Kurt H. Wolff, 1950). Some typical and useful titles include: Lenenis Kruse, *Privatheit als Problem und Gegenstand der Psychologie* (1980), which focuses on the social psychology of privacy; Ferdinand David Schoeman, *Privacy and Social Freedom* (1992), which thoughtfully studies the philosophical dimension; Judith C. Inness, *Privacy, Intimacy, and Isolation* (1992), which pursues the legal implications; and Patricia Boling, *Privacy and the Politics of Intimate Life* (1996), which critically analyzes some feminist positions. For changes in the housing of Londoners, see esp. Donald J. Olsen's fine *The Growth of Victorian London* (1976). The lack of privacy in American Puritan households is well brought out by John Demos, *A Little Commonwealth: Family Life in Plymouth Colony* (1970). Karen Chase and Michael Levenson, *The Spectacle of Intimacy: A Public Life for the Victorian Family* (2000), travels through sensational Victorian trials, novels, reform clothing, and the like.

[p. 254] *"which vexed me exceedingly"*: "Nanci" Berlioz, diary, April 14, 1822. Cairns, *Berlioz,* vol. I, *The Making of an Artist, 1803–1832* (1989; 2d ed., 1999), 106.

[p. 254] *"greatly to my annoyance"*: "Nanci" Berlioz, diary, May 7, 1822. Ibid., 107.

[p. 254] *"my diary's stammering"*: Alma Schindler-Werfel, *Diaries 1898–1902,* selected and ed. Antony Beaumont (1998; trans. Beaumont and Susanne Rode-Breyman, 1999), xiii.

[p. 256] *"many other things of the same sort"*: Stephen, *Liberty, Equality, Fraternity,* 106.

[p. 256] *"the right to be let alone"*: Samuel D. Warren and Louis D. Brandeis, "The Right to Privacy," *Harvard Law Review* (1890), IV, 193–220, passim.

[pp. 256–57] *"Secrecy is one"* . . . *"the haunts of privacy"*: C. E. Sargent, *Our Home: Or, the Key to a Nobler Life* (1888), 5–6.

[p. 257] *impressive breaches in the fortifications of privacy*: See James Jackson Kilpatrick, *The Smut Peddlers* (1960), 243.

[p. 259] *"utterly abhorrent to the public feeling"*: Thomas Babington Macaulay. Denis Mack Smith, *Mazzini* (1994), 42.

[p. 259] *"far fataler forms of scoundrelism"*: Thomas Carlyle, "To the Editor of the Times," *The Times* [London], June 19, 1844, p. 6.

[p. 261] *"expression peculiar to itself"*: G. Stanley Hall, *Adolescence: Its Psychology and Its Relations to Physiology, Anthropology, Sociology, Sex, Crime, Religion and Education*, 2 vols. (1904), I, 589.

[p. 262] *"I am only fourteen years old"*: Julie Manet, *Journal (1893–1899)*, ed. Jean Griot (1979), 9.

[p. 262] *"incredibly moved"*: A.S., June 18, 1897, *Tagebuch*, II, 257.

[p. 262] *"Agitated me greatly"*: A.S., April 24, 1898, ibid., 283.

[p. 262] *"once and for all"*: A.S., July 7, 1902, ibid., 374.

[p. 263] *"anything but interesting"*: Marie Bashkirtseff, *Journal*, 2 vols. (1898), I, 5.

[p. 263] *"old journal"*: Mabel Loomis, November 7, 1872, Journal, I, Mabel Loomis Todd Papers, Yale — Manuscripts and Archives.

[p. 263] *"and grateful friend, Mabel Loomis"*: March 5, 1879, Journal, II, ibid.

[p. 263] *"I can leave behind"*: Henri-Frédéric Amiel, July 36, 1876, *Journal intime*, trans. Mrs. Humphrey Ward (1887), 213.

[p. 264] *"for my delight in future years"*: Friedrich Hebbel, March 23, 1835, *Tagebücher, 1835–1863*, ed. Karl Pörnbacher, 3 vols. (1966–67; ed., 1984), I, 7.

[p. 264] *"to tell a story fairly"*: Thomas Henry Huxley, April 6, 1850. *Diary of the Voyage of H.M.S. Rattlesnake*, ed. Julian Huxley (1935), 266.

[p. 264] *"with redoubled force to my mind"*: Asa Fitch, August 16, 1839, diary, Asa Fitch Papers, box 2, Yale — Manuscripts and Archives.

[p. 266] *"Klimt had kissed me!"*: Schindler-Werfel, *Diaries, 1898–1902*, xiii.

[p. 266] *"complete physical union"*: Ibid., May 1, 1899, 125.

[p. 267] *"even if it's only a kiss"*: Ibid., December 13, 1900, 355.

[p. 267] "not even Klimt!!": Ibid., June 4, 1901, 410.

[p. 267] *"Whoever it might be."*: Ibid., July 24, 1901, 421.

[p. 267] *"My poor, poor husband!"*: Ibid., January 1, 1902, 467.

[p. 268] *"and retired roués"*: Anon., "American Domestic Life Described by an American," *The Leisure Hour*, XVIII (1869), 111.

[p. 268] *"and be alone"*: Robert Kerr, *The Gentleman's House: or, How to Plan English Residences, from the Parsonage to the Palace* (1864; 2d rev. and enl. ed., 1865), 67–68.

[p. 269] *"other apartments in the house"*: Konstanze von Franken, *Handbuch des guten Tones und der feinen Sitten* (23d rev. ed., 1900), 47.

[p. 269] *"is required for each"*: G. A. T. Middleton, *Modern Buildings: Their Planning, Construction and Equipment*, 6 vols. (1905), I, 44.

[p. 271] *"comfort, propriety, and health"*: The Builder (1864), XXII, 94. Olsen, *Growth of Victorian London*, 160.

[p. 271] *"sacrificed to the sitting rooms"*: Building News (1877), XXXII, 484. Ibid., 131.

[p. 272] *"in all communities"*: Veblen, *Theory of the Leisure Class*, 112–13.

[p. 272] *"I did the best I could"*: Droz, *Monsieur, Madame et Bébé*, 287–89.

[p. 274] *"knew only about egoism"*: Alexis de Tocqueville, *Democracy in America*, 2 vols. (1835–40; trans. George Lawrence, ed. J. P. Mayer and Max Lerner, 1966, 2 vols. in l), 477 [vol. II, part 2, ch. 2].

[p. 274] *"to look after itself"*: Ibid.

[p. 275] *"part, corporation and family"*: Jacob Burckhardt, *The Civilization of the Renais-*

sance in Italy: An Essay (1860; trans. S.G.C. Middlemore, 1878; 2d rev. ed., 1945), 81 [part II].

[p. 275] *a "spiritual* individual": Ibid.

[p. 277] *"one way or the other"*: Freud, *The Ego and the Id* (1923), Standard Edition, XIX, 50n.

[p. 277] *"that particular man, but mankind"*: Thomas Hobbes, *Leviathan, or the Matter, Forme and Power of a Commonwealth Ecclesiastical and Civil* (1651), The Introduction.

[p. 277] *"the path to fundamental problems"*: Friedrich Nietzsche, *Beyond Good and Evil* (1886), part I, no. 23.

[p. 278] *"the delusions of Selflove"*: Gladstone, September 16, 1841, *Gladstone Diaries*, III, 140.

[p. 278] "Qu'est-ce que le *moi?"*: Stendhal, *Rome, Naples et Florence* (1826; ed., 1987), 307.

[p. 279] *"self-knowledge"*: A.S., August 15, 1895, *Tagebuch*, II, 149.

[p. 279] *"acts of meanness and stupidity"*: A.S., March 13, 1900, ibid., 324.

CODA

[p. 283] *"we were not bitter"*: Ray Stannard Baker, *American Chronicle* (1945), 226.

[p. 283] *"industrial town in the Midlands"*: J. A. Hobson, *Confessions of an Economic Heretic* (1938), 15.

[p. 284] *"a most revolutionary part"*: Marx and Engels, *Communist Manifesto*, 83.

[p. 288] *"'the triumph of reason'"*: A.S., March 3, 1914, *Tagebuch*, V, 103.

[p. 289] *"Everybody is at a loss"*: A.S., August 5, 1914, ibid., 128–29.

Bibliography

In writing this book, I have relied almost wholly on primary materials whenever I had anything to say about Schnitzler: the four-volume edition of his writings, *Gesammelte Werke* (1961–62), consisting of *Die dramatischen Werke*, 2 vols., and *Die erzählenden Schriften*, 2 vols.; *"Aphorismen und Betrachtungen," Buch der Sprüche und Bedenken*, I (1927; ed. 1993); *Entworfenes und Verworfenes*, ed. Reinhard Urbach (1977), which collected interesting unpublished drafts; his letters, *Briefe, 1875–1912*, ed. Therese Nickl and Heinrich Schnitzler (1981), and *Briefe 1913–1931*, ed. Peter Michael Braunwarth, Richard Miklin, Susanne Pertlik, and Heinrich Schnitzler (1984); his autobiography, *My Youth in Vienna* (1968; trans. Catherine Hutter, 1970); his abundant and revealing diaries, *Tagebücher*, ed. Peter Michael Braunwarth et al., 10 vols. (1987–2000); and his papers, at the University of New York at Binghamton. There are several collections of Schnitzler's correspondence; perhaps the most fascinating is *Dilly. Adele Sandrock und Arthur Schnitzler. Geschichte einer Liebe in Briefen, Bildern und Dokumenten*, gathered by Renate Wagner (1975), a collection that documents Schnitzler's passionate, if brief, love affair with a remarkable actress. *Arthur Schnitzler. Sein Leben und seine Zeit*, ed. Heinrich Schnitzler, Christian Brandstätter, and Reinhard Urbach (1981), is a well-designed picture biography.

Schnitzler is scarcely a neglected author. Harmut Scheible's *Schnitzler* (1976) is a terse life in the Rowohlt series of illustrated monographs, with a lavish bibliography. Bruce Thompson's *Schnitzler's Vienna: Image of a Society* (1990) keeps the promise of its title. There are numerous volumes on the history of Schnitzler's Austria, and his Vienna, of varying merit. For a terse general survey of recent Austrian history, see A. J. P. Taylor, *The Habsburg Monarchy, 1809–1918* (1948), typically energetic and aphoristic. John W. Boyer,

Political Radicalism in Late Imperial Vienna: Origins of the Christian Social Movement, 1858–1897 (1981), may seem a little austere, but its dependable coverage of the rise of modern anti-Semitic politics is invaluable. David F. Good, *The Economic Rise of the Habsburg Empire, 1750–1914* (1984), may be read in conjunction with Alan Sked, *The Decline and Fall of the Habsburg Empire, 1815–1918* (1989). For an orderly account, see William M. Johnston, *The Austrian Mind: An Intellectual and Social History, 1848–1938* (1972). There are two dependable studies of Jews in Vienna that complement one another: Marsha L. Rosenblit, *The Jews of Vienna, 1867–1914* (1983), and Steven Beller, *Vienna and the Jews, 1867–1938* (1989). Ilsa Barea, *Vienna* (1966), is a highly personal but evocative history of the city. *Jugend in Wien. Literatur um 1900*, ed. Ludwig Greve and Werner Volke (1974), is a helpful exhibition catalogue. Carl E. Schorske, *Fin-de-Siècle Vienna: Politics and Culture* (1980), is a justly well known, readable set of connected essays, including those on the Ringstrasse, on Klimt, on Freud (from which, with its suggestion that psychoanalysis was a kind of counterpolitics for Freud—a way to achieve fame closed to him by anti-Semitism—I dissent), and others. And see Frederic Morton's suggestive *A Nervous Splendour: Vienna 1888/1889* (1980).

Among studies of Schnitzler's culture, I have derived most profit from Edward Timms, *Karl Kraus, Apocalyptic Satirist: Culture and Catastrophe in Habsburg Vienna* (1986); David S. Luft, *Robert Musil and the Crisis of European Culture, 1880–1942* (1980); and Hermann Broch, *Hugo von Hofmannsthal and His Time* (1984).

Acknowledgments

I owe thanks to archivists, who considerably eased my research with their expertise and their cordiality, and who supplied priceless materials for this book: Dr. Jürgen Wetzel, Director of the Landesarchiv Berlin, and Dr. Christiane Schuchard at the same institution; Judith Schiff, Chief Research Archivist at the Manuscripts and Archives division, University Library, Yale; Zephorine L. Stickney, Archivist and Special Collections Curator; Madeleine Clark Wallace Library at Wheaton College. Professor Rosmarie T. Morewedge, Chairman, Department of German, Russian and East Asian Languages at the State University of New York at Binghamton, guided me through the important Arthur Schnitzler Collection.

I am obliged to a number of former students with whom I talked through some of the central issues in this work, and whose dissertations (though I never suggested any of their topics) furnished precious pieces of evidence, especially Jennifer Hall, Meike Werner, Helmut Walser Smith, George Williamson, and Jeffrey Auerbach. Through the years I have discussed the Victorians with two other former students, now my friends, Robert Dietle and Mark Micale, to whom I have dedicated this book. My gratitude, too, goes to fellows of the first class (1999–2000) at the Center for Scholars and Writers at the New York Public Library: Greg Dreicer suggested titles for the chapter on privacy; Andrew Delbanco found a diary entry of Hawthorne's for me; Tony Holden, biographer, poet, and poker player, shared with me his intimate knowledge of nineteenth-century literature and thoughtfully kept me out of his game; Howard Markel suggested some texts on venereal disease, Marion Kaplan, Ada Louise Huxtable, Harvey Sachs, Allen Kurzweil—indeed all the fellows—listened and talked to my purpose: an unforeseen but, it turned out, a noteworthy dividend that has come my way for being their "director." A second year fellow, Bernhard Schlink, kindly discussed German electoral practices with me; Ileen DeVault helped with Frederick Taylor. I also want to thank Paul LeClerc, President of the New York Public Library, for his faith in my work.

A number of friends and acquaintances supplied an address or a usable title, or just had "business" lunches with me, notably Lynn Gamwell, Ernest Goodman, Frank Mecklenburg, Frederic Morton, Ellen Ross, Anne Skillion, Isser Woloch. Alain Corbin graciously suggested recent books on nineteenth-century sexuality in France. Jens Malte Fischer put me in his debt by sending me his sophisticated writings on the fin-de siècle. Gaby Katwan, good comrade (and truly insightful psychoanalyst) in Berlin, greatly helped me to understand Schnitzler's intricate, in some ways shocking character. She and other old friends were there for me as they have been through the years, particularly Stefan Collini, Quentin Skinner, Henry Turner. During our meetings at the "Club," Doron Ben-Atar joined me to kick around problems and titles greatly improving my grasp on both. Gladys Topkis gave the kind of assistance, fondly, wisely, and wittily, that I have long come to expect. John Merriman read the manuscript, paying close attention to the historical context, much to its benefit. Bob Webb, as fine an editor as he is historian, subjected it to an examination that gave me much (needed) work, a reading to which the hackneyed phrase "fine-tooth comb" fully applies and which I gratefully acknowledge.

Bob Weil has been a fostering editor. I warmly thank him; two others at Norton, Drake McFeely and Jeannie Luciano, for their collegial discussions with me, a rare pleasure in modern publishing; and my copyeditor, Ann Adelman, for her perceptive eye and light hand. As so often before, my wife, Ruth, set aside pressing work of her own to go over my text with meticulous attention, usually more than once, and markedly improved it. My readers will be grateful to her, as am I.

—PETER GAY
Hamden, Connecticut, and New York City, January 2001

Index

Acton, William, 81–82, 83, 85, 86
Addison, Richard, 32, 103
Adler, Otto, 83
adolescence, 260–62, 273
Adolescence (Hall), 261
Adolphe (Constant), 133
adultery, 44, 69, 79–80, 255
aggression, 97–126
    bourgeois attitudes toward, xxiv, 97–99
    discipline as form of, 102–6
    in evolution, 97–98
    instinct for, 97–99
    racial, 110–17
    rationalization of, 99, 100, 116–17, 22–25
    religious justifications for, 99, 118
    sexuality and, 83–84, 105, 122, 140
    state-sanctioned, 107–10, 117–25
agnosticism, 157, 158, 168, 172–73, 181
Akademische Gymnasium (Vienna), xxvii, 115
À la recherche du temps perdu (Proust), xxvii
Albert, Prince-Consort of Queen Victoria, 144, 228
Albrecht, J. F., 80–81, 89
Alcott, Louisa May, 218
Alcott, William, 132
Alger, Horatio, 9
alienation, 135, 275–76, 284
Allen, William, 119
Alte Pinakothek, 10, 11–12
American Woman's Home, The (Beecher), 271

Amiel, Henri-Frédéric, 263
Anatol cycle (Schnitzler), 69–70
Anatomy of Melancholy, The (Burton), 134
And the Bridge Is Love (Schindler), 266
Anglican Church, 161, 171, 180, 187
Anna Karenina (Tolstoy), 146, 236
anomie, 135, 276
"Answer to the Question: What Is
    Enlightenment?" (Kant), 273, 274
anti-clericalism, 162–63, 168, 170, 171, 188
anti-Semitism, 21, 64, 111, 112, 114–17, 126, 143,
    162, 166–67, 169, 226, 244, 251
anxiety, 129–54
    as bourgeois ailment, 126, 129–32, 69, 279
    change as cause of, 141–47, 287
    defenses against, 140, 153–54
    as neurasthenia, 129, 132–38
    sexual origins of, 130–32, 138–40, 47–49
    social origins of, 132–38, 140, 287
Argenson, René-Louis de Voyer de Paulmy,
    marquis d', 242
aristocracy:
    bourgeoisie vs., 7, 10–12, 23, 27–28, 29, 32,
        140, 198, 287
    cultural institutions supported by, 10–11, 23,
        228, 229
    political influence of, 21
    privacy of, 255
Armory Show (1915), 239
Arnhold, Eduard, 226

Arnold, Matthew, 132, 144
art:
  bourgeois taste in, xxiv, 236–37, 248–50,
    285–86
  collectors of, 196, 222–27, 236, 245–46, 285–86
  "doctrine of distance" in, 236–37
  exhibitions of, 226–28, 230, 231, 236, 237
  market for, 24, 223–24, 231, 247, 248–50
  modern, xxi, 10, 222–30, 239, 248
  museums of, 5, 10, 229, 230, 231, 232, 245–48,
    285
  women as portrayed in, 136–37
Arthur Schnitzler (Schmutzer), 62
artisans, 198–99, 255
artists:
  avant-garde, 6, 222–28, 234–35, 250, 285–86
  patronage of, 196, 222–27
  women, 231
Aryan race, 58, 112, 174
Ashton, James, 55–56
atheism, 157, 168, 169, 172, 174, 175, 185
Austro-Hungarian Empire:
  bourgeoisie of, 21–23, 102, 233
  economic collapse of (1873), 30
  Jewish population of, 3, 21, 22, 115–17, 143,
    162
  political situation in, 21–23, 115–17
  postal service of, 258
  see also Vienna

Bach, Johann Sebastian, 245
Baden-Powell, Robert, 151
Baedeker guidebooks, 233–34
Baker, Ray Stannard, 283
Balzac, Honoré de, 47, 241, 243
Barbey d'Aurevilly, Jules-Amédée, 28
Barrie, James M., 206
Barye, Louis, 238
Bashkirtseff, Marie, 262–63
Baudelaire, Charles, xxiv, 38, 131, 240, 241, 243,
  286
Bavaria, 10–12, 50, 68, 105, 228, 258
Bayle, Pierre, 159
Bayreuth opera house, 11, 174, 244, 245
Beard, George M., 132, 135–37, 138, 139, 153
"Beard Trimming Chart," 1
Beaumarchais, Pierre-Augustin Caron de, 32
Beccaria, Cesare, 120–21, 123
Beecher, Catharine, 271
Beer-Hofmann, Richard, 4
Beeton, Isabella, 45–46, 55, 202, 256
Bel-Ami (Maupassant), 225–26
Belgium, 20, 112–13, 114, 120, 123
belle dame sans merci, La (Keats), 205
Benkert, Karoly Maria, 66
Bentham, Jeremy, 30, 121
Bergmann, Wilhelm, 138
Berlin, 5, 11, 143, 226

Berlin Philharmonic Orchestra, 11
Berlin Secession, 223
Berlioz, Hector, 254
Berlioz, Joséphine, 94
Berlioz, Louis, 94
Berlioz, "Nanci," 254
Besant, Annie, 53–54, 90–91
bête humaine, La (Zola), 146
Betham-Edwards, Miss, 49
Beyond Good and Evil (Nietzsche), 277
Bible, 48, 55, 67, 106, 118, 159–61, 165, 167, 178,
  186, 192
Birmingham, England, 11–12
birth control, 40, 50–55, 257, 258, 270, 298n
Bishop, Francis, 119
Bismarck, Otto von, 16, 17, 59, 167, 210–11,
  284
Blake, William, 117
Blavatsky, Madame, 174, 182
Bleak House (Dickens), 121
Bleichröder, Samuel, 59
"Blessed be drudgery" (Gannett), 213–14
Bloy, Léon, 169
Blunt, Wilfrid Scawen, 91
Bolles, Edwin C., 227
Bonheur, Rosa, 208
Bonnard, Pierre, xxi
Book of Hanging Gardens (Schoenberg), 221
Book of Household Management (Beeton), 45–46,
  202
Book of Songs (Heine), 205
Boston Symphony Orchestra, 11
Boucicaut, Aristide, 7–8
Boudin, Eugène, 249
Bouguereau, Adolphe-William, 226, 249
Bouilhet, Louis, 29
Bourbon Restoration, 14–15, 19, 50, 68
Bourgeois Experience: Victoria to Freud, The (Gay),
  xxiii–xxiv, 310n
bourgeoisie, Victorian:
  attitudes of, 4–6, 9, 25–26, 45, 64, 126
  Austrian vs. German, 22
  author's analysis of, xxiii–xxiv, 281–82, 287
  avant-garde artists vs., 6, 222–28, 234–35, 250,
    285–86
  biography of, xix–xxv
  class distinctions within, 4–7, 24–28, 294n
  conformity by, 32, 105
  conscience of, 18, 100, 111, 112, 140, 215,
    216–17
  conservative vs. liberal, 16–18, 21, 125, 284
  cultural aspirations of, xxiv, 9–12, 23, 221–50,
    285–86
  dominance vs. subservience of, 9–12, 13
  English vs. German, 9–12
  enterprise of, 9–10, 22
  ethical standards of, 25–26
  grand, 6, 42, 102, 226, 233, 253, 270

heroes of, 102, 152, 286–87
historical analysis of, xxiii–xxiv, 4, 5–6, 9, 12, 30–31, 281–82, 287, 289
hostile critiques of, 5–6, 18, 28–31, 45, 78–79, 80, 90, 125, 138, 140–41, 195, 234–35, 281, 282, 283, 285–86
leisure activities of, 199, 219, 221–50, 285
as "middling orders," 4–6, 16, 25, 42, 57, 59, 140, 141, 198, 206, 217, 234, 255, 286
new wealth as basis of, 5, 6, 7–9, 17, 25, 40, 43, 53, 186–87, 198
petty, 6, 7, 21, 24–25, 59, 140–41, 200, 202, 208–9, 232–33, 246, 253, 287
prestige desired by, 6–7, 199
pyramid structure of, 24–25, 232–33
security as important to, xxix, 8
self-analysis of, 277–79, 283–88
self-confidence of, 9–12, 13, 28–29, 107, 126
sentimentality of, 125
shared identity of, 24–28, 30, 31–33, 53, 57, 217, 286–87
as social ideal, 32–33
squeamishness lacked by, 45–47
supportive critiques of, 30–31
bourgeoisophobes, 28–30, 78, 90, 234–35, 282
Bourget, Paul, 169
Bradlaugh, Charles, 53–54
Brahms, Johannes, 238–39, 244–45, 286
Brancusi, Constantin, 239
Brandeis, Louis D., 256
breast feeding, xxiv, 45–46, 256, 272–73
Briefgeheimnis (secrets of letters), 258
Bromfield, James, 167
Browne, Hablot ("Phiz"), *34*, 272–73
Bruckner, Anton, 221, 243, 244
Bruyas, Alexandre, 225
Bücher, Karl, 213
Buddenbrooks (Mann), 194–95
Bülow, Cosima von, 47
Burckhard, Max, 267
Burckhardt, Jacob, 143, 275
Bürgertum, see bourgeoisie, Victorian
Burke, Edmund, 107
Burton, Robert, 134
Butler, Josephine, 76

Cabanel, Alexandre, 230, 249
Caesarism, 17–18
Calhoun, George R., 148
Cammarano, Michele, 197
Camp, Maxime du, 110
capitalism:
    casualties of, 135, 143, 186, 217, 218–19
    criticism of, 135, 153–54, 282–83
    exploitation by, 111, 126, 134–35, 186, 210–18, 282
    free markets in, 285
    scientific, 173–74

welfare state vs., 287
work ethic and, 197–98, 211–12, 215, 217
capitalists:
    cultural institutions supported by, 9–10
    emotional diminishment of, 218–19
    as "robber barons," 28, 238
    stereotypes of, 225, 284
capital punishment, 68, 117–25
Carlyle, Thomas, 28, 111, 142–43, 173, 192–93, 217, 259
Carmen (Bizet), 205
Carnegie, Andrew, 7, 238
Carneri, Bartholomäus von, 136
Caspari, Otto, 130
Cassatt, Mary, 237, 239, 249
castration, 196, 204, 205
Casual Love (Schnitzler), 64
Causeries du Lundi (Sainte-Beuve), 242–43
Cézanne, Paul, 223–24, 225, 228, 237
Chamberlain, Houston Stewart, 174
"Changes at Home" ("Phiz"), *34*, 272
Character (Smiles), 198
Chateaubriand, François-René de, 164–65
Chekhov, Anton, xxi, xxii
Chevalier, Michel, 14
children:
    aggressiveness of, 100–101, 103
    anxiety of, 130, 133
    bodily conditions witnessed by, 46–47, 89
    bourgeois vs. working-class, 188
    discipline of, 25, 77, 102–6, 125
    idleness of, 196
    legal status of, 50
    manners taught to, 25, 42, 256
    mortality rates for, 41
    necessity of, 50, 52–53, 87–88
    parental devotion to, 40, 41, 42, 44, 77–78, 102–3, 297n
    privacy of, 256, 260–62, 268, 269–70
    punishment of, 102–6, 126, 212, 256
    sexual knowledge of, 89–93
    tastes of, 235
    in work force, 18, 25, 111, 210, 212, 215
Chocquet, Victor, 224
Christian, Jules, 151
Christianity:
    alienation from, 185–89, 285
    anti-Semitism in, 114, 115
    colonialism and propagation of, 114
    compassion as basis of, 98, 172, 278
    corporal punishment justified by, 106
    original sin as doctrine of, 106, 200
    sectarian hatreds in, 166–67, 171–72
    secular criticism of, 159–61, 164, 181–82
    see also specific denominations
Christian Science, 174–75
Christian Socials, 21, 188
Church, Frederic, 238

civilization, modern:
adolescence and, 261
aggressive impulses in, 102, 110
anxiety as result of, 132–38, 140
colonialism as propagation of, 112
progress in, 141–47
Civilization of the Renaissance in Italy, The
(Burckhardt), 275
Civil War (U.S.), 19, 51–52
Claretie, Jules, 146
class:
conflicts of, 13, 110, 218
exploitation and, 64–65
hierarchical structure of, 4, 24–25
Claudel, Paul, 169
cleanliness, household, 201–2
clerks, 25, 208–9, 232–33
Cobbe, Frances Power, 49
Codding, Milo D., 118
coitus interruptus, 55–56
Cole, Thomas, 238
Coleridge, Samuel Taylor, 278
colonialism, 112–14
Communist Manifesto, The (Marx and Engels), 31,
284
Comstock, Anthony, 257
Comte, Auguste, 173
condoms, 54–55, 56
confessions, 178, 265–67, 277
Congo Free State, 112–13, 114
conspicuous consumption, 199
Constant, Benjamin, 133
Constitution (U.S.), 162
Contagious Diseases Act (Brit.), 76
contraception, 40, 50–55, 257, 258, 270, 298*n*
Cooper, Thomas, 165
Courbet, Gustave, 225, 237
crime, 68, 122–23
Criminal Law Amendment Act (Brit.), 68
critics, 237, 240–48
Cruikshank, George, *96*

Darwin, Charles, 97–98, 140, 142, 161, 163, 172,
177–78, 188, 264
Daumier, Honoré-Victorin, *220*, 272
David Copperfield (Dickens), 79, 106, 272–73
Davis, Andrew Jack, 176
d'Azeglio, Massimo, 4
Debay, Auguste, 184
Decamps, Alexandre, 226–27
Declaration of Independence, 111
Defective Sexual Feelings of Women, The (Adler), 83
defenses, psychological, 140, 153–54
Degas, Edgar, 228, 237, 249, 250
deism, 159–60, 170, 172, 185
Delacroix, Eugène, 224
Demeaux, J.-B.-D., 147, 149
democracy, 16–18, 104, 228, 274–75

Democracy in America (Tocqueville), 274–75
depression, 72, 133, 134
diaries, 253–54, 255, 258–67, 278–79, 286
Diary of a Nobody (Grossmith and Grossmith), 44
Dickens, Charles, 47, 79, 86, 105, 106, 121, 122,
123, 146, 187, 272–73
Dictionary of Accepted Ideas (Flaubert), 152
Dictionnaire encyclopédique des sciences médicales
(Christian), 151
Dictionnaire philosophique (Voltaire), 160
Diderot, Denis, 28, 159, 169–70
Dietetic of the Soul (Feuchtersleben), 137
disciple, Le (Bourget), 169
Disraeli, Benjamin, 112
Dissenters, 165, 180, 187
distance, doctrine of, 236–37
divorce, 18, 36, 50
Doll's House, A (Ibsen), 236
Dombey and Son (Dickens), 47, 146
domesticity, cult of, 40, 43–44, 60
Doyle, Arthur Conan, 178
Drake, Henry A., 103
Dreyfus affair, 114–15, 116, 260, 287
Droz, Gustave, 92–93, 106, 272
Drummond, Edward, 119
Dubois, Jean, 298*n*
Duchamps, Marcel, 239
dueling, xxii, 64, 102, 260
Dujardin, Edouard, xxii
Dumas, Alexandre, fils, 224–25
Duncan, J. Matthews, 86, 92
Durand-Ruel, Paul, 248–50
Durkheim, Emile, 135, 168–69
Duty (Smiles), 198

Eastlake, Charles, 229
Eastlake, Lady, 229
Ebers, Georg, 46
economics, 211, 218
Eddy, Mary Baker, 174
education:
discipline in, 102–6
family values and, 44
private, 9, 27, 42, 103–4
salaries in, 24
state support for, 5, 10, 43
universal, 20
see also teachers
Effi Briest (Fontane), 259–60
Elder, Louisine, 237
Eliot, George, 161, 208, 235
Elisabeth, Empress of Austria, 30
Ellis, Havelock, 54, 67
"Emancipator of Labor and the Honest Working-
People, The" (Nast), *190*
"Emilie" (Schnitzler's mistress), xxvii–xxix, 63
Eminent Victorians (Strachey), 281
Enfantin, Barthélemy Prosper, 173

Engels, Friedrich, 21, 30–31, 212–13, 215,
    216–17, 284
England:
    art collections in, 229, 231
    bourgeoisie in, 9–12, 20–21, 30
    capital punishment in, 119–22, 123
    corporal punishment in, 104–6
    family life in, 42, 44
    governmental repression in, 107–8
    homosexuality in, 68
    industrialization in, 210–11, 214–18
    Jewish population of, 161
    marriage in, 57, 58
    midwives in, 207
    parish system of, 217–18
    Parliament of, 123, 161, 214–18
    political situation in, 16, 20–21
    postal system of, 258, 259
    religious census of (1851), 187
    secret ballot introduced by (1872), 276
    secularism in, 159, 161, 187
    spiritualism in, 179–80
    venereal disease in, 130
    women's condition in, 49–50, 202, 209
Enlightenment, 32, 40, 103, 106, 114, 120, 141,
    142, 144, 159, 169–71, 185, 255, 274
Eros, 76, 79, 94
Eugénie Grandet (Balzac), 47
European Workers (Le Play), 40–42
evolution, 97–98, 111, 142, 177–78, 211
executions, public, 121–22
Exposition Décennale (1900), 227–28, 236

factories, 210–18
    Engels vs. Ure on, 212–13, 216
    government regulation of, 214–18
    owners of, 28, 212–13
    workers in, 25, 27, 134–35, 186, 210–18
Factory Act (Brit.), 215–16
Faguet, Emile, 164
Fairy Tale, The (Schnitzler), 60, 99
Falkenhorst, C., 133
families, 35–60
    as bourgeois institution, 33, 36, 296n
    decline of, 36, 40–42
    emotional dynamics of, 39–40, 44, 100–101
    extended, 41, 43
    Freud's analysis of, 39–40
    individualism encouraged by, 40, 41, 42–43
    living quarters for, 44, 60, 255, 268–72
    paternalistic, 41, 42, 43–44, 47, 77, 103
    privacy in, 255–59, 285
    prosperity as important to, 40, 43
    size of, 36, 41–42, 43, 51, 52–53, 54
    social role of, 43–44
    sociology of, 36, 40–42
    women's role in, 49–50, 51, 200–204
    see also children; parents

Family, The (Riehl), 40–42
Farrer, James Anson, 123, 124
Father and Son (Gosse), 167
fathers:
    as disciplinarians, 77, 103
    as domestic tyrants, 47
    families headed by, 41, 42, 43–44, 47
    fear of, 164
    remarriage of, 41
    sons' revolt against (Oedipus complex), 35,
        38–40
Faust (Goethe), 157–58
feminism, 47, 48, 76, 126, 166, 173, 200, 204, 205,
    209, 273–74
Féré, Charles, 213
Feuchtersleben, Ernst Freiherr von, 137, 138
Feuerbach, Ludwig, 159
"Few Thoughts for a Young Man, A" (Mann),
    196–97
Feydeau, Ernest, 110
"Fifi" (Schnitzler's mistress), 71–72
First Amendment (U.S.), 162
Fitch, Asa, 264
Flaubert, Gustave, 28–29, 38, 44, 110, 152, 165,
    242, 282
flogging, 104, 105, 113
Fontane, Theodor, 240, 259–60
Foote, Mary Halleck, 54–55
Forster, E. M., 235
Fournier, Dora, 50
"Four-Pointed Urethral Ring," 128
Fowler, O. S., 150
France, 270
    anti-Semitism in, 114–15
    art exhibitions in, 226–28, 231, 237, 240,
        248–50
    Bourbon Restoration in, 14–15, 19, 50, 68
    bourgeoisie in, xxv, 6, 13–15, 248
    capital punishment in, 118–19, 120–21, 122
    contraception in, 53
    corporal punishment in, 104–5
    family life in, 44
    governmental repression in, 108, 109–10
    homosexuality in, 67–68
    industrialization in, 210, 215
    July Monarchy of, 19–20
    marriage in, 57–58, 94
    midwives in, 207
    political situation in, 14–15, 19–20
    revolutions of, 13, 14–15, 27–28, 36, 50, 107,
        108, 109–10, 111, 113, 158–59, 170, 173,
        228, 276, 284
    Romantic movement in, 242
    Second Empire of, 15, 248
    secularism in, 161–62, 164, 169, 187
    venereal disease in, 130
    women's condition in, 48, 49, 50, 202
France, Anatole, 166

Francis I, King of France, 131
Franken, Konstanze von, 268–69
Frankfurt, Germany, 16–17, 270–71
Franz Ferdinand, Archduke, 288
Franz Joseph, Emperor of Austria, 21, 30
Frazer, James, 164
Freemasons, 159
Freer, Charles L., 238
French Revolution, 14, 27–28, 36, 50, 107, 111,
    158–59, 170, 173, 228, 284
Freud, Martha Bernays, 26, 27, 206
Freud, Sigmund, xxiii, 171, 270
    anxiety as viewed by, 134, 138–41
    bourgeois background of, 26, 27, 207
    Jewish heritage of, 22
    masturbation as viewed by, 151
    neurosis as viewed by, 75, 154
    "normal" love defined by, 59
    Oedipus complex formulated by, 35, 38–40
    psychoanalytic technique of, 276–77
    religion as viewed by, 164, 174
    Schnitzler compared with, 66
    self-analysis by, 39, 279
    sexuality investigated by, 66, 88
    women's role as viewed by, 206–7
    work ethic as viewed by, 23, 195
Frick, Henry Clay, 238
Friedrich, David, 247
Fruits of Philosophy (Knowlton), 53–54
Functions and Disorders of the Reproductive Organs, The
    (Acton), 81–82

Gachet, Paul, 224
Gambetta, Léon, 163
Gannett, William, 213–14
Gardner, Isabella Stewart, 238
Garibaldi, Giuseppe, 178
Gaskell, Elizabeth, 137
Gauguin, Paul, 223, 225, 236
Gautier, Théophile, 110
Genius of Christianity (Chateaubriand), 164–65
Gentleman's House, The (Kerr), 268
George, Stefan, 221
German Southwest Africa, 113–14
Germany, 16-17, 42
    art exhibitions in, 223, 231, 246–48
    bourgeoisie in, xxv, 6, 7, 9–12, 22, 29, 233,
        246–48, 284
    capital punishment in, 119, 122
    colonies of, 113–14
    corporal punishment in, 105
    homosexuality in, 68
    industrialization in, 210–11
    Jewish population of, 226
    marriage in, 57–59
    national elections of (1907), 113
    religious conflict in, 166–67
    Romantic movement in, 169–71

secularism in, 159, 163
spiritualism in, 176
women's condition in, 50, 201, 202
germ theory, 142, 201–2
Gibbon, Edward, 169–70
Gladstone, Catherine, xxiv, 46, 47
Gladstone, William Ewart, xxiv, 46, 47, 103, 278
Gluck, Christoph Willibald, 233, 245
Glümer, Marie ("Mz."), 65, 70–72, 75, 262
Goethe, Johann Wolfgang von, 28, 116, 157–58,
    243
Golden Bough, The (Frazer), 164
Goldschmidt, B. H., 59
Goncourt, Edmond and Jules, 98, 204, 242
gonorrhea, 130, 148
Goodyear, Charles, 56
Gosse, Edmund, 167
governesses, 42, 207
government:
    aggression by, 107–10, 117–25
    bureaucracy of, 25, 145, 246
    economic policies of, 211
    employees of, 23, 25, 209
    regulation by, 214–18, 285
Graham, Sylvester, 148–49
Great Exhibition (1851), 144, 228
Great Expectations (Dickens), 105
Greece, ancient, 35, 39, 100, 135, 254, 255, 277
Gropius, Walter, 266
Grossbürgertum, 6
Grossmith, George and Weedon, 44
Grosvenor Gallery, 231
guillotine, 120, 122
Guizot, François, 195
Gulbransson, Olaf, 156
Günther, Louis, 124

Hall, G. Stanley, 261, 262
Hall, S. C., 175, 178
Hallé, Charles, 10
Hallé Orchestra, 10, 233
Halliday, Andrew, 106
Hamburg, Germany, 246–47
Hamlet (Shakespeare), 39, 100
Hamsun, Knut, xxi
hangings, 121–22
Hanslick, Eduard, 23, 243–45
Hard Times (Dickens), 86
Hardy, Thomas, 163
Hartford Atheneum, 238
Havemeyer, Henry O., 237, 238
Hawthorne, Nathaniel, 168
Hebbel, Friedrich, 263–64
Heeger, Anna "Jeanette," 64–65, 210
Hegel, Georg Wilhelm Friedrich, 135
Hegetschweiler, Johannes, 12
Heine, Heinrich, 14, 165, 173, 205
Henry IV, King of France, 120

Herbart, Johann Friedrich, 278
heredity, 66, 106, 134
Hereros, 113–14
Herzl, Theodor, 116
Hill, Rowland, 258
Hippocrates, 134, 150
Hirschfeld, Magnus, 67
Hirsekorn, August Friedrich, 193, 198, 218
Hirsekorn, Carl August, 193, 218
History of England (Macaulay), 103
Hobbes, Thomas, 100, 159, 277
Hobson, J. A., 113, 283
Hoffmann, Josef, 271
Hofmannsthal, Hugo von, 4, 195, 262
Hofstadter, Richard, 301*n*
Home Life in France (Betham-Edwards), 49
homosexuality, 65–69, 105, 274
Howells, William Dean, 240
Hughes, Thomas, 203–4
Hugo, Victor, 121, 242
Hume, David, 169–70, 232
Huxley, T. H., 140, 172–73, 181, 264
Huysmans, Joris-Karl, 169, 184–85
hypochondria, 72, 158, 194–95

Ibsen, Henrik, xxi, 70, 195, 236, 283
Idleness and Work (Cammarano), 197
illness, xxviii, 41, 46–47, 131–32, 148, 303*n*
Immermann, Karl, 183
Imperialism, 99, 112–14, 282
Imperialism (Hobson), 113
Importance of Being Earnest, The (Wilde), 265
Impressionism, 33, 222–28, 230, 231, 236, 237, 247, 249, 285–86
income:
    disparities in, 24–25
    disposable, 53, 219, 269
    sources of, 24–25, 232–33
Independent Salon (1847), 231
Indians, American, 111
individualism, 40, 41, 42–43, 135, 213, 274–76
industrialization, 13, 22, 25, 36, 43, 134–36, 141–42, 145, 174, 210–18, 284
Ingersoll, Robert, 159
Ingres, Jean-Auguste-Dominique, 230
Interpretation of Dreams, The (Freud), 39
Iphigenia in Tauris (Gluck), 233
Italy:
    bourgeoisie in, xxv, 12–13
    electoral reform in (1882), 20
    marriage in, 57
    nationalist movement in, 259
    political situation in, 12–13, 20

James, Henry, 47, 181, 225, 236, 240, 241
James, William, 98, 180–81, 182, 278
James Dixon & Sons, 233
Jaurès, Jean, 283

Jerome, Jerome K., 192
"Jesus and Voltaire" (Roberts), 177
Jewish Disabilities Bill (Brit.), 161
Jewish Question, 64, 116
Jews, 175
    as art collectors, 225–26
    assimilation of, 58, 115–16
    in Austro-Hungarian Empire, 3, 21, 22, 115–17, 143, 162
    in bourgeoisie, 3, 8
    cult of virginity and, 76
    in England, 161
    in Germany, 226
    liberal vs. Orthodox, 171
    marriages of, 58–59
    pogroms against, 114–15
    prejudice against, 21, 64, 111, 114–17, 126, 143, 162, 166–67, 169, 226, 244, 251
Johnson, Samuel, 144
journalists, 15, 22, 241, 260, 262, 282, 283
Joyce, James, xxi, xxii
Judaism, 164, 175
July Monarchy (1831), 19–20
Jungle, The (Sinclair), 282–83
Juvenal, 185

Kaden, Julie, 42
Kandinsky, Vassily, xxi, 223
Kant, Immanuel, 171, 273, 274
Kaposi, Moritz, xxviii
Kauffmann, Angelica, 234
Keats, John, 205
Kerner, Justinus, 176–77, 178
Kerr, Robert, 268
Key, Ellen, 42
Keynes, John Maynard, 183
Kiehnle, Hermine, 201
Kiehnle-Kochbuch, 201
Kiesewetter, Carl, 176, 177–78, 179
Kingsley, Charles, 173
Kiss, The (Brancusi), 239
Kleinbürgertum, 6
Klimt, Gustav, 222, 266, 267
Knowlton, Charles, 53–54
Koehler, Bernhard, 225
Koehler, R., 56–57
Kokoschka, Oskar, 266
Krafft-Ebing, Richard Freiherr von, 67, 75–76, 82–83, 133
Krupp, Alfred, xxiv, 7
Kuyper, Abraham, 168

labor:
    division of, 134–35, 202, 276
    specialization of, 154, 261, 276
Labouchere Amendment (Brit.), 68
Lapouge, Georges Vacher de, 112
Last Day of a Convict, The (Hugo), 121

lauriers sont coupés, Les (Dujardin), xxi–xxii
lawyers, 19, 24, 38
Leixner, Otto von, 234
Leopold II, King of Belgium, 112–13
Le Play, Frédéric, 40–42
Lesseps, Ferdinand de, 174
Lessing, Gotthold Ephraim, 171
letters, 253–54, 255, 258–67, 286
Letters on the Aesthetic Education of Mankind
　　(Schiller), 135
Levi, Hermann, 11
Leviathan (Hobbes), 277
libraries, 229–30, 237, 238
Lichtwark, Alfred, 246–47
Liebelei (Schnitzler), 234
Liebermann, Max, 222, 223, 247–48
Liebknecht, Wilhelm, 283
Lieutenant Gustl (Schnitzler), xxi–xxii, 64
Life of Jesus, Critically Examined (Strauss), 160–61
Lind, Jenny, 229
Link, Sophie, 69
Linton, Eliza Lynn, 205
Liszt, Franz, 229
literacy, 13, 111, 255, 285
literature:
　　bourgeois tastes in, 235–36
　　criticism of, 240–43
　　"peasant," 183
　　on sexuality, 53–55, 79–85
　　success, 9, 197–98, 218–19
Locke, John, 106
Lodge, Oliver, 178
Lohmeyr, Friedrich, 7
Lombroso, Cesare, 208
London *Examiner,* 132
Lorelei (Heine), 205
Louis XV, King of France, 242
Lourdes religious shrine, 166, 179, 184–85
love, 97
　　as basis of marriage, 57–60, 88
　　"normal," 59
　　romantic, 57–60, 88, 94
　　sexual, 63–64, 78–94
Lucas, Charles Jean-Marie, 118–19
Ludwig I, King of Bavaria, 10
Ludwig II, King of Bavaria, 10–11
Lueger, Karl, 21, 116
Lutheran Church, 165, 166, 171
Lutyens, Emily Lytton, Lady, 91–92
Lyman, Joseph, 84–85
Lyman, Laura, xxiv, 84–85, 286

Macaulay, Thomas Babington, 103, 259
Madame Bovary (Flaubert), 165, 242
Maecenas, 223, 225
Magendi, A., 196
Mahler, Gustav, 116, 137, 221, 266, 267
"Mais si, ma femme . . ." (Daumier), *220*

Malthus, Thomas, 52–53
Manchester, England, 9–10, 107–8, 288
Manet, Edouard, 223, 237, 238, 248–49, 262, 286
Manet, Julie, 46–47, 262
manliness, ideal of, 43, 99, 104, 114, 117, 151,
　　196, 282
Mann, Horace, 104, 196–97
Mann, Thomas, xxi, 194–95
Mann, Thomas Johann, 194
manners, 25, 42, 256
Mantegazza, Paolo, 82, 133
Marc, Franz, 225
Mariage de Figaro, Le (Beaumarchais), 32
Mariano, Raffaele, 118
Markbreiter, Otto, 78
marriages:
　　arranged, 57–59
　　of convenience, 68, 69
　　financial considerations in, 57–59, 60
　　manuals for, 80–81
　　romantic love and, 57–60, 88, 94
　　second, 41
　　sexual initiation in, 90–93
　　venereal disease and, 130–31
　　of virgins, 75–77
　　women's legal standing in, 49–50, 59, 203
　　women's role in, 203–6
Married Women's Property Act, 50
Martin, H. Newell, 82
Marx, Karl, 14–15, 17, 30–31, 135, 163, 168, 186,
　　188, 216, 284
Mary Magdalene, 236
"Mask of Anarchy, The" (Shelley), 108
masturbation, 89–90, 147–51
materialism, 168, 175, 177–78, 218–19
Matisse, Henri, 225, 228, 239
Maupassant, Guy de, 131, 225–26
Maximilian II, King of Bavaria, 10
Mazzini, Giuseppe, xxiv, 259
"McCounter Jumper repents of an Easter Trip in
　　a Third-Class Carriage," 2
medicine, xxviii, 4, 8, 22, 24, 35–38, 48, 158, 207,
　　208, 210
Meissonier, Jean-Louis, 230, 235
Meistersinger von Nürnberg, Die (Wagner), 244
Melville, Herman, 168
Mendelssohn, Felix, 233
Menzel, Adolph, 6
merchants, 5, 29–30, 255
Mérimée, Prosper, 205
Metropolitan Museum of Art, 237, 238
Metternich, Prince Klemens Wenzel Nepomuk
　　Lothar von, 16, 24, 284
Michelangelo Buonarroti, 208
Michelet, Jules, 48
Middlemarch (Eliot), 235
Middleton, G. A. T., 269
Midsummer Night's Dream, A (Mendelssohn), 233

midwives, 46, 207
Mill, John Stuart, 15, 21, 30, 49–50, 111, 142, 154, 173, 206–7, 218
miracles, 166, 179, 181
M'Naghten case, 119
Modernism, xx, xxi, 282, 287
monarchy, 17, 21, 23, 100, 102, 104, 109, 110, 228, 250
Mondrian, Piet, 223
Monet, Claude, 24, 224, 231, 237, 247, 249
Monsieur, Madame et Bébé (Droz), 92–93, 106, 272
Montesquieu, Charles-Louis de Secondat, Baron de La Brède et de, 274
Montez, Lola, 10
"Monument to Napoleon" (Cruikshank), *96*
morality:
    decline of, 41
    family values and, 43
    guardians of, 54
    laws of, 160
    sexual urges restrained by, 80, 81, 138–39
    of work ethic, 192–95
Moreau, Gustave, 205
Morgan, J. P., 15
Morisot, Berthe, 46–47, 231, 262
Morley, John, 160
mortality rates, 41, 152
Mosher, Clelia, 86
Mosher Survey, 86–88
mothers:
    breast feeding by, xxiv, 45–46, 256, 272–73
    childbirth by, 46, 47, 272
    mortality rates for, 41
muckrakers, 282–83, 284
Munch, Edvard, 228, 236
Münchhausen (Immermann), 183
Munger, Theodore H., 195–96
Munich, Germany, 5, 9, 10–12
Murray, Gilbert, 78
museums, 5, 10, 229, 230, 231, 232, 237, 238, 245–48, 250, 285
music:
    amateur performances of, 271
    atonal, xxii, 221–22, 223
    of Brahms vs. Wagner, 244–45
    criticism of, 243–45
    modern, xxii, 221–22, 223, 238–39
    patronage of, 228–29, 250
    religious, 165
    in Vienna, 23, 221–22, 229, 243–45
Musical Times, 226, 240
Mysteries of Females or the Secrets of Nature (Albrecht), 80–81

"Names, Numbers, and Location of the Organs," *155*
Napoleon I, Emperor of France, xxiv–xxv, 14, 15, 18, 24, 108, 141, 145, 236

Napoleon III, Emperor of France, 14, 15, 18, 242, 248
Nast, Thomas, *190*
nationalism, 99, 110, 126, 259, 282
Nat Turner's Rebellion, 109
nature, 52, 53, 66, 94, 100, 139, 145, 160, 163–64, 169, 207
Netherlands, 11, 20, 68, 123
neurasthenia, 129, 132–38
neurosis, 75, 164, 205
Newcastle, England, 198–99
New Christianity, The (Saint-Simon), 173–74
New Haven Leader, 133, 137–38
newspapers, 15, 22, 53, 215
New Testament, 160–61
Newton, Isaac, 208
New York Society for the Suppression of Vice, 257
New York Times, 92n
Niethammer, Marie, 176–77
Nietzsche, Friedrich, xx, 138, 163, 164, 168, 277–78
nineteenth century:
    as "age of transition," 142
    as "our century of nerves," 133
    progress in 141–47
    religion vs. science in, 163–64
    twentieth century compared with, 287–88
North and South (Gaskell), 137
Noyes, John Humphrey, 52
Nude Descending a Staircase (Duchamps), 239

Oberhof, Der (Immermann), 183
Oedipus complex, 35, 38–40
Oedipus Rex (Sophocles), 39
Of Crimes and Punishments (Beccaria), 120, 123
Old and the New Faith, The (Strauss), 161
Old Testament, 55, 67, 106, 160
Olympia (Manet), 237
Onanisme, L' (Tissot), 148
"On the Railroad" (Plönnies), 146
On the Threshold (Munger), 195–96
opera houses, 11, 174, 228–29, 234, 239–40
orgasms, 37, 64–65, 83–88, 298n
Origin of Species, The (Darwin), 97–98, 188
Our Home: Or, the Key to a Nobler Life (Sargent), 256–57
Our Mutual Friend (Dickens), 79
"Overwrought Person, The" (Schnitzler), 72–73
Owen, Robert, 188

Paganini, Niccolò, 229
Paget, James, 151
Paine's Celery Compound, 133
paintings:
    academic, 226–27, 247
    collections of, 196, 222–27, 236, 285–86
    modern, xxi, 24, 222–30, 239, 248–50

Paracelsus (Schnitzler), xxix, 133
parents:
    authority of, 36–40, 41
    devotion of, 40, 41, 42, 44, 77–78, 102–3, 297*n*
    marriages arranged by, 57–59
    sex education by, 89–93
    step-, 41
    see also fathers; mothers
Paris Commune, 109–10, 113
Paris Salon (1846), 226–27
Paris Salon (1865), 237
Party of Order, 15, 27–28
Pascal, Blaise, 181, 242, 277
Past and Present (Carlyle), 192
Pasteur, Louis, 152
Patmore, Coventry, 83
Peabody, George, 8
peasants, 17, 26, 111, 183–84, 197
Peel, Robert, 119, 123
Péguy, Charles, 169
penile rings, 149
Péreire brothers, 15, 173–74
"Peterloo Massacre," 107–8
Peter Pan (Barrie), 206
Petersen, Carl, 247–48
petite bourgeoisie, 6
philanthropy, 9–12, 186–87, 226, 284
philosophes, xxiii, 120, 142, 169–70, 172
Philosophy of Manufacturers, The (Ure), 212–15
physicians, xxviii, 4, 8, 22, 24, 35–38, 48, 158,
    207, 208, 210
Picasso, Pablo, 222, 223, 228, 236, 239
piety, 157–58, 164, 166, 167, 169, 184, 194–95,
    216
pilgrimages, religious, 184–85
Pissarro, Camille, 224, 230, 231, 235, 249, 250
Pius IX, Pope, 163
Plato, 67, 100, 277
Plönnies, Luise von, 146
poetry, 170, 196
politics:
    bourgeois influence in, 12–24, 27–28, 31
    corruption in, 13, 16, 20, 116–17, 276
    elite control of, 15
    factionalism in, 107
    indifference to, 22–23
    of industrialization, 211, 214–15
    mass, 116–17, 142
    opposition parties in, 16, 107
    parliamentarian, 16–18
    radicalism in, 249–50
    reform movements in, 16–18, 22, 111, 118–19,
        123, 276, 282–83, 284
    religion and, 162–63, 164, 166, 169
    World War I and, xx, 22
Pope, Alexander, 170–71
population, 19, 52–53, 143, 187
Portraits littéraires (Sainte-Beuve), 242

Port-Royal (Sainte-Beuve), 242
Post-Impressionism, 222, 223
poverty, 13, 40, 46, 143, 158, 185, 188, 256, 285
*Practical Treatise on Nervous Exhaustion
    (Neurasthenia), Its Symptoms, Nature,
    Sequences, Treatment, A* (Beard), 136–37
press:
    freedom of, 22
    literary reviews in, 241
    popular, 15, 22, 53, 111, 215, 227, 260, 283
    see also journalists
printing, 141, 232, 245
prison reform, 117, 118–19, 122
privacy:
    bourgeois attitudes towards, xxii, xxiv, 20,
        253–79, 312*n*
    of diaries and letters, 253–54, 255, 258–67, 286
    in families, 255–59, 285
    individualism and, 40, 41, 42–43, 135, 213,
        274–76
    introspection allowed by, 277–79
    of personal space, 268–72, 276
    public sphere vs., 194, 254–56, 257, 267, 274
    violation of, xxviii–xxix, 253–54
"private parts," 254–55
Problem in Greek Ethics, A (Symonds), 67
Professor Bernhardi (Schnitzler), 38
proletariat, *see* working class
"Proper Use of Time, A," 197
prostitution:
    bourgeois attitudes towards, 27, 40, 70, 71, 76,
        79–80, 82, 121, 231
    marriage as legalized, 88
    masturbation vs., 89–90
    venereal disease and, 130–31
Protestant Ethic and the Spirit of Capitalism, The
    (Weber), 153–54
Protestantism, 76, 141, 165, 166–67, 175, 178
Proust, Marcel, xxi, xxvii, 89–90, 243
Prussia, 17, 50, 68, 105, 109, 167, 207, 248
psychiatry, 37, 132, 154
psychoanalysis:
    criticism of, 39
    cultural history analyzed by, xxiii
    patient-therapist relationship in, 276–77
    sexuality investigated by, 66, 138–40, 151, 196
psychology, 180–81, 277–79
*Psychology as Science, Newly Founded on Experience,
    Metaphysics and Mathematics* (Herbart), 278
Psychopathia Sexualis (Krafft-Ebing), 67, 82–83
publishers, 24, 233–34
punishment:
    capital, 68, 117–25
    corporal, 102–6, 126, 212
Pure Food and Drug Act (U.S.), 282–83
Puritans, 255, 257

Quinn, John, 239

railroads, 5, 142, 145–47, 153
Ravaillac, François, 120
reading, xx, xxi–xxii, 69, 116, 169, 232, 235–36, 240–43
Redgrave, Richard, 233
Reform Act, First (Brit.), 20, 123
Reform Act, Second (Brit.), 20
Regnault, Jean-Baptiste, *61*
Reigen (Schnitzler), xxi, 81
Reinhard, Marie ("Mz. II"), 51, 73–75, 78, 207
religion, 157–89
    aesthetic element in, 164–66
    aggression justified by, 99, 118
    bourgeois attitudes toward, 13, 18, 29, 157–89, 306n
    capital punishment justified by, 118
    as "collective neurosis," 164
    decline of, 41, 177–78, 180–83, 185–89
    family values and, 43, 44
    indifference to, 185–89, 285
    institutions of, 32, 163, 175
    politics and, 162–63, 164, 166, 169
    resurgence of, 164–67
    in Romantic movement, 169–71
    science vs., 140, 159–61, 163–64, 172–74, 177–78, 180–83
    secularism vs., 157–89
    spiritualism vs., 174–82
    unconscious dimension of, 164, 165–66
    unorthodox beliefs vs., 172–80
    work ethic and, 194–95, 214
    working class attitudes towards, 183–88, 284
    see also Christianity
Rembrandt van Rijn, 238
Renaissance, 141, 275
Renoir, Pierre-Auguste, 224, 231, 247, 249
revolution of 1830, 14
revolution of 1848, 13, 15, 108
Rhodes, Cecil, 114
Riehl, Wilhelm Heinrich, 40–42
Roberts, J. E., 177
Rockefeller, John D., 7, 283
Roe, Arthur and Emma, 51–52
Romantic movement, 29, 84, 103, 169–71, 242
Roosevelt, Theodore, 53, 196, 199, 282, 283
Rosé Quartet, 221–22
Rosières, Raoul, 168
Rousseau, Jean-Jacques, 106, 170, 277
Rousseau, Théodore, 249
Runge, Philipp Otto, 170, 247
Ruskin, John, 232
Russell, Bertrand, 78
Russia:
    bourgeoisie in, 24
    pogroms in, 114–15
    spiritualism in, 179
    women physicians in, 208

Sadler, Michael, 215
Sainte-Beuve, Charles Augustin, 172–73, 242
Saint-Simon, Claude-Henri de Rouvroy, comte de, 173–74, 265, 286
salaries, 24–25, 232–33
Salten, Felix, 4, 102
Sand, George, 29, 208
Sandrock, Adele, 72, 84, 85
Sargent, C. E., 256–57
Sartor Resartus (Carlyle), 192–93
Schiele, Egon, 222
Schiller, Friedrich, 135, 192
Schindler, Alma, 254, 265–67
Schlegel, August Wilhelm, 170
Schmutzer, Ferdinand, *62*
Schneider, Eugène and Adolphe, 7
Schnitzler, Arthur:
    aesthetic tastes of, xxii, 221–22, 223
    as amateur pianist, 3, 101–2
    anxiety of, 129–32
    aphorisms of, 97
    autobiography of, xxviii, 77, 116
    as bachelor, 4, 64, 131–32, 191
    bourgeois background of, xxvii, 3–4, 26, 29, 35–36, 64, 72, 101, 207
    childhood of, xxvii–xxix, 35, 63, 65–66, 77–78
    correspondence of, 69, 70–71, 84
    cosmopolitan culture of, xx, xxii
    dialogues of, 72–73
    diaries of, xx, xxvii–xxix, 3, 22–23, 29, 36, 37, 49, 63, 64–65, 69, 74–75, 77, 78, 90, 97n, 102–3, 115–17, 129, 130–31, 157–58, 195, 221–22, 253–54, 262, 278–79, 288–89
    dramas of, 33, 63–64, 65, 69, 73, 133, 233, 234, 279
    education of, xxvii, 22, 36–38
    family of, 35–36
    fiction of, xxi–xxii, 60, 64, 69–70, 99, 233, 279
    homoerotic impulses of, 65–66
    hypochondria of, 72, 158
    jealousy of, 70–72
    Jewish heritage of, 3, 8, 58, 115–17, 158
    marriage of, 4, 74, 262
    mistresses of, xxvii–xxix, 49, 50, 63, 64–65, 69–75, 78, 207, 210, 262
    in nineteenth and twentieth centuries, xx, 222
    orgasms recorded by, 37, 64–65
    as physician, 4, 36–38, 191
    poetry of, 63
    political opinions of, 22–23, 102, 110, 115–17
    privacy valued by, xxviii–xxix, 253
    reading by, xx, xxi–xxii, 69, 116, 169
    religious beliefs of, 157–58, 164, 172, 177
    reputation of, 65
    royalties of, 233
    sexual experiences of, xxvii–xxix, 4, 26, 37, 49, 50–51, 63–66, 69–75, 78, 81, 94, 101–2, 130–32, 191, 195, 207, 210, 262, 287

Schnitzler, Arthur (*continued*)
 as Viennese, xx, xxviii, 3–4, 36
 as witness to bourgeois world, xix–xxii, 33, 60, 72, 250
 women as viewed by, 49, 69–75, 88, 207
 as writer, xxi–xxii, 4, 37–38, 131, 157, 191, 195
 writings of, xix, xxi–xxii, 33, 63–64, 81
Schnitzler, Gisela, 35
Schnitzler, Johann:
 background of, 8
 death of, 101
 Jewish heritage of, 8, 22, 116
 as physician, xxviii, 8, 22, 35–36, 158
 Schnitzler's diary found by, xxvii–xxix, 35, 63, 90, 130–31, 158, 191, 253–54, 262
 Schnitzler's relationship with, 35–38, 77, 90, 100, 130–31, 132, 191–92
 writings of, 38
Schnitzler, Julius, 35
Schnitzler, Louise, 35, 77–78, 101–2
Schnitzler, Olga Grossmann, 262
Schoenberg, Arnold, xxi, xxii, 221–22, 223
Scholar Gypsy, The (Arnold), 132
Schütz, Heinrich, 245
science:
 bourgeois attitude towards, 85–86
 facts as basis of, 85–88
 religion vs., 140, 159–61, 163–64, 172–74, 177–78, 180–83
 truth as object of, 160–61
séances, 176–77
secolo nevrosico, Il (Mantegazza), 133
Second, The (Schnitzler), 64
self-censorship, 89, 100
Self-Help (Smiles), 197–98, 218–19
"Sentiment of Rationality, The," 181
servants, 3, 27, 126, 183, 200, 201, 202, 203–4, 268, 272
Seventh Symphony (Bruckner), 243
sexuality, 63–94
 aggression and, 83–84, 105, 122, 140
 anxiety about, 130–32, 138–40, 147–49
 bourgeois attitudes towards, xxiv, xxvii, 45, 51–52, 54–55, 64, 78–94, 282, 298n
 compatibility in, 59–60, 86–88
 dysfunctional, 81–85, 86, 138, 148, 267, 282
 erotic drive in, 80, 81, 82–83, 139–40
 gratification in, 81–88
 guilt and, 151
 infant, 254–55
 knowledge of, 89–93
 literature on, 53–55, 79–85
 perversions in, 65–66, 67, 69, 181
 privacy of, 269, 274, 286
 psychoanalytic investigation of, 66, 138–40, 151, 196
 scientific investigation of, 85–88
 suppression of, 80, 81, 105, 122, 138–39

 taboos in, 66
 unsatisfied, 79–80
 of women, 59–60, 76, 81–88, 90–93, 138
Shakespeare, William, 39, 100, 232, 233
Shaw, George Bernard, xxi, 241, 283
Shchukin, Sergei, 225
Shelley, Percy Bysshe, 108
Sidgwick, Henry, 181–82
Siebert, Friedrich, 92
Simmel, Georg, 98
Simon, James, 226
Sinclair, Upton, 282–83
slavery, 18, 19, 109, 111, 117, 211, 284
slums, 27, 210, 215, 256
Smiles, Samuel, 197–98, 200, 218–19
Smith, Adam, 134–35, 213
Social Darwinism, 98, 188, 301n
Social Darwinism in American Life (Hofstadter), 301n
Social Democrats, 22, 126, 188, 284
socialism, 188, 213, 283, 288
society:
 hierarchical arrangement of, 4, 24–25, 29
 individualism vs., 274–76
 law and order in, 15, 27–28, 107–10, 122–25, 185–86, 188
 upward mobility in, 7–9
Society for Psychical Research, 181–82
Society for the Diffusion of Knowledge Respecting the Punishment of Death and the Improvement of Prison Discipline, 118–19
Socrates, 277
Some Mistakes of Moses (Ingersoll), 159
"Song of the Bell, The" (Schiller), 192
Sophocles, 39
Sorrows of Young Werther, The (Goethe), 29
Soubirous, Bernadette, 179, 184
Spinoza, Baruch, 159
spiritualism, 174–82
Spitzweg, Carl, 235
Steele, Joseph, 103
Steffens, Lincoln, 283
Stehkragenproletarier, 6
Stendhal, 12, 278
Stephen, James Fitzgerald, 125
Stephen, James Fitzjames, 256
Stevenson, Robert Louis, 234–35
Stieglitz, Alfred, 239
Stolz, Alban, 166
Strachey, Lytton, 281
Straus, Rahel, 58
Straus, Trude, 58
Strauss, David Friedrich, 160–61
Strindberg, August, xxi
Studies on the Psychology of Sex (Ellis), 54
Subjection of Women, The (Mill), 49–50, 206–7
suffrage, 5, 13, 17–20, 27

secularization and, 162–63
survival of the fittest, 97–98, 111, 211
Suttner, Bertha von, 288
Swift, Jonathan, 170–71
Swinburne, Algernon Charles, 105, 205
Sybel, Heinrich von, 48
Symonds, John Addington, 67, 68
syphilis, xxviii, 130–32

Taine, Hippolyte, 13, 44
Tanguy, Julien François, 223–24
Tarbell, Ida, 283
taste:
    bourgeois, xxiv, 221–50, 285–86
    expenditures for, 232–35
    formation of, 232, 240–48
Taylor, Frederick W., 214
teachers, 24, 207, 208, 209, 210
Ten Hour Bill (Brit.), 215, 217
Tennyson, Alfred Lord, 6
Terre, La (Zola), 183–84
Thackeray, William Makepeace, 121, 145–46, 195
theaters, 232, 234
theology, 29
    naturalistic, 159–60
    sexuality as viewed by, 81, 87–88
Theory of the Leisure Class (Veblen), 199
Theosophy, 174, 178
Thompson, Joseph P., 118
Thoré, Théophile, 226–27
Three Essays on the Theory of Sexuality (Freud), 66
Thrift (Smiles), 198
Tissot, Claude-Joseph, 124–25
Tissot, James, 231
Tissot, Samuel-Auguste-André-David, 147–48, 150
"To a Locomotive in Winter" (Whitman), 146
Tocqueville, Alexis de, 14, 31, 274–75
Todd, Mabel Loomis, 263
Tolstoy, Leo, xxii, 36, 146, 213, 236
Tom Brown at Oxford (Hughes), 203–4
Tom Brown's Schooldays (Hughes), 203
"To the preacher of morals in Cologne on the Rhine" (Gulbransson), 156
trade unions, 143, 214–15, 287
train 17, Le (Claretie), 146
Tristan und Isolde (Wagner), 244
trois grâces, Les (Regnault), vi, 61
Trollope, Anthony, 232–33
Turner, Nat, 109
Twain, Mark, 162, 174–75

unconscious, 139–40, 164, 165–66
United States:
    art collections in, 237–38, 249
    bourgeoisie in, xxv, 7, 8–9
    corporal punishment in, 103–4
    culture of, 19, 176, 237–38
    family life in, 42
    governmental repression in, 109
    immigration to, 143
    individualism in, 274–75
    marriage in, 57, 58
    music in, 238–39
    political situation in, 16, 18–19, 107
    secularism in, 158, 162
    spiritualism in, 176
    universal suffrage in, 18–19
    upward mobility in, 7, 8–9
    women's condition in, 202–3, 208, 209
urbanization, 141, 143, 145, 183, 285
Ure, Andrew, 212–15, 216, 217

Van Gogh, Vincent, 222–23, 224, 225, 236
Varieties of Religious Experience, The (James), 180
Veblen, Thorstein, 199, 271–72
venereal disease, xxviii, 130–32, 148, 303n
vengeance, 118, 124–25
Vera, A., 118
Vermeer, Jan, 226–27
Victoria, Queen of England, xxiv–xxv, 10, 78, 103, 120, 123, 126, 206, 273
Vienna:
    anti-Semitism in, 21, 115–17, 162
    bourgeois culture of, 3–4, 30
    Jewish population of, 3, 21, 22, 115–17, 143, 162
    music in, 23, 221–22, 229, 243–45
    population of, 143
    stock market crash in (1873), 116
    Vorstadt district of, 4
Vienne, France, 186
Vintras, Eugène, 179
Virchow, Rudolf, 48
Virgil, 192
virginity, cult of, 69, 70, 74, 75–77, 91, 99, 266–67
Virgin Mary, 76, 163, 166, 179, 181, 184–85
Voltaire, 32, 120–21, 147–48, 160, 169–70, 171, 177, 185
Volupté (Sainte-Beuve), 242
Vuillard, Edouard, xxi

Wachenheim, Hedwig, 270
Wade, John, 108
Wadsworth, Daniel, 238
Wagner, Cosima, 262
Wagner, Richard, 11, 47, 174, 244–45
Wagner, Siegfried, 47
Walter, Bruno, 137, 221
Walters, William T., 238
Warren, Samuel D., 256
Washington Square (James), 47
Waterloo, Battle of, 14, 108
Watts, George Frederic, 231
wealth, 143, 153–54, 218–19
    displays of, 199, 271–72

wealth (*continued*)
    new, 5, 6, 7–9, 17, 25, 40, 43, 53, 186–87, 198
    sharing of, 9–12, 186–87
    see also income
Wealth of Nations, The (Smith), 134–35
Webb, Beatrice Potter, 270
Weber, Max, 153–54, 169, 218
Werfel, Franz, 266
wet nurses, 45–46, 256
What Every Woman Knows (Barrie), 206
Whistler, James McNeill, 231, 238
Whitman, Walt, 68, 146
Wild Duck, The (Ibsen), 70
Wilde, Oscar, 66, 68–69, 241–42, 257, 265
Wilhelm II, Emperor of Germany, 226, 246
"Will to Believe, The" (James), 180
Wittelsbach monarchy, 10–12
women:
    as artists, 231
    bourgeois, 32–33, 72–73, 75–77, 208–9
    breast feeding by, xxiv, 45–46, 256, 272–73
    domestic duties of, 32–33, 43, 45, 47–50, 51,
        200–204, 207, 218, 255
    dowries of, 57–58
    education of, 59, 179, 208, 209–10
    equality of, 47–50, 76, 201, 202, 203, 208–9,
        273–74, 282
    exploitation of, 64–65, 126, 184, 206–7
    "fallen," 73, 76–77
    fear of, 204–5
    frigidity of, 81–85, 86, 138, 267, 282
    as helpmeets, 203–6
    intelligence of, 208, 209
    legal status of, 48, 49–50, 59, 203
    life expectancy of, 152
    male obsession with, 69–72
    menstruation of, 48, 208
    Mosher Survey on, 86–88
    national differences in, 136–37
    nervousness of, 132, 138, 141
    peasant, 184
    power of, 203–6
    privacy of, 273–74
    professional careers of, xxii, 207–10
    sexuality of, 59–60, 76, 81–88, 90–93, 138
    social role of, 5, 32–33, 47–50, 205–7
    suffrage for, 19, 76, 111, 166, 207, 209–10
    virginity of, 69, 70, 74, 75–77, 91, 99, 266–67
    work ethic and, 200–210, 218
    in work force, 40, 43, 48, 59, 206, 207–10

Woolf, Virginia, 235, 274
Wordsworth, William, 106
Work: A Story of Experience (Alcott), 218
Work and Pleasure (Féré), 213
work day, length of, 111, 213, 215–16, 217
work ethic, 191–219
    anxiety and, 140–41
    as bourgeois ideal, xxii, 38, 153–54, 158,
        191–95, 198–200, 210, 213, 216, 219, 308*n*
    in capitalism, 197–98, 211–12, 215, 217
    character formed by, 196–98, 200, 218–19
    dehumanization and, 202–3, 212–14, 218–19
    idleness vs., 191–92, 194–97, 213
    industrialization and, 13, 22, 36, 43, 134–36,
        141–42, 145, 174, 210–18
    moderation in, 193–95
    moral improvement and, 192–95
    original sin and, 192
    religion and, 194–95, 214
    Schnitzler's views on, 158, 191–92, 195
    in self-help literature, 197–98, 218–19
    women and, 200–210, 218
    for working class, 198, 200, 210–18
working class:
    bourgeoisie vs., 7, 13, 15, 17, 20, 25–28, 140,
        185–88, 189, 198, 213, 216–17, 287
    culture available to, 234, 285
    exploitation of, 111, 126, 134–35, 186, 210–18,
        282
    political power of, 13, 17–18, 26, 27–28, 183
    religious beliefs of, 183–88, 284
    social protests by, 107–8
    subjugation of, 185–86, 188
    unchanging reality of, 141
    work ethic as applied to, 198, 200, 210–18
workplace, home separated from, 41, 43
World War I, xx, xxiv–xxv, 22, 27, 59, 102, 138,
    179, 225, 239, 282, 288–89
World War II, 36
Wundt, Wilhelm, 278

Year-Book of Spiritualism for 1871, The, 179–80
Yeats, W. B., 174
Youth in Vienna (Schnitzler), xxviii, 77

Zemlinsky, Alex von, 267
Zionism, 116
Zola, Emile, 28, 44, 121, 142, 146, 183–84, 195,
    240, 241, 282

About the Author

Peter Gay is Sterling Professor of History Emeritus at Yale University and, since 1997, Director of the Center for Scholars and Writers at the New York Public Library. A prolific cultural historian with a strong, if rational commitment to psychoanalysis, he has ranged from the seventeenth to the twentieth centuries. Among his books are *Freud: A Life for Our Time* (1988), which has been translated into nine languages; a two-volume study, *The Enlightenment: An Interpretation* (1966–69), of which the first volume won the National Book Award; and a memoir, *My German Question: Growing Up in Nazi Berlin* (1998), which was honored with the Geschwister Scholl Prize. His five-volume study, *The Bourgeois Experience: Victoria to Freud* (1984–98), was the impetus for the present book. He lives in Hamden, Connecticut, and New York City with his wife, Ruth, a writer.